WHERE · TO · GO
· IN ·
BRITAIN

W.W. NORTON & COMPANY
New York · London

WHERE · TO · GO
IN
BRITAIN

∎

Contributors:
Richard Cavendish (The West Country, The North Country)
Gilbert Summers (Scotland)
Hugh Westacott (South and South-East England)
Geoffrey Wright (Wales and the Marches)
Michael Wright (Central England and East Anglia)

Editors:
Edwina Johnson and Sue Gordon

Published in the UK by The Automobile Association, Fanum
House, Basingstoke, Hampshire RG21 2EA

Copyright © 1992 The Automobile Association

Cartography © 1992 The Automobile Association

First American Edition 1993

ISBN 0-393-03459-3

Typesetting by Servis Filmsetting Ltd, Manchester.
Colour reproduction by Daylight Colour Art Pte. Ltd, Singapore
Printed by Graficromo S.A. Spain
Set in 9/10½pt Bembo

W.W. Norton & Company, Inc.,
500 Fifth Avenue, New York, NY 10110
W.W. Norton & Company, Ltd.
10 Coptic Street, London WC1A 1PU

1 2 3 4 5 6 7 8 9 0

∎

Front Cover:
V K Guy Ltd, Lands End; *Nature Photographers Ltd*, Pearl-bordered fritillary; *AA Photo Library*,
Edinburgh Castle (D Corrance), Stonehenge (E Meacher), Portmeirion (T D Timms), Guard
(R Victor).

Back Cover:
AA Photo Library, Grasmere Island (E A Bowness), Chatsworth House (V Greaves), Sally Lunn Plaque,
Bath Royal Circus (E Meacher), River Ant at How Hill (A Souter), Ann Hathaway's Cottage
(T Wood).

CONTENTS

■

REGIONAL MAP
6

INTRODUCTION
7

THE WEST COUNTRY
8

SOUTH AND SOUTH-EAST ENGLAND
46

CENTRAL ENGLAND AND EAST ANGLIA
88

WALES AND THE MARCHES
124

THE NORTH COUNTRY
152

SCOTLAND
192

INDEX
220

ACKNOWLEDGEMENTS
224

■

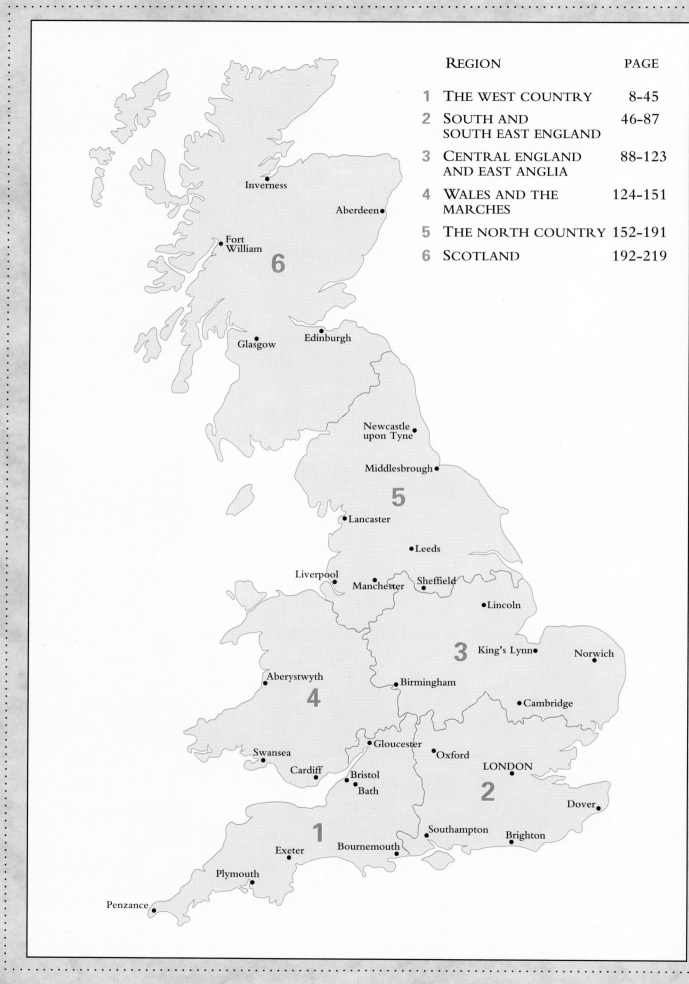

	REGION	PAGE
1	THE WEST COUNTRY	8–45
2	SOUTH AND SOUTH EAST ENGLAND	46–87
3	CENTRAL ENGLAND AND EAST ANGLIA	88–123
4	WALES AND THE MARCHES	124–151
5	THE NORTH COUNTRY	152–191
6	SCOTLAND	192–219

■

INTRODUCTION

■

Where to go in Britain? The answer could almost be, anywhere and everywhere, so richly endowed are the British Isles both with entrancing countryside and a history that has left the traces and monuments of every century on the landscape. To include all these innumerable attractions in a book of this size is impossible. Instead some 500 of the best have been selected and described.

The variety is almost endless. There is fine mountain scenery here, from the Cairngorms to the Lake District. There are prehistoric and Roman sites, frowning medieval castles and glamorous stately residences. There are places connected with famous people from the Brontës to the Beatles. There are cathedrals, churches and ruined monasteries. Historic cities include Canterbury and Cardiff, Edinburgh and Exeter, Gloucester and Glasgow. There are picturesque fishing harbours, lovingly tended gardens, museums and galleries stocked with the beautiful and the unusual. There are rare breeds farms, zoos, safari parks and white-knuckle rides in amusement parks, cheek by jowl with steam railways, and collections of bygones that bring 'all our yesterdays' into today.

HOW TO USE THIS BOOK

The book is divided into sections, each covering a region of Great Britain, each with a map locating the attractions in that region, and each with a short introduction to set the scene. Within the section, the entries are in alphabetical order. The county and geographical location of entries are indicated whenever helpful. To avoid confusion, in the section covering Scotland attractions are assigned both their old county and their new region. For example, Inveraray, formerly in Argyllshire and now in the vast region of Strathclyde, is given both county and regional names. In just one instance, Fife, are these identical. Eight cities have detailed plans to help you find your way about. If you are uncertain about the region in which to find a particular place, refer to the complete index at the end of the book.

A brief indication of opening times has been given for each attraction. These change on an alarmingly frequent basis and, to avoid disappointment, should **always be checked** before setting out. No indication of the *hours* has been provided, and a venue that is described as being *Open: daily* may open only each morning or each afternoon. Where no month is given, it should be assumed that the attraction is open throughout the year. Of course, even places open every day, all year round, often close on Christmas Day and one or two other days. Admission charges have not been included. To check that a place you want to go to is open when you wish to visit it, you should always consult the attraction itself or the nearest tourist information centre. The following organisations are indicated by abbreviations after the relevant opening times: **Cadw** (Welsh Historic Monuments); **EH** (English Heritage); **HS** (Historic Scotland); **NT** (National Trust); **NTS** (National Trust for Scotland). Membership of these bodies normally carries free admission to most or all of their sites.

■

THE WEST COUNTRY

No region in Britain outdoes the West Country in the range of its attractions, from titanic cliffs and gull-haunted fishing harbours to the heights of Dartmoor and Exmoor, or from cathedral cities to quiet villages. It is here that two of the most famous views in England can be enjoyed. One is the prospect of Salisbury Cathedral as John Constable painted it, where over the water meadows, even the cud-chewing cows seem to have arranged themselves in appropriate dispositions. The second view is the magical view of St Michael's Mount from the mainland, like a fairy castle safe on its sea-ringed island in Mount's Bay.

Nature and man have combined to create many other jewels: the harbour at Boscastle, deep between its sheltering headlands; the village of Clovelly tumbling down its north Devon cliff; the ruins of Tintagel Castle on its hulking, sea-defying rock; or the weird moonscape of Cornwall's china clay country. And there is the region's treasure of gardens, from the Arcadian temples of Stourhead and the sweeping sward of Bowood to the secret rococo paradise at Painswick and the noble glades of Westonbirt.

Human beings have been working their wonders in the West Country for a very long time. Stonehenge has stood in its present form, grey and eerie on Salisbury Plain, while 120 generations of men and women have come and gone. Of equal antiquity are the stone circles at Avebury, which some find even more atmospheric. The Iron Age village at Chysauster is another fascinating prehistoric site, while in Bath are some of the country's richest Roman remains – and at Cirencester are some glowing Roman mosaics.

Europe's most extensive miniature railway can be ridden at Dobwall's, and the world's biggest collection of working bees is busy buzzing at the Quince Honey Farm. There are collections of shoes in Street and buttons in Shaftesbury. You can go letterboxing on Dartmoor or underground in Exeter or drive a tank simulator at the Tank Museum. There are lawnmowers to admire at Trerice and the shell and feather decorations created by the two Miss Parminters in their eccentric polygonal citadel of A La Ronde. Miss Chichester of Arlington Court liked shells, too, and also model ships.

The stark ruins of Corfe Castle contrast with Castle Drogo's 1920s baronial comfort, and in between are medieval fortresses turned into civilised homes, like Berkeley Castle and Sudeley Castle. From delectable Athelhampton or Montacute or charming Sheldon Manor with its platypus-skin quilt, the graph of stately homes curves up to the palatial magnificence of Longleat with its guardian lions. There are swans at Abbotsbury and Slimbridge, wild ponies on Dartmoor and Exmoor, seals and woolly monkeys in Cornish sanctuaries. Georgian Bath and Regency Cheltenham await the visitor, with maritime Bristol and naval Plymouth, while churches range from the Gothic sublimity of Gloucester, Wells and Tewkesbury to remote little Culbone and mermaid-haunted Zennor. No shortage, here, of experiences to savour.

A LA RONDE
DEVON

■ JUST OFF THE A376, 2 MILES (3KM) NORTH OF EXMOUTH ■

Below: a swan glides gracefully on the water at Abbotsbury swannery, where Britain's only managed herd of mute swans has reared its young for at least 600 years, and perhaps longer, in a meadow where a small stream flows down to the Fleet lagoon, sheltered behind the Chesil Bank

Left: perched above the estuary of the Exe, this charming, oddly shaped house was built for two spinster ladies at the end of the 18th century. Inside are weird and engaging examples of shells and featherwork and decorations in cut paper, with which the ladies ornamented their residence

This delightfully eccentric, 16-sided house, acquired by the National Trust in 1991, was built in the 1790s for two maiden ladies who were cousins, Miss Jane and Miss Mary Parminter. They lived here until their deaths and were buried in a tiny chapel that they had built near the house. According to family tradition, the building was inspired by the octagonal Byzantine church of San Vitale in Ravenna, which the cousins had seen on a visit to Italy. Settling at Exmouth after their return in 1795, they built their house on land just outside the town which still has a sweeping view over the estuary of the Exe to the Powderham Castle estate. The two ladies intended their home to pass only to their unmarried female descendants, but in fact in 1883 it was inherited by a clergyman named Reichel, who made some alterations. Among other things, he replaced the original thatched roof with tiles.

The polygonal shape of the building occasioned strangely shaped rooms, with funny little stray spaces here and there. Considerable ingenuity was displayed in making the most use of space. In the Octagon, which rises 35ft (10.5m) high at the centre of the house, for instance, there are hinged flaps on the door jambs which could be let down to serve as seats or shelves.

The Octagon commands a view of the extraordinary, grotto-like gallery above, which was covered with shells and feather decorations by the ladies themselves. Many of the rooms have decorations of some kind, with portraits and pictures made from sand and seaweed. The drawingroom has a frieze of feathers and a weird fireplace, with a watercolour of St Michael's Mount surrounded by shells and engravings. The house is altogether a delightful curiosity. *Open: daily, late Apr–Oct (NT).*

ABBOTSBURY
DORSET

■ ON THE B3157 BETWEEN BRIDPORT AND WEYMOUTH ■

The village is best-known for its **swannery**, which was started by the Benedictine monks of the local monastery in the 14th century or earlier and is still going strong. The monks kept the swans to supply meat for the table in lean winter months. When the monastery was closed down by Henry VIII, the swannery was preserved by the Fox-Strangeways family, local landowners who became Earls of Ilchester. Today the swannery has the only managed herd of mute swans in the country.

The path to the swannery leads pleasantly beside a stream to the nesting-ground on the edge of the **Fleet lagoon**, one of the strangest features of Britain's coastline. This 9-mile (14.5km) stretch of water, protected from the force of the sea by the natural pebble beach of **Chesil Bank**, is a sheltered haven not only for swans, but many other birds. They range from little terns to herons, cormorants, great crested grebes, bunting and warblers, and tiny goldcrests. The crowds of wintering wildfowl include mallard, teal and widgeon.

The number of swans wanting to breed varies considerably from one year to another, from 20 pairs to as many as 100. They start to prepare their nests in February and some return to exactly the same spot year after year. As there is not room for all the pairs to rear their cygnets, some are placed in special breeding pens.

The duck decoy is one of the few still working in Britain, and the reed bed

DUCK DECOYS

Duck decoys were first devised in Holland and were introduced to England in the 17th century. The ducks are craftily enticed into a succession of netted tunnels, called 'pipes'. Once they are well inside, the decoyman shows himself at the wide entrance and drives them up the narrowing tunnel into a small, detachable bag at the far end. At Abbotsbury the ducks are lured into the pipes by corn, which is scattered on the surface of the water. Nowadays they are caught to be ringed and released again, not killed for the pot as in the past. Ringing started at Abbotsbury in 1937.

The Gill family were decoymen at Abbotsbury for many years. Gregory Gill was decoyman from 1879 until 1922. In his seventies he was succeeded by his son Joe, who retired in 1950 leaving Fred Lexster, a nephew, in charge.

provides material for the swans' nests, as well as good thatch for local houses.

The village, with its stone and thatched cottages, is 1 mile (1.6km) inland from the swannery. Its inhabitants used to live principally by fishing and plundering wrecks. There are some tumbled ruins, once a monastery, but the most impressive survival is a splendid 15th-century **tithe barn**.

The **Subtropical Gardens** on the B3157, in a sheltered position close to the shore, were created in the 18th century by the first Lady Ilchester and enlarged by subsequent generations. Rare and tender plants flourish here and the spring brings marvellous displays of camellias, magnolias, azaleas and rhododendrons. Set apart on a low hill is **St Catherine's Chapel**, once used as a lighthouse. *Open: daily, Apr–Oct (swannery): daily, mid-Mar–mid-Oct (gardens): daily (chapel).*

ARLINGTON COURT
DEVON

■ ON THE A39, 8 MILES (13KM) NORTH-EAST OF BARNSTAPLE ■

Set in a beautiful landscape of woods, lakes and green pastures, the Regency house of the Chichester family was left to the National Trust by the last of the line, Miss Rosalie Chichester, a recluse who died aged 84 in 1949. Her collections of ship models, shells, fans and other trinkets that took her fancy add charm to a stern Greek Revival mansion of the 1820s, designed by a Barnstaple architect, Thomas Lee. There is a good collection of carriages in the stables, with Jacob sheep, Shetland ponies and peacocks in the grounds, and a Victorian conservatory. *Open: Sun–Fri and BH Sat, Apr–Oct (NT).*

ATHELHAMPTON HOUSE
DORSET

■ ON THE A35, 1½ MILES (2½KM) WEST OF TOLPUDDLE ■

In a deep dream of peace among its formal gardens beside the River Puddle. Athelhampton is one of England's most charming and beautiful houses. Its mellow walls and battlements go back to the 15th and 16th centuries, when it was built by the Martyn family. The great hall, with its linenfold panelling, is hung with tapestries. The house is the Athelhall of Thomas Hardy's Dorset novels and, according to tradition, stands on the site of the palace of 10th-century King Athelstan. The gardens were laid out in the 1890s. *Open: Wed, Thu, Sun, BH, Eas–Oct; also Tues, May–Sep and Mon, Aug.*

AVEBURY
WILTSHIRE

■ ON THE A361, 7 MILES (11KM) WEST OF MARLBOROUGH ■

The village of Avebury grew up in and among the hulking standing stones of one of Britain's most impressive prehistoric sites, constructed more than 4,500 years ago. Two stone circles are surrounded by an outer circle, the largest in Europe, which is itself surrounded by a henge, consisting of a ditch and a massive bank. The bank originally stood some 55ft (17m) high and its chalk gleamed a brilliant white. The huge stones of the various circles, weighing 40 tons (41 tonnes) or more apiece, were dragged here from the downlands to the east. From the southern entrance the remains of a stone avenue, presumably used for processions, can be seen running to the south-east. Also in the village is the **Great Barn Museum of Wiltshire Life**. *Open: daily, all year (stone circle, EH, NT): daily, mid-Mar–Oct; Sat, Sun, Nov–mid-Mar (Great Barn, NT).*

■ ANCIENT SITES

The stone circles at Avebury are part of one of the biggest prehistoric complexes in Europe. A mile (1.5km) or so to the north-west, on Windmill Hill, are the sparse remains of an earthwork camp constructed some 5,500 years ago. There are also numerous barrows in the area, including West Kennet Long Barrow in a field south of the A4, which is of roughly the same date as the Windmill Hill camp. Close to Avebury is Silbury Hill, a huge manmade mound dating from the same period as the stone circles and covering 5½ acres (2¼ha). No-one knows what is was for

■

■

Below: eerie and awesome in their massive size and immense antiquity, the stone circles at Avebury are what is left of one of the major religious centres of prehistoric Britain. People probably came from long distances to attend spectacular ceremonies here

■

■ DON'T MISS

■ The sand and seaweed pictures (A La Ronde)

■ Seashell decorations (A La Ronde and Arlington Court)

■ The skeleton under the floor (Great Barn Museum, Avebury)

FOR CHILDREN

■ Cygnets at the swannery in May (Abbotsbury)

ANYONE WHO WAS ANYONE WENT TO BATH

TO TAKE THE WATERS IN THE 18TH CENTURY,

WHEN ENGLAND'S MOST ELEGANT GEORGIAN

BATH
AVON

TOWN WAS PLANNED TO RESTORE ITS

ROMAN SPLENDOUR

The roster of Bath's visitors in its palmy days in the 18th century includes virtually everyone of fashion and note of the time: from Queen Anne to Jane Austen, Dr Johnson to Sir Walter Scott, Clive of India to Nelson. The professional gambler Beau Nash was appointed master of ceremonies to preside over assemblies, balls and card parties in the days of sedan chairs, fluttering fans and powdered wigs.

Fashionable society went to Bath to see and be seen, but some went also to wallow in the healthful water of the hot springs, as the Romans had done before them.

GEORGIAN BATH
The Georgian city of today, with its crescents and terraces in local stone ranged decorously

on the steep hillside above the River Avon, was fundamentally the creation of three men. Ralph Allen, a self-made businessman, supplied the stone from the quarries he owned at Combe Down, on the outskirts of Bath. The

principal architects of the city were two John Woods, father and son. John Wood the Elder arrived in Bath in 1727. Among his achievements are Queen Square, where he lived himself, and Gay Street, but his masterpiece is acknowledged to be the **Circus**, inspired by the Colosseum in Rome and so planned that whichever street you take into it, a graceful unbroken crescent confronts you. The Circus was built to his plan after his death in 1754 by his son, John Wood the Younger, who also designed magnificent **Royal Crescent** close by. This glorious curve of identical houses was completed in 1774. **No. 1** has been restored and furnished by the Bath Preservation Trust to give a flavour of life in the city in the late-18th century. *Open: Tue–Sun, Mar–Oct.*

'WATER IS BEST'
John Wood the Elder's original intention was to make Bath the Rome of Britain, to recreate the grandeur of its Roman past on a larger scale. The town's history as a resort goes back to Roman times and far beyond, for the hot springs had been discovered at least 5,000 years before the Romans arrived in the 1st century AD. They saw it as an ideal place for an elaborate bathing complex with a temple to the goddess Minerva (the Celtic goddess Sulis already had a shrine there). The main spring bubbles up from deep underground at a rate of 250,000 gallons (1,137,500

Below: looking down at the steamy green water of the Great Bath and the foundations of Roman columns. In the background rises the pinnacled tower of Bath Abbey.

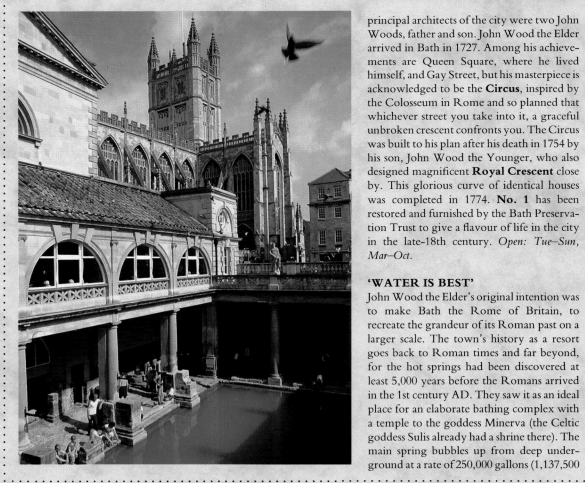

Above: the elegant line of Royal Crescent curves away behind a balloon and its attendants in 18th-century dress. Although it contains 30 separate houses, Royal Crescent is built like a grand palace, with 114 Ionic columns supporting a continuous cornice and balustrade

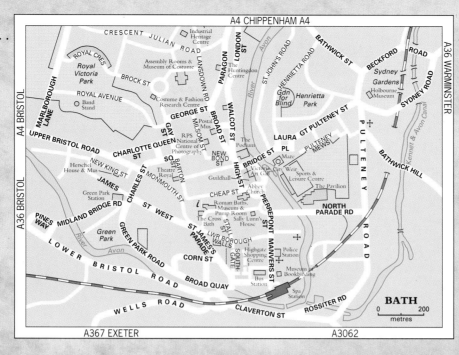

CRESCENT JULIAN ROAD — Industrial Heritage Centre — A4 CHIPPENHAM A4

Below: William
Herschel's house in
Bath is now a museum
to his memory

Below: the Museum of
Costume has a wealth
of exhibits from many
periods

Above: graceful
Pulteney Bridge

You can sample Cherry
Ciderette and Lemon
Juice Soda at J B
Bowler's soft drinks
factory and
engineering works. Mr
Bowler started in
business in 1872 and
tackled jobs of any

litres) of water a day, at a steady temperature of 116 degrees F (46.5 degrees C).

Visitors to the **Roman Baths Museum** today can see the results of recent archaeological work, with finds ranging from coins and other offerings thrown into the spring, to gems and brooches, lead piping, carved stones, altars, mosaics and a fine head of Minerva. *Open: daily.*

Looking down over the Roman Baths, which are 20ft (6m) below ground level today, is the 18th-century **Pump Room**. On the outside is an inscription in Greek proclaiming that 'Water is best', and inside you can buy a glass of spring water, or eat in the restaurant.

A PLACE TO EXPLORE

Close to the Pump Room is **Bath Abbey**, the last important church built in England before the Reformation. Inside is a host of tablets to Bath notables, including Beau Nash and Sir Isaac Pitman, inventor of Pitman's shorthand.

Another reminder of the 18th century is **Sally Lunn's House** close by, said to be Bath's oldest house. It is now a restaurant, where you can enjoy a Bath bun.

Bath is a charming place to explore, the sort of town where you go into a bank to find it has a ceiling that would grace a ducal palace. There is an excellent range of shops, museums and galleries. The **Holburne Museum**, in a noble building at the end of imposingly grand **Great Pulteney Street**, has lavish displays of Old Master paintings, silver, porcelain, Italian majolica, glass and furniture. Look out for the garden roller inscribed by Eric Gill. *Open: daily, mid-Feb–mid-Dec.*

kind, great or small.
The works finally
closed down when his
grandson retired in
1969. In all that time,
practically nothing was
thrown away. The
place has now been
lovingly recreated in all
its muddled glory

MUSEUMS AND GALLERIES

The **Victoria Art Gallery** also has an interesting collection, with paintings by Thomas Barker and other Bath artists. Up the hill, next to the Countess of Huntingdon's Chapel, don't miss the **Museum of English Naïve Art**, with its touching and sometimes eccentric pictures of street scenes, ships, bare-fisted pugilists and improbable sheep. *Open: Mon–Sat (Victoria Art Gallery): daily, Apr–Oct (Museum of Naïve Art).*

Not far away and deeply nostalgic, at the **Industrial Heritage Centre**, is J B Bowler's alarmingly dangerous Victorian brass foundry and engineering works, all unguarded machinery and flapping fan belts, which has been preserved entire since it closed down. Mr Bowler had a sideline making fizzy drinks. *Open: daily.*

The **Museum of Costume** has one of the world's best collections of its kind. Its exhibits cover 400 years of fashion, from linen shirts of 1590 to Italian styles of the 1990s. The displays are in the stately **Assembly Rooms**, designed by John Wood the Younger. The building was burned out by incendiary bombs in 1942, and in the 1950s it was restored with 18th-century decor by Oliver Messel. *Open: daily.*

The **National Centre of Photography** has a good exhibition on the early days of the camera, while **Herschel House**, built in 1766, is a museum to the astronomer. *Open: daily (National Centre of Photography): daily, Mar–Oct; Sat and Sun, Nov–Feb (Herschel House).* Also of interest are **Bath Postal Museum**, the **Geology Museum** and the **Museum of Bookbinding**. *All open: Mon–Fri.* Just outside Bath, at Claverton Manor, is **The American Museum**, with 18 period furnished rooms and a superb collection of quilts.

BERKELEY
GLOUCESTERSHIRE

■ OFF THE B4066, 17 MILES (27KM) SOUTH OF GLOUCESTER ■

King Edward II was brutally murdered at **Berkeley Castle** in 1327 and the room in which he was killed can still be seen. In one corner is a deep hole like a well – the 28ft (8.5m) deep dungeon into which prisoners of lowlier rank were flung and left to rot.

The castle was built in the 12th century, with substantial additions in the 14th, and the Berkeley family have lived there for more than 800 years (they also owned Berkeley Square in London). In that time they have turned their barbaric fortress, whose walls are 14ft (4m) thick, into a civilised home, stocked with family portraits, fine furniture, silver, china and paintings. All the same, the stout Norman keep still looks ready to stand siege. It was besieged in 1645, when a Parliamentary army stormed it. A medieval kitchen can also be seen, as well as the 14th-century great hall with its splendid timber roof. From the house there is a view over the Elizabethan terraced gardens to water meadows, where cattle graze in as tranquil a scene as any in England. In the butterfly house tropical butterflies flutter and swoop.

The lords of Berkeley were buried in the **church of St Mary**, on a hill overlooking the castle. It has a separate belltower, an unusual feature built in 1753. The 14th-century church door still shows bullet holes and axe marks from the siege of 1645. Nearby, the Georgian **home of Edward Jenner**, who discovered the smallpox vaccine, is kept as a museum to him. His tomb can be seen in the church.

Open: daily, Apr–Sep; Sun only, Oct (Castle and Jenner Museum).

BICKLEIGH
DEVON

■ ON THE A396, 5 MILES (8KM) SOUTH OF TIVERTON ■

A display of devices and gadgets used by prisoners-of-war attempting escapes is an unusual attraction at **Bickleigh Castle**. The moated manor house was the home of the Carew family from the 16th century. *Open: Eas; Wed, Sun, BH to end May; daily except Sat Jun–Oct.*

Bickleigh Mill is now used as a craft centre, with workshops and showrooms. Shire horses work on the farm and children can handle pigmy goats, Vietnamese pot-bellied pigs and other endearing animals. There is also a bird park and a motor centre. *Open: daily, Apr–Dec; Sat, Sun, Jan–Mar.*

BOSCASTLE
CORNWALL

■ ON THE B3263, 10 MILES (16KM) EAST OF TINTAGEL ■

A winding, S-shaped inlet between towering cliffs leads in from the sea to the long, narrow harbour at Boscastle on the wild north Cornish coast. It would be hard to imagine many places looking more like the

■

EDWARD JENNER

Edward Jenner, who lived almost all his life at Berkeley in Gloucestershire, was one of the great benefactors of the human race. He was born in this village, where his father was vicar, in 1749. As a young man Jenner studied medicine in London under John Hunter, the great surgeon, and returned to Berkeley as a country doctor. An enthusiastic naturalist, he was interested in hedgehogs and cuckoos, and in the country belief that people who caught cowpox would never catch

smallpox. He experimented by transmitting cowpox from sufferers to healthy people, so as to immunise them against smallpox. He published his results in 1798 in a pamphlet which was translated into many languages, and was to become the foundation of modern immunological medicine.

■

■

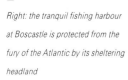

Right: the tranquil fishing harbour at Boscastle is protected from the fury of the Atlantic by its sheltering headland

■

headquarters of wreckers and smugglers, but Boscastle was a respectable port in its time, exporting slate in sailing ships which had to be hauled through the harbour entrance. The curving inner jetty goes back to the 17th century and the outer one has been rebuilt by the National Trust, which owns the harbour, since a stray mine blew it up during the Second World War. The stone, slate-roofed houses crowd together on the steep hill down to the harbour, where there is a **Museum of Witchcraft**. *Open: daily, Apr–Oct.*

BOURTON-ON-THE-WATER
GLOUCESTERSHIRE

■ OFF THE A429, 4 MILES (6KM) SOUTH OF STOW ON THE WOLD ■

The River Windrush flows under charming little bridges along the main street of this Cotswold tourist honeypot. An exhibition of perfumery adds to the scented attractions of the **Cotswold Perfumery** in Victoria Street. Other things to see include penguins, parrots and the feathered denizens of **Birdland**; the **Model Village**, a miniature replica of Bourton made in the 1930s and one-ninth life size; the vintage vehicles in the **Cotswold Motor Museum**; and the **Village Life Exhibition** of bygones. *All open: daily (Motor Museum, Feb–Nov only).*

BOWOOD HOUSE
WILTSHIRE

■ OFF THE A4, 5 MILES (8KM) WEST OF CHIPPENHAM ■

The ravishing **park** at Bowood, landscaped by 'Capability' Brown in the 1760s, must be one of the half-dozen most beautiful in all England. With magnificent trees in exactly the right positions, and garlanded with daffodils in spring, the grassy sward curves sweetly down to a slender artificial lake, with an island and classical temple. Nearby a cascade tumbles down the rocks beside a hermit's cave, which is lined with fossils and mineral specimens. In a completely separate garden are bluebell woods with serried ranks of rhododendrons, and a mausoleum by Robert Adam. Adam also designed the south front of the house – originally the service quarters of the main house, which was pulled down in 1955. There is a beautiful terraced garden in front, and inside a satisfying collection of paintings, sculpture and objects from India. *Open: daily, Apr–Nov.*

BRYMPTON D'EVERCY
SOMERSET

■ OFF THE A30, JUST WEST OF YEOVIL ■

The smallest legal distillery in Britain is one of the attractions of this exquisite manor house in local stone, cut from quarries on nearby Ham Hill. Brympton apple brandy is on sale, along with cider and wine from the estate vineyard. There is also the I Zingari cricket club collection and a museum of country life. The main front of the house is Tudor and Elizabethan, while the beautiful south front dates from the late 17th century. Close by is the parish church of St Andrew, which goes back to the 14th century. *Open: Sat–Wed, May–Sep; also Eas weekend (house).*

BUCKFAST ABBEY
DEVON

■ OFF THE A38 NEAR BUCKFASTLEIGH, 21 MILES (34KM) SOUTH-WEST OF EXETER ■

A monastery was founded on this site beside the River Dart far back in the 11th century, well before the Norman Conquest of 1066. In the Middle Ages it prospered under the Cistercians, but it was closed down in 1539 during the Reformation. Long afterwards, in 1882, Benedictine monks returned here. In 1907 they began to rebuild the abbey church on its medieval foundations, learning how to do it more or less as they went along, and it was completed in 1938. Inside there is a fine mosaic pavement. The abbey is known for its tonic wine and honey. *Open: daily.*

There is also a **butterfly farm** and **otter sanctuary** nearby, and at Buckfastleigh station **steam trains** run on through the scenic Dart Valley to Totnes. *Open: daily, Eas–Oct (butterfly farm): Eas–Sep (South Devon Railway).*

■

Above: clipping one of the tall yews on the terrace at Bowood, a colourful foreground to the Robert Adam front of the house. Hundreds of roses bloom here in the summer, in beds divided by stone steps and balustrades, with classical urns along the walls

■

■

DON'T MISS

■ The murder room (Berkeley Castle)

■ Lord Byron's Albanian fancy dress and Queen Victoria's wedding chair (**Bowood**)

■ Apple brandy (**Brympton d'Evercy**)

FOR CHILDREN

■ Rides on the rocking-horse (Bickleigh Castle)

■ Pot-bellied pigs (Bickleigh Mill)

■ Scent-sampling (Cotswold Perfumery, Bourton-on-the-Water)

IN ITS HEYDAY BRISTOL WAS BRITAIN'S

SECOND MOST IMPORTANT PORT, AFTER

LONDON. IT IS STILL ONE OF THE LIVELIEST,

BRISTOL
AVON

MOST INVIGORATING AND ENJOYABLE CITIES

IN THE COUNTRY

It was from Bristol and with the backing of Bristol merchant venturers that John Cabot sailed to discover the mainland of North America in 1497. In the 18th century Bristol merchants and financiers made fortunes in the slave trade. At the handsome old Llandoger Trow Inn in King Street, Bristol, Daniel Defoe met the real-life original of 'Robinson Crusoe' and in Robert Louis Stevenson's *Treasure Island*, young Jim Hawkins sailed with Long John Silver from the city. Bristol money backed Isambard Kingdom Brunel, whose Great Western Railway steamed triumphantly into the city from London in 1841. Brunel's pioneering ocean greyhound, the *Great Western*, first of the transatlantic steam liners, was launched from the city docks, and in the 1840s his iron ship, the *Great Britain*, was built there.

All this activity centred on Bristol's inland harbour. Until well into the 19th century the middle of the city was a forest of masts and spars of sailing ships, while the quays and taverns echoed to half the languages of the globe. When new docks were built at Avonmouth the **old port** languished, but it has now been turned into a most attractive waterside area, with boat trips, cobbled wharves and floating restaurants. The **Arnolfini Gallery** specialises in modern art exhibitions. *Open: daily.*

INDUSTRIAL HERITAGE

On the southern side of the water, behind a screen of towering cranes, **Bristol Industrial Museum** covers the city's pioneering involvements with land, sea and air transport. On display are the world's oldest self-propelled passenger-carrying road vehicles, the world's oldest tug and the great-grandfather of all leisure caravans, which was built in Bristol in

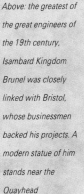

■

Above: the greatest of the great engineers of the 19th century, Isambard Kingdom Brunel was closely linked with Bristol, whose businessmen backed his projects. A modern statue of him stands near the Quayhead

■

■

Above: soaring across the Avon gorge, Clifton Suspension Bridge was designed by Brunel and built after his death as a monument to his genius. It became a favourite spot with people determined to commit suicide

■

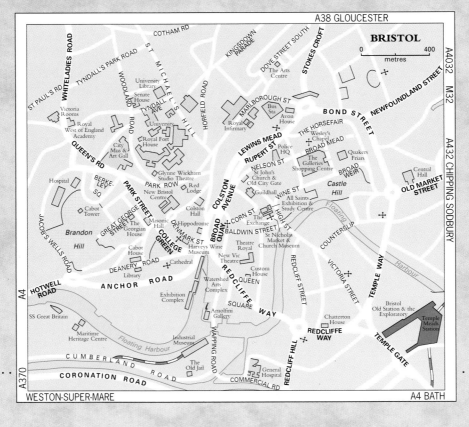

the 1880s. Also of interest are Bristol cars and lorries, Rolls Royce aero engines and the role Bristol played in the development of *Concorde*. *Open: Sat–Wed.*

Further along is the **Maritime Heritage Centre**, housing the collection of a former Bristol ship-building firm, Hill and Sons. Brunel's iron masterpiece, **SS Great Britain**, is being restored to her original majesty nearby. *Open: daily (heritage centre and SS Great Britain).*

CHURCHES AND CHAPELS

From the harbour there are fine views of the **church of St Mary Redcliffe**, with its graceful 290ft (88m) spire, rebuilt in the 15th century and one of the biggest and most impressive parish churches in Britain. Outside the south door is the tomb of the church cat, a tabby of godly habit which used to attend all the services and dearly loved processions.

Bristol Cathedral on the other side of the water is not as impressive a church as might be expected. The nave and the two western towers were sensitively designed in the 19th century by G E Street, who added

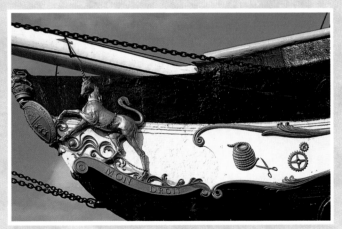

them on to the 14th-century east end of the building. A third church which is well worth seeing is the **New Room**. Concealed in Broadmead shopping precinct, it is the oldest Methodist chapel in the world, a graceful 18th-century building with many links with the early Wesleyan movement. *Open: Mon–Sat, Apr–Sep; Mon, Tue, Thu–Sat, Oct–Mar.*

CITY LANDMARKS

Bristol was heavily bombed and badly damaged during the Second World War, but the handsome **Corn Exchange** of 1743 by the great Bath architect, John Wood the Elder, came through safely. The big covered market here is thoroughly enjoyable and in Broad Street nearby is the astonishing Art Nouveau façade of the **Edward Everard**

Building, a symphony of brightly coloured tiles in praise of the art of printing which no visitor should miss.

Bristol's only surviving medieval gateway is at the foot of Broad Street. Not far away is the picturesque alleyway called **Christmas Steps**, built in 1669 at the personal expense of a rich wine merchant. At the top is the little 15th-century chapel of the Three Kings. Wine, and in particular sherry, has always been a Bristol speciality. You can follow the story of Bristol Cream and Bristol Milk instructively at **Harveys Wine Museum**. *Open: Fri.*

There is another Brunel link at Temple Meads station, where the original building, designed by the great man himself and 80ft (24m) longer than the cathedral, is now home to the **Exploratory Hands-On Science Centre**. The splendid train shed has a mock hammerbeam roof, with the widest span of its day. *Open: daily.*

IN AND AROUND BRISTOL

Bristol is a hilly place, but is fortunately well equipped with restaurants, cafés and pubs of character to pause and rest in. Up the hill at the top of Park Street is the **university**, dominated by the **Wills Memorial Tower**, 215ft (65m) high and housing a bell called Great George, which weighs 10 tons (10.2 tonnes). It is a family monument to the Wills tobacco dynasty, who have been great benefactors to the city. The **City Museum and Art Gallery** here is one of the best provincial museums in the country. In a handsome building designed by Sir Frank Wills are magnificent displays of Oriental art, ceramics, ivories and lacquerware. There is delectable Bristol Blue glass to relish, as well geology, archaeology, Egyptology and natural history galleries. Works by Bristol artists form part of an exceptional collection of paintings. *Open: daily.*

The museum also runs **Red Lodge**, whose decorous Georgian exterior conceals rooms rioting in uproarious 16th-century panelling. One of them has an internal porch of phenomenal proportions. Oddly enough, this was the setting for Britain's first reform school for girls, which was established here in 1854. *Open: Mon–Sat.*

Further out from the centre are the 18th-century terraces of Clifton and **Bristol Zoo**, which is rated as one of the best in the country. *Open: daily.*

BUCKLAND ABBEY
DEVON

■ OFF THE A386, 6 MILES (9KM) SOUTH OF TAVISTOCK ■

Two of Britain's most redoubtable sea-dogs lived in this house, Sir Richard Grenville of the *Revenge* and Sir Francis Drake. It was Grenville who converted the nave and chancel of the Cistercian monastery church into an extremely unusual house. Drake bought the house soon afterwards, in 1581. There are relics of both men in the house, including Drake's drum. *Open: Fri–Wed, Eas–Oct; Sat, Sun, Nov–Mar (NT).*

CASTLE COMBE
WILTSHIRE

■ OFF THE B4039, 5 MILES (8KM) NORTH-WEST OF CHIPPENHAM ■

In one of the prettiest villages in England, the main street of simple stone houses runs down past an old market cross to a picturesque bridge over the Bybrook. Here a row of cottages was magically transformed into a bustling fishing port for the film *Dr Doolittle*. The **church** has an ancient, faceless clock and over the south door is an unusual royal coat of arms, placed there on the death of Oliver Cromwell in 1658.

CASTLE DROGO
DEVON

■ OFF THE A382, 4 MILES (6KM) NORTH-EAST OF CHAGFORD ■

One of the last grandly baronial houses in England, poised dramatically above the valley of the Teign, Castle Drogo was designed by Sir Edwin Lutyens for the tycoon Julius Drewe and completed in 1930 in a style which convincingly combines grandeur and comfort. The **gardens** are special, too. *Open: daily (garden); Sat–Thu, Eas–Oct (Castle).*

CHEDDAR GORGE
SOMERSET

■ ON THE B3135, IMMEDIATELY NORTH-EAST OF CHEDDAR ■

Dramatically steep and narrow, the gorge winds between limestone cliffs more than 400ft (120m) high. The best approach is

■

Above: legends grew up about Sir Francis Drake after his death at sea in 1596, and there were those in Devon who refused to accept that he was dead. The story that his aid for England could be summoned by striking his drum seems to have been invented in the 1890s by Henry Newbolt, author of Drake's Drum

■

■

Below: cars snake their way past the looming walls of Cheddar Gorge, where nature trails explore the woods and conifer plantations. The caves, which are now commercial attractions, were once home to Stone Age hunters, who tracked their prey here as much as 14,000 years ago

■

from the north, with the road descending gradually at first. Near the foot of the gorge are **Cox's Cave** and **Gough's Cave**, with spectacular stalactites, stalagmites and rock formations. The **Cheddar Showcaves Museum** displays Stone Age artefacts and finds from the caves and the gorge, including the skeleton of a young man aged about 23 from Gough's Cave, where he was buried about 12,000 years ago. Examination of his teeth has shown that he cleaned them regularly. It is possible that the cave was then a kind of factory, turning out flint implements. *Open: daily (caves and museum).*

In Cheddar village nearby, the **church of St Andrew** has good stained glass, brasses and bench ends.

CHELTENHAM
GLOUCESTERSHIRE

THE CHELTENHAM GOLD CUP
Run over a course of approximately 3 miles (5km) in March, the Cheltenham Gold Cup is the most prestigious steeplechase in the National Hunt calendar. The greatest horses in the sport have contested the race since 1924. Golden Miller won it five years in a row in the 1930s and in 1934 was the first horse ever to win the Gold Cup and the Grand National in the same season. More recently, Arkle won the Gold Cup three years in succession in the 1960s. There are always good Irish challengers for the trophy, and a strong contingent of Irish racegoers helps to bring Cheltenham to life for three days in March.

■

The great Duke of Wellington went to Cheltenham in 1816 to cure a liver complaint he had contracted, by taking the spa water. His approval made the town's fortune, attracted other liverish servicemen and encouraged speculators to transform Cheltenham into a stylish Regency spa town. Elegant terraces look out over flowery gardens, from balconies and verandas adorned with delicate lacy ironwork. Among the gems are the tree-lined **Promenade**, the **Queen's Hotel**, **Montpellier Walk** with its smart shops and classical caryatids, the **Rotunda** (which is now a bank), and the domed **Pittville Pump Room**. This was inspired by an Athenian temple when it was built in the 1820s, and set in a spacious park. Today it contains costume and jewellery galleries, and exhibits covering Cheltenham's history. *Open: Tue–Sun, Apr–Oct; Tue–Sat, Nov–Mar; also Eas, BH Mons.*

The history of the spa goes back well before the Regency period, to the early 18th century. At this time a medicinal spring was discovered by chance in a field, on the spot where Cheltenham Ladies College stands today. A small spa was created in the 1730s and a visit by George III in 1788 gave the town a boost. Few buildings are left from this period, however.

Cheltenham Art Gallery and Museum has a particularly distinguished collection of Arts and Crafts metalwork, textiles, and ceramics. It also contains furniture by Ernest Gimson and others, as well as good Dutch 17th-century paintings, English paintings and an oriental gallery of Chinese ceramics and costume. Local history and archaeology are also covered. *Open: daily, May–Sep; Mon–Sat, Oct–Apr.*

The **Gustav Holst Birthplace Museum** honours the memory of the composer of *The Planets*, who was born here in 1874. *Open: Tue–Sat.*

Since the 19th century the town has been known for its schools, and the ample Victorian buildings and playing fields of Cheltenham College for boys are a pleasing backdrop for the annual cricket festival. Cheltenham prides itself on its smart shops, and on the remarkable 'wishing fish' clock in the modern **Regent Arcade**. It also boasts gardens and parks, and a lively cultural life, with two theatres and annual festivals of music (in July) and literature (in October). Meanwhile the racecourse at **Prestbury Park**, in a beautiful Cotswold setting, is one of the strongholds of steeplechasing.

■

DON'T MISS

■ The royal coat-of-arms (Castle Combe church)

■ The staircase (Castle Drogo)

■ Montpellier Walk (Cheltenham)

■ The Arts and Crafts collection (Cheltenham Art Gallery and Museum)

FOR CHILDREN

■ Drake's Drum (Buckland Abbey)

■ The Stone Age skeleton and the caves (Cheddar Gorge)

CHYSAUSTER ANCIENT VILLAGE
CORNWALL

■ OFF THE B3311, 2½ MILES (4KM) NORTH OF GULVAL ■

Cared for by English Heritage, the surprisingly substantial remains of a hamlet inhabited 2,000 years ago stand silent on a draughty Cornish hillside. There are eight houses, with walls up to 6ft (2m) high and rooms opening off a central courtyard. They had paved floors, covered drains and small gardens. The inhabitants probably panned for tin in the nearby stream, and the hillfort of Castle an Dinas, a mile (1.6km) away to the east, would have given them refuge in danger. *Open: daily, Apr–Sep; Tue–Sun, Oct–Mar (EH).*

CIRENCESTER
GLOUCESTERSHIRE

Known locally as 'Siren', this amiable market town is best known for its wool church and Roman collection in the Corinium Museum. As *Corinium*, Cirencester was one of the largest towns in Roman Britain. In the Middle Ages it grew prosperous on the wool trade, and the **church of St John the Baptist** – one of the biggest parish churches in England – was rebuilt in the sumptuous Perpendicular style in the 15th century. It has a mighty tower and is entered through a three-storey south porch of astonishing dimensions. Inside there is a rare 'wineglass' pulpit, fine fan-vaulting and numerous brasses.

The showpieces in the **Corinium Museum** are Roman mosaics. There are also tombstones, sculptures and many household and everyday objects. Although the focus is mainly Roman, the museum also has prehistory displays, and material relating to the town's later history. *Open: daily.*

■

Above: part of the charming Hare Mosaic in the Corinium Museum, Cirencester. Discovered in the town in 1971, it is a fine example of the Roman technique. Mosaics were made from small cubes of stone in different colours, and in this case cubes of glass were used on the hare's back to accentuate the pattern

■

CLOVELLY
DEVON

■ OFF THE A39, 10 MILES (16KM) WEST OF BIDEFORD ■

The houses of this famously photogenic village on the North Devon coast stand almost on top of each other, so steep are the cliffs above the harbour, with its sturdy 16th-century stone quay. The main street is far too steep for cars and descends in cobbled steps (a Land Rover will bring you back up by a different way). There is a good visitor centre at the car park. The remains of Iron Age earthworks can be seen at **Clovelly Cross**, at the top of the village, off the A39, and the delightful **Hobby Drive**, built by an 18th-century squire, winds through the woods with delectable views over Bideford Bay.

COMPTON ACRES GARDENS
DORSET

■ ON THE B3065 AT CANFORD CLIFFS, BETWEEN POOLE AND BOURNEMOUTH ■

With fine views over Poole Harbour and the Purbeck Hills, these celebrated gardens were planned by T W Simpson in 1914 as a set of separate areas of strikingly different character. In the Italian Garden there are formal flower beds and a lake with water-lilies and a temple. The Japanese Garden is also elegant, with a pagoda, a tea-house draped in wisteria and a lake crossed by stepping-stones. There is also a Roman Garden and a Rock and Water Garden, and more besides. *Open: daily, Mar–Oct.*

■

Above: small boats in Clovelly harbour at low tide. Donkeys used to carry visitors up the village street, but no more

■

CORFE CASTLE
DORSET

■ ON THE A351, BETWEEN WAREHAM AND SWANAGE ■

The ruined bastions and curtain walls of the **castle** climb grimly up the steep hill above the village to the jagged keep at the top. The fortress was blown up by order of Parliament in 1646, after a long siege in which it was stoutly held for the King by Lady Bankes, wife of the Royalist owner. The castle fell only when one of her officers treacherously opened the gates to the enemy. Today the stronghold is one of England's most dramatic ruins.

The castle and the village below are both built of local grey Purbeck stone. The keep dates from soon after the Norman Conquest, and by 1300 the surrounding walls and towers had also been completed. In the inner ward are the remains of a house King John built for himself, with a chapel and garden. Much earlier, before the castle was built, the Anglo-Saxon kings had a hunting lodge here, where the youthful King Edward was murdered in 978 by his stepmother. This made way for her own son, known to history as Ethelred the Unready, to ascend the throne. *Open: daily, Feb–Oct; weekends, Nov–Jan (NT).*

CORNISH SEAL SANCTUARY
CORNWALL

■ AT GWEEK, 4 MILES (6KM) EAST OF HELSTON ■

This hospital for the treatment of injured seals, dolphins, birds and other casualties found around the coast is set on the banks of the beautiful River Helford. The patients, who include young seals dashed against rocks in gales, can be seen recovering in pools. When they are well enough, they are returned to the sea. **Nature trails** lead through the woods. There are attractive old houses in the village of **Gweek**, which in the Middle Ages, before the harbour silted up, was the port for Helston. *Open: daily.*

CORSHAM COURT
WILTSHIRE

■ OFF THE A4, 4 MILES (6KM) SOUTH-WEST OF CHIPPENHAM ■

Corsham is an attractive little town in pale Bath stone, with an 18th-century town hall and a handsome church. Lord Methuen's imposing mansion, set back from its handsome gateway and lawn where peacocks promenade, is less a stately home than a gallery for an absorbing display of Old Master paintings by Van Dyck, Veronese, Rubens, Reynolds, Romney and dozens more. There are fine chimneypieces and carpets, and the furniture includes pieces by Chippendale and Robert Adam. The oldest part of the house is Elizabethan. The state rooms were added in 1760 by 'Capability' Brown, who also laid out the park. *Open: Tue–Thu, Sat, Sun, Jan–Nov.*

■

THE BATHURSTS OF CIRENCESTER PARK

The towering yew hedge which shields Earl Bathurst's Georgian mansion in Cirencester from irreverent public view stands 40ft (12m) high and is said to be the tallest in Europe. It was planted in 1818. The Bathursts, whose family vault is in the parish church, have been great benefactors to the town. The 4th Earl founded the Corinium Museum in the 1850s to preserve the Roman antiquities which were being discovered in such profusion, and his ancestor, the 1st Earl, laid out the delightful wooded grounds of Cirencester Park in the 18th century, together with his friend Alexander Pope. Pope liked to muse upon the scene from the summerhouse where seven rides meet, now called Pope's Seat. The park is open to the public today. Polo is played there and the Broad Ride runs for more than a mile (1.6km) between spreading chestnut trees.

■

Below: blown up with gunpowder and mines on the instructions of a vengeful Parliament in 1646, the jagged fangs and stumps of Corfe Castle's medieval fortifications still defy time and weather. Strategically sited on the Isle of Purbeck, the site has a long history of treachery and death

■

■

DON'T MISS

■ The cup made for Anne Boleyn (Cirencester parish church)

■ Roman mosaics (the Corinium Museum, Cirencester)

■ The Hobby Drive (Clovelly)

■ Views over the River Helford (the Cornish Seal Sanctuary)

■ Michelangelo's *Sleeping Cupid* (Corsham Court)

FOR CHILDREN

■ Seals and other patients (the Cornish Seal Sanctuary)

COTEHELE HOUSE
CORNWALL

■ OFF THE A390, 8 MILES (13KM) SOUTH-EAST OF TAVISTOCK ■

The Edgcumbe family moved away to the outskirts of Plymouth and their stately mansion of Mount Edgecumbe House in the 17th century, leaving their old grey granite home at Cotehele (pronounced C'teel) to slumber through the rest of the centuries almost unchanged. The National Trust preserves it today, with its original armour and tapestry, pewter, embroidery and furniture.

Set above the valley of the Tamar, the old house has a **garden** on different levels down to the river. A restored sailing barge, the *Shamrock*, is moored at the quay, with dock buildings of the 18th and 19th centuries. There is also a medieval dovecote, a restored watermill and a cider press. *Open: Sat–Thu, Apr–Oct (house): daily (garden).*

COTSWOLD FARM PARK
GLOUCESTERSHIRE

■ OFF THE B4077, 6½ MILES (10KM) WEST OF STOW ON THE WOLD ■

The rare-breed farm animals assembled here constitute the best collection of the kind in the country. Weird Loughtan sheep from Isle of Man parade about under the weight of up to six horns apiece. Shaggy red Highland cattle look prehistoric, and Iron Age pigs have been specially bred here. There are Gloucester Old Spot pigs, goats with a villainous expression, and a small army of sheep, hens and rabbits. Seasonal events include lambing and shearing. *Open: daily, Apr–Sep.*

■

Below: the land-locked estuary of the River Dart shelters ships in Dartmouth Harbour, which once traded prosperously in cloth, wine and cod. In the background is the grand Edwardian bulk of the Royal Naval College, designed by Sir Aston Webb, which dominates the town

■

■

Left: mare, foal and an old-fashioned farm cart make a pretty picture at the Heavy Horse Centre, Cricket St Thomas. The leading wildlife park in the West Country, it has been developed in the grounds of Cricket House, rebuilt by Sir John Soane in the 1800s for Admiral Hood

■

CRICKET ST THOMAS
SOMERSET

■ ON THE A30, BETWEEN CHARD AND CREWKERNE ■

The television series *To the Manor Born* was filmed at Cricket House, a 19th-century manor. Kept out of shot were elephants, leopards, roaming zebras and wallabies, which all help to make its **wildlife park** an enjoyable outing. Visitors can go on the Jungle Safari Ride and on a miniature railway through the grounds. Add to this a children's farm, a Heavy Horse Centre, a tropical aviary and a craft centre, and you will find there is no shortage of things to do. *Open: daily.*

DARTMOUTH
DEVON

When Second World War American troops left Dartmouth for the invasion of Europe in 1944, they were following in the illustrious wake of the soldiers who had embarked for the Crusades from this venerable port 800 years before. In summer today you can take a peaceful cruise the other way, up the scenic **River Dart** to Totnes (see page 41). Dartmouth is also home to the Royal Naval College.

In the town the narrow streets close to the waterside include the restored, four-storey 17th-century Butterwalk, a heavily carved arcade where there is now a small **maritime museum**. The ruins of a 16th-century **fort** stand on the cobbled quay at Bayard's Cove whose cobbled quay was used as the set for *The Onedin Line*. In the **church of St Saviour** is a celebrated early 15th-century brass to John Hanley, thought to be one of the characters in Chaucer's *Canterbury Tales*. Sea-lapped **Dartmouth Castle** was built in 1481 to protect the harbour. *Open: daily, Eas–Sep; Tue–Sun, Oct–Eas (EH).*

DOBWALLS FAMILY ADVENTURE PARK
CORNWALL
■ OFF THE A38, 3 MILES (5KM) WEST OF LISKEARD ■

On Europe's most extensive miniature railway system, 10 scaled-down replicas of American 'Iron Horse' locomotives – some steam, some diesel – haul trains and passengers through tunnels and deep cuttings, across canyons, and through forests. There is an adventure playground and fairground as well, while Mr Thorburn's Edwardian Countryside is devoted to the famous wildlife artist Archibald Thorburn, who died in 1935. More than 200 of his paintings are on view and there is a recreation of his studio. *Open: daily Eas–Oct; Nov–Eas, check with local tourist information centre.*

DORCHESTER
DORSET

Dorset's attractive county town still has something of the atmosphere immortalised in Thomas Hardy's novels, in which it appears as Casterbridge. The **Dorset County Museum**, which has substantial material on Hardy – and on another local literary figure, the 19th-century poet William Barnes – traces Dorchester's history back to its remote origins as an Iron Age settlement and subsequently as a Roman town. The museum is also strong on geology, natural history and country crafts. *Open: daily.*

A statue of Barnes stands outside the Perpendicular **parish church of St Peter**. Judge Jeffreys presided savagely over the Bloody Assizes in what is now the Antelope Hotel, and the Tolpuddle martyrs were tried in the Old Courts. The King's Arms Hotel with its fine portico appears in Hardy's *Mayor of Casterbridge*. The **Dorset Military Museum** covers the history of the Dorset Regiment, and the **Dinosaur Museum** has skeletons, fossils and lifesize reconstructions of the giant beasts. *Open: Mon–Sat (Military Museum): daily (Dinosaur Museum).*

DUNSTER
SOMERSET
■ ON THE A39, 2 MILES (3KM) EAST OF MINEHEAD ■

The High Street widens out to accommodate the octagonal Yarn Market, built in the 17th century, where local weavers brought their cloth to be sold. Like the medieval butter cross and Gallox Bridge, the two-arched stone packhorse bridge over the mill stream, it is now looked after by English Heritage. **Dunster Castle** was the home of the Luttrell family for six centuries, and now belongs to the National Trust. It was extensively remodelled in the 19th century by the architect Anthony Salvin, to dramatically pleasing effect. *Open: Sat–Wed, Apr–Nov (castle); daily, Feb–Dec (gardens), NT.*

Above: the tremendous oak staircase at Dunster Castle, with its elaborately carved balustrade, was added to the house after Francis Luttrell married an heiress in 1680 and spent money on improvements. He also raised an infantry regiment, which became the Green Howards

■

DON'T MISS

■ The Tamar barge *Shamrock* (Cotehele)

■ The 'Shipman' brass (St Saviour's Church, Dartmouth)

■ Thomas Hardy's study (Dorset County Museum, Dorchester)

FOR CHILDREN

■ Exotic animals (Cricket St Thomas Wildlife Park)

■ Miniature train rides (Dobwalls Family Adventure Park)

■ Dinosaurs (Dorchester Dinosaur Museum)

Above: a mosaic from Roman Dorchester. The Romans stormed the massive ramparts of Maiden Castle, outside the town to the south, in AD43

■

THOMAS HARDY

Dorchester has close links with Thomas Hardy. The great poet and novelist lived at Max Gate on the outskirts of the town, and died there in 1928. It is owned by the National Trust now, but is not open to visitors. The Trust also owns the cottage at Higher Bockhampton outside Dorchester, where Hardy was born in 1840: it can be visited by appointment. Hardy's body was buried with ceremony in Westminster Abbey, but his heart was interred separately in the quiet churchyard at Stinsford, where he lies with his country ancestors.

■

DARTMOOR
DEVON

Dartmoor's best-known animal, the Hound of the Baskervilles, does not exist, and its best-known building is not open to tourists. This is the famous **Dartmoor Prison**, which can be seen in its grimness in Princetown or from the B3357. It was built in 1806 for French prisoners-of-war captured in the struggle against Napoleon. They helped to build the **church of St Michael** in Princetown. 'The Moor' has been an ordinary prison since 1850.

GEOLOGY AND LANDSCAPE

Both the mythical Hound and the real prison contribute to the sense of eeriness, bleakness and danger on Dartmoor. Dartmoor was declared a National Park in 1961 and covers 365 square miles (945 square km) of high granite moorland, with areas of heath and bog. Parts are used as firing ranges by the Army and are not open to the public. About 30,000 people live in the National Park, most employed in farming, and they are far outnumbered by visitors in the summer.

Dartmoor is essentially a hump of granite sticking up above the surrounding lowland. The moor rises to 'tors', piles of boulders heaped up on each other, the remains of higher summits that have been eroded and shaped by thousands of years of weather. Below a tor there is often a mass of scattered rocks, or 'clitter', lying on the surface. It was these rocks that were used for building houses, barns, bridges and field walls all through the human history of Dartmoor, until late in the 19th century.

ANCIENT SETTLEMENTS

Human occupation goes back to prehistoric times. At **Grimspound**, on the moor near Postbridge, the protective wall of a village occupied perhaps 3,000 years ago can still be

Below: view of Dartmoor, with one of its tors in the foreground. These curious outcrops of granite rock have been worn and sculptured by wind and weather ever since the Ice Age

seen. The wall originally stood 6ft (2m) high and 9ft (3m) thick, and the villagers would bring their cows and sheep inside it at night. The site is in the charge of English Heritage. So are the standing stones and village remains at **Merrivale**. Here stones and hut foundations are scattered over miles of the Plym Valley, east of Yelverton. They date from the Stone Age to the present century. The remains of an abandoned medieval village below **Hound Tor**, south of Manaton, can also be visited. *All open: any reasonable time.*

Farm is home to an engaging assortment of old-style farm animals and poultry. *Open: daily, Apr–Oct.*

To the west lie the charming **Beccy Falls**, where the Becca Brook cascades over boulders in a wooded glen on its way to the River Bovey. South of Drewsteignton is **Fingle Gorge**, with picturesque Fingle Bridge at the heart of what R C Blackmore (author of *Lorna Doone*) called 'the finest scene in England'.

THE DARTMOOR PONIES
The open moors are grazed by sheep and cattle, and roamed by Dartmoor ponies. All these animals, including the ponies, belong to the 'commoners' who own the unenclosed land on Dartmoor, generally by inheritance from medieval farmers, and who still have the right to pasture stock on it. Although the ponies live wild, they are rounded up every autumn so that the year's foals can be marked or branded by their owners.

A Dartmoor oddity is letterboxing. Boxes are hidden in all sorts of places on the moors. Each box has inside it a visitor's book, a rubber stamp and an inkpad. The idea is to find as many as you can, leaving each box intact. Letterboxing can add considerably to the enjoyment of a moorland walk or ride. Besides walking and riding, pony trekking, rock climbing and fishing all draw visitors to Dartmoor.

LOCAL HISTORY
To get a flavour of life as it used to be on Dartmoor, explore the **Museum of Dartmoor Life**, which occupies a Regency watermill in Okehampton. There are displays on tin and copper mining, which for centuries were flourishing Dartmoor industries. At Sticklepath nearby, the **Museum of Waterpower** is a restored tool-making works. Waterwheels drive working trip hammers and shears, which operated here from 1814 until 1960. *Open: Mon–Sat, Mar–mid-Nov; also Sun, Jun–Sep (both museums).*

WOODS, RIVERS AND RAVINES
Lydford Gorge, where the River Lyd leaves the western edge of Dartmoor through a narrow ravine, is a celebrated beauty spot owned by the National Trust, along with the **Devil's Cauldron** pothole and the 90ft (27m) **White Lady Falls**. Nearby is the 12th-century stone keep of **Lydford Castle**, which gave its name to the local brand of 'Lydford law': hang first and hear the evidence afterwards. **Brentor** is a spectacular isolated hill, with the ruined church of St Michael perched high on top, and astonishing views. *All open: daily.*

Over on the eastern edge, the River Bovey runs through woods at **Parke**, another National Trust beauty spot near Bovey Tracey, and the **Parke Rare Breeds**

EXETER
DEVON

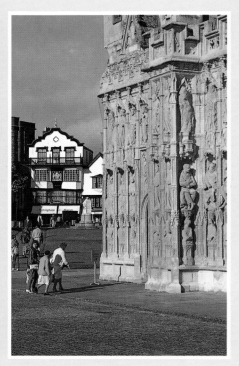

Under the city streets runs a network of narrow, claustrophobic **underground passages** which were originally built in the Middle Ages to bring water into the town, and were used until the 19th century. The citizens used to haul up buckets of water through holes in the tunnel roof. Dry now, or only dripping a little, the tunnels make an unusual guided tour. People queue up at the entrance in Princesshay shopping precinct to get in.

Up above ground, the focus of the city is the **cathedral**. The hulking Norman towers at the ends of the transepts are an unusual feature: the battlements and pinnacles were added later. Most of the rest of the building dates from the 13th and 14th centuries. Inside, above the soaring nave, is the world's longest unbroken stretch of Gothic vaulting. It runs for more than 100yds (90m) and standing under it has been likened to being inside a monstrous whale. The tall 14th-century bishop's throne is intricately carved, and there are other delightful medieval carvings beneath the seats in the choir. They include what is probably the first picture of an elephant ever attempted in this country.

The chapel of St James was knocked flat by a bomb in 1942 and rebuilt after the war, with charming carvings by the cathedral's master mason, George Down. Among them are a rugby player and the one-eyed cathedral cat. Also keep an eye out for the 15th-century clock and the memorial window to the men of HMS *Exeter*, sunk in action in 1942. In the cathedral library, the *Exeter Book* contains the largest collection of Anglo-Saxon poetry that has survived in this country.

Attractive old houses surround the cathedral close, and up a side alley is the low-beamed **Ship Inn**, which was Sir Francis Drake's favourite Exeter tavern. There are elegant Georgian streets to be admired, especially **Southernhay**, and stretches of the old **city wall** in the local red stone, originally built to protect the Roman town. This grew up round a fort, built above the River Exe at the highest point into which ships could sail from the English Channel. The city wall was strengthened and kept in repair ever afterwards.

The crumbly red local stone was also used to build the little churches that were squeezed at odd angles inside the cramped and swarming medieval city, which thrived on the wool trade. It was run by its merchant guilds and the city regalia can be seen today in the **Guildhall**. *Open: Mon–Fri.*

There is a notable collection of Exeter silver in the **Royal Albert Memorial Museum**, which also has English paintings, and archaeology and natural history displays. Meanwhile cascades of lace shimmer in the **Museum of Costume and Lace** in Rougemont House. *Open: Tue–Sat (Royal Albert Memorial Museum); Mon–Sat (Museum of Costume and Lace).*

The ruins of the Norman **castle** and the **Rougemont Gardens**, stocked with shrubs by the famous Exeter firm of Veitch are also well worth a visit.

Of special interest is the **Exeter Maritime Museum** in the old canal basin. It displays one of the world's biggest collections of boats. Brought from all over the globe, they range from coracles and a Chinese junk, to a tug and a steam dredger. *Open: daily, Apr–end Sep; for winter opening, check with tourist information centre.*

■
Above: looking past the corner of Exeter Cathedral across the close to Mol's Coffee House, which dates from the 1590s (the Dutch gable was added later). The great Devon sea-dogs of Elizabethan days – Drake, Hawkins, Frobisher – used to meet there

■
Above: a collection of brightly painted fishing boats from Portugal is one of the attractions of the Maritime Museum, which was opened in 1969 in the old canal basin close to the River Exe. It has since built up an interesting display of boats from around the world
■

FORDE ABBEY
DORSET
■ OFF THE B3162, 4 MILES (6KM) SOUTH-EAST OF CHARD ■

Cushioned in its 30 acres (12ha) of grounds in the valley of the River Axe on the Dorset–Somerset border, the house is a captivating blend of medieval Cistercian monastery and 17th-century country mansion. The last abbot built himself a princely dwelling in Perpendicular style here, and Sir Edward Prideaux, a wealthy lawyer, converted it into his home in the 1650s. Indoors, the pride and joy of the house is the set of early 18th-century Mortlake tapestries. Outdoors are fine **gardens**, an unusual bog garden and a lake. *Open: Sun, Wed and BH afternoons, Eas–mid-Oct (house); daily (gardens).*

FOREST OF DEAN
GLOUCESTERSHIRE

The Dean still extends over more than 50 square miles (129 km²) of upland between the Wye and the Severn. In the Middle Ages it was a royal hunting ground, and much larger. There are many trails through the woods, which are now managed by the Forestry Commission. The area has a long history of coal mining, in tiny pits that might have been worked by a single family for generations. Iron mining is also a time-honoured occupation here, and one of the most fascinating placs to visit is **Clearwell Caves Ancient Iron Mines**. These mines date back to prehistoric and Roman times, and have an eerie atmosphere. *Open: daily, Mar–Oct.*

Dean Heritage Centre at Soudley provides an introduction to the area, with nature trails and picnic spots, while steam locomotives whistle hoarsely in the woods at **Dean Forest Railway** outside Lydney. Nearby at **Lydney Park**, the ruins of a Roman healing temple command a spacious view over the Severn, and there is a small, interesting museum. *Open: daily (Dean Heritage Centre and Forest Railway); Wed, Sun and BH, Eas–Sep (Lydney Park).*

Below: seen at its most commanding, rising from a morning mist, Glastonbury Tor has a mystery and an awe about it. It was probably a pagan sacred site long before Christianity, and its terraces may be an ancient processional path to the summit

GLASTONBURY
SOMERSET

Glastonbury has the strongest links with the legends of King Arthur and the Holy Grail of any place in Britain, which accounts for the occult bookshops, vegetarian cafés and alternative therapy centres in this otherwise stolid Somerset town. The haunting ruins of the great medieval **abbey** stand on the site where, according to ancient tradition, the first Christian church in Britain was built. This is where King Arthur and Queen Guinevere were buried, it is said, and the site of Arthur's grave is marked. Growing here is a descendant of the famous holy thorn tree, which flowers at Christmas. *Open: daily.*

There is another holy thorn outside the **parish church of St John the Baptist**, with its handsome Perpendicular tower. The George and Pilgrims' Inn was originally a 15th-century hostel for pilgrims. The **Tribunal**, the abbey courthouse, is now a local archaeology and history museum, and the **Somerset Rural Life Museum** occupies the abbey tithe barn. *Open: daily (both museums).*

Above the town rises the eerie shape of **Glastonbury Tor**, topped by a church tower and commanding a tremendous view. At its foot is the healing spring of **Chalice Well**.

GLENDURGAN GARDEN
CORNWALL
■ NEAR MAWNAN SMITH, 4 MILES (6KM) SOUTH-WEST OF FALMOUTH ■

Looking out over the bewitching estuary of the Helford River, the garden was created in the 19th century by the Fox family of Falmouth, which is why a pair of stone foxes stand guard at the gate. The grounds follow the valley of a small stream down to the estuary, with winding paths and a laurel maze. Subtropical plants prosper in this sheltered place: tulip trees, swamp and Mexican cypresses, tree ferns, bamboos. Daffodils and bluebells run riot in the spring, and there are enticing glimpses of the estuary and the sea. The garden was given to the National Trust in 1962. *Open: Tue–Sat and BH Mon, Mar–Oct.*

■

THE HOLY GRAIL

The Holy Grail of Arthurian legend was a profoundly sacred and magical relic, which the great paladins of the Round Table rode out to seek – Sir Lancelot, Sir Gawain, Sir Galahad and many more. It was the chalice of the Last Supper, the cup into which Christ himself poured the wine of the first communion service. It was also, in legend, the chalice in which Joseph of Arimathea caught some of the blood which dripped from Christ's wounded side on the cross. It consequently had a double connection with the redeeming blood of the Christian Saviour.

According to the traditions of Glastonbury Abbey, Joseph of Arimathea and a group of companions came to Glastonbury and established the first Christian foundation in Britain. They built the revered 'old church' on the site where the abbey ruins stand today. It was natural to wonder whether Joseph brought the Holy Grail with him, and whether the precious relic was kept in secret there over the centuries. The monks never made any such claim, but the name of Chalice Well was not given by accident.

■

■
DON'T MISS

■ The bog garden (**Forde Abbey**)

■ The underground passages (**Exeter**)

■ Carvings of an elephant and the cathedral cat (**Exeter Cathedral**)

■ The view on a clear day (**the summit, Glastonbury Tor**)

FOR CHILDREN

■ Spooky passageways (**Clearwell Caves Ancient Iron Mines, Forest of Dean**)

EXMOOR
SOMERSET AND DEVON

With red deer and wild ponies, high moors and venerable oak woods, winding lanes, plunging valleys and sparkling streams – not to mention miles of spectacular coastline – Exmoor delights the eye and heart at every season. The 265 square miles (686km²) of the Exmoor National Park, designated in 1954, have a year-round population of only about 10,000 people and is one of the less visited parks of its kind. It still has lonely places.

The National Park straddles the Devon–Somerset border, with close to three-quarters of its area on the Somerset side. Rather more than half of it is farmland. The moors rise to above 1,300ft (400m) and the highest point is **Dunkery Beacon**, at 1,704ft (520m).

The National Trust protects thousands of acres of Exmoor, and Dunkery Beacon is part of its most notable Exmoor property, the Holnicote estate, south of Porlock, with more than 6,000 acres (2,400ha) of wild moorland grazed by ponies and the occasional deer, while buzzards wheel overhead. It includes the ancient oak woodland of **Horner Vale**, with its nature trails, where the challenging bellowing of the stags rings through the woods in the autumn. The Trust also owns the picture-postcard village of **Selworthy**, originally built for the estate's pensioners in the 1820s, with its thatched houses and cottage gardens bursting with hollyhocks and delphiniums: and most of the villages of **Allerford**, **Bossington** and **Luccombe** as well. The area is rich in medieval dovecotes and packhorse bridges, prehistoric barrows and hill forts.

There is no shortage of prehistoric remains on Exmoor. Some of the most rewarding are found in the remote area called **The Chains**, north-west of Simonsbath. The most dramatic of them is **Long Stone**, a 9ft (3m) pillar of slate tucked away in a dip in the moorland. Other standing stones and burial mounds on the moors are silent reminders of long-forgotten lives here many centuries ago.

LORNA DOONE COUNTRY
In the country west of Porlock, **Badgeworthy Water** is a magnet to visitors drawn to Exmoor by R D Blackmore's historical novel *Lorna Doone*. From Malmsmead at the foot of Badgeworthy Water a path leads into the 'Doone Country' in the valley of the Hoccombe Water, where the remains of old houses are probably those in which Blackmore imagined his wild and wicked outlaws living, late in the 17th century. A 'must' for

admirers of the book is **Oare Church**, where Lorna Doone married John Ridd, and you can see the window through which the villainous Carver Doone fired at her.

PARKS AND MANOR HOUSES
To the west again, **Watersmeet** is another favourite spot owned by the National Trust, where Hoaroak Water joins East Lyn River. You may see salmon leaping up the rapids, and there are delightful walks by the waterside and through woods rich in oak and beech, larch and whitebeam. The focal point is **Watersmeet House**, built as a fishing lodge in the 1830s. *Open: daily, Eas—Oct.*

Over on the south-eastern edge of the National Park are woodland walks and picnic spots at **Wimbleball Lake**, below Haddon Hill, a 374-acre (151ha) reservoir completed in the 1970s. *Open: daily.*

A tree discovery walk is one of the attractions of **Combe Sydenham Country Park**, along with the deer park. The 16th-century house was the home of Elizabeth Sydenham, who married Sir Francis Drake. **Gaulden Manor** at Tolland was the Somerset home of the Turberville family (the D'Urbervilles of Hardy's *Tess of the D'Urbervilles*). Their charming old house in local red sandstone has fine ceilings and furniture, and a bog garden in the grounds. *Open: Sun–Fri, Apr–Oct (Combe Sydenham Country Park): Sun, Thu and BH Mon, May–Aug (Gaulden Manor).*

MANMADE PLEASURES
To the north, English Heritage has charge of the ruins of **Cleeve Abbey**, a Cistercian monastery at Washford. Saved

at the Dissolution by being turned into a house, it has a remarkably complete set of cloister buildings. *Open: daily.* Also at Washford, in stark contrast, is **Tropiquaria**, where an indoor replica jungle has been created inside a 1930s BBC transmitting station, for visitors to make the closer acquaintance of snakes, lizards, iguanas, toads and free-flying tropical birds. *Open: daily, Mar–Oct; weekends and school holidays, rest of year.*

There are manmade pleasures on the western outskirts of Exmoor, too, where the

■

Above: Tarr Steps, a celebrated beauty spot near Hawkridge in the southern part of Exmoor. The River Barle is crossed by an old packhorse bridge about 180ft (55m) long. The bridge has been washed away and rebuilt many times

■

■

Above: Oare Church, where, in real life, novelist R D Blackmore's grandfather was rector

■

village of Combe Martin follows its long main street down the valley of the River Umber to the sea. A successful gambler built the Pack of Cards Inn, or so tradition has it. The **Combe Martin Motorcycle Collection** is a nostalgic last resting-place for old British motorbikes and petrol pumps, while at the **Combe Martin Wildlife Park** otters, meerkats and other animals thrive among woods and cascades. South of Berrydown there are farm animals to be seen at **Bodstone Barton Farmworld**, a working farm since the 17th century. At Stowford, penguins and tropical birds parade at the **Exmoor Bird Gardens**. *Open: daily (Bird Gardens and Bodstone Barton Farmworld); daily, Mar–Nov (Combe Martin Wildlife Park); Eas, then daily, May–Sep (Combe Martin Motorcycle Collection).*

COASTAL EXMOOR

The coastline of Exmoor is graced by the highest cliffs and some of the most spectacular scenery in England. The **South West Coast Path** runs all the way from Combe Martin eastwards, past the 1,043ft (318m) bulk of the **Great Hangman**. The National Trust owns the stretch from Trentishoe past Highveer Point to Woody Bay. At **Martinhoe** are the remains of a Roman signal station, where a watch was kept against raiders coming across the Bristol Channel from Wales. The cliffs above **Woody Bay** are a breeding ground for guillemots, shags and gulls in their myriads. The **Valley of the Rocks** is famous for its eroded rock pillars, which have fanciful names like Ragged Jack, White Lady and the Devil's Chimney. In *Lorna Doone*, John Ridd went to consult a witch who lived in a cave here.

Lynmouth became a popular seaside resort after Wordsworth and Coleridge sang its praises. It is on the coast where the valleys of the West Lyn and the East Lyn join, and in 1952 it was badly devastated by a sudden and horrific flood. Perched 430ft (130m) up above the cliff is Lynton, connected to Lynmouth by a cliff railway, whose cars run on the weight of the water in their tanks. At Lynton the **Lyn and Exmoor Museum**, in an 18th-century cottage, has a collection of bygones from the area and a reconstruction of an old Exmoor kitchen. *Open: Mon–Fri, Sun, Apr–Oct.*

To the east is **Countisbury Common**, where soaring cliffs rise 991ft (302m) above the sea. There are miles of footpaths on National Trust land in this area, and tremendous views across to South Wales. Further east again is the hamlet of **Culbone**, whose

tiny church is one of the smallest in the country. It measures 34ft (10m) long by 12ft (4m) wide, and only 30 people fill it. There is a legend that Jesus came here as a boy.

There are handsome churches at **Porlock** – dedicated to St Dubricius, who according to legend conducted the marriage service of King Arthur and Queen Guinevere – and at **Minehead**, a busy and popular seaside resort with a pleasant old harbour and a big holiday camp. Both places make useful bases for exploring the quieter depths of Exmoor.

GLOUCESTER
GLOUCESTERSHIRE

The mighty, pinnacled tower of the **cathedral**, rising 225ft (68m) high, dominates the city of Gloucester and can be seen miles away in the Vale of Severn and along the Cotswold edge to the east. It was built, in effect, on the proceeds of a murder.

In 1327 King Edward II was brutally killed at nearby Berkeley Castle. Buried in the abbey church of St Peter at Gloucester, he swiftly became an unofficial saint. There were stories of miraculous cures at his tomb and pilgrims came in droves to visit it. Their offerings enabled the monks to rebuild the church, which they did in creamy Cotswold stone in the brand-new and sumptuous Perpendicular style of architecture. The fan-vaulting in the cloister is possibly the earliest in the country. Behind the high altar the walls of the church were splayed out to make room for the colossal east window, at almost 3,000 square feet (279m²), the largest in Britain. Edward II's tomb, with its effigy of the murdered king, can still be seen close to the altar. Not far away is the curious figure of Robert Curthose, Duke of Normandy, son of William the Conqueror. He was buried here, in the earlier church on the site, after 28 years of captivity in Cardiff Castle; even in death his effigy is held in an iron cage.

The church became the cathedral of the new diocese of Gloucester in the 16th century, after the abbey was closed down by Henry VIII. Gloucester had been an important town for many centuries before that, because of its position at the crossing of two major routes, from London across the Severn to Wales, and from the South West up the Severn Valley, to the Midlands and the North. It grew up originally round a Roman fort commanding the Severn, and a few scattered Roman remains are still to be seen.

There are Roman mosaics and sculptures in the **City Museum and Art Gallery**, as well as 18th-century furniture, barometers, coin hoards and marine paintings. The enjoyable **Folk Museum** has lively displays on traditional fishing for eels and elvers, lampreys and salmon in the Severn, along with objects for keeping witches at bay. A Double Gloucester dairy and models of early steam engines are set off in half-timbered buildings of about 1500, whose floors slope at lunatic angles. *Open: Mon–Sat (both museums),*.

Gloucester's dock area has been rescued from dereliction as the home of the **National Waterways Museum**, which covers the history and crafts of Britain's canals and inland waterways. The old Custom House accommodates the **Regiments of Gloucestershire Museum**: the 'glorious Glosters' being one of the Army's most famous infantry formations. *Open: daily (both museums)*.

Nearby, in the refurbished Albert Warehouse is something on no account to miss. The Robert Opie Collection, which forms the **Museum of Packaging and Advertising**, is a deeply nostalgic array of thousands of items from yesterday's kitchen cupboards, pantries and shop shelves: tins and cartons and containers of household products, from Vim to Cherry Blossom shoe polish; cigarettes and cereal packets; posters and old enamel advertising signs. *Open: daily*.

■

Left: one of Gloucester's new shopping precincts has been brightened up with a colourful decoration, while Father Time, John Bull, and grotesque figures of 1904 chime bells above a jeweller and watchmaker's shop in Southgate Street

■

HIDCOTE MANOR GARDEN
GLOUCESTERSHIRE
■ OFF THE B4081, 4 MILES (6KM) NORTH-EAST OF CHIPPING CAMPDEN ■

One of Britain's most photographed and influential gardens was created on a bare Cotswold hillside by Lawrence Johnston, principally between the two World Wars. It became internationally famous, and after his death in 1958 was sympathetically restored by the National Trust. It is organised as a series of garden 'rooms' with distinctive colour schemes, separated by walls and hedges and connected by narrow paths. *Open: Sat–Mon, Wed, Thu, Apr–Oct (NT).*

Next door at **Kiftsgate Court** is another delightful garden created in friendly rivalry to Hidcote. It boasts the largest rose in England. *Open: Wed, Thur, Sun, BH, Apr–Sep.*

KILLERTON
DEVON
■ ON THE B3181, 7 MILES (11KM) NORTH-EAST OF EXETER ■

The simple 18th-century house, home to generations of the Acland family and now owned by the National Trust, stands in a resplendent park. Beeches and oaks, conifers and maples, bamboos and pampas grass, magnolias and rhododendrons climb the steep hill behind the house to the Iron Age hill fort on top. The **park** was laid out by Sir Thomas Acland early in the 19th century. Daffodils bloom here in spring, and the autumn colours are magnificent. In the house a costume collection is shown in period rooms. *Open: daily (except Tue), Apr–Oct (house); daily (gardens).*

KNIGHTSHAYES COURT
DEVON
■ OFF THE A396 AT BOLHAM, 2 MILES (3KM) NORTH OF TIVERTON ■

The National Trust owns this 1870s Victorian house, whose most fascinating feature is its romantic, mock-medieval decorative scheme, brainchild of the architect William Burges. Unfortunately, the owner, John Heathcoat-Amory of the Tiverton lace dynasty, fired Burges and had the house finished by J D Crace, but there are still weird and wonderful things to be seen inside in the way of Gothic arches, vaulted ceilings and vast, bulging chimneypieces. Outside is a beautiful **garden**, developed after 1950 by a later generation of Heathcoat-Amorys, with formal terraces, willows and rare shrubs. It attracts many garden enthusiasts. *Open: daily, Apr–Oct (house closed Fri), NT.*

LACOCK
WILTSHIRE
■ OFF THE A350, 3 MILES (5KM) SOUTH OF CHIPPENHAM ■

The village of Lacock is one of the brightest jewels in the crown of the National Trust. The buildings, in mellow local stone interspersed with occasional brick and half-timbering, and roofed with local stone tiles, have remained largely unaltered for centuries. The oldest cottages go back to the 13th century, and there is also a 14th-century tithe barn. The venerable Angel Inn dates from the 15th century. The character of the village was preserved by generations of the Talbot family. The last of them, Miss Matilda Talbot, gave the estate to the Trust in the 1940s.

Lacock grew round an **abbey** of nuns, founded here in the 13th century. It prospered up until the 18th century on the wool trade. When the abbey was closed down in 1539 and the nuns pensioned off, the estate was bought by Sir William Sharington. He converted the abbey into a house, though parts of the nunnery are still standing. In the 1750s a big new entrance hall was built for John Ivory Talbot, designed in the 'Gothick' manner by Sanderson Millar.

William Henry Fox Talbot, the pioneer of photography, lived here and produced the first-ever photographic negative in 1831, showing the small oriel window in the south gallery of the house. The **Fox Talbot Museum**, housed in a 16th-century barn, commemorates him. *Open: Wed–Mon, Apr–Oct (house and museum); daily, Apr–Oct (grounds), NT.*

■

WILLIAM HENRY FOX TALBOT

William Henry Fox Talbot, one of the founders of modern photography, was born in 1800 and inherited Lacock as a young man. He was a many-sided scientist and an expert on the decipherment of Assyrian cuneiform writing, although it was as a mathematician that he was elected a Fellow of the Royal Society in 1831. His first efforts at photography were inspired by the beautiful scenery of Lake Como in Italy in 1834. He called his photographs 'calotypes', from a Greek word meaning 'beautiful'. His results were first made public in 1839, and his book *Pencil of Nature* was the first commercial publication to use photographs as

illustrations. Oddly enough, Fox Talbot rarely allowed photographs to be taken of himself. He died in 1877.

■

LAND'S END
CORNWALL

The most westerly point on England's mainland has long attracted visitors, partly for this reason alone, and partly for its thrilling scenery of 60ft (18m) granite cliffs, thundering waves and flying spray. The **South West Coast Path** runs all round the headland, and some of the land here is owned by the National Trust. On a clear day you can see the Isles of Scilly, 25 miles (40km) out to sea in the west. Wolf Rock lighthouse is 9 miles (14km) away to the south-west, and immediately ahead is Longships lighthouse. Land's End has been developed as a major amusement centre, with exhibitions ('Man Against the Sea' and 'the Spirit of Cornwall'), a galleon adventure playground, shire horses, a model village, souvenir shops, craft workshops, restaurants and the Last Labyrinth electronic theatre experience.

LANHYDROCK HOUSE
CORNWALL
■ ON THE B3268, 2½ MILES (4KM) SOUTH-EAST OF BODMIN ■

The grandest house in Cornwall was completed in about 1640, but had to be largely rebuilt after a ferociously destructive fire in 1881. The outside was reconstructed in the 17th-century manner, but the interior is amply Victorian, including the palatial kitchen, with its larders and cellars, bakehouse and dairy, where meals of gargantuan proportions were prepared for house parties. The main rooms have impressive plaster ceilings; the one in the long

Below: beyond its reserved and formal Victorian garden lies stately Lanhydrock, where the Robartes family, Viscounts Clifden and originally rich bankers in Truro, held sway for many generations. Many of the trees behind the house were planted between the Wars and there are fine copper beeches, flowering ashes and tulip trees

gallery illustrates Old Testament stories. Family portraits bring to life various members of the Robartes dynasty, who owned the estate until it was given to the National Trust in 1953. Outside, there is a Victorian formal garden of parterres and clipped yews. The house is approached along a noble avenue of trees and is set in 450 acres (180ha) of wooded **grounds**, with a delightful walk down to the River Fowey. *Open: Tue–Sat, and BH Mon, Apr–Oct (house); daily (grounds).*

LONGLEAT HOUSE
WILTSHIRE
■ OFF THE A362, 2 MILES (3KM) WEST OF WARMINSTER ■

One of England's most princely houses, Longleat is a combination of stately home and park, amusement centre and wild animal reserve. It belongs to the Thynne family, Marquesses of Bath, who pioneered the stately home business after the Second World War and in 1966 opened Britain's first drive-through **safari park**, in collaboration with Jimmy Chipperfield of the famous circus family, an experienced supplier of animals to zoos. Longleat has always been known for its lions, but visitors can also admire roaming rhinos, camels, giraffes, cheetahs and mischievous monkeys. Additional attractions include a rare white tiger, and a boat trip to see the hippos.

The house itself was completed in 1580 for Sir John Thynne and the great hall

LONGLEAT AND THE THYNNES
The name Longleat comes from a long watercourse, or leat, built for the medieval priory's mill. The estate came into the hands of Sir John Thynne in the 16th century, who had made a fortune in the tangled and dangerous politics of the time. One of his successors, Thomas Thynne (known as 'Tom of Ten Thousand' for his wealth), secretly married the Percy heiress, Elizabeth Percy, though she was only 15 and the union was unconsummated. One of her admirers was a Swedish nobleman, Count Königsmark, who vainly challenged Thynne to a duel and eventually had him shot and mortally wounded in his coach in London in 1682. Thynne's enormous monument in Westminster Abbey shows the murder.

retains its Elizabethan character. The other rooms were redesigned early in the 1800s by Sir Jeffry Wyatville and later in the century Italianate decoration of the utmost grandeur was added by J C Crace. The house is full of treasures: portraits, paintings, fine marble and marquetry work, rare books and manuscripts.

The grounds were superbly landscaped by 'Capability' Brown in the 18th century. There are enjoyable walks and an entrancing view from 'Heaven's Gate'. Also to be enjoyed are a maze, an adventure castle and pets' corner, a narrow-gauge railway, a butterfly garden, a Dr Who exhibition and a display of dolls' houses. *Open: daily (house); daily, mid-Mar–Oct (safari park); daily, Eas–Oct (other attractions).*

Just across the A362 from the main gate is **Cley Hill**, an 800ft (240m) chalk mound owned by the National Trust, a dramatic landmark crowned by the ramparts of an Iron Age hill fort.

MILTON ABBAS
DORSET

Set in the smiling Dorset countryside among the Winterbornes, the village was planned and built all of a piece around 1780. Joseph Damer, afterwards Earl of Dorchester, had decided that he did not want the old village cluttering up the grounds and atmosphere of Milton Abbey, his private mansion, and ruthlessly destroyed it. In its place, situated well out of sight and mind, he built today's neat and tidy thatched houses with their own church.

Milton Abbey itself, which was built for Damer by Sir William Chambers, is now a boy's school, bristling with schoolmasterly notices of a hectoring character, ordering visitors about. The massive **church** with its 15th-century tower is worth visiting all the same. There is a most unusual font by J A Jerichau, a 19th-century Danish sculptor, and a stained-glass window by Pugin, as well as a beautiful 15th-century hanging tabernacle in oak and memorials to the Hambros, who owned the estate until the 1930s. *Open: daily (church); spring and summer school holidays (abbey).*

MONTACUTE HOUSE
SOMERSET
■ OFF THE A3088, 4 MILES (6KM) WEST OF YEOVIL ■

Built of golden stone from the quarries on nearby Ham Hill, this gracious Elizabethan mansion was constructed to show off the wealth and cultivated taste of Sir Edward Phelips, a successful lawyer who became Speaker of the House of Commons and Master of the Rolls. He opened for the prosecution at the trial of Guy Fawkes in 1605. His house was finished in the 1590s and did him full justice, with a particularly impressive entrance front adorned by statues of the Nine Worthies in Roman armour (the worthies being heroic personages such as King Arthur, Julius Caesar and Charlemagne). The house was restored earlier this century by Lord Curzon and now belongs to the National Trust. Inside there is a richness of heraldry, tapestries, plasterwork, panelling and elaborate fireplaces, with Tudor and Jacobean portraits on loan from the National Portrait Gallery in London. *Open: daily Wed–Mon, Apr–Oct (house); Wed–Mon (park), NT.*

MORWELLHAM QUAY
DEVON
■ OFF THE A390, 4 MILES (6KM) SOUTH-WEST OF TAVISTOCK ■

Actors in costume help to bring back to life a copper mine and a busy Victorian inland port on the River Tamar. Morwellham was the highest point on the Tamar to which ships of any size could navigate, and until the railways arrived the river was far the quickest and most efficient way of transporting the copper from the mine at the site. Today an electric tramway carries visitors deep into the black bowels of the mine, which has been restored to its condition in 1868. Other enjoyable attractions include riverside walks, carriage drives, period workshops and museums, lime kilns, a farm and a school, adding up to a rewarding family day out. *Open: daily.*

■

Above: the table is set sumptuously at Longleat House in the lower dining room, which is crowned by its vast 19th-century ceiling. The huge house has more than 100 rooms and is built on the site of a medieval priory, closed down in 1529

■

■

DON'T MISS

■ The Victorian kitchen (Lanhydrock)

■ The Elizabethan carved chimneypiece (**the great hall, Longleat House**)

■ Lord Curzon's bathtub (**Montacute House**)

■ The Victorian school (**Morwellham Quay**)

FOR CHILDREN

■ The galleon adventure playground (**Land's End**)

■ The lions (**Longleat House**)

■ Trying on 19th-century costumes (**Morwellham Quay**)

■

Below: the assayer in his office and laboratory at Morwellham Quay, where he tested ores. Built in the late 18th century, the laboratory has a specially high ceiling to allow poisonous vapours given off during smelting to rise above the heads of the workmen

■

PAINSWICK ROCOCO GARDEN
GLOUCESTERSHIRE

■ ON THE B4073, ¼ MILE (800M) NORTH OF PAINSWICK ■

Hidden away in a little Cotswold valley, a secret garden was constructed in the briefly fashionable rococo style in the 18th century by Benjamin Hyett, the owner of Painswick House. Fortunately he commissioned a local artist named Thomas Robins to paint its picture in 1748: or possibly the picture was Robins's design for the garden. Whichever it was, the painting has been used in the restoration of the enchanting garden, with its lake, plunge pool and woodland walks. *Open: daily, Feb–mid-Dec.*

PECORAMA PLEASURE GARDENS
DEVON

■ OFF THE B3174 AT BEER ■

Up above the old fishing village of Beer, the gardens offer a fabulous view out over Lyme Bay. Visitors can ride on a miniature railway and model railway layouts are on view in the main building, along with an exhibition of nostalgic railwayana. There is also an aviary, a nature trail and a children's activity area. *Open: times vary. Check with local tourist information centre.*

PLYMOUTH
DEVON

As a major naval base, Plymouth was severely bombed during the Second World War. There are still narrow streets and Tudor houses in the area of the old harbour that Sir Francis Drake knew, and where the Mayflower Stone commemorates the departure of the Pilgrim Fathers for New England in 1620. The **Merchant's House** tells the story of Plymouth's past. *Open: Tue–Sun.* **Prysten House** is another merchant's mansion of the 15th century. *Open: Mon–Fri, Apr–Oct.*

By Plymouth Sound are the lawns of the **Hoe**, the famous promenade where Drake disdained to interrupt his game of bowls for the Spanish Armada, or so legend has it. **Smeaton's Tower** is part of the old Eddystone lighthouse. **Plymouth Dome** offers a hi-tech time-travel experience, from a galleon's deck to today's satellite weather pictures. *Open: daily, May–Oct (tower): daily, all year (dome).* It would be a shame to visit Plymouth without taking to the water to enjoy **boat trips** on the Sound, a water tour of the Royal Naval Dockyard on the Tamar Estuary (with a view of Brunel's great railway bridge of 1859), or longer trips to Eddystone and the River Tamar. A passenger ferry will take you to **Mount Edgcumbe**, whose stately grounds command lordly views of the Sound. *Open: daily.*

In Plympton, an eastern suburb of Plymouth, are the Georgian splendours of the National Trust's **Saltram House**. It has rooms designed by Robert Adam, magnificent plasterwork and fine period furniture. *Open: Sun–Thu, Apr–Oct (NT).*

■

Above: there is a fine view from the top of Smeaton's Tower, the upper part of the lighthouse placed on Eddystone Rock in 1759. Designed by John Smeaton, it was replaced in 1882 because the foundations were wearing away.

■

Right: Saltram is known for its Adam interior and paintings by Reynolds

■

■

ON PLYMOUTH HOE

Sutton Harbour, from which Drake, Hawkins and other great Elizabethan seadogs sailed, was the original port of Plymouth. In 1588 the English fleet gathered in Plymouth Sound to await the Spanish Armada, a far superior force. According to the well-known story, Sir Francis Drake was playing bowls on Plymouth Hoe when word came that the Armada had been sighted. Refusing to be hurried, he said the Dons must wait their turn, and calmly finished his game. The story is very likely true. A display of coolness would certainly have been good for everyone's morale.

■

■

DON'T MISS

■ The view from the Doric Seat (Painswick Rococo Garden)

■ A seaside stroll (Plymouth Hoe)

■ Moonlit towers and castle battlements (St Michael's Mount)

FOR CHILDREN

■ Model railways (Pecorama Pleasure Gardens)

■ The aquarium (Plymouth)

■ An underground tour (Poldark Mine)

■ The bees (Quince Honey Farm)

POLDARK MINE
CORNWALL

■ ON THE B3297, 2 MILES (3KM) NORTH OF HELSTON ■

After a long period of decline, tin mining in Cornwall seems finally to have met its Waterloo, but visitors can experience something of what life was like for the miners at Poldark Mine. A one-hour tour explores three underground levels. On the surface the museum, heritage collections and cinema tell the industry's story. There are gardens and children's amusements and rides, plus a collection of working antiques including a beam engine 40ft (12m) high. *Open: daily, Eas–Oct.*

POWDERHAM CASTLE
DEVON

■ OFF THE A379, 8 MILES (13KM) SOUTH-WEST OF EXETER ■

Sir Philip Courtenay, ancestor of the Earls of Devon, built Powderham Castle to command the Exe estuary some 600 years ago. It has been the family home ever since, although it was substantially altered and rebuilt in the 18th and 19th centuries. Inside are family portraits, fine furniture and tapestries, and a gorgeous music room designed by James Wyatt. A tortoise of staggering antiquity lives in the rose garden, and deer browse in the park. *Open: Sun–Thu, mid-May–mid-Sep.*

QUINCE HONEY FARM
DEVON

■ ON THE A361, 3½ MILES (6KM) WEST OF SOUTH MOLTON ■

Founded in 1948 with two hives, Quince Honey Farm is now Britain's largest, and home to more than a million honey bees. Visitors can watch the bees at work, safe from stings behind glass, and observe every detail of their busy lives. Even the queen bee can be seen at the heart of her hive, with larvae and newly hatched bees in the comb cells. The extracting and bottling equipment is also on view, and honey and beeswax products are on sale. *Open: daily.*

■

Below: one of the most famous and dramatic views in England, which Milton called 'the great vision of the guarded mount'. A Benedictine priory was founded on St Michael's Mount in the 11th century, where according to legend St Michael had appeared to a hermit 500 years before

■

■

Above: bees will take over anything that is handy, like this old red pillarbox at Quince Honey Farm, where the world's largest display of living and working honey bees is on view. Their stings are kept on the other side of the glass

■

ST MICHAEL'S MOUNT
CORNWALL

■ REACHED ON FOOT (AT LOW TIDE), OR BY BOAT FROM MARAZION ■

Intensely romantic on its island in Mount's Bay, the castle dates back to medieval times, though what can be seen today is largely of the 17th to 19th centuries, when the fortress belonged to the St Aubyn family, Lords St Levan. The National Trust acquired it in 1954. The highest point of the castle is the tower of the chapel, 200ft (60m) above the waves. Some of the rooms are in the 18th-century 'Gothick' style, and the fiercely battlemented south-east wing was designed in the 19th century by the architect Piers St Aubyn. Visitors can decide whether to take a ferry or alternatively to walk across the causeway to the island at low tide. *Open: Mon–Fri, Apr–Oct.*

SALISBURY
WILTSHIRE

GREAT MEN AND MONUMENTS

Among the most interesting and most touching memorials in Salisbury Cathedral are those which commemorate famous figures connected with the city and its shire. Behind the Gorges tomb a stained-glass window by Christopher Wordsworth honours the saintly poet George Herbert, who spent his last years as parson of Bemerton, just outside Salisbury. He died in 1633 and the stained glass window illustrates one of his poems.

In the north-west transept there is a bust of Richard Jefferies, the Wiltshire natural history writer and author of *Bevis,* who was born at Coate Farm (now a museum to him, near Swindon), in 1848. Not far away is a figure in white marble, seated in a chair. This is Sir Richard Colt Hoare of Stourhead, the author of innumerable volumes on Wiltshire history and antiquities and member of a rich banking family. As in life, he is shown busy scribbling away at a book with a quill pen.

The Whistler family lived in the cathedral Close before the Second World War and the memorial to artist Rex Whistler is a glass prism, etched by his brother Laurence. It can be found in the north-east transept.

The view of **Salisbury Cathedral** from the water meadows, as Constable painted it, with the tallest spire in the country pointing seraphically to the heavens, is a magnificent prospect. The visitor can still enjoy it by approaching from the south-west, along Town Path from Harnham Mill. The cathedral was built in local grey stone within 40 years, starting in 1220, when bishop Richard Poore and his clergy decided to move down from the draughty mound of Old Sarum immediately to the north. Because it was built so quickly, the church is all in one style, a plain and austere Gothic. The slender 404ft (123m) spire was added in the following century and the top leans 2½ft (75cm) out of true. It has been a cause of constant anxiety over the centuries. The original timber framework is still inside and can be seen on one of the interesting guided tours.

The interior is even more austere than it might have been, thanks to the activities of the architect James Wyatt, who earned the nickname 'Destroyer' for what he did here. Called in by the clergy in 1788, he ruthlessly swept away chapels and screens, smashed stained glass, and arranged the tombs in tidy rows. Fortunately, the cathedral still boasts many points of interest, including Europe's oldest clock mechanism and an enchanting glass memorial to Rex Whistler.

To 'Destroyer' Wyatt's credit is **Cathedral Close**, which was laid out by him and has an unsurpassed and tranquil loveliness. Two of the substantial houses are now museums. The **Salisbury and South Wiltshire Museum** is known for its prehistoric collections from Stonehenge and other Wiltshire sites, but has lively material on the city's history. *Open: Mon–Sat, all year; also Sun Jul, Aug.* The **Museum of the Duke of Edinburgh's Royal Regiment**, housing exhibits of the former Berkshire and Wiltshire regiments, is also rewarding. *Open: daily, May–Oct; Sun–Fri, Apr, Nov; Mon–Fri, Feb, Mar.* **Mompesson House** rejoices in elegant 18th-century plasterwork. *Open: Sat–Wed, Apr–Oct (NT).* There is more plasterwork in **Malmesbury House**, where Charles II is said to have been hidden in 1651. *Open: Tue–Thu and BH Mon, Apr–Sep.*

After founding the cathedral, the bishop and his clergy laid out a new town, with a neat grid of streets and a large marketplace. The city prospered and Salisbury market has been going strong ever since. Buildings of all periods and styles lean comfortably against each other in the streets.

On a hill in the northern outskirts loom the huge earthworks of **Old Sarum**, an Iron Age hill fort which the Romans took over as a base. It was subsequently a Saxon town and then a Norman stronghold. The outline of the Norman cathedral can be seen in the grounds. *Open: daily, Eas–Sep; Tue–Sun, Oct–Eas (NT).*

Above: seen against a threatening sunset, the graceful spire of Salisbury Cathedral points reassuringly to heaven. The effect is not unlike that achieved in John Constable's great painting Salisbury Cathedral from the Meadows, *a classic image of serenity against a stormy sky*

Left: one of the stately rooms in Mompesson House, showing some of the delectable plasterwork. The handsome house in Salisbury's Cathedral Close was built early in the 18th century for Charles Mompesson. The plasterwork and interior decoration date from about 1740

SEALIFE PARK
DORSET

■ ON THE A353, NORTH-EAST OF WEYMOUTH ■

Opened in 1983 and boasting the biggest tank in Europe, the giant oceanarium teems with dolphins and porpoises, squid and octopus, conger eels which go to any lengths, and vast shoals of fish. The great blue whale has a special splash pool, and there is a shark observatory. Additional attractions include touch pools for children, an adventureland and an ocean film cinema. The aquarium is in **Lodmore Country Park**, where the RSPB has a nature reserve which attracts lapwings and snipe.

Not far away, at **Radipole Lake**, is another RSPB bird sanctuary which offers some excellent urban birdwatching, with extensive reedbeds being home to many species of warbler. *Open: daily (sealife park).*

SEZINCOTE
GLOUCESTERSHIRE

■ OFF THE A44, 1½ MILES (2½ KM) WEST OF MORETON-IN-MARSH ■

Although it looks as if a passing Mogul Emperor dropped it here from a magic carpet, Sezincote somehow seems at home in its green and leafy Cotswold parkland. (The name is pronounced *Season-cut*). Sir Charles Cockerell had it designed by his architect brother, Samuel Pepys Cockerell, in the early 1800s, to remind him of his time in India. Sir Charles slept in the resplendent octagonal tent room, which was decorated with a canopy supported by wooden spears and connected to the main house by a curving passage.

There is, however, nothing oriental about the interior of the main house itself, which is in Regency style.

In the **gardens** a temple to the Hindu sun god stands above an ornamental lake, and the stately bridge over the stream is guarded by figures of brahmin bulls. The stream trickles down to the Snake Pool, in the middle of which a snake winds itself round a tree stump. Next to the house an elegant orangery, which is guarded by more Brahma bulls, gazes out on an Indian paradise garden. The effects are exotic and stylish. *Open: Thu and Fri, May–Jul and Sep (house); Thu, Fri and BH Mon, Jan–Nov (gardens).*

■

Below: domed in exotic Mogul splendour, the mansion at Sezincote attracted the Prince Regent, who came to admire it. After seeing the house he decided to have the Royal Pavilion at Brighton built in Indian style. Years later, Sir John Betjeman visited Sezincote and wrote admiring verse about it

■

SHAFTESBURY
DORSET

Gold Hill is Shaftesbury's most famous street, its cottages and cobbled road staggering picturesquely up to the top of a 700ft (213m) spur from which the town surveys the countryside. The **Local History Museum** has a collection of buttons that were once made here, with exhibitions of needlework, toys and other bygones. *Open: daily Eas–Sep.*

Shaftesbury grew up around the richest **nunnery** in medieval England, founded by King Alfred in the 9th century. It was destroyed during the Dissolution of the Monasteries in 1539. Its sparse ruins can be seen today, with a small accompanying museum. There is also an attractive re-creation of an Anglo-Saxon herb garden. *Open: daily Apr–Oct.*

SHELDON MANOR
WILTSHIRE

■ OFF THE A420, 4¼ MILES (7KM) WEST OF CHIPPENHAM ■

The sole survivor of a long-vanished medieval village, this smiling manor house has been a family home for more than 700 years. The main porch dates from 1282 and there is a little 15th-century chapel where family weddings are still held. In the house are fine panelling and oak furniture, with a miscellany of other remarkable objects ranging from Nailsea glass and Persian carpet saddlebags, to a quilt made from the skin of 88 Australian duckbilled platypuses.

The house nestles among informal **gardens** with vast old yews, apple trees, old-fashioned roses and a variety of unusual shrubs in a setting as timeless and idyllic as itself. *Open: East, then Sun, Thu, BH to early Oct.*

■

DON'T MISS

■ The view of Salisbury Cathedral (from the **water meadows**)

■ The Salisbury Giant (**Salisbury and South Wiltshire Museum**)

■ The Indian temple and lake (Sezincote)

■ The platypus-skin bedcover (Sheldon Manor)

FOR CHILDREN

■ The stuffed mongrel which won the Afghan Medal (**The Museum of the Duke of Edinburgh's Royal Regiment**, Salisbury)

■ Touch pools (Sealife Park)

SHEPPY'S CIDER FARM
SOMERSET
■ ON THE A38, BETWEEN WELLINGTON AND TAUNTON ■

The Sheppy family have been making cider in the West Country since the 18th century and keep up the traditions of the days when each farm made its own. Their orchards grow apples with richly romantic names, like Tremlett's Bitters, Stoke Red, Kingston Black and Yarlington Mill. Visitors can explore the cellar and press room, where the apples are processed in the autumn. Antique cider equipment is on view in the museum, and visitors can buy the product, naturally. *Open: Mon–Sat; also Sun, Eas–Dec.*

SHOE MUSEUM
SOMERSET
■ HIGH STREET, STREET ■

The things people have put on their feet – shoes and boots, slippers and pumps, clogs and galoshes, sandals and stiletto heels –

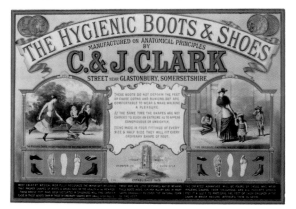

range from the practical to the weird. They can be seen in this museum, housed in the factory which Cyrus Clark founded in Street in 1825. Besides shoes from Roman days to the present, there are cobbler's tools and shoe-making machinery, Georgian shoe buckles, caricatures, costume illustrations, fashion plates and advertisements. There is also a section about the history of C & J Clark's itself. The business began as a tannery and then expanded, making sheep-wool slippers for local cottagers. *Open: Mon–Sat, Eas–Oct,*

SLIMBRIDGE WILDFOWL REFUGE
GLOUCESTERSHIRE
■ OFF THE A38, 13 MILES (20KM) SOUTH OF GLOUCESTER ■

Thousands of swans, geese and ducks throng this reserve on the marshes and mudflats of the River Severn. It is run by the Wildfowl Trust, founded by the late Sir Peter Scott in 1946, and there are many rare birds to be seen from the walks, hides and towers. Some of the wintering swans return year after year and are sadly missed if they fail to appear. The reserve covers some 800 acres (325ha) and anything up to 8,000 birds take refuge here in a cold winter. A decoy is used to catch ducks for ringing, and there are flamingos and a tropical house with hummingbirds. *Open: daily.*

SNOWSHILL MANOR
GLOUCESTERSHIRE
■ OFF THE A44, 2 MILES (3KM) SOUTH OF BROADWAY ■

In 1919 an architect named Charles Wade bought a tumbledown manor house at Snowshill, in the Cotswolds. He restored it and then filled it with an astonishing collection of objects, assembled on the magpie principle. Today the National Trust preserves it in all its glorious oddity.

Charles Wade had a local reputation as a wizard, which he deliberately cultivated

---

■

PREHISTORIC SITES

More prehistoric remains are crowded into a few miles round Stonehenge than in any other area of comparable size in Britain. Even a casual drive or stroll nearby will reveal the humps of ancient barrows, or grave mounds. Men were buried here with their weapons – stone battleaxes and bronze daggers – and women with necklaces and ornaments. Finds can be seen in museums in Salisbury and Devizes.

Much less obvious, just to the north of Stonehenge, are the remains of a long, narrow enclosure with earth banks. Called the Cursus, it may have been used for religious processions or perhaps funeral games, including races, held on the death of a king or powerful chieftain.

Approaching Stonehenge itself is a ceremonial avenue, best seen from aerial photographs. From the River Avon to the south-east, it once led to the Heel Stone by a curving course.

About 2 miles (3km) to the north-east of Stonehenge (on the A345) is Woodhenge. All that can be seen today are concrete posts, marking the positions of wooden posts which once supported a sizeable circular building. There were others immediately to the north, at Durrington Walls. They may have been special buildings for colleges of priests who carried out the rituals at Stonehenge.

■

■

Above: advertising for Sheppy's Cider has a traditional ring, appropriate to a business that prides itself in keeping old ways alive

■

Right: the C & J Clark's poster promotes the firm's 'Hygienic' range of boots and shoes, introduced in 1883

■

by appearing mysteriously to visitors from hidden passages and dark doorways. His tastes were catholic, and he collected items ranging from antique spectacles and barometers to pistols, ship models, Javanese masks and Burmese rice jars, besides toys and dolls, musical instruments, Islamic rugs, looms and mangles, spinning wheels, bicycles and Italian church furniture. In one of the upstairs rooms, figures of Japanese samurai in armour and weird helmets glare savagely from the gloom. The innumerable clocks keep 'Wade time' – which means that they strike and chime when they feel like it. Outside is a pleasant terraced garden, also created by Wade, but it is the jackdaw's paradise inside that compels attention. *Open: Eas, then Wed– Sun, May–Sep; Sat, Sun, Apr and Oct (NT).*

STONEHENGE
WILTSHIRE
■ OFF THE A303, 2 MILES (3KM) WEST OF AMESBURY ■

Stonehenge attracts visitors in such numbers that the public is no longer allowed near the stones. It can also be difficult to get views of them unhindered by camera-happy tourists and noisy school parties.

■

Above: stark and solemn against the sky, Stonehenge has attracted all sorts of theories about its origins and purpose. Suggested builders range from the ancient Druids to beings from outer space. That there is something compelling about it is attested by the number of visitors drawn to it

■

The unique feature of Stonehenge is the central section of standing stones, up to 24ft (7m) high and weighing up to 50 tons (51 tonnes) apiece, arranged in pairs. A massive lintel stone lies across the top of each pair, held in position by mortice-and-tenon joints. These stones are about 4,000 years old, but the site itself goes back another 1,000 years before that. The great monument was frequently altered before reaching its present arrangement. The huge standing stones, or sarsens, were probably dragged to the site on wooden rollers and erected using earth ramps. Until recently it was accepted that the smaller bluestones were brought from the Prescelly Mountains in south-west Wales, probably by raft up the Bristol Chanel and then along rivers for most of the way. It has alternatively been suggested that they were carried to this part of Wiltshire by Ice Age glaciers, and were comparatively close at hand for building purposes.

Arguments about the purpose and meaning of Stonehenge have raged for years. It was clearly an important religious and ritual centre, and the many burial mounds close to it suggest that it was considered an exceptionally sacred place. The central horseshoe of sarsens is orientated towards midsummer sunrise over the Heel Stone, a 35-ton (36-tonne) pillar now leaning at an angle. This suggests that Stonehenge was constructed to relate closely to astronomy and the calendar. *Open: daily (EH).*

STOURHEAD
WILTSHIRE
■ OFF THE B3092, 3 MILES (5KM) NORTH OF MERE ■

Stourhead House was designed in a restrained Palladian style in the 1720s by Colen Campbell for the Hoare family, wealthy bankers. It contains good furniture and an interesting collection of pictures, but makes far less impact than the **grounds**. It was in the 1740s that Henry Hoare (known as 'the magnificent'), started to create today's enchanting Arcadian landscape garden. Damming a stream to form a lake, he planted trees on the hillside. Among them were placed graceful classical temples and rotundas, a Gothic cottage and a grotto, in positions calculated to please the eye and elevate the spirit. A walk round the lake today is still a breathtaking experience. *Open: Sat–Wed Apr–Oct (house); daily from 8.00am (gardens), NT.*

■

DON'T MISS

■ Women's fashions (**The Shoe Museum**)

■ The eccentric exhibits (**Snowshill Manor**)

■ A perambulation (**Stonehenge**)

■ A walk (**Stourhead**)

FOR CHILDREN

■ Feeding the birds (**Slimbridge**)

■ Japanese armour (**Snowshill Manor**)

SUDELEY CASTLE
GLOUCESTERSHIRE
■ OFF THE A46, SOUTH OF WINCHCOMBE ■

A compelling mixture of ruined fortress and Victorian gentleman's residence, built in the local stone, the castle is set in wooded countryside below the Cotswold scarp. It was built in the 15th century and was subsequently owned by both Edward IV and Richard III, but it is best-known as the home of Katherine Parr, last wife and widow of Henry VIII. She lived here after his death in 1547 and among her household was the ill-fated Lady Jane Grey. The castle was later owned by the Brydges family, Lords Chandos, and in 1644 was attached and badly knocked about by Parliamentary troops. Parts of it are still glamorously ruined, but the estate was bought in the 19th century by the rich Dent family, Worcester glovers who had the house partly restored by Sir George Gilbert Scott. He designed the beautiful tomb of Katherine Parr in the church. The house contains an interesting collection of curios, porcelain, tapestries and paintings by Van Dyck, Rubens and Turner and is set in attractive gardens. *Open: daily, Apr–Oct.*

TANK MUSEUM
DORSET
■ OFF THE A352 IN BOVINGTON CAMP, NEAR WAREHAM ■

The museum of the **Royal Tank Regiment** and the **Royal Armoured Corps** contains enough lumbering battlefield monsters to mount an alarming assault if they were all mobilised, and a strange and frightening sight they would make. There are more than 250 armoured fighting vehicles from countries which include Germany, Japan and the United States, as well as Britain, and they provide convincing evidence of human ingenuity in the field of war. Efficiently displayed and explained, they range from tanks of the type used on the Somme in the First World War to those of the Second World War and to the Gulf War. You can climb inside some tanks and experience driving one, with simulators. There are complementary displays of uniforms, medals, cups and trophies, photographs, cartoons and toy tanks. *Open: daily.*

TEWKESBURY
GLOUCESTERSHIRE

Massive and magnificent, the great **abbey church** dominates Tewkesbury as it has ever since the Middle Ages. Work on it began after the Norman Conquest, and the central tower is the biggest of that period in existence. The church was restored in the 1870s by Sir George Gilbert Scott, prompting William Morris to found the Society for the Preservation of Ancient Buildings.

■
Below: an unusual view of Tewkesbury, with the River Severn in the foreground. The Severn is joined at Tewkesbury by the Warwickshire Avon. Traffic on its rivers and the richness of its water meadows have contributed to the town's prosperity over the centuries

■

Inside, the nave is supported by tall Norman pillars and above is a gorgeous 14th-century roof. The church has a famous organ with a 16th-century case, splendid stained glass and a number of exceptionally fine tombs. Among them is one of the grisliest monuments in the country – the cenotaph of John Wakeman, the last abbot, with the effigy of a decaying corpse being eaten by worms, a mouse, a frog and a beetle. Close by, the bones of the 15th-century Duke of Clarence, who was drowned in a butt of Malmsey wine, repose in a glass case under a grating in the floor.

In the town, the **museum** covers local history. *Open: daily, Apr–Oct.*

To the south and well worth seeing, at **Wallsworth Hall** off the A38, is a thoroughly enjoyable collection of wildlife paintings, called 'Nature in Art'. *Open: Tue–Sun and BH Mon.*

TINTAGEL CASTLE
CORNWALL

■ OFF THE B3263, 5 MILES (8KM) NORTH-WEST OF CAMELFORD ■

At this dramatic and legend-haunted site the ruins of the stronghold cling to a headland rearing high above the roaring breakers of the north Cornish coast. It is reached by a narrow spine of rock and precipitous steps, and there are more ruins of the fortress on the landward side. In legend this was where King Arthur was conceived, and although the ruins are medieval, there was probably a royal centre here long before. The castle ruins are now in the care of English Heritage. *Open: daily, Apr–Sep; Tue–Sun, Oct–Mar (EH).*

Tintagel village is very commercialised, but the 14th-century **Old Post Office** stands out among the buildings. *Open: daily, Apr–Oct.*

TOTNES
DEVON

A charming old town of character on the River Dart, Totnes has recovered in fine style from a serious fire a few years ago. The main street is spanned by the medieval **east gate** and close to it is the 15th-century **church of St Mary** in crumbly red stone. At the top of the hill the keep of **Totnes Castle** glares grimly over the surrounding country. *Open: daily Apr–Sep; Tue–Sun, Oct–Mar (EH).*

Local bygones can be enjoyed in **Totnes Museum**, but the **Guildhall**, the **Period Costume Collection** and **Totnes Motor Museum** are also of interest. *Open: Mon–Fri and BH, Etr–Oct (museum): Mon–Fri. Eas–Sep (Guildhall): Mon–Fri and Sun, Spring BH– Oct (costume collection): daily, Eas–Oct (motor museum).*

TRELISSICK GARDEN
CORNWALL

■ ON THE B3289, 4 MILES (6KM) SOUTH OF TRURO ■

Looking out over Carrick Roads, the park was created by the Gilbert family, who owned it until 1913. The gardens were laid out by later owners, the Copelands, who gave the property to the National Trust in 1955. With rhododendrons and azaleas, summer-flowering shrubs, ferns, oaks and beeches, cypresses and cedars and spreading lawns, the gardens are a delight all year round. *Open: Mon–Sat, Mar–Oct; all year (woodland walk), NT.*

TRERICE
CORNWALL

■ OFF THE A3058, 3 MILES (5KM) SOUTH-EAST OF NEWQUAY ■

A museum of lawnmowers is one of the pleasures of the old Elizabethan manor house of the Arundells, set among narrow lanes in quiet Cornish countryside. Sir John Arundell rebuilt it in the 1570s and adorned it with gables in the Dutch fashion. There are fine ceilings and fireplaces, oak and walnut furniture and tapestries, and the great hall is lit by a window containing no fewer than 576 pieces of glass. The house belongs to the National Trust. *Open: Wed–Mon, Apr–Oct (NT).*

■

Above: behind a blaze of rhododendrons a stone cottage nestles among the protective trees in Trelissick Garden. Set in a stately park above the broad harbour of Carrick Roads, it has camellias and hydrangeas, ivy and fig gardens, and a dell of ferns

■

■

MERLIN AND TINTAGEL

According to legend, it was at Tintagel that King Arthur was conceived, through the wiles of Merlin, the great enchanter. The story goes that Uther Pendragon, King of Britain, fell passionately in love with Ygraine, the beautiful wife of the Duke of Cornwall. The Duke shut her up in impregnable Tintagel Castle on its stupendous, sea-beaten headland. By magic art Merlin transformed King Uther into the likeness of the Duke, and in this disguise he gained entry to the castle and Ygraine's bed. The story was first written down in the 12th century and certainly the castle makes a suitably romantic setting for it.

■

■

DON'T MISS

■ Katherine Parr's tomb (**Sudeley Castle**)

■ Tank simulators (**the Tank Museum, Bovington Camp**)

■ The effigy of Abbot Wakeman (**Tewkesbury**)

■ The heights above Merlin's Cave (**Tintagel**)

■ The waterside (**Totnes**)

WELLS
SOMERSET

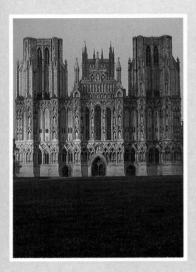

Tucked quietly below the Mendip Hills, Wells is an unobtrusive Somerset market town transformed by a **cathedral** of astonishing loveliness. Some people consider it the most beautiful cathedral in England, and the dramatic west front, seen rising beyond the cathedral green, is a triumph of medieval architecture. Standing in niches across the symmetrical façade are almost 300 statues of angels, saints, kings and other figures – many now too worn by time to be identified. This huge screen was designed by a master mason named Thomas Norreys in the 13th century. It forms part of a long history of building, which lasted from about 1180 until the beginning of the 16th century.

Inside the cathedral there is immediately another dramatic visual effect, as the eye is carried along the creamy columns of the nave to one of the titanic scissor arches that were put in place in the 14th century to support the massive central tower, which was beginning to tilt. They were designed by another brilliant master mason, William Joy. The rood in the upper arch, with figures of the crucified Christ, the Virgin Mary and St John, was designed in 1920 by Sir William Nicholson.

The local sculptors who made the west front statues let themselves go inside the church, with lively carvings of animals and demons and scenes of country life, which include culprits stealing apples from an orchard and several painful depictions of people suffering agonies from toothache. Also not to be missed is the splendid medieval clock, with its four knights on horseback who come charging round a castle every quarter of an hour, fighting a tournament. The same rider gets knocked flat every time. The clock's three dials indicate the hours, minutes and days of the lunar month. Dating from about 1390, it is one of the oldest clocks in the country.

Below the clock, the figure of Christ rising from the grave is a work of the 1950s by a local carver, Estcourt Clack. Curving stone stairs, deeply worn by the tread of clerical feet over the centuries, lead up to the octagonal chapter house, with its central supporting pillar like a giant palm tree.

The cathedral is approached from the market place by a 15th-century gateway, known as 'Penniless Porch' because local beggars used to gather hopefully there. A companion gate, known as 'the Bishop's Eye', leads to the moated and battlemented **Bishop's Palace**. The swans in the moat ring a bell by the drawbridge with their beaks at feeding time: at least they used to, but nowadays they are fed so much by visitors that they cannot always be bothered. The palace has a 13th-century chapel, a beautiful ruined medieval hall and Victorian state rooms. The spacious grounds – with a peculiar statue of Adam and Eve by Estcourt Clack, carved from a single yew trunk – lead to the pool where 40 million gallons of spring water a day well up from below ground, giving the town its name. *Open: Sun and Thu, Eas–Oct; daily in Aug; also BH Mon.*

To the north of the cathedral, one of the sights of the city is **Vicars' Close**, a picturesque 14th-century street of small houses where the clergy who carried out services in the cathedral lived. The enjoyable old-fashioned **Wells Museum** nearby has a rewarding jumble of objects, from prehistoric remains to plaster casts of some of the cathedral statues, as well as horse brasses, pipe stoppers, a bath chair and the skeleton of the so-called 'Witch of Wookey'. *Open: daily, Eas–Sep; Wed–Sun, Oct–Eas.*

Wells is England's smallest city. It is a pleasant place to stroll or shop in, with old coaching inns, an 18th-century town hall and the **parish church of St Cuthbert**, with a handsome pinnacled tower.

Above: the west front at Wells is like a gigantic altar screen for the display of a multitude of statues. Based on a simple geometric ratio, it is divided by buttresses into five sections, rising in five tiers. Above them are the gable and flanking towers

Above: the statues on the west front of the cathedral were produced by a local school of craftsmen. There were more than 400 statues originally, painted in glowing colours with what must have been a blazing effect. Time and weather have worn them away, and some have been restored or replaced

WESTONBIRT ARBORETUM
GLOUCESTERSHIRE
■ ON THE A433, 3 MILES (5KM) SOUTH-WEST OF TETBURY

One of the best collections of trees and shrubs in Europe occupies 600 acres (240ha) of ground, with 17 miles (27km) of paths and rides and an ample supply of waymarked trails, in an arboretum which was designed from the beginning to please the eye as well as instruct the mind. Now owned and run by the Forestry Commission, Westonbirt was started in 1829, at a time when many new conifers were being introduced from North America. Today it shows off Douglas firs and redwoods, pines and sequoias, arranged along glades and avenues and set off by flowering trees and shrubs. There is a wonderful glade of ornamental cherry trees, and the old oak woods shimmer in spring with primroses and bluebells. The autumn colours are entrancing and in winter the distinctive barks of the birch and maple trees are particularly pleasing. There is an informative exhibition and video programme at the visitor centre. Nearby **Westonbirt House** was designed by Lewis Vulliamy in the 19th century. It is now a girls' private school, but its Italian-style gardens are occasionally open to the public in school holidays. *Open: daily (arboretum).*

WHEAL MARTYN MUSEUM
CORNWALL
■ ON THE A391, 2 MILES (5KM) NORTH OF ST AUSTELL ■

The weird moonscape north of St Austel, with its gleaming humps and craters, has been created over the last 200 years or so by the mining of china clay, which is used in pottery and papermaking. The story of the industry is vividly told in indoor displays at Wheal Martyn, where the workings go back to the 1820s and the 19th-century works have been restored. Cornwall's largest working water wheel, 35ft (11m) in diameter, was used to pump clay slurry up from the pit. Visitors can see lesser wheels, tramways and inclines, the blueing house where slurry was dyed, settling tanks with their granite walls, and the 220ft (67m) long pan kiln, in which the material was dried. Also to be seen are tools and examples of Plymouth porcelain, in which china clay was first used in Britain in the 18th century. There are veteran lorries and locomotives on view and heavy wagons that used to carry sacks of dried clay until the 1920s. They were eventually replaced by pipelines. Outside there is a spectacular viewing area of a modern china clay pit.

Besides history, there is a rewarding **nature trail** to enjoy. It leads through the woodland and around the old tips, giving spectacular views of today's working pits. The trail demonstrates the remarkable way in which wildlife can adapt itself and thrive in a changed and, on the face of things, harshly hostile environment. Grass and shrubs flourish below the discarded tips, sheltering bees and grasshoppers. Ivy cloaks a deserted engine house, and a tunnel leads into pine and beech woods. Also here are a pottery, picnic area and adventure trail. *Open: daily, Apr–Oct.*

WILTON HOUSE
WILTSHIRE
■ ON THE A30, 3 MILES (5KM) WEST OF SALISBURY ■

Two of the most famous rooms in England can be enjoyed in the palatial house of the Herbert family, Earls of Pembroke. Both were designed by Inigo Jones for the 4th Earl, who was also one of Shakespeare's patrons. The Single Cube Room is 30ft (9m) long by 30ft (9m) wide and 30ft (9m) high, panelled in dazzling white and gold. It has a painted ceiling with scenes from Sir Philip Sidney's *Arcadia*. This remarkable literary work, concerned mainly with love, was written during visits to the house. The Double Cube Room, an apartment of the utmost grandeur and widely regarded as the best-proportioned room in England, 60ft (18m) long by 30ft (9m) wide and 30ft (9m) high, has superb plasterwork, pictures created especially for the room by Van Dyck, and Chippendale furniture.

Also in this magnificent mansion are fine paintings, statues and furniture, curios and family memorabilia, and cloisters in the Gothic style by James Wyatt, who was called in to make the house more comfortable, and warmer, in 1801. There is a large collection of model soldiers (7,000 of them in all) on view, engaged in battles and tableaux, a model railway, a dolls' house, a 250-piece Viennese dinner service, a garden centre and an adventure playground, besides beautiful lawns and grounds.

The parkland has some especially elegant cedars. *Open: daily, Apr–Oct.*

■

Above: the stately Palladian bridge is reflected in the water of the Nadder in the grounds of Wilton House. It was built in 1737 by the 9th Earl of Pembroke, a skilful architect. He widened the river and landscaped the grounds to create an effect of delightful rustic tranquillity

■

■

CHINA CLAY

It was only in the late 18th century that European potteries, first at Meissen and later elsewhere, discovered the secret of using china clay, or kaolin, in the making of porcelain. The Chinese had kept the technique to themselves for many centuries. A Quaker chemist from Plymouth named William Cookworthy found deposits of china clay in the St Austell area in the 1740s. He eventually opened a pottery in Plymouth making the first true porcelain in England. The principal Staffordshire potters, led by the formidable Josiah Wedgwood, soon opened their own pits in Cornwall to supply their factories. The result is the strange manmade landscape outside St Austell today.

■

■

DON'T MISS

■ The medieval clock with jousting knights (Wells Cathedral)

■ Autumn tints (Westonbirt Arboretum)

■ The china clay workings (Wheal Martyn)

■ The Single and Double Cube Rooms (Wilton House)

FOR CHILDREN

■ Carvings (Wells Cathedral)

■ Model soldiers (Wilton House)

THE WITCH OF WOOKEY

There is an old story that Wookey Hole caves were once the home of a witch. When local archaeologist H E Balch excavated the caves early this century, he found – along with the remains of long-extinct woolly rhinoceroses and a cave bear – the skeleton of a woman with a few pitiful belongings, together with the bones of two tethered goats. Presumably, this poor goatherd was the original 'witch'. She is pictured (above) in a drawing by J Hassell. The museum at Wookey has her skeleton on display.

WIMBORNE MINSTER
DORSET

The handsome old market town, with its solid Georgian houses and imperturbably prosperouos air, takes its name from its imposingly large **church**, a clumsy-looking building in chequered grey and brown stone. It is dedicated to St Cuthburga, a Saxon princess who founded a nunnery on the site early in the 8th century. She can be seen in a stained-glass window near the north porch, holding a model of the church in her hands.

The huge central tower is basically Norman, and the bulky west tower was added in the 15th century. Inside, the church is rich in interest. A glittering panoply of trumpets protrudes from the organ and a rarity is the chained library of 240 books, established in 1686. The columns and arches below the central tower of the church date from about 1120 and are the oldest part of the building. The west tower houses the brightly painted 14th-century astronomical clock, with its 24-hour dial, on which the sun, moon and stars revolve around the earth. A quarterjack strikes bells every quarter of an hour. On the opposite wall is a tablet to a local character named Gulliver, one of the most successful smugglers in Dorset history.

In one of the chapels is a curious 17th-century monument to Sir Edward Uvedale. The oddity is that his effigy has two left feet, the result of a mistake when the monument was restored. Another oddity is the coffin of Anthony Ettricke, who died in 1703 after solemnly vowing not to be buried either in the church or out of it. He craftily got round this inconvenient commitment by having a recess made in the church wall.

Near the church, in one of the town's oldest houses, is **Priest's House Museum** with an enjoyable local history collection, a working Victorian kitchen, a 1920s ironmonger's shop, a rural life gallery and a charming walled garden. *Open: daily, Apr–Oct; Sat, Sun Nov–Jan.*

Another attraction is **Wimborne Model Town**, a model of the town to one-tenth scale, exactly as it was in the early 1950s. *Open: Fri–Wed, Eas–Oct.*

WOOKEY HOLE
SOMERSET

■ OFF THE A371, 2 MILES (3KM) NORTH-WEST OF WELLS ■

The Mendip Hills are honeycombed with caves, potholes and underground rivers. Among the most impressive of the limestone caverns are those at Wookey Hole, with their stalactites and stalagmites, spectacular lighting effects and strange rock formations. These include the menacing figure of the 'Witch of Wookey', who can be seen with her dog in the **Witch's Chamber**. The River Axe emerges from the hills through these caves, which were occupied by human beings long ago in the Stone Age. Their stone axes, flint scrapers and cutters have been found by archaeologists, as well as the bones of hyenas, mammoths, woolly rhinoceroses and a cave bear. The caves are now run by Madame Tussaud's. There is a museum, a fairground exhibition, an Edwardian penny-pier arcade and demonstrations of papermaking in the 19th-century mill which took its power from the Axe. *Open: daily.*

WOOLLY MONKEY SANCTUARY
CORNWALL

■ OFF THE B3253, 3 MILES (5KM) NORTH-EAST OF LOOE ■

The sanctuary was founded in 1964 by zoology writer, Leonard Williams, as a home for Amazon woolly monkeys, which have been flourishing happily there ever since. They have pens and long runs through the trees, and are allowed to roam free and swing about in the branches at times. Cuddly, mischievous and friendly, they can be seen at close quarters under the supervision of their human attendants. *Open: Sun–Thu, May–Sep, and Eas.*

WORLDWIDE BUTTERFLIES
DORSET

■ ON THE A30, 2 MILES (3KM) EAST OF YEOVIL ■

At Compton House, in its dignified 19th-century Tudor style, butterflies and moths from all over the world flutter about in reconstructions of their natural habitats, including a palm house and jungles. Miraculously colourful, they strike an exotic note in the quiet Dorset countryside. Also here is **Lullingstone Silk Farm**, which produces the silk for royal wedding dresses and coronation gowns. *Open: daily, Apr–Oct.*

ZENNOR
CORNWALL

■ ON THE B3306, 3 MILES (5KM) WEST OF ST IVES ■

It was at Zennor during the First World War that D H Lawrence finished his novel *Women in Love*. Which is not inappropriate, for the best-known Zennor story is the tale of a beautiful mermaid, who fell in love with the squire's son. She lured him away to her bower deep beneath the waves and he was never seen again. She can be seen with her comb and looking-glass, carved on a wooden bench-end in the 12th-century **church of St Senara**. Buried in the churchyard is John Davey, who died in 1891. He is said to have been the last person to understand Cornish as his native language. The **Wayside Museum** has a fascinating collection of bygones. *Open: daily, mid-Mar–Oct.* Nearby is the Stone Age tomb of **Zennor Quoit**.

■

Below: looking west towards Gurnard's Head along the sea-beaten, adamantine cliffs of the west Cornish coast from Zennor. Pendour Cove in the foreground is where a mermaid is said to have enticed her human lover to his fate in her watery home

■

■

DON'T MISS

■ The effigy with two left feet (Wimborne Minster)

■ The mermaid carving (Zennor Church)

FOR CHILDREN

■ The miniature model town (Wimborne Minster)

■ The caves (Wookey Hole)

■ Monkeys (the Woolly Monkey Sanctuary)

■ Colourful butterflies and strange moths (Worldwide Butterflies)

SOUTH
AND
SOUTH-EAST ENGLAND

The most prosperous area of England, embracing the corridors of power in London and easily accessible to influences from the Continent, southern and south-eastern England is correspondingly rich in stately mansions, memorable gardens, treasures of art and craftsmanship, prosperous towns and spick-and-span villages.

The great houses include some of the biggest and grandest in Britain. At the Sackville palace of Knole in its Kentish deer park, it is said you could spend each day of the year in a different room. There are some 200 rooms in Blenheim Palace, the colossal pile Sir John Vanbrugh laid on the groaning Oxfordshire earth as the nation's tribute to the Duke of Marlborough. Another great soldier of a later generation, the Duke of Wellington, contented himself with the more modest Hampshire comforts of Stratfield Saye, though he had Apsley House as his grand London residence, filled with fine paintings, lavish table services and a life-size statue of Napoleon in the nude.

The roll of gracious houses unfolds from medieval times to the present century. Reflected dream-like in its moat, Ightham Mote has stood since the 14th century. Tudor architecture has left us charming Chenies Manor with its physic garden, the imposing brickwork of Layer Marney Tower and the culminating splendour of Hampton Court. With the 17th century come the palatial splendours of Audley End and Hatfield House, while the 18th brings Stowe and Goodwood with its attendant racecourse, and the Regency period introduces the oriental delights of Sezincote and the Royal Pavilion in Brighton. The 19th-century crop of sumptuous residences includes Queen Victoria's Osborne House and Waddeson Manor in its Rothschild glory of objects beautiful and rare, while Edwardian opulence can be savoured at Hever Castle and high society glimpsed at Polesden Lacey.

Links with famous figures of politics, literature and art are abundant: Sir Winston Churchill at Blenheim and Chartwell; Rudyard Kipling at Bateman's in his beloved Sussex; Gilbert White at Selborne and Jane Austen nearby at Chawton; Charles Dickens in London and Rochester; the Bloomsbury Group at Charleston Farmhouse. Turner painted the park at Petworth and Sir Stanley Spencer painted heaven in Cookham.

Castles include photogenic Bodiam in its lily moat, Pevensey where William the Conqueror landed, and the royal majesty of Windsor. St Martin's Church in Canterbury was used for Christian worship even before St Augustine landed in the 6th century. In Winchester Cathedral the bones of King Canute oddly repose in two different boxes. The Roman lighthouse at Dover and Colchester's town walls equally speak of the distant past, while at Chichester you can see the cathedral's venerable weathercock pocked with bullet marks from a Second World War dogfight above the dreaming spire.

More dreaming spires at Oxford which, with towns from Burford to Romsey and Rye to Southampton, has all the centuries at its back. There is enough of interest in London, of course, to last a lifetime and space permits us only a trawl through its riches here, while Portsmouth mounts the most powerful broadside of naval attractions in the kingdom, with Nelson's *Victory* in the van.

■

Broughton
Castle
● Banbury

Stowe
Landscape
Gardens

Bedford ■

Shuttleworth
Collection

Audley End ■

Milton Keynes ■

BEDFORDSHIRE

Rousham
House

Claydon
House

Woburn
Abbey

Dunstable ■

Luton ●
Luton
Hoo

Stevenage ●
Knebworth
House

Bishop's
Stortford ●

ESSEX

Colchester ■

Layer
Marney
Tower

Minster
Lovell

Blenheim
Palace

BUCKINGHAMSHIRE

Waddesdon
Manor

Aylesbury ●

Whipsnade
Zoo

Chelmsford ■

Burford ■

Cotswold
Wildlife Park

Oxford ●

Zoological
Museum

Hatfield ■

HERTFORDSHIRE

St Albans ■

Hatfield
House

Harlow ■

Brentwood ■

OXFORDSHIRE

West
Wycombe

Chenies
Manor
House

Watford ●

Enfield ●

Basildon ●

High Wycombe ●

Beaconsfield ●

Southend-on-Sea ●

Didcot
Railway
Centre

Stonor Park

Cookham-on-Thames

**GREATER
LONDON**

Woolwich ●

Tilbury ●

Sheerness ●

Margate ●

Fawley
Court

Courage
Shire Horse
Centre

Dorney
Court

Slough ●

LONDON ■

Dartford ●

Ramsgate ●

Mapledurham
House

Reading ●

Windsor ●

Staines ●

Kingston ●

Bromley ●

Rochester ●

Chatham
Historic Dockyard

Canterbury

Newbury ●

BERKSHIRE

Thorpe
Park

Chessington
World
of Adventure

Croydon ●

Maidstone ●

Chilham

Stratfield
Saye

Wisley
Gardens

Painshill Park

Sevenoaks ●

Knole

Ightham
Mote

Leeds
Castle

Dover ●

Highclere
Castle

Clandon
Park

Polesden
Lacey

Chartwell

KENT

Ashford ●

Basingstoke ●

Guildford ●

Loseley
House

Dorking ●

Reigate ●

Hever Castle

Penshurst
Place

Tonbridge ●

Folkestone ●

Hawk
Conservancy

SURREY

Crawley ●

East Grinstead ●

Hammerwood
Park

Royal
Tunbridge Wells ●

Scotney
Castle

Port Lympne
Zoo Park

Chawton

Selborne

Horsham ●

Leonardslee
Gardens

Bluebell
Railway

Bateman's

Bodiam
Castle

Great Dixter

Rye ●

Alresford

Petersfield ●

HAMPSHIRE

Winchester ●

Romsey ●

Marwell Zoo

Petworth

**WEST
SUSSEX**

**EAST
SUSSEX**

Pevensey
Castle

Hastings ●

Weald & Downland
Open Air Museum

Goodwood

Lewes ●

Battle ■

Southampton ●

Arundel ●

Charleston
Farmhouse

Eastbourne ●

**New
Forest**

Beaulieu
● Exbury
Gardens

Chichester ●

Worthing ●

Brighton ●

Portsmouth ●

Bognor Regis ●

Isle of Wight

0	10	20	30	40	50 miles
0	20	40	60	80 kms	

ALRESFORD
HAMPSHIRE

■ ON THE A31, 7 MILES (11KM) EAST OF WINCHESTER ■

Two Alresfords are marked on maps — **Old Alresford** and **New Alresford**. The latter is new only in the sense that it was founded in the 13th century, when the Bishop of Winchester dammed the river to improve navigation between Winchester and Southampton. New Alresford is an attractive, tree-lined village. It was the birthplace in 1787 of the novelist Mary Russell Mitford, author of *Our Village*. It has been ravaged by fires over the centuries, and today there are few buildings left that date from before the 18th century. The steam-hauled '**Watercress Line**' operated by the Mid-Hants Railway runs from Alresford to Alton.

ARUNDEL
WEST SUSSEX

■ OFF THE A27, 10 MILES (16KM) EAST OF CHICHESTER ■

This charming little town, full of delightful 18th- and 19th-century buildings, is dominated by its castle and neo-Gothic Roman Catholic cathedral. After the Norman Conquest Roger de Montgomery built the **castle**, which was besieged by Parliamentary forces during the Civil War and severely damaged by cannon shot. The seat of the Dukes of Norfolk, hereditary Earl Marshalls of England, it was restored in the late 18th century and virtually rebuilt at the end of the 19th century. It is full of interest and treasures, including Old Masters and fine furniture. The extensive park is popular with visitors. *Open: Sun–Fri, Eas–Oct (castle); daily, all year (grounds).*

The fine **parish church** was built at the end of the 14th century. It contains the Fitzalan Chapel, the private chapel of the Dukes of Norfolk, which at one time was separated from the rest of the church by brickwork. This is a rare example of a Roman Catholic chapel in an Anglican parish church, in which Mass is celebrated. In the past, the chapel could only be reached from the castle. In these more tolerant times the wall separating it from the church has been replaced by an iron grille. The imposing Roman Catholic **cathedral church of St Philip Neri** was built at the end of the 19th century.

AUDLEY END
ESSEX

■ OFF THE B1383, 1 MILE (1.6KM) WEST OF SAFFRON WALDEN ■

This great Jacobean mansion, built by Thomas Howard, Earl of Suffolk and Lord Treasurer to James I, was so large that it proved difficult to maintain. It has suffered many vicissitudes and alterations since. The great outer court was demolished and the house was gradually reduced in size, until it reached its present shape in about 1750. Much remodelling was carried out by Sir John Vanbrugh and Robert Adam, and 'Capability' Brown landscaped the grounds. The principal features of interest are the magnificent Jacobean great hall and the state rooms, designed by Robert Adam. *Open: Tue–Sat, Eas–Sep.*

■

Above: a fine 'W' class locomotive, built in 1925, on the privately owned Mid-Hants Railway. The line runs for 10 miles (16km) between New Alresford and Alton. It is popularly known as the 'Watercress Line' because quantities of this plant are cultivated in the area

■

■

Right: the great hall of Audley End was built in the early 17th century The furnishings and pictures were placed here in the 1820s to recreate the look of a Jacobean hall

■

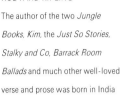

RUDYARD KIPLING

The author of the two *Jungle Books*, *Kim*, the *Just So Stories*, *Stalky and Co*, *Barrack Room Ballads* and much other well-loved verse and prose was born in India

in 1865. Sent back to England for schooling, he endured years of misery in Southsea before returning to India in 1880 to work as a journalist. His early publications earned him a reputation in England and he came back to live in London in 1889. Kipling (above) declined the post of Poet Laureate, but accepted the Nobel Prize for Literature in 1907. He loved the English countryside and had a particular affection for Sussex, where he lived at Bateman's. There are many mementoes of the author in this house, and also at Wimpole Hall in Cambridgeshire, his daughter's home for many years.

■

BATEMAN'S
EAST SUSSEX

■ OFF THE A265, 16 MILES (26KM) NORTH OF EASTBOURNE ■

This fine Sussex ironmaster's house was built in 1634 and was the home of Rudyard Kipling from 1902 until his death in 1936. Kipling, who was born in India, had a romantic attachment to Sussex, his adopted county. Kipling and his American wife, Carrie, laid out the gardens and harnessed the power of the watermill to generate electricity. The house contains many mementoes of his life. *Open: daily, Eas–Oct (NT).*

BATTLE
EAST SUSSEX

A pleasant small town, mostly Georgian in character. Battle derives its name from the Benedictine **Abbey of St Martin**. The abbey was built by William the Conqueror to celebrate his victory over the Saxons at the Battle of Hastings in 1066, and its high altar is supposed to stand on the site where King Harold fell. The abbey is now in ruins. Of more interest to visitors are the plans showing the course of the Battle of Hastings, which are placed at significant points on the battlefield. *Open: daily (abbey, EH, and battlefield).*

BEAULIEU
HAMPSHIRE

■ ON THE B3056, 6 MILES (10KM) SOUTH-EAST OF LYNDHURST ■

An uneasy mixture of history and Disneyland characterises the entertainment centre of Beaulieu. Originally a Cistercian abbey, it passed into the hands of the Montagu family following the Dissolution in 1538 the 16th-century Palace House, receives scant mention in Beaulieu's publicity. The emphasis is given to the nationally important motor museum, the model railway, and the monorail. *Open: daily.*

BEDFORD
BEDFORDSHIRE

The attractive county town of Bedfordshire, located on the River Ouse, is chiefly famous for its four excellent schools. In 1556, Sir William Harpur, Lord Mayor of London and a native of Bedford, endowed the 'free and perpetual school' for which Edward VI had granted a patent in 1552. Later, three more schools were funded by the Harpur Trust.

John Bunyan (1628–88) is also associated with Bedford. He was an itinerant preacher and the author of the religious and literary classic, *The Pilgrim's Progress*. His spiritual autobiography, *Grace Abounding to the Chief of Sinners*, was written during his imprisonment in Bedford's **County Gaol**. Many of the places mentioned in *The Pilgrim's Progress* have been identified in and around Bedford. The **Bunyan Meeting Library and Museum** contains relics. *Open: Tue–Sun.*

■

Below: the National Motor Museum at Beaulieu contains an outstanding collection of historic cars, motorcycles, vans and lorries

■

■
DON'T MISS

■ The 'Watercress Line' (**New Alresford**)

■ The view (**Arundel Castle**)

■ The saloon, and the vista from the Temple of Concord (**Audley End**)

FOR CHILDREN

■ The monorail and the model railway (**Beaulieu**)

BLENHEIM PALACE
OXFORDSHIRE

■ OFF THE A34 AT WOODSTOCK, 8 MILES (13KM) NORTH-WEST OF OXFORD ■

The Manor of Woodstock was granted to John Churchill, 1st Duke of Marlborough, in 1704 by a grateful Parliament, in appreciation of his victory over the French at the Battle of Blenheim, in Bavaria, during the War of the Spanish Succession. The building of Blenheim Palace commenced in 1705, but it was not completed until after Marlborough's death. Today it is one of the great palaces of England, a masterpiece of classical architecture with everything conceived on the grandest and most sumptuous scale. It was designed by Sir John Vanbrugh, with some assistance from Nicholas Hawksmoor, and remains much as it was when first built. The magnificent grounds were laid out by Vanbrugh and Henry Wise, but were later altered by 'Capability' Brown, who installed two lakes. Early in this century, parts of the grounds were restored to Vanbrugh's original designs.

Blenheim was the birthplace of Sir Winston Churchill and it contains an exhibition of his life and work, together with some personal mementoes. Other, more meretricious attractions include an adventure playground, boat rides on the lake, and a miniature train in the park. Pop concerts and similar events are sometimes held here. *Open: daily, Eas–Oct.*

BLUEBELL RAILWAY
EAST SUSSEX

■ OFF THE A275, 10 MILES (16KM) SOUTH OF EAST GRINSTEAD ■

A steam-hauled line that runs for several miles from Sheffield Park to Horsted Keynes, the Bluebell Railway passes through delightful countryside, carpeted with bluebells in late spring. The station at Sheffield Park has been restored to its former glory in the days of the London, Brighton & South Coast Railway, while Horsted Keynes station is decorated with the livery of the Southern Railway. *Open: daily, May–Sep; weekends at other times.*

BODIAM CASTLE
EAST SUSSEX

■ OFF THE A229, 10 MILES (16KM) NORTH OF HASTINGS ■

This castle is in a beautiful setting, and when it is approached across the fields it is difficult to believe that it is little more than a shell surrounded by a romantic, lily-filled moat. After the French sacked Rye in 1377, Sir Edward Dalyngrydge applied to the king for permission to construct a castle at Bodiam. His aim was to protect the upper reaches of the River Rother, which was then navigable and could have provided an invasion route. The castle was not completed until the end of the 14th century, just before such fortifications were rendered largely obsolete by the introduction of cannon. It has survived as an outstanding example of late medieval military architecture, perhaps because it never saw a shot fired in anger – although the Parliamentarians took the precaution of slighting it. *Open: daily, Apr–Oct; Mon–Sat, Nov–Mar (NT).*

Above: the Bluebell Railway runs through 5 miles (8km) of woodland glades and pastures, and is a wonderfully scenic route. There are exhibitions of old locomotives and carriages at both ends of the line

■

Right: Sir Edward Dalyngrydge's splendid, late medieval castle at Bodiam has guarded the Rother Valley for 600 years

■

SIR WINSTON CHURCHILL

The bedroom in which Winston Churchill first saw the light of day can be seen at Blenheim Palace. His grave is also only a mile or two away, in the quiet country churchyard at Bladon, where he rests among his ancestors.

Churchill was the grandson of the 7th Duke of Marlborough. Born in 1874, he went to school at Harrow, for which he retained a lifelong affection. He joined the army and saw action at the Battle of Omdurman in the Sudan in 1898, before becoming a Member of Parliament in 1900. He served in the cabinet in the First World War, but for most of the period between the Wars he was out of step with the Conservative party. He was 65 when, in 1940, he became Prime Minister and led his country against Hitler. Refusing any higher honours, he was knighted in 1953 and in the same year he won the Nobel Prize for Literature. Churchill died in 1965. Apart from the collection at Blenheim, there are also many mementoes of him at Chartwell in Kent, where he lived for many years.

■

DON'T MISS

■ The view from the grand bridge (Blenheim Palace)

■ A steam-hauled ride (the Bluebell Railway)

■ The Royal Pavilion and the Lanes (Brighton)

BRIGHTON
EAST SUSSEX

Often known as 'London-by-the-Sea', Brighton is a curious mixture of the brash vulgarity of seaside piers, winkles, candy floss, 'kiss-me-quick' hats, furtive, adulterous weekends, and Regency elegance. Until the middle of the 18th century, it was a small fishing village called Brighthelmstone. In 1750, Dr Richard Russell published a Latin treatise extolling the virtues of sea water for drinking and bathing, and Brighton's popularity began. Suddenly it became fashionable to 'take the waters', and royalty, literati and the upper classes were pushed down the beach in bathing machines to plunge modestly into the sea. The growth of Brighton was encouraged by the arrival of the railway, which brought increasing numbers of day-trippers to disport themselves on the pebbly beach.

The future King George IV was so taken with the town that he commissioned Henry Holland to build the **Royal Pavilion**. It was later altered and extended by John Nash in Indian and Chinese styles, although these were based purely on the architects's *conception* of the oriental. Despite its bizarre character, the Royal Pavilion is a delight to anyone who appreciates the unusual and eccentric. It has been lovingly restored by Brighton Corporation and gives an interesting insight into the manners and mores of the Regency period. *Open: daily*.

The influence of the Prince Regent is to be found throughout Brighton and Hove in elegant crescents and bow-fronted villas, with charming balconies enclosed with ornamental railings. Behind the Royal Pavilion lie **The Lanes**, which form the oldest part of the town. This area, still based on a medieval street system, is a maze of narrow roads and alleyways, largely given over to boutiques and the antiques trade.

Brighton is justly famous for its parks and beautiful floral displays. The sea front is less attractive, although sections of the Promenade are pleasant. At the eastern end of the town is a huge marina. Volk's Electric Railway, opened in Brighton in 1883, was the first railway to be powered by electricity in Britain.

■

Below: the minaret-like domes of the Prince Regent's architectural fantasy, the Royal Pavilion, Brighton. Here he escaped from London life to eat, drink, flirt, and play cards

■

BROUGHTON CASTLE
OXFORDSHIRE

■ ON THE B4035, 3 MILES (5KM) SOUTH-WEST OF BANBURY ■

A house has stood on this site since the 13th century. The present building was enlarged and moated in about 1300 by Sir John de Broughton and dates mainly from the early 14th century. It was owned by William of Wykeham, who was Bishop of Winchester from 1367 to 1404 and also Chancellor of England. Today the castle is the home of Lord and Lady Saye and Sele; it has been in their family for the last 600 years. A splendid mansion with a 16th-century north front, it contains fine linenfold panelling, beautiful fireplaces, splendid plaster ceilings and good furniture. *Open: May–Sep (check exact days with local tourist information centres).*

BURFORD
OXFORDSHIRE

This enchanting little town which, like so many in the Cotswolds, derived its wealth from the wool trade, is built on a hillside that slopes down to the River Windrush. The main street, which runs down to a handsome bridge over the river, is a delightful jumble of ashlar-fronted Tudor and Georgian houses. The fine parish church contains some Norman and Early English work, but is chiefly notable for its splendid chapels in Perpendicular style. Nowadays, Burford derives its wealth from tourism and the antiques trade.

CANTERBURY
KENT

Canterbury was the site of a prehistoric settlement before Roman times. The Romans chose the spot to found their city of *Durovernum*, which the Saxons renamed *Cantwarabyrig* – 'the borough of the men of Kent'. It retains the flavour of a medieval walled city, even though much was destroyed in the Second World War and rebuilt in the new 'brutalist' style of modern architecture.

It is impossible to escape the religious importance of Canterbury. It was the main centre of Christianity in England until the Reformation, and today it is the focus of the worldwide Anglican Communion. The **Cathedral Church of Christ** was built by Lanfranc, the first Norman archbishop, and became a centre of pilgrimage after the martyrdom of St Thomas à Becket in 1170 that so outraged the whole of Christendom. A magnificent shrine (later destroyed on the orders of Henry VIII), was built, and Canterbury became a centre of pilgrimage. Some of the enormous revenues received from the devout were used to rebuild the cathedral on a much larger scale. The present nave and transepts were built 200 years later. The cathedral was finally completed with the addition of the magnificent Bell Harry Tower.

■

CANTERBURY PILGRIMS

The murder of Archbishop Thomas à Becket in 1170 horrified all Christendom, and miraculous cures were soon reported from his tomb in Canterbury Cathedral. Pilgrims (below) flocked to Canterbury, to share in the sanctity of the place. It was against this background that Geoffrey Chaucer set his famous *Canterbury Tales* in the 14th century. Chaucer's pilgrims are on their way from London to Canterbury, and each tells a tale to enliven the journey. The gallery of characters includes the pious Knight, the earthy Miller, the prim Prioress, the Merchant, the lugubrious Monk and the vigorous and much-married Wife of Bath.

■

Left: the stately west front of Canterbury Cathedral, the mother church of the worldwide Anglican Communion, viewed from Christ Church Gate

■

The interior is full of interest. There is a simple memorial to St Thomas on the spot where he was murdered in the north-west transept. Contrasting in style is a series of magnificent tombs, including that of the Black Prince. Other major points of interest are the cloisters, the crypt, the monastic buildings and beautiful Christ Church Gate, built in Perpendicular style.

In the old part of the city is **Mercery Lane**, a fine medieval street. Other places of interest include the **Hospital of St Thomas**, founded in 1180 for poor pilgrims and the **Weavers' House**, once used by Huguenot refugees. Canterbury is also home of one of the most famous, and picturesque, cricket grounds in the world. A magnificent lime tree stands within the boundary.

CHARLESTON FARMHOUSE
EAST SUSSEX

■ OFF THE A27, 10 MILES (16KM) NORTH-WEST OF EASTBOURNE ■

This unpretentious farmhouse was built in the 18th century. In the early years of the 20th, it became the home of Clive Bell, the critic, his artist wife, Vanessa, and her lover, the painter Duncan Grant, who formed a country branch of the Bloomsbury Group. The interior was decorated by Vanessa and Duncan, who spent much energy painting abstract and naturalistic designs on the panelling, walls, bedheads, tables and chairs in the house. *Open: Eas–Sep (specific days only. Check with local tourist information centres).*

CHARTWELL
KENT

■ OFF THE B2026, 2 MILES (3KM) SOUTH OF WESTERHAM ■

An undistinguished country house that was Sir Winston Churchill's home from 1924 until his death in 1965, Chartwell is full of mementoes of his life, ranging from walking sticks to his numerous uniforms of state. One of the most interesting rooms is the study, in which Churchill wrote some of his most memorable books.

Around the Golden Rose Garden, planted to celebrate the Churchills' golden wedding, is the famous 8ft (2.4m) high wall that Churchill built. Nearby is his studio, containing many of his paintings. *Open: Tue–Thu, Sat, Sun and BH Mon, Mar–Oct (house, garden and studio), NT.*

CHATHAM HISTORIC DOCKYARD
KENT

■ OFF THE A231, IN CHATHAM ■

The Dockyard was founded in 1547 by Henry VIII and remained in service for over 400 years until it was closed in 1984. It is Britain's most complete dockyard dating from the days of 'wooden walls'. There are 80 acres (32ha) of working museum space, including the enormous Sail and Colour Loft, the Ropery and the Covered Slipways, and eight galleries illustrating the history of shipbuilding with animated displays. *Open: Wed–Sun and BH Mon.*

CHAWTON
HAMPSHIRE

■ OFF THE A31, 1½ MILES (2KM) SOUTH-WEST OF ALTON ■

The attractive little village of Chawton, with its thatched cottages and green, is chiefly known for its associations with Jane Austen, who lived in a house here from 1809 to 1817. Today Jane Austen's house is furnished in the style of the early 19th century, and contains mementoes and memorabilia associated with the author. Visitors can still see and hear the creaking door that led to the room in which she wrote and which warned her to hide her manuscript from prying eyes. *Open: daily, Apr–Oct; Wed–Sat, Nov, Dec and Mar.*

■

Above: the 'Wooden Walls' exhibition at the Historic Dockyard in Chatham illustrates the building of an 18th-century warship, and shows what life in the Royal Navy was like before the age of steam

■

■

Below: the interior of Jane Austen's house at Chawton. In this modest home some of the finest novels in the English language were written

■

■

DON'T MISS

■ The site of Thomas à Becket's martyrdom (**Canterbury Cathedral**)

■ The tomb of the Black Prince (**Canterbury Cathedral**)

■ The painted furniture (**Charleston Farmhouse**)

■ Sir Winston Churchill's study (**Chartwell**)

FOR CHILDREN

■ The 'Wooden Walls' animated display (**Chatham Historic Dockyard**)

CHENIES MANOR HOUSE
BUCKINGHAMSHIRE

■ OFF THE A404, 6 MILES (10KM) WEST OF WATFORD ■

Chenies Manor House was originally the home of the Earls and Dukes of Bedford. The red-brick house has been altered significantly over the centuries, but the south wing with its splendid chimneys, long gallery, and curious projections containing closets and privies is predominantly Tudor. The delightful grounds include a penitential maze and a physic garden. *Open: Apr–Oct (check exact days with local tourist information centres).*

CHESSINGTON WORLD OF ADVENTURES
SURREY

■ ON THE A243 AT CHESSINGTON, 4½ MILES (7KM) SOUTH OF KINGSTON-UPON-THAMES ■

Once known prosaically as Chessington Zoo, Chessington World of Adventures has added a Disneyland-style theme park to traditional attractions. Visit the American Wild West, take a river ride through the mystic East, see a ruined Norman castle and walk through a computer screen to discover the fantasy world of the fifth dimension. *Open: daily.*

CHICHESTER
WEST SUSSEX

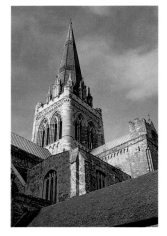

Chichester, the county town of West Sussex, was the important Roman city of *Regnum*, which was linked to London by Stane Street. Many significant Roman remains have been found in the vicinity, including the vast **Fishbourne Palace** dating from about AD75. *Open: daily, Mar–Nov; Sun, Dec–Feb.*

The modern city is built on the Roman street plan and is predominantly Georgian in character, with many handsome houses (especially in the **Pallants**). The **cathedral** is mostly Norman, with comparatively few additions and alterations. Flying buttresses were employed to take the weight of the roof when it was renewed in stone after a disastrous fire. The retro-choir was also rebuilt and some side-chapels and decorated windows were installed. The Lady Chapel was added about 1300, and the unusual detached campanile was erected 100 years later. A spire was added at the same time but this collapsed in 1861 and had to be rebuilt. There are interesting tombs and memorials, as well as a fine modern tapestry by John Piper, a Graham Sutherland painting, and a window by Marc Chagall.

In St Martin's Square is the remarkable **St Mary's Hospital**. This was built at the end of the 13th century for the care of the sick and was converted into almshouses for the aged poor in the 16th century and is still used for that purpose.

Chichester has an annual arts festival, based at its modern Festival Theatre in Oaklands Park, and the harbour is a yachtsman's paradise.

CHILHAM
KENT

■ OFF THE A252, 6 MILES (10KM) SOUTH-WEST OF CANTERBURY ■

One of the show places of Kent, Chilham is best visited outside the tourist season. The village is a delightful jumble of half-timbered Tudor and Jacobean houses built round a square. The parish church has a Perpendicular tower and some fine monuments.

Chilham Castle has an octagonal keep and is tucked away behind the fine Jacobean mansion built by Sir Dudley Digges in the early 17th century. The plan is hexagonal, with one side missing to form a courtyard. The gardens fall in a series of terraces to a lake. It is thought that the park may have been laid out by 'Capability' Brown.

Medieval banquets, displays of jousting and falconry and similar flummeries are held in the castle gardens during the summer. *Open: specified weekdays, Eas–Oct (mansion); daily, Eas–Oct (castle gardens).*

CLANDON PARK
SURREY

■ OFF THE A25, 3 MILES (5KM) EAST OF GUILDFORD ■

A superb Palladian mansion, built in red brick in the 1730s for the 2nd Earl of Onslow, Clandon Park was designed by the Venetian architect, Giacomo Leoni, to replace the original 17th-century house. The exterior was restored in 1876, which affected the harmony of the original design. However, the interior is magnificent, with perfectly proportioned rooms and much fine baroque plasterwork that has been beautifully restored to its former glory by the National Trust. Concerts are sometimes held in the Marble Hall. The house contains the Gubbay collection of furniture, needlework and porcelain, as well as the **Queen's Royal Surrey Regimental Museum.**

The gardens have a parterre and grotto, and a Maori house from New Zealand. *Open: Sat–Wed and BH Mon, Mar–Oct (NT).*

CLAYDON HOUSE
BUCKINGHAMSHIRE

■ OFF THE A413, 6 MILES (10KM) SOUTH OF BUCKINGHAM ■

This is the home of the Verneys, who have lived here for well over 500 years. The present house was built in the middle of the 18th century, and although the exterior is not particularly distinguished, the interior is remarkable; some of the rococo rooms are the finest in England. The wrought-iron and mahogany staircase, the Library, the Pink Room and the Chinese Drawingroom are particularly fine. Florence Nightingale was the sister of Sir Harry Verney's wife, Parthenope, and the house contains her bedroom and a museum with many mementoes of her.

Concerts are held in the house during the summer months. The landscaped park is crossed by a public path, and contains a series of lakes. *Open: Sat–Wed and BH Mon, Mar–Oct (NT).*

■

'THE LADY OF THE LAMP'
Florence Nightingale (below) had a room at Claydon House in Buckinghamshire which contains her four-poster bed and a picture of her pet owl. Although she had a house in South Street, London, 'the lady of the lamp' visited Claydon regularly after her sister Parthenope married Sir Harry Verney in 1858. After the death of 'Parthe' in 1890 Florence took a characteristically strong-minded interest in the Claydon estate, investigating the condition of the cottages and the state of the water supply and sanitation, and taking vigorous corrective measures. Sir Harry died in 1894 and after that, although she was still welcome at Claydon, Florence stopped going there. After 1896 she never left her bedroom in South Street, where she died in 1910 at the age of 90.

■

■

The Chinese Drawingroom at Claydon House, one of the finest examples of rococo art in England

■

■

DON'T MISS

■ The penitential maze (Chenies Manor House)

■ The Safari Skyway (Chessington World of Adventures)

■ Medieval tournaments (Chilham Castle)

COLCHESTER
ESSEX

An attractive town, famous for its oyster beds, Colchester was once the capital of the Iron Age chieftain Cunobelin. In AD44 it was captured by the Romans, who named it *Camulodunum*. They established their first English *colonia*, or settlement here, which was stormed by Boudicca in AD62. Considerable sections of the Roman city walls remain, including the impressive ruins of the Balkerne Gate. The **castle**, built partly with Roman bricks on what had been the site of a Roman temple, was constructed after the Norman Conquest. It has the largest keep in Europe, with walls 12ft (3.5m) thick. *Open: daily.*

The town suffered considerable damage during the Civil War, when it supported the king and was besieged by parliamentary forces for 11 weeks. There are three ruined abbeys in Colchester besides seven medieval churches, a considerable number of pleasing Georgian houses, and a fine 15th-century inn, the Red Lion Hotel. Some interesting half-timbered buildings still stand in the section of the town that was once occupied by Flemish weavers.

COOKHAM-ON-THAMES
BERKSHIRE

This attractive riverside village on the Thames has somehow managed to remain unspoilt and keep its charm. Kenneth Grahame used the river banks around Cookham as the setting for *The Wind in the Willows*. But Cookham is chiefly famous as the birthplace of the eccentric artist, Sir Stanley Spencer (1891–1949). The **Stanley Spencer Gallery** contains a collection of his works. *Open: daily, Eas–Oct; Sat, Sun and BH, Nov–Eas.*

COTSWOLD WILDLIFE PARK
OXFORDSHIRE
■ OFF THE A361, 3 MILES (5KM) SOUTH OF BURFORD ■

A zoo in the modern style, pioneered at Whipsnade, the wildlife park keeps animals in paddocks rather than cages. The absence of fences – in most cases the animals are separated from the public by impassable ditches – enables the visitor to accept the illusion that he is close to nature. The collection, set in 200 acres (80ha) of gardens and woodland, contains a number of exotic mammals and reptiles, as well as fish and insects. The Butterfly House has the largest flight cage in Britain. There are also woodland walks, an adventure playground, a narrow-gauge railway, and a brass-rubbing centre. *Open: daily.*

COURAGE SHIRE HORSE CENTRE
BERKSHIRE
■ OFF THE A4, 3 MILES (5KM) WEST OF MAIDENHEAD ■

The centre is devoted to the breeding, rearing and training of the famous shire horses used by the Courage brewery as walking advertisements for their beer. The centre also houses a museum of farm carts and agricultural implements. There is a collection of small animals, and a children's playground. *Open: daily, Eas–Oct.*

■ **DON'T MISS**

■ The Stanley Spencer Art Gallery (Cookham)

■ The Roman lighthouse (Dover Castle)

FOR CHILDREN

■ The Butterfly House (Cotswold Wildlife Park)

■ Steam locomotives (Didcot Railway Centre)

DIDCOT RAILWAY CENTRE
OXFORDSHIRE

This is a fascinating exercise in nostalgia as well as an important contribution to industrial archaeology. The splendid engine shed at Didcot recreates the golden age of steam and the old Great Western Railway (sometimes known from its initials as 'God's Wonderful Railway'), as it was in 1932 before it was nationalised. There are a number of lovingly restored GWR locomotives and fine examples of rolling stock which, especially on steaming days, may be enjoyed in all their glory. There is a museum of GWR relics and memorabilia, and displays of signalling equipment, as well as a fascinating working exhibition of Isambard Kingdom Brunel's broad-gauge railway, which ran from London to Bristol. Visitors may take rides on a section of track in restored railway carriages. *Open: daily, Eas–Sep; weekends, rest of year.*

DORNEY COURT
BUCKINGHAMSHIRE

■ ON THE B3026 AT DORNEY, 2 MILES (3KM) WEST OF WINDSOR ■

A remarkably complete example of a large Tudor house, Dorney Court is everybody's idea of what a half-timbered manor should look like. A false classical front protected the original timbers of the house for several centuries. When it was removed it revealed a gabled, red-brick exterior in a remarkable state of preservation. Today the house is a Grade I listed building of outstanding architectural and historical interest. It contains, among many other interesting objects, 12 generations of portraits of the Palmer family, a priest's hole and the Palmer Needlework, an Elizabethan tapestry depicting the life of triplets. The house also enjoys historical associations with Charles II, who visited his mistress, Barbara Palmer, Countess of Castlemaine, here in the 17th century. *Open: Eas–Sep (days vary; check with tourist information centres).*

DOVER
KENT

This large and important port is the English terminus of the Channel Tunnel. Its famous white cliffs, from which France is clearly visible on a fine day, symbolise British detachment from Europe. The town suffered bombing and shelling during the Second World War, and much of the post-war reconstruction is undistinguished.

The **castle**, overlooking the town, was built at the end of the 12th century by Henry II. In 1803 the curtain walls were lowered to make gun platforms, to repel any French invasion. The keep contains two chapels and a 250ft (75m) well, dug to provide the garrison with water. Adjacent to the castle are the impressive remains of the **pharos**, a lighthouse built by the Romans as a navigational aid. Originally it was about 100ft (30m) high. Even though only about 40ft (12m) of it remain today, it is still a remarkable monument. The Saxons used it as a bell tower for the little church of St Mary in Castro. *Open: daily (castle, EH).*

There are a number of interesting buildings in the town. In the High Street is the town hall, which incorporates the **Maison Dieu Hospital**, built in the 13th century as a hostel for pilgrims travelling to Canterbury, Rome, Compostella and the Holy Land. Next door is **Maison Dieu House**, built in 1665. Nearby, in Priory Road, is **St Edmund's Chapel**, consecrated by St Richard of Chichester in 1253. It is one of several claimants to the title of smallest church in Britain. During construction of a car park in New Street, a **Roman painted house** was discovered, and it has been preserved in a special exhibition area. Dover College, in Effingham Street, incorporates part of the old Benedictine Priory of St Martin in its structure. *Open: Tue–Sun, Apr–Oct; also BH Mon and Mon Jul, Aug (Roman painted house).*

■

ROYAL TREAT

A stone pineapple in the great hall at Dorney Court commemorates the fact that it was here that the first fruit of its kind was grown in England. The story has it that King Charles II cut off the top of a pineapple brought from Barbados, and gave it to Roger Palmer (the husband of Charles' mistress Barbara, Countess of Castlemaine), during a dinner at Mansion House. From this, in 1665, matured the first pineapple to be grown in England, in the gardens of Dorney. A painting in the hosue shows the head gardener, Rose, presenting the fruit of his labours to King Charles II.

■

■

Above: the Pharos, *or lighthouse, built by the Romans to guide their galleys from Gaul. Dover Castle can be seen in the background*

■

■

Below: the famous White Cliffs at Dover are seen by millions of travellers returning to England

■

EXBURY GARDENS
HAMPSHIRE

■ NEAR SOUTHAMPTON, 3 MILES (5KM) SOUTH-WEST OF FAWLEY ■

Lionel de Rothschild and his son have created what is claimed to be the world's finest collection of hybrid rhododendrons in a 200-acre (80ha) garden set in woodland. Other plants and shrubs include azaleas and camellias, and there are some fine specimen trees. A striking feature that has been developed in the past few years is the 2-acre (1ha) rock garden, containing many exotic species. There are picnic areas, a tea room and a gallery, where works of art are displayed. Visitors may purchase horticultural products from the plant centre. *Open: daily, Mar–Jul and mid-Sep–end Oct.*

FAWLEY COURT
BUCKINGHAMSHIRE

■ OFF THE A4155, 2 MILES (3KM) NORTH OF HENLEY-ON-THAMES ■

Fawley Court lies on the banks of the River Thames. It was built in the middle of the 17th century, replacing a mansion that had been destroyed by fire in 1642. The new design was by Sir Christopher Wren, in red brick with stone quoins and a hipped roof. The exterior was altered later by James Wyatt, who added an Ionic colonnade. The interior contains some original plasterwork, as well as Adam-style additions by Wyatt and decorations by Grinling Gibbons. The house contains a Polish Museum.

The grounds were landscaped by 'Capability' Brown in the 18th century. Temple Island once belonged to Fawley Court, but is now owned by Henley Royal Regatta. *Open: Mar–Nov (days vary; check with tourist information centres).*

GOODWOOD
WEST SUSSEX

■ OFF THE A285, 3 MILES (5KM) NORTH-EAST OF CHICHESTER ■

Goodwood House, the seat of the Duke of Richmond and Gordon, was designed by James Wyatt and built between 1780 and 1800, replacing a modest brick house. It is remarkable that such a large mansion should be constructed entirely of flint. The intention was to make it very much larger, but the money ran out and Wyatt's grandiose plan, based on an enormous octagon, had to be curtailed. In the event only the porticoed wing and two side wings were constructed. The house contains a fine collection of paintings, including works by Canaletto, Kneller, Lely, Van Dyck and Reynolds. There are some excellent pieces of furniture, as well as family mementoes and Napoleonic relics. *Open: Eas–Oct (days vary; check with local tourist information centres).*

The famous **racecourse**, known universally as 'Glorious Goodwood', claims to be the most beautiful in England. It was laid out on the South Downs in 1801 by the 3rd Duke of Richmond. Near the racecourse is **The Trundle**, an Iron Age hill fort which is often used as a vantage point by racegoers.

GREAT DIXTER
EAST SUSSEX

■ OFF THE A28 AT NORTHIAM, 6 MILES (10KM) SOUTH-WEST OF TENTERDEN ■

A fine example of a 15th-century half-timbered Tudor manor house, Great Dixter was purchased in 1910 by Nathaniel Lloyd, who employed the great architect, Sir Edwin Lutyens to restore it. He incorporated a small 16th-century hall house into the structure, which was brought, timber by timber, from Benenden. The Great Hall is magnificent, with a huge hammerbeam roof carved with armorial bearings. Lutyens also designed the gardens which include yew hedges and fantastic topiary in the form of pyramids, birds, and crenellations. *Open: Tue–Sun and BH Mon, Apr–mid-Oct.*

HAMMERWOOD PARK
WEST SUSSEX

■ ON THE A264, 3 MILES (5KM) EAST OF EAST GRINSTEAD ■

Hammerwood Park was designed by Benjamin Latrobe in 1792, the first major commission of the English-born architect of the Capitol in Washington, DC. This late Georgian house has been restored, and recently won a Special Award from the Institut International des Chateaux Historiques. There are guided tours, and displays of costumes and kitchen equipment. *Open: Wed, Sat and BH Mon, Apr–Sep.*

HATFIELD HOUSE
HERTFORDSHIRE

■ OFF THE A1000, JUST EAST OF HATFIELD ■

Robert Cecil, Chief Secretary and Lord Treasurer to King James I, built a magnificent mansion (now destroyed) at Theobalds. James persuaded Cecil to exchange his manor for the 15th-century Royal Palace at Hatfield. Cecil had the old palace demolished (except for the great hall which still survives), and built Hatfield House in its place. Today, Hatfield is one of England's showpieces.

This Jacobean palace was designed principally by Robert Lyminge, and built between 1607 and 1611. The principal features of the interior are the magnificent grand staircase and the sumptuously appointed state rooms. There are many relics of Elizabeth I on view. She was held in confinement at Hatfield, and heard news of her accession to the throne in 1558 under an oak tree in the park. There are also portraits by Hilliard and Zucchero, fine paintings by Van Dyck, Mytens, Kneller and Reynolds, outstanding furniture and tapestries, and ornate plasterwork and fireplaces.

There are splendid formal gardens outside, and an extensive park in which the world's first successful tank trials took place in 1916. Hatfield House is home to the **National Collection of Model Soldiers**, and there are often special exhibitions. *Open: Tue–Sun, Eas–Oct.*

■

GOOD QUEEN BESS

The future Elizabeth I (below) had a frightening upbringing among the threatening currents of Tudor politics. Her mother, Anne Boleyn, was beheaded when the little girl was only two years old. Her terrifying father, Henry VIII, died in 1547 and under his two successors, Edward VI and Mary I, Elizabeth was suspected of intriguing. She spent much of her time under house arrest at the old Royal Palace of Hatfield. It must have been with heartfelt relief that the princess received news, under an oak tree in the park, that she had become queen in 1558.

■

■

Right: the 'rainbow' portrait of Queen Elizabeth I, one of three at Hatfield House. Elizabeth spent much of her girlhood at the old Royal Palace of Hatfield, of which only one wing has survived. Hatfield House as it is today (below) is mainly Jacobean

■

HAWK CONSERVANCY
HAMPSHIRE

■ OFF THE A303 AT WEYHILL, 4 MILES (6KM) WEST OF ANDOVER ■

As its name implies, the Hawk Conservancy is a specialist centre for the breeding and study of birds of prey from all over the world. Traditional methods are used to train owls, hawks, falcons and eagles, which are shown and flown (weather permitting) for visitors in a wild garden setting. The more adventurous visitors are allowed to hold and feed the birds. *Open: daily, Eas–Oct.*

HEVER CASTLE
KENT

■ OFF THE B2027, 7½ MILES (12KM) SOUTH-WEST OF SEVENOAKS ■

Hever Castle is fascinating, but needs to be observed with detachment because much of it is bogus. Originally it was a 13th-century fortified and moated manor house. In 1506 Thomas Bullen, the father of Anne Boleyn (she gentrified the spelling of her name), inherited it. Anne was probably born here, and it was certainly her childhood home. Hever acquired status when Anne became the second wife of Henry VIII and the mother of Queen Elizabeth I. Her father died five years after her execution, and Henry VIII gave Hever to Anne of Cleves, whom he had divorced. After these sad events, history passed the castle by until it was purchased in 1903 by the American multi-millionaire, William Waldorf Astor.

For 80 years the Astors laboured to restore and transform Hever. The interior was filled with fake panelling and plasterwork, and a village of 'Tudor' cottages was built in the grounds for the use of guests and servants. These efforts are still much appreciated by the directors of historical films, who often use Hever as a location. Less controversially, a beautiful garden was created containing lakes, a yew maze, splendid topiary and a magnificent Italian garden with genuine classical statuary and sculpture.

Right: Hever Castle, the childhood home of Henry VIII's second wife, Anne Boleyn. She was beheaded on a charge of adultery in 1536

Hever contains an outstanding collection of Tudor royal portraits, including Henry VII by Mabuse, Henry VIII by Holbein, Queen Elizabeth I by Geerarts, and Anne Boleyn by an unknown artist. The book of hours that Anne carried with her to the execution block is exhibited, and there is a tableau of her life. *Open: daily, Eas–Nov.*

HIGHCLERE CASTLE
HAMPSHIRE

■ OFF THE A34, 6 MILES (10KM) SOUTH OF NEWBURY ■

This extravagant, High Gothic Victorian mansion was designed for the 3rd Earl of Carnarvon by Charles Barry in 1830. The rooms range in style from Moorish to Church Gothic and Gentleman's Club, and contain some fine furniture, including Napoleon's desk. There is also a Van Dyck, and a collection of 18th-century paintings. Highclere Castle was the home of the 5th Earl of Carnarvon, who discovered Tutankhamun's tomb in 1922. Some of his early Egyptian finds are now on display.

The interesting grounds include an orangery, a fernery and a secret garden. *Open: Wed–Sun, Jul–Sep.*

■

Left: High Victorian splendour at
Highclere Castle

■

IGHTHAM MOTE
KENT

■ OFF THE A227, 4½ MILES (7KM) NORTH OF TONBRIDGE ■

This is a beautiful moated manor house, dating from the 14th century. Three families – the Cawnes, the Allens and the Selbys – have left their mark on its buildings and their memorials may be seen in Ightham parish church. The name 'Mote' is not a corruption of 'moat' but of 'moot', an Anglo-Saxon meeting-place at which legal and administrative matters were discussed. Despite its harmonious appearance, the construction of the present house has been spread over three centuries, and the only incongruous note is struck by the large Palladian window in the drawingroom. The oldest part is the great hall, probably built in 1340 by Sir Thomas Cawne. It has massive oak beams, and a stone arch with decorated corbels supporting the roof.

This relatively small manor house contains two chapels. Above the great hall, next to the solar (or drawingroom) is a medieval chapel containing a squint, so that Mass can be seen and heard by those in the solar. There is also a beautiful Tudor chapel containing linenfold panelling, a fine painted ceiling and a sanctuary ring for those escaping from justice.

A number of stories and legends are associated with Ightham Mote. The Allens were Roman Catholics and were suspected of harbouring priests and keeping 'a vile and papisticall house'. The house was raided by the authorities but nothing treasonable was uncovered. A walled-up skeleton is supposed to have been found in a cupboard in the great hall. In the 17th century a Cromwellian soldier was drowned in the moat while attempting to gain access to the house to press his suit with one of the Selby ladies. It is said that a suit of armour in the great hall belonged to him.

Open: Sun, Mon, Wed–Fri and BH Mon, Mar–Oct.

■

Below: a heraldic figure at
Knebworth House, the former
home of the Victorian historical
novelist Edward Bulwer-Lytton

■

KNEBWORTH HOUSE
HERTFORDSHIRE

■ ON THE B656, 2 MILES (3KM) SOUTH-WEST OF STEVENAGE ■

Knebworth has been the ancestral home of the Lyttons since 1492. Little of the original Tudor mansion has survived, except for the banqueting hall, which was incorporated into the present house when it was substantially rebuilt in 1843 in High Gothic style. The driving-force behind the conversion was Edward Bulwer-Lytton, 1st Baron Lytton (1803–73). Bulwer-Lytton is chiefly known as the author of several well-researched, popular historical novels, including *The Last Days of Pompeii* and *The Last of the Barons*.

The banqueting hall contains some fine panelling and a Jacobean carved screen. There is also good furniture, family portraits and some of Bulwer Lytton's manuscripts. In the extensive grounds is a Grecian mausoleum, containing classical monuments to the Lytton family. The gardens were laid out by Sir Edwin Lutyens, and include the Jekyll herb garden. The park is now given over to the public who can amuse themselves at the funfair and frolic round the 16th-century tithe barn.

Open: Eas–Sep (check exact days with tourist information centre).

■

DON'T MISS

■ Displays of falconry (**the Hawk**
Conservancy)

■ The royal portraits and gardens
(**Hever Castle**)

■ The great hall and two chapels
(**Ightham Mote**)

■ The Jekyll herb garden
(**Knebworth House**)

ISLE OF WIGHT

The Isle of Wight is a hilly, lozenge-shaped island measuring 23 miles (37km) from east to west and 14 miles (22km) from north to south. It lies a short distance from the Hampshire coast and protects the entrance to Southampton Water. The island enjoys an exceptionally mild climate, which in the past has attracted the Romans, and today brings modern retirees. Queen Victoria was a regular visitor and helped to make the island a popular venue for yachtsmen and tourists.

Despite its popularity with holiday-makers and day-trippers, the beautifully manicured chalk landscape remains relatively unspoilt away from the coastal towns. There is a dense network of well maintained foot-paths, including a coastal path that encircles the island, enabling visitors to explore the many delights of the Isle of Wight.

THE WEST OF THE ISLAND
On the extreme western tip of the Isle of Wight is **Alum Bay**, famous for its multi-coloured sands which can be seen in the contorted strata of the cliffs. Marconi conducted wireless experiments from the bay in 1897. Nearby is **The Needles Old Battery**, a recently restored fort built by Palmerston in 1862, which gives splendid views of the famous Needles lighthouse. *Open: Apr–Nov (days may vary; check first with tourist information centres), NT.*

Freshwater, to the north-east of Alum, is a small village with Tennysonian associations. There are some splendid chalk cliffs to the west of the town, and a shipping-marker has been erected on **Tennyson Down** as a memorial to the poet.

North of Freshwater and 9 miles (14km)

west of Newport is **Yarmouth**, an attractive small ferry port and yachting centre. Near the Victorian pier is the **castle**, one of the chain built for coastal defence by Henry VIII. Situated a mile or so (1.6km) to the west is **Fort Victoria Country Park**. Fort Victoria was built to defend the western approach to the Solent. It now contains exhibitions and an aquarium, and its grounds have been made into a country park. *Open: daily (castle): daily (park); Mar–Nov (aquarium).*

Calbourne, 5 miles (8km) west of Newport, is an attractive village with an interesting church and a restored watermill. *Open: daily, Eas–Oct.*

Further along the B3401, 1 mile (1.6km) south-west of Newport, is **Carisbrooke**, originally the principal town of the island. It has an interesting parish church, which was once the chapel of a Cistercian priory dissolved by Henry VIII, but the town is chiefly notable for its Norman **castle**, It was constructed on the site of a Roman fort and enclosed by an additional wall in Elizabethan times. Visitors can still see a team of donkeys working the donkey wheel, housed in a 16th-century wellhouse. There is also a museum of local antiquities containing mementoes of Charles I, who was imprisoned here for a year before his execution. *Open: daily (EH).*

THE COWES AND NEWPORT AREA
Cowes, at the northern extremity of the island, is divided by the River Medina into West Cowes, the more attractive part of the town, and East Cowes. It is the chief yachting centre on the island, and during **Cowes Week** (the first week in August), it enjoys international importance. The **castle** was originally built by Henry VIII and is now the headquarters of the Royal Yacht Squadron.

Queen Victoria stayed as a child at **Norris**

Top: bottles of coloured sands from Alum bay make popular souvenirs.

Above: sailing boats and cannon can be seen at the Royal Yacht Squadron, whose base is at Cowes Castle

Left: the Needles off Alum Bay are one of the most hazardous places for shipping on the English coast

Castle in East Cowes, which was built by James Wyatt in 1805 in the style of a Norman castle. *Open: specified days (grounds only). Check with tourist information centre.*

Osborne House, just south of East Cowes, is probably the most interesting and popular attraction on the island. It was built by Thomas Cubitt in the 1840s for Queen Victoria and Prince Albert, who helped design it. Osborne became their private home, where they could escape from the cares of state. After Albert's death in 1861, Victoria preserved it as it was in his lifetime. She died here in 1901, and it remains a remarkable monument to royal taste in the Victorian age. There are some splendid and extraordinary rooms, such as the Durbar Room, decorated in Indian style, but it is the small, intimate objects in the house that many visitors find most moving. *Open: daily, Eas–Oct (EH).*

Further south is **Newport**, the largest town and 'capital' of the island. It has some pleasing 18th-century houses in the High Street, a Roman villa and a fine Guildhall designed by John Nash. The **church of St Thomas** contains the grave of Princess Elizabeth, the daughter of Charles I, and a memorial to her commissioned by Queen Victoria.

THE EAST OF THE ISLAND
Children and adults alike will enjoy a trip to **Butterfly World** betweeen Newport and Wootton, where butterflies from all over the world fly free in tropical indoor gardens. *Open: daily, Eas–Oct.*

At Havenstreet station, is the **Isle of Wight Steam Railway**. *Open: Apr–Oct (days vary; check with tourist information centres).*

Ryde, six miles (10km) east of Newport, is a large resort containing many attractive 19th-century buildings. The **Cothey Bottom Heritage Centre** contains a fine collection of vintage and veteran vehicles. At **Puckpool Park** is a mortar battery, part of the Solent defences built in 1862. *Open: daily, Eas–Oct (heritage centre): guided tours specified days (park).*

To the far east of the island is the yachting centre of **Bembridge**. It has a **Maritime Museum**, which specialises in the history of diving, an old **windmill**, a lifeboat station and the unusual, boat-shaped **Pilot Boat Inn**. *Open: daily, Mar–Oct (museum): Sun–Fri, Apr–Nov; daily, Jul, Aug (windmill, NT).*

Brading, south-west of Bembridge, has a **Roman villa**, the **Isle of Wight Wax Museum**, the **Lilliput Museum of Antique Dolls and Toys** and the **Old Town Hall Museum**, with stocks and a whipping post. *Open: daily, Apr–Sep (Roman villa): daily, (wax museum): daily, mid Mar–mid Jan (museum of antique dolls and toys): open at specified times (check with tourist information centre) (old town hall museum).*

The brash seaside resort of **Sandown**, with its fine sands, is home to the **Isle of Wight Zoo**. Nearby **Shanklin** is more genteel and attractive. The famous **Shanklin Chine** is a 300ft- (90m-) deep ravine, containing rare plants. *Open: daily, Eas–Oct; Sun, Nov–Eas (zoo): daily, Eas–Oct (chine).*

Further south is **Ventnor**, the Isle of Wight's most attractive seaside resort. It is built in a series of terraces climbing the cliff face. Attractions include **Ventnor Botanic Garden**, which contains a large collection of sub-tropical plants, and a **Museum of Smuggling History**. *Open: daily (garden): daily, Eas–Oct (museum).*

Godshill, north-west of Ventnor, is *the* show village of the island. In summer coachloads of tourists come to admire the delightful thatched cottages grouped round the church. Other attractions include **Godshill Toy Museum**; the **Natural History Centre** and the **Model Village**, a one-tenth scale model of Godshill. *Open: daily, Eas–Oct (toy museum and model village: daily, Eas–Aug (natural history centre).*

North of Godshill is **Arreton Manor**, dating from 1612, with an interesting **collection of toys and dolls**, as well as the **National Wireless Museum**. Nearby is **Arreton Country Craft Village**, where craftsmen sell their products. *Open: Sun, Mon–Fri and BH Sat (manor): daily (craft village).*

KNOLE
KENT

■ ON THE A225, 1 MILE (1.6KM) SOUTH OF SEVENOAKS ■

One of the largest and most interesting of the great houses of England, Knole is fortunate to be in the loving hands of the National Trust, and has escaped the tawdriness too often associated with the income-generating activities of comparable buildings. The original house was medieval and was purchased by Thomas Bourchier, Archbishop of Canterbury, from Lord Saye

Above: herds of fallow and Japanese deer trim the grass in the park at Knole. Rabbits also live in its open expanses of turf, which were enclosed in 1456 by Archbishop Bouchier.

■

Above, right: the Green Court is the largest of Knole's seven courtyards. The two-storey range was probably built to lodge Henry VIII's attendants – hence the number of small doorways and narrow windows

■

and Sele in 1456. Bourchier virtually rebuilt it, and in 1533 it passed to Archbishop Thomas Cranmer. When he realised that Henry VIII coveted Knole because of its dry position on the knoll from whence it derives its name, Cranmer, remembering the precedent set by Cardinal Wolsey, who once owned Hampton Court, wisely handed it over to the king. It remained in royal hands for 30 years, until Queen Elizabeth leased it to her cousin, Thomas Sackville, Earl of Dorset, in 1566. He purchased the freehold in 1603, and Knole has been the home of the Sackvilles ever since.

Legend has it that Knole contains seven courtyards, 52 staircases, and 365 rooms, but this association with the measurement of time seems almost too good to be true. The exterior has a collegiate appearance, but behind the façade lies a medieval great hall and magnificently appointed state apartments. These contain fine plasterwork, furniture dating from the 17th century (including magnificent canopied beds and silverwork), and pictures by Van Dyck, Kneller, Gainsborough and Reynolds.

Knole is not all grandeur. One of the most interesting suites was occupied for 40 years during the 18th century by Lady Betty Germain, a friend of the Sackvilles. Her rooms exude a cosy intimacy appropriate to a lady who occupied her time with needlework, correspondence and making pot-pourri.

The gardens, which extend to over 26 acres (10.0ha), have changed little since the 17th century. They are enclosed by a wall and are laid out with formal walks, flower beds, shrubs and trees. Beyond is the deer park, covering 1,000 acres (405ha). *Open: Wed–Sun and BH Mon, Mar–Oct (house); first Wed of month, May–Sep (garden); daily, all year (park), NT.*

LAYER MARNEY TOWER
ESSEX

■ OFF THE B1022, 6 MILES (10KM) SOUTH-WEST OF COLCHESTER ■

This extraordinary structure was built in 1520 by Sir Henry Marney, who rose from humble beginnings to serve under Henry VII, and eventually became a member of Henry VIII's privy council. He amassed a fortune and in 1520 decided to display his wealth by building a magnificent house constructed in brick and designed in the latest fashion. But the money ran out and only the gatehouse was actually built. It gives an impressive indication, however, of the scale of Lord Marney's vaulting ambition: Layer Marney Tower is the tallest gatehouse in the country, the main structure above the entrance having three storeys. There are towers that are eight storeys high on each of the four corners, with extensive views over the Essex countryside and the Blackwater Estuary.

Deer and rare breeds of farm animals are kept in the grounds. Next to the garden is the parish church, which contains tombs and memorials of the Marney family. *Open: Apr–Sep (days vary; check with tourist information centres).*

■

DON'T MISS ____

■ Lady Betty Germain's apartments (**Knole**)

■ The dog collar museum (**Leeds Castle**)

■ The blossom in springtime (**Leonardslee Gardens**)

LEEDS CASTLE
KENT
■ OFF THE A20, 5 MILES (8KM) SOUTH-EAST OF MAIDSTONE ■

Leeds Castle is built in a natural moat on two islands in the River Len, and is most people's idea of what a medieval castle should look like. The name 'Leeds' is derived from Led, a 9th-century advisor to the Kentish king, Ethelbert IV. Leeds has sometimes been known as 'Ladies' Castle, because it was the home of eight medieval queens, including the two wives of Edward I, Eleanor of Castile and Margaret of France; Edward III's queen, Philippa of Hainault; and Henry V's queen, Catherine of Valois. In the 17th century it was the home of Lord Culpeper, who was Governor of Virgina from 1680–3.

The Saxon lands were given by William the Conqueror to Robert de Crevecoeur, who constructed a keep at the beginning of the 12th century. At the end of the 13th it reverted to the Crown, and Edward I had a gatehouse and barbican constructed.

The interior is as interesting as the exterior, containing a magnificent banqueting hall in which Henry VIII feasted, a Norman cellar, a private royal chapel, and a suite of rooms prepared for the reception of Henry V and his consort, Catherine of Valois. An unusual museum of dog collars in the gatehouse, and a fine collection of Impressionist paintings, medieval furnishings, tapestries and French and English furniture, complete the picture.

The grounds contain aviaries of rare tropical birds and the Culpeper garden, with fragant and old-fashioned flowers. There is a maze planted in 1987, with a shell-lined grotto nearby, containing a waterfall gushing from the face of a god, and an exit through a rock-lined tunnel. The park (but not the golf course), was landscaped in the 18th century by 'Capability' Brown, and the attractive, reed-fringed lake is now home to many varieties of waterfowl.

Leeds Castle is an international conference centre and regularly hosts events and festivals. *Open: daily, Eas–Oct; weekends, rest of year.*

LEONARDSLEE GARDENS
WEST SUSSEX
■ ON THE A281, 4 MILES (6.4KM) SOUTH-EAST OF HORSHAM ■

These magnificent gardens have been laid out in a valley containing a string of lakes that are one of the sources of the River Adur. They are the brainchild of Sir Edmund Loder, who began to create them in 1889. He was particularly interested in rhododendrons and he gave his name to the *Loderi* variety, many examples of which may be seen at Leonardslee. It is a wonderful experience to visit the gardens in springtime and wander amid the splendid displays of rhododendrons, camellias, magnolias, acers, azaleas and other exotic shrubs adorning the lakes and waterfalls, and to observe the reflections of the water. In October there are spectacular displays of autumn colours. *Open: daily, Apr–Jun; weekends in Oct.*

CANINE NECKWEAR

The earliest dog collars on show in the museum at Leeds Castle are alarming-looking 16th-century iron contraptions, studded with sharp spikes. They were to protect a hound's vulnerable neck against bears and wolves. From later times come more graceful and elaborate examples, combining decorative purposes with ease of identification. There is one of leather, covered with red velvet and bearing the arms of the Archbishop of Salzburg. Brass collars from the 19th century include one with the inscription: 'I am Mr Pratt's Dog, King St. Nr. Wokingham, Berks. Whose dog are you?' There are silver collars, awarded as prizes to coursing and show champions, and even one which looks like a man's starched shirt collar, with a bowtie at the front. The collection is unique and delightful.

LONDON'S IMPERIAL PAST, WHEN A QUARTER

OF THE WORLD WAS RULED FROM THIS GREAT

CITY, IS REFLECTED IN THE RICHNESS OF ITS

LONDON

BUILDINGS, MUSEUMS, STATUES AND ART

TREASURES

■

Above: the Nereid Monument in the British Museum, dating from the 5th century BC, once stood in a Greek colony at Lycia in Asia Minor. It has been reconstructed into a facade, showing the Nereids (wind spirits) as dancing maidens with flowing garments

■

Right: the imposing front of Buckingham Palace was erected in 1913, hiding an earlier one by John Nash. In the foreground is the Victoria Memorial

■

The capital of the United Kingdom is easily the largest and most important city in the country. It is also one of the world's great treasure-houses and is the centre of British state ceremonial, tradition and culture. London has some of the world's finest museums, art collections and theatres, as well as some outstanding public buildings. It would take many lifetimes to become familiar with all its treasures, and the places of interest described in this section can give only an indication of the flavour and diversity of London and its environs.

APSLEY HOUSE

Standing at the Hyde Park Corner end of Piccadilly, Apsley House was the London home of the Duke of Wellington. It is one of London's grandest houses and was designed in 1778 by Robert Adam, with alterations and additions by James Wyatt in 1829.

Particularly noteworthy are the **Piccadilly Drawingroom**, the **Portico Room**, the **Yellow Drawingroom**, the **Striped Drawingroom** and the **dining-room**. The Waterloo Banquet was held annually in the magnificent **Waterloo Gallery** until the Duke's death in 1852. There are numerous paintings collected by the 'Iron Duke', as well as portraits, busts, mementoes and relics of his campaigns. *Open: Tue–Sat.*

BRITISH MUSEUM

One of the most important and remarkable museums in the world is housed in an imposing classical building in Great Russell Street, Bloomsbury. The collection includes outstanding works of art and artefacts from the ancient and classical world, There are also displays of British archaeological finds, as well as manuscripts, prints and drawings, and the magnificent reading room of the **British Library**. *Open: daily (museum); daily (reading room – ticket holders only).*

BUCKINGHAM PALACE

The official residence of the sovereign since 1837, Buckingham Palace was originally built in 1703 and enlarged and remodelled by John Nash in the 1820s. The palace is

■

Above: Covent Garden has become a popular centre for tourists. Here there are shops, craft stalls and antiques markets, as well as street entertainers

■

never open to the public, but the ceremony of the **Changing of the Guard** (which takes place at 11.30am daily in summer, and at the same time every other day in

winter), may be watched through the railings.

The palace stands in a commanding position at the south-west end of The Mall, overlooking St James' Park and Green Park. In the centre of the circus, in front of the palace, is an allegorical **memorial to Queen Victoria**, erected in 1911.

The **Royal Mews** in Buckingham Palace Road contain the stables for the royal horses, and some state carriages. *Open: Wed and Thu.*

At Buckingham Gate nearby is the **Queen's Gallery**, which has changing exhibitions of works of art from the royal collection. *Open: Tue–Sun and BH Mon.*

COVENT GARDEN
Covent Garden was originally the convent garden of the monks of Westminster Abbey, and was also London's principal vegetable market until it was removed to Nine Elms in 1974. Today the area is home to a lively, Continental-style piazza with boutiques, cafés and street theatre. Attractions include the **London Transport Museum**, which contains a fine collection of buses and tube trains. *Open: daily.*

The classical portico of **St Paul's**, 'the actors' church', designed by Inigo Jones, can be viewed nearby, and the **Theatre Museum** in Russell Street is well worth visiting. *Open: Tue–Sun.*

Several theatres can be found in the area, including the **Royal Opera House** and the **Theatre Royal**, known as 'Drury Lane'.

DICKENS' HOUSE
Situated at 48 Doughty Street, off Gray's Inn Road, this modest house was the home of the novelist Charles Dickens from 1837 to 1839. It is furnished in early Victorian style, and the basement kitchen is modelled on that of Dingley Dell in *Pickwick Papers*. There are also manuscripts, first editions, mementoes of Dickens' life and a fine library.

DR JOHNSON'S HOUSE
No. 17 Gough Square, just off New Fetter Lane, was the home of Dr Samuel Johnson, lexicographer, essayist, novelist, poet, moralist and sage, from 1749 to 1758. The house was built in about 1700 and contains portraits, letters and early editions of his works. *Open: Mon–Sat.*

GREENWICH
Situated on the south side of the Thames, this attractive area of London is famous for its park and magnificent Renaissance buildings. The **Royal Naval College** on the waterfront was originally built as a royal palace for Charles II by John Webb, and was later altered by Sir Christopher Wren and Nicholas

■

Below: the figurehead of the Cutty Sark, one of the last and fastest tea clippers, breasted the waves to China in the 19th century. She can now be seen in dry dock by Greenwich Pier

■

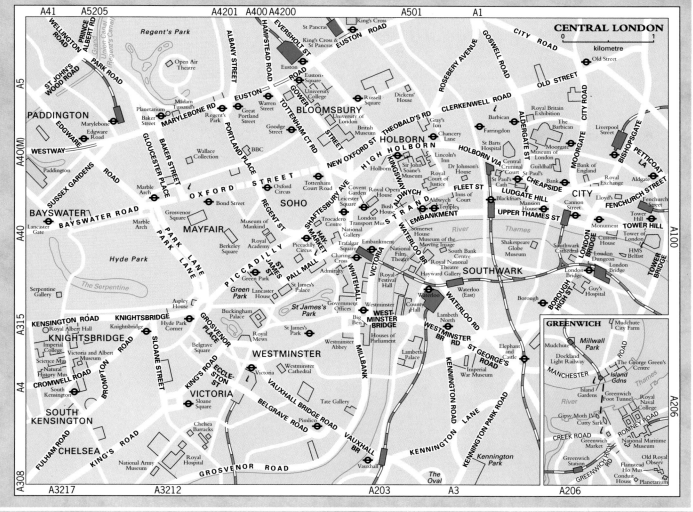

CENTRAL LONDON

■

■

Hawksmoor. *Open: Fri–Wed (Painted Hall and chapel).*

Nearby are the famous tea clipper the *Cutty Sark*, and Sir Francis Chichester's ship, *Gipsy Moth IV*, in which he single-handedly circumnavigated the globe. *Open: daily (both).*

Behind the Royal Naval College is the **National Maritime Museum**. Originally the only building here was the **Queen's House**, a Palladian villa designed by Inigo Jones in the early 17th century. Two wings were added in the 19th century and these are now home to the museum. It houses the most important maritime collection in the country, covering all aspects of nautical history. *Open: daily (museum and house).*

Greenwich Park, designed by André Le Nôtre, who laid out the famous gardens at Versailles, con-

tains the **Old Royal Observatory**. Flamsteed House nearby was designed by Sir Christopher Wren. The Prime Meridian of the World, on which all the world's clock time is based, was laid out in 1884 and can be seen in the 18th-century **Meridian Building**. The Old Royal Observatory is now a museum. *Open: daily.*

HAM HOUSE

On the River Thames, 1 mile (1.6km) south of Richmond, lies Ham House. It was built in 1610 and enlarged in 1672 by the Duke of Lauderdale, who was famous for his lavish entertaining.

The house stands in attractive 17th-century gardens, and contains a fine collection of works of art including Mortlake tapestries, costumes, textiles, a miniature of Queen Elizabeth I by Nicholas Hil-

liard, and paintings by Lely, Reynolds, Van de Velde, Kneller and Constable. *Open: Tue–Sun, (NT).*

HAMPSTEAD

An attractive area of north London, Hampstead has long been the haunt of the literati. The many fine and interesting old houses include **Keats' House** in Keats' Grove. It contains mementoes of the poet, who lived in Hampstead shortly before his death in 1821. *Open: daily.*

Fenton House, built in 1695, contains collections of ceramics and musical instruments and is host to concerts in summer. *Open: Mon–Wed and Sat–Sun, Apr–Oct; Sat–Sun in Mar.*

Hampstead Heath, a large area of open space, grass and woodland, has always been one of London's places of recreation. **Kenwood House**, on the Heath, was given to the nation by the Earl of Iveagh in 1927. The house was remodelled by Robert Adam in the 18th century and the grounds were landscaped by Humphry Repton. Today it contains an outstanding collection of paintings. *Open: daily (EH).*

HAMPTON COURT

This magnificent palace on the River Thames, 13 miles (21km) west of London, was originally built by Cardinal Wolsey in the early 16th century. He gave it to King Henry VIII in 1529, and it remained a royal palace until the accession of George III in 1760. Parts of the Tudor palace were rebuilt by Sir Christopher Wren. Of particular interest are the state apartments, the great hall, the royal chapel, the Tudor kitchens, and the superb collection of paintings, furniture and tapestries.

The magnificent gardens include an Elizabethan knot garden, a Tudor pond garden, and a 17th-century Italian Garden. The world-famous maze was planted at the beginning of the 18th century.

HIGHGATE CEMETERY

This fascinating corner of north London is located in Swains Lane, near Highgate Hill. The cemetery is in two parts. The eastern section is still in use and contains many famous graves, including those of George Eliot, Sir Leslie Stephen and other literary figures. Karl Marx has a large and unmistakable monument. *Open: daily.*

The western part is no longer open for burials. Overgrown, and

■

■

Above: Take-Off *by Dame Laura Knight, a painting at the Imperial War Museum, brings the interior of a Second World War bomber aircraft vividly to life*

hardly maintained, it was first put into use in 1838. Today it is crowded with vaults and gravestones, urns and angels, catacombs and several huge mausoleums. *Open: daily (guided tours only).*

HMS *BELFAST*

This, the last of the British big-gun cruisers, may be reached by ferry from Tower Pier. HMS *Belfast* was the largest British cruiser ever built and displaces 11,000 tons (11,220 tonnes). Her 8in (20cm) guns saw action at the Battle of the North Cape, the D-Day landings, and in the Korean War. She is now a naval museum. *Open: daily.*

HOUSES OF PARLIAMENT

The Palace of Westminster, as the Houses of Parliament are officially known, stands beside Westminster Abbey, on the banks of the Thames.

The splendid Gothic buildings that we know today were designed by Sir Charles Barry and Augustus Pugin after a disastrous fire of 1834. *Open: by arrangement only, for those attending debates, lobbying, or taking part in a tour organised by an MP or Peer.*

The **clocktower**, 320ft (98m) high, is known throughout the world as Big Ben, although the name actually refers to its famous $13\frac{1}{2}$ ton (14 tonne) bell.

IMPERIAL WAR MUSEUM

This museum lies south of the river, on Lambeth Road. It is housed in the handsome old Bethlehem Hospital, once an asylum for the insane, popularly known as 'Bedlam'. The Imperial War Museum contains exhibits explaining and illustrating British military history since 1914. There are realistic recreations of First World War trenches and an excellent gallery of paintings by war artists. *Open: daily.*

KEW GARDENS

The Royal Botanic Gardens, popularly known as Kew Gardens, are a collection of 50,000 specimens of plants, trees and shrubs from around the world. They have been built up over the last 250 years by numerous dedicated collectors.

The Royal Botanic Gardens today not only provide the general public with beautiful seasonal displays of the gardener's art, but are also an important research institute. *Open: daily.*

MADAME TUSSAUD'S

This, the most famous waxworks museum in the world, is found in Marylebone Road, near its junction with Baker Street. The figures are all life-size and include historical personages, members of royalty, statesmen, politicians, entertainers and other famous people of today and yesterday. Downstairs, in the Chamber of Horrors, there are recreations of sensational murder cases and grisly displays of instruments of torture. *Open: daily.*

NATIONAL GALLERY

The nation's most important art gallery is found on the north side of Trafalgar Square, in a neo-classical building by William Wilkins of 1832 with a new wing by Robert Venturi. The National Gallery has one of the world's greatest collections of Western painting, including outstanding examples of all major European schools. *Open: daily.*

NATIONAL PORTRAIT GALLERY

This interesting art gallery in St Martin's Place, just behind the National Gallery, contains over 8,000 portraits, drawings and photographs of Britons, dating from Tudor times to the present. The interest is in the sitter rather than the artist, so although there are works by Gainsborough, Kneller and Reynolds in the collection, there are also many works by lesser-known and amateur artists. *Open: daily.*

NATURAL HISTORY MUSEUM

An exciting museum located in Cromwell Road, South Kensington, the Natural History Museum contains specimens and exhibits of plant and animal life, rocks, fossils and meteorites, as well as displays about evolution, human biology and those children's favourites, dinosaurs. *Open: daily.*

OLD BAILEY

The Central Criminal Court, or the Old Bailey, as it is popularly known, is situated at the junction of Old Bailey and Newgate Street in the City of London. It occupies the site of the once-notorious Newgate Prison, the site of public executions.

Number One Court is the most famous, and it is here that some of Britain's most notorious cases have been tried. *Open: when the court is sitting (public galleries only).*

PETTICOAT LANE

A market held on Sunday mornings in Middlesex Street, between Liverpool Street station and Aldgate underground station, Petticoat Lane derives its name from its association with the second-hand clothing trade. Clothing is still sold, but so are household goods, pets, dubious antiques and jewellery. Many visitors go just to savour the raucous and colourful atmosphere. Trading starts as early as 4.00am. *Open: Sun.*

The splendid entrance to the Natural History Museum in South Kensington was designed by Alfred Waterhouse and opened in 1880

PICCADILLY

One of London's principal thoroughfares, Piccadilly runs from Piccadilly Circus to Hyde Park Corner.

Piccadilly Circus, once regarded as 'the hub of the capital', now contains a range of tawdry amusements, souvenir shops and places to eat, and is frequented by prostitutes and drug addicts. The famous **statue of Eros** was designed in 1893 as a memorial to Lord Shaftesbury, and was originally entitled 'The Angel of Charity'.

Piccadilly proper is a much more distinguished street, and includes quality shops and hotels. The elegant **St James's Church**, designed by Sir Christopher Wren, contains an altarpiece and font by Grinling Gibbons. Burlington House, on the north side, is the home of the **Royal Academy of Arts**, which holds important exhibitions. Attractive **Burlington Arcade** nearby contains a number of fashionable shops and boutiques, while the **clock** above Fortnum & Mason, with its revolving figures in 18th-century dress, is also of interest.

PLANETARIUM

The London Planetarium is in the Marylebone Road, next to Madame Tussaud's. It is a fascinating scale model of the heavens, showing the position of the stars and planets as they appear from any place on earth and at any moment in time from 50 years before the birth of Christ to some 2,000 years into the future. *Open: daily.*

REGENT'S CANAL

This 8½-mile (14km) waterway links the Thames with the **Grand Union Canal** at Paddington Basin. A stroll along this hidden waterway shows the visitor unusual aspects of London. It runs through **Regent's Park** to **Camden Lock**, which is frequented by artists and craftsmen.

ROYAL PARKS

London is justly famous for the number and beauty of its parks. The five royal parks described below are located in or close to the city centre.

Green Park lies between Buckingham Palace and Piccadilly. It is an informal park, created in 1668 and used by King Charles II for picnics.

Hyde Park was acquired by Henry VIII after the Dissolution of the Monasteries. He enclosed it as a deer park and hunted here with his daughter, the future Queen Elizabeth I, and it was not until the reign of Charles I that it was opened to the public. **Marble Arch**, on the edge of the park, was designed by John Nash for Buckingham Palace in the 19th century but it proved too narrow for the state carriage and was removed to its present site. Nearby is **Speaker's Corner** where, on Sunday afternoons, people harangue the public from soap-boxes.

Kensington Gardens are a more formal park, and once formed part of Kensington Palace. They were laid out by Charles Bridgeman in 1731 and contain a statue of **Peter Pan**, as well as the Round Pond.

St James's Park lies between The Mall and Birdcage Walk, to the east of Buckingham Palace. It was popular with Henry VIII and was later laid out as a park for Charles II by André Le Nôtre. It contains a lake which is a well-known haunt of waterfowl.

Regent's Park was once used by Henry VIII as a hunting-ground. The present park was laid out by John Nash in 1812 and named after the Prince Regent. It contains the famous **Zoological Gardens**, the **Open-Air Theatre** and the beautiful **Queen Mary's Rose Garden**.

ST PAUL'S CATHEDRAL

A magnificent cathedral on Ludgate Hill, in the City of London, St Paul's is Sir Christopher Wren's masterpiece and was completed in 1697. It is built on the site of an earlier cathedral destroyed in the Great Fire of London in 1666. St Paul's suffered direct hits during the London Blitz, but has survived remarkably unscathed.

As well as being notable for the perfection of its classical design, St Paul's is interesting as a British valhalla. It contains the tombs and monuments of innumerable military men, including the particularly splendid sarcophogi of Nelson and Wellington.

The famous dome is actually double. The outer dome is of wood and lead, and the inner of stone. The interior of the dome can best be viewed from the Whispering Gallery, so-called because a word whispered on one side of the gallery can be heard clearly on the other. *Open: daily (restricted admittance during services); Mon–Sat (crypt and gallery).*

SCIENCE MUSEUM

This interesting and lively museum, in Exhibition Road, South Kensington, is housed in a handsome building completed in 1928. It was founded in 1856 and is devoted to science and technology. Here there are exhibits of machinery and working models, from the early days of steam to the space age, with plenty to appeal to children. *Open: daily.*

SIR JOHN SOANE'S MUSEUM

One of the most idiosyncratic and unusual museums to be found anywhere in London is Sir John Soane's Museum, at 13 Lincoln's Inn Fields. The collection of sculptures, drawings, paintings, curios and *objets d'art* in the house was amassed by Sir John Soane (1753–1837), who bequeathed his home and his collection to the nation on condition that it should remain exactly as he left it. Visitors to the house today can see the sarcophagus of Seti I and an excellent selection of paintings by William Hogarth. *Open: Tue–Sat.*

TATE GALLERY

An art gallery on Millbank, fronting the Thames, the Tate was founded by Sir Henry Tate, the sugar magnate. Its neo-classical building was designed by Sidney J R Smith and opened in 1897. It has been extended several times since. The collection is devoted to British art of all periods and modern foreign art, from the Impressionists to the present day. The Clore Gallery houses the Turner collection of 300 paintings and 20,000 drawings, sketches and notebooks. *Opern: daily.*

TOWER OF LONDON

The Tower is one of London's most famous landmarks. Its oldest part is the **White Tower**, which was built by William the Conqueror to impress the citizens of London. For parts of its history it has served as a prison and a place of execution for many a famous name.

Particular features of interest are the Norman Chapel of St John, the Chapel of St Peter ad Vincula, Traitor's Gate, the armouries (which contain a wonderful collection of arms and armour), the exhibition of the **Crown Jewels** and, of course, the Beefeaters in their Tudor uniform. *Open: daily, Mar–Oct; Mon–Sat, Nov–Feb.*

Tower Green nearby has a plaque marking the site of the scaffold that was used to execute the Tower's prisoners.

TRAFALGAR SQUARE

London's most famous square was laid out between 1830 and 1850 and is dominated by **Nelson's Column**. Famous buildings surrounding the square include Admiralty Arch, the National Gallery, and the classical church of St Martin-in-the-Fields, designed by James Gibbs and completed in 1724.

Trafalgar Square is a centre for public rallies and demonstrations, as well as the traditional location for Londoners to see in the New Year.

VICTORIA & ALBERT MUSEUM

This museum, affectionately known as 'the V&A', is located in Cromwell Road. It contains an enormous collection of applied art from all over the world. The exhibits include tapestries, sculpture, stained glass, ivories, furniture, ceramics, silver, rooms from demolished houses, wallpapers, carpets, jade, costumes and musical instruments. *Open: daily.*

■

Below: indomitable St Paul's Cathedral was a symbol of hope to the nation during the Blitz

■

WESTMINSTER ABBEY

The national church and shrine of England is Westminster Abbey. William the Conqueror and almost all of his successors have been crowned here. An outstanding example of English Gothic architecture, the abbey has over 1,000 tombs and memorials to royal sovereigns, the great and the good, as well as the poignant Tomb of the Unknown Warrior, whose body was taken from the battlefields of France after the First World War.

WHITEHALL

The name given to the street that runs from Trafalgar Square to Parliament Square. Nowadays, 'Whitehall' is generally used as a term for the administrative arm of government, for some of the most important ministries are located here. In the centre of Whitehall is the **Cenotaph**, designed by Sir Edwin Lutyens in 1919 and used today as a memorial to the dead of both World Wars.

Off Whitehall is **Downing Street**. No. 10 is occupied by the Prime Minister, no. 11 by the Chancellor of the Exchequer, and no. 12 by the government's Chief Whip.

Horse Guards Parade is where **Trooping the Colour** takes place each year on the Saturday nearest to 11 June, the Queen's official birthday. The **Cabinet War Rooms** may be reached from Horse Guards. These 19 bomb-proof, underground rooms were built during the Second World War. Visitors can see Churchill's bedroom, the Transatlantic Telephone Room for communicating with President Roosevelt, and the Map Room. *Open: daily.*

■

Left: the White Tower, built between 1077 and 1097 for William the Conqueror, is the oldest part of the Tower of London

■

■

Above: Nelson has been standing atop his 172ft (52m) granite column in Trafalgar Square since 1842

■

LOSELEY HOUSE
SURREY

■ OFF THE A3100, 2 MILES (3KM) SOUTH-WEST OF GUILDFORD ■

A fine Elizabethan mansion built in the 1560s by Sir William More, from stone taken from nearby Waverley Abbey. Extensions were made in the 17th century. Loseley is still owned by Sir William's descendants. The house contains some fine Tudor panelling, which may have come from Henry VIII's long-vanished palace of Nonsuch at Esher. Other items of interest are a huge chimneypiece carved from a solid block of chalk, fine furniture, tapestries and needlework.

The Loseley herd of Jersey cattle is justly famous, and Loseley Hall icecreams and yoghurts are widely marketed. *Open: Wed–Sat, Jun–Sep.*

■

Left: Luton Hoo houses the magnificent Wernher collection. Designed by Robert Adam, it was finally completed by Sir Robert Smirke in 1816

■

LUTON HOO
BEDFORDSHIRE

■ OFF JUNCTION 10 OF THE M1, NEAR LUTON ■

This great house has had a chequered architectural history. It was designed and commenced by Robert Adam in 1767 but was completed by Sir Robert Smirke in 1816. It suffered severely from a fire in 1843 and the interior was extensively remodelled at the beginning of the century. The 1,500-acre (600ha) park was landscaped by 'Capability' Brown, but the house is chiefly notable for the **Wernher collection** of old masters, china, ivories, silverware, and works of art connected with the Russian imperial family, including Fabergé jewellery and portraits. *Open: Tue–Sun and BH, Eas–Oct.*

MAPLEDURHAM HOUSE
OXFORDSHIRE

■ OFF THE A329, 4 MILES (6KM) NORTH-WEST OF READING ■

A large Elizabethan mansion, built by Sir Michael Blount in 1588 on the banks of the River Thames, Mapledurham is still owned by Sir Michael's descendants. The mellow house has a fine oak staircase, some Tudor plasterwork and a good collection of family portraits. An interesting feature is the Strawberry Hill Gothick chapel of 1797. The attractive grounds contain the 12th-century remains of the old manor house of Mapledurham Gumey, and a 15th-century working watermill, which has been lovingly restored. *Open: Sat, Sun and BH, Eas–Sep.*

MARWELL ZOO
HAMPSHIRE

■ OFF THE B2177, 7 MILES (11KM) SOUTH OF WINCHESTER ■

This zoological park, which opened in 1972, specialises in the breeding and conservation of endangered species. The animals are kept in large paddocks and enclosures which once formed part of nearby Marwell Hall. As well as its collection of big cats, it has camels, giraffes, monkeys and rare species like Siberian tigers and Asian lions. *Open: daily.*

■

Below: giraffes take a quizzical interest in visitors at Marwell Zoo near Winchester, where the animals can be viewed in large enclosures, or roaming through paddocks. Marwell is one of the bigger zoos in Britain and is particularly concerned with breeding endangered species

■

■

DON'T MISS

■ The solid chalk chimneypiece (Loseley Hall)

■ Fabergé jewellery (Luton Hoo)

FOR CHILDREN

■ The working watermill (Mapledurham House)

■ The miniature railway (Marwell Zoo)

■ The toy museum (Penshurst Place)

MINSTER LOVELL
OXFORDSHIRE

■ OFF THE B4047, 2 MILES (3KM) WEST OF WITNEY ■

Minster Lovell is a charming village on the River Windrush. The main feature of interest is the ruined **Minster Lovell Hall**, dismantled in the 18th century. It was built by the Lovell family, who lost their lands after the defeat of Richard III at Bosworth in 1485. According to a gruesome legend, Francis Lovell supported the rebellion of Lambert Simnel during Henry VII's reign. Fearing capture, he hid in a secret chamber whose whereabouts were known only to his servant. The servant died in an accident, and Lovell starved to death. In 1708 workmen repairing the building discovered the skeletons of a man and a dog. Nearby is a splendid dovecote. *Open: daily, Eas–Sep.*

PAINSHILL PARK
SURREY

■ ON THE A245 NEAR THE JUNCTION WITH THE A3 AT COBHAM ■

A magnificent, recently restored, 18th-century landscaped garden, Painshill was created by Charles Hamilton. He transformed barren heathland into an ornamental pleasure-ground. The park contains a lake fed from the river by an enormous waterwheel, a grotto, a temple, a ruined abbey, a Chinese bridge, a castellated tower, and a mausoleum. *Open: Sun, Apr–Oct.*

PENSHURST PLACE
KENT

■ ON THE B2176, 4½ MILES (6KM) NORTH-WEST OF TUNBRIDGE WELLS ■

The manor house of Penshurst Place, is a delightful jumble of styles and periods. The earliest part is the great hall, built in about 1340 by Sir John de Pulteney, who was four times Lord Mayor of London. This magnificent example of a medieval great hall, which has changed little since it was first built, has a roof supported on massive beams of chestnut on which are carved grotesque figures. Considerable additions were made to the house when it came into the possession of the Sidneys in 1552. The solar became what is now the state diningroom, and the long gallery and the nether gallery were built. There is a 10-acre (4ha) walled garden, and an adventure playground and nature trail. Children will also enjoy the collection in the Toy Museum.

Penshurst has many literary associations. It was owned in the 15th century by Humphrey, Duke of Gloucester, who bequeathed his library to Oxford university. The poet, courtier and soldier, Sir Philip Sidney, was born here in 1554, and the dramatist, Ben Johnson, was a frequent visitor in the 17th century. He described Penshurst in *The Forest. Open: Tue–Sun and BH, Eas–Sep.*

LOVELL THE DOG

The romantic ruins of Minster Lovell Hall in Oxfordshire (below), with the Windrush rippling gently past crumbling arches and green lawns, are all that is left of the pride and wealth of a family that backed the wrong side. In the 15th century Sir Francis Lovell was a loyal friend and ally of King Richard III. (He is portrayed as 'Lovell the dog' in Shakespeare's pro-Tudor play, *Richard III*.) Rewarded with numerous profitable appointments, he fought for Richard at Bosworth in 1485, when Henry Tudor won the crown of England. Lovell escaped and spent time in hiding abroad before joining Lambert Simnel's uprising which was defeated in battle at Stoke. Lovell was last seen riding away from the battlefield and swimming his horse across the Trent. It is assumed that his was the skeleton found at Minster Lovell Hall in 1708. His only mistake was loyalty.

Right: Penshurst Place is one of England's finest country houses, situated in an area of great natural beauty. The rather gaunt and impressive house is set off by Tudor gardens and a park

NEW FOREST
HAMPSHIRE

William the Conqueror, who 'loved the tall deer as if he were their father', created the New Forest as his hunting-ground, and its landscape has changed little in the last 900 years. It is a mixture of majestic trees and open glades, a habitat that the red deer favours. There are also considerable areas of heather-covered heathland that are entirely bereft of trees. The forest extends to approximately 93,000 acres (37,665ha), of which more than two-thirds belong to the Crown. In 1992 it was given the protection of National Park status.

A WOODLAND HABITAT

When the New Forest was a royal hunting preserve, it was protected by special laws which were rigorously enforced by the Court of Verderers. Their duties and responsibilities have been curtailed over the centuries; nowadays they make by-laws and look after the interests of commoners who have the right to graze animals in the forest.

The New Forest is handily placed near the one-time shipbuilding centres of Southampton, Portsmouth and Bucklers Hard. Its mighty oaks were much in demand as timber for shipbuilding, especially during the Napoleonic Wars, when steps had to be taken to replenish the dwindling stocks of trees.

Many species of animals, including badgers, red deer and the more numerous fallow, roe and muntjac deer, make their home in the forest. Ponies are in evidence everywhere. The shy adder, Britain's only native venomous snake, is quite common but rarely seen, and almost never strikes.

EXPLORING THE FOREST

The best way to see and enjoy the New Forest is on foot. Rights of way are not marked distinctively on Ordnance Survey maps of the area, but as much of the forest is common land, virtually all paths shown on a map may be used.

Lyndhurst makes a good centre from which to explore the New Forest. It is known as 'the Capital of the Forest'. The **church** contains a painting by Lord Leighton and some stained glass by William Morris. In the graveyard is the **tomb of Alice Hargreaves** (Mrs Reginald Hargreaves). As Alice Liddell she was the little girl for whom Lewis Carroll wrote *Alice in Wonderland*.

In the town-centre car park is an interesting display illustrating the life of the forest. The **Court of Verderers** meets six times a year in a hall next to the Queen's House, and conducts its business according to ancient ceremonials.

HAMLETS AND VILLAGES

Seven miles (11km) north-east of Lymington is **Bucklers Hard**, a pretty hamlet of two rows of terraced cottages, sloping down to the Beaulieu River. It was an important centre of shipbuilding in the 18th and 19th centuries. A **museum** displays models of ships built on the Hard. Some cottages are open to the public. *Open: daily*.

Boldre, 2 miles (3km) north of Lymington, is a beautiful village with an interesting Norman church situated on a hill. It contains a memorial to the officers and men of HMS *Hood* who died in action against the *Bismarck* during the Second World War. The poet and biographer of Nelson, Robert Southey, married his second wife, Catherine Bowles, here in 1839. William Gilpin, who propounded the theory of the picturesque, was vicar at this church from 1777 to 1804, and funded the village school from the proceeds of his popular *Picturesque Tours*. He is buried in the churchyard and has a memorial in the north chapel.

SALT MINES, SOLDIERS AND SNAKES

The picturesque old town of **Lymington** has many attractive 18th- and 19th-century buildings. It is both a ferry port and a yachting centre, and lies on the River Lymington. It was once a centre of shipbuilding and salt-refining. Salt was obtained by digging shallow pans in the marshes. The water was partially evaporated by the sun and the brine was drawn off into boiling-houses, where it was heated. The salt residue was then refined.

The **parish church** was occupied by parliamentary troops during the Civil War and was badly damaged.

Brockenhurst, 3 miles (5km) south of Lyndhurst, is a pleasant small town. The **parish church** contains the graves of a number of New Zealand soldiers who died of wounds in the nearby military hospitals during the First World War.

'Brusher' Mills, one of the great forest characters of the 19th century, is buried under a marble gravestone with a hut and snakes carved on it. Brusher – who got his name from the careful way in which he brushed cricket pitches – earned his living by catching adders, which he sold to London Zoo to be fed live to larger snakes. He lived in an illegally built hut near Hollands Wood. It was burned down one day before the 30 years were up which would have allowed him to claim his home under ancient forest law.

A DAY OUT IN THE FOREST

Furzey Gardens, at Minstead, 2 miles (3km) north of Lyndhurst, are set in 8 acres (3ha) of grounds surrounding a delightful thatched cottage. The **Will Selwood Gallery** exhibits the work of local artists and craftsmen. *Open: daily*.

The **Rufus Stone**, $4\frac{1}{2}$ miles (7km) north-west of Lyndhurst, marks the spot where William II was killed in 1170. He was the son of William the Conqueror and known as 'Rufus' due to his ruddy complexion. He was killed by an arrow from an unknown source while out hunting in the forest. William was very unpopular, and scholars are unsure whether his death was a genuine accident or murder. Some even maintain that the king was ritually murdered by believers in the Old Religion. It is even possible that he was killed not here, but near Beaulieu.

Children and adults alike will enjoy the **New Forest Butterfly Farm** at Ashurst, 3 miles (5km) north-east of Lyndhurst. It is an indoor tropical garden, containing butterflies and moths from all over the world. *Open: daily, end Mar–Oct*.

■

Above: a ship's figurehead at Bucklers Hard

■

Bottom: one of the New Forest's beautiful glades

■

Below: the silver studded butterfly is found on heathland in the forest

■

MATTHEW ARNOLD'S 'CITY OF DREAMING

SPIRES' IS THE HOME OF THE OLDEST UNIVER-

SITY IN THE UNITED KINGDOM, AND IS ONE OF

OXFORD

OXFORDSHIRE

THE LOVELIEST AND MOST INTERESTING

CITIES IN EUROPE

Oxford is not only a beautiful and ancient university town, but also an important and bustling city. There is so much to see that it is impossible to do justice to it in one visit. Visitors are recommended to start at the **Oxford Story** in Broad Street, an audio-visual display that explains the history of the city and the workings of the university. *Open: daily.*

Then walk round the city, perhaps following the itinerary below. There are many interesting buildings to study, and the colleges are sometimes open to the public.

BALLIOL TO THE BODLEIAN

Balliol College, which fronts St Giles and Broad Street, was founded in 1266 by John de Balliol, although most of its buildings are Victorian. A plaque on the wall in Broad Street records the fact that Bishops Latimer and Ridley, and Archbishop Cranmer, were burnt at the stake nearby during the 16th-century Marian terror.

Further along Broad Street is **Trinity College**, which has one of Oxford's most attractive quadrangles. It was founded in 1555 by Sir Thomas Pope on the site of the much older Durham College, parts of which are incorporated into the existing buildings. Sir Christopher Wren designed the fine classical buildings of the **Garden Quadrangle**.

Cross the road and walk past Exeter College to the **Sheldonian Theatre**, which was built in 1668 by Sir Christopher Wren and was inspired by the Theatre of Marcellus in Rome. It is used for university ceremonies. Next door is the **Clarendon Building**, designed by Nicholas Hawksmoor and financed from the profits of Clarendon's *History of the Rebellion*. It was the headquarters of Oxford University Press until 1830.

The **Bodleian Library**, situated behind the Clarendon Building in Old Schools Quadrangle, dates from the early 16th century. Its enormous collection of books and priceless manuscripts has overflowed into the New Bodleian Library and the Radcliffe Camera. Visitors may view the library and enjoy its numerous exhibitions. *Open: daily.*

THE RADCLIFFE CAMERA, AND BEYOND

Beyond Old Schools' Quad is the **Radcliffe Camera**, a classical rotunda designed by James Gibbs in 1739, surmounted by a dome. It housed the library of Dr Radcliffe, the court physician.

On the left, at the junction of Catte Street and the High Street, is **All Souls College**, which was founded in 1438 by Henry Chichele, Archbishop of Canterbury, as a chantry for the souls of those killed in the Hundred Years' War. The gateway and the first quadrangle date from the 15th century. The second quadrangle was designed by Nicholas Hawksmoor. The college has a fine Perpendicular chapel.

On the right of Catte Street is **St Mary the Virgin**, the university church. John Henry Newman, the 19th-century theologian and founder of the Oxford Movement, was vicar here before his conversion to

Above: rowing past Merton and Christ Church Colleges

Above: these famille verte *porcelain figures are among the interesting exhibits at the Ashmolean Museum*

Right: the Radcliffe Camera is now part of the Bodleian Library Its domed rotunda was designed by James Gibbs in 1739

Above: participants in Oxford's colourful May Day celebrations, which have been a feature of town life for centuries

the Roman obedience. **Queen's College** in the High Street was rebuilt between 1692 and 1716 by Nicholas Hawksmoor and Sir Christopher Wren. The foundation was for a Provost, 12 fellows and 70 poor boys, representing Christ, the 12 apostles and his disciples.

MAGDALEN AND MERTON

Magdalen College, at the bottom of the High Street, is often regarded as Oxford's most beautiful college. On May Day morning the college choir climbs to the top of the chapel bell tower to sing a eucharistic hymn. Nearby is graceful **Magdalen Bridge**.

Retrace your route on the other side of the High Street and turn left along Merton Street to **Merton College**, the oldest and one of the most interesting Oxford colleges. It was founded by William de Merton in 1264, and some parts of its buildings date from this period. The library is probably the finest medieval example in the country. The chapel, which dates from the end of the 13th century, is full of interest and contains some exceptionally fine medieval glass.

FROM CORPUS CHRISTI TO CHRIST CHURCH

Corpus Christi College has a quadrangle and gateway unchanged since the college was founded by Bishop Foxe in 1517. Other features of interest include a 16th-century sundial, incorporating a perpetual calendar, the hall, with its fine hammerbeam roof, and the chapel's altarpiece, attributed to Rubens.

Take the path that runs between Corpus Christi and Merton and leads into Broad Walk. Turn right past **Christ Church College**, founded by Cardinal Wolsey in 1525. The priory church is now both the college chapel and Oxford's cathedral. Above Wolsey's Gateway leading to the Great Quadrangle, known as Tom Quad, is Tom Tower, designed by Sir

Christopher Wren. In it hangs Great Tom, a huge bell. The college overlooks **Christ Church Meadows**.

ALICE'S SHOP AND THE ASHMOLEAN

Alice's Shop, at 83 St Aldgate's, is the original shop described by Lewis Carroll in *Through the Looking-Glass. Open: daily.*

Continue along St Aldgate's to **Carfax Tower**, the centre of the old city. The tower dates from the 14th century and is all that remains of St Martin's Church. The jacks on the old clock still mark the passing of time.

Follow Cornmarket Street to the **Saxon Tower** of St Michael's Church, built in the middle of the 11th century. It was originally one of the watchtowers of the city wall, but was then incorporated into the church.

Continue along Magdalen Street to **Martyrs' Memorial** in St Giles. It records the appalling execution by burning of several Protestant martyrs during the reign of Queen Mary in the 16th century.

Almost opposite is the **Ashmolean Museum**, one of the finest museums in the country, with an outstanding collection of art and archaeology. *Open: Tue–Sat, all year (except Easter, Christmas and early Sep).*

1   Balliol College
2   New Bodleian Library
3   Manchester College
4   Saxon Tower
5   The Oxford Story
6   Sheldonian Theatre
7   Bodleian Library
8   Hertford College
9   Radcliffe Camera
10 Clarendon Centre
11 Carfax Tower
12 St Edmund Hall
13 University College
14 Museum of Modern Art
15 Pembroke College
16 St Cross (Pusey House)
17 Corpus Christi College

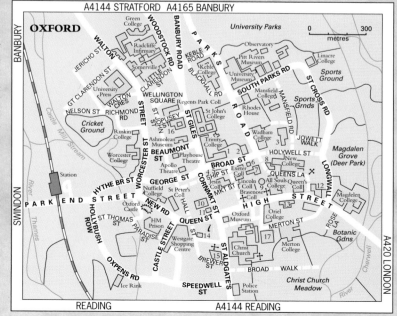

PETWORTH
WEST SUSSEX

Petworth is a delightful small town with winding, narrow streets, especially round the little market place, some good half-timbered buildings and handsome, Georgian houses. It is dominated by the gatehouse of **Petworth House** which, in its present form, was built by Charles Seymour, 6th Duke of Somerset, in 1688. The 'Proud Duke', as he was known, rebuilt the 12th-century house originally owned and crenellated by the Percy family. Only the chapel and cellars are left to remind us of the old house. The park and pleasure grounds landscaped in 1751 by the young 'Capability' Brown, extend to 700 acres (280ha) and are enclosed by a 14-mile (22km) wall. The house contains a magnificent collection of pictures including works by Lely, Van Dyck, Claude, Reynolds, Kneller, Poussin, Titian, Turner and Gainsborough. *Open: Sat, Sun, Tue–Thu and BH, Eas–Oct (NT).*

PEVENSEY CASTLE
EAST SUSSEX
■ ON THE A259, 5 MILES (8KM) NORTH-EAST OF EASTBOURNE ■

At Pevensey are the remarkable remains of the splendid Roman castle of *Anderida* whose 12ft-thick outer walls still stand today. It was constructed *c.*AD280 and continued to protect the Saxon shore from marauding raiders after the Romans withdrew from England in AD410. It was attacked by the Saxons in 477, and the garrison was put to the sword. After William the Conqueror landed at Pevensey in 1066 to commence his conquest of England, the Normans built a keep and gatehouse within the Roman walls, which withstood sieges in 1088 and 1264. Pevensey was one of the Cinque Ports, and was required to provide ships for the king in times of war. It was an important port in Tudor times, before the harbour silted up. During the Second World War a gun emplacement was constructed and the castle became part of the coastal defences. Ancient fireplaces and dungeons can be seen. *Open: daily, Eas–Sep; Tue–Sun, Oct–Eas (EH).*

POLESDEN LACEY
SURREY
■ OFF THE A24, 3 MILES (5KM) NORTH-WEST OF DORKING ■

Polesden Lacey is a fine Regency villa, built in 1824 by Thomas Cubitt of the famous construction family. It replaced the original 17th-century house, which was built by Sir Anthony Rous and subsequently owned by the dramatist, Richard Brinsley Sheridan. The house is set in a fine 18th-century garden, surrounded by 1,000 acres (400ha) of magnificent parkland, with views over the surrounding countryside. There is a superb walled rose garden.

From 1906 the house was owned by the Hon Mrs Ronald Greville, the famous Edwardian society hostess, who remodelled it to display her husband's collection of paintings, tapestries and furniture. King George VI and Queen Elizabeth (now the Queen Mother) spent part of their honeymoon here. On display are photographs from Mrs Greville's albums. During the summer months plays are often staged in the grounds. *Open: Wed–Sun, end-Mar–end-Oct, Sat and Sun only in Mar and Nov (house); daily, all year (grounds), NT.*

PORT LYMPNE ZOO PARK
KENT

■ ON THE B2067, 8 MILES (13KM) SOUTH-EAST OF ASHFORD ■

This zoological park, owned by John Aspinall, is set in 270 acres (110ha) on a splendid site on the escarpment of the North Downs overlooking Romney Marsh. The animals, which include tigers, African buffaloes, cheetahs and tapirs, are kept in paddocks to simulate, as far as possible, their natural habitat. There is a 2½-mile (4km) 'Zoo Trek' through fields and woodlands, and a safari trailer for the less energetic. The splendid house contains several exotic features. *Open: daily.*

PORTSMOUTH
HAMPSHIRE

Portsmouth, or 'Pompey' as it has been known to countless generations of sailors, is an important naval base and ferry terminal. The well-protected deepwater harbour of Portsmouth has been used from prehistoric times. Henry VII constructed the world's first dry dock at Portsmouth, and it has been a naval base ever since. Portsmouth suffered heavily from bomb damage during the Second World War, when much of the old city was destroyed.

The centre of interest is the Royal Dockyard. Here, in a specially constructed dry dock, is Nelson's flagship, **HMS Victory**, which was launched in 1765 and is still in commission. There are conducted tours of the ship and visitors are shown Nelson's great cabin, as well as the spot where he died on the orlop deck. Nearby, in a specially designed building, are the fascinating remains of the **Mary Rose**, Henry VIII's flagship that sank with all hands off Spithead in 1545 while sailing to intercept a French fleet. Our knowledge of Tudor life and naval architecture has been immeasurably increased by the raising of this ship. Opposite the *Victory* is the **Royal Naval Museum**, which contains an interesting collection of naval relics, Nelsonia, and a panorama of the Battle of Trafalgar. A recent addition to the dockyard is **HMS Warrior**, which was the first iron-hulled warship. *All open: daily.*

A little to the south, in old Portsmouth, is an interesting jumble of streets that still has the flavour of the old city. On the waterfront are a number of ancient fortifications. The house in which Charles Dickens was born in Old Commercial Road is now the **Charles Dickens Birthplace Museum**. *Open: daily, Mar–Oct.*

Southsea is Portsmouth's seaside resort. It contains elegant houses, attractive public gardens, two piers and a long promenade, on which are sited a number of naval memorials. At the far end is **Southsea Castle**, part of a chain of castles built by Henry VIII to defend the south coast. *Open: daily.*

■

Above: Horatio Nelson, Britain's greatest admiral, still keeps watch over the sea at Portsmouth

■

■

Below: HMS Victory *flying Nelson's famous signal, 'England expects that this day each man will do his duty' on Trafalgar Day at Portsmouth (21 October)*

■

ROCHESTER
KENT

This ancient city and port on the River Medway has a small Norman **cathedral**, constructed on the site of a ruined Saxon church. Its principle features are the striking Norman west front, pierced by a large Perpendicular window, and the crypt, which contains some fine Early English vaulting with medieval graffiti in the piers.

The ruined **castle**, completed by William de Corbeuil by about 1130, is still one

Left: historic Rochester's Norman cathedral with its famous west front, viewed through a space in the ruined castle walls

of the finest surviving examples of Norman military architecture in England. *Open: daily, Eas–Sep; Tue–Sun, Oct–Eas (EH).*

Rochester features in several novels and stories by Charles Dickens, in which it is known variously as 'Dullborough', 'Mudfog' and 'Cloisterham'. Restoration House in Maidstone Road is a handsome Tudor mansion that was the model for Miss Haversham's house in *Great Expectations*; Uncle Pumblechook lived in one of the Tudor houses in the High Street.

CHARLES DICKENS AND ROCHESTER

The city of Rochester is proud of its connections with Charles Dickens, and the great novelist is honoured at a special Dickens Festival every year at the turn of May and June. Local people dress up in Victorian costumes, there are readings and plays, and famous characters from Dickens' novels put in an appearance to encourage the celebrations. At Christmas time local people don their costumes once again to indulge in some Dickensian carol singing (above).

Dickens grew up in Chatham, where his father was a clerk in the Dockyard, but it was Rochester that he loved. He bought Gad's Hill House (now a school), just outside the town, and lived there from 1857 until his death in 1870. He would have liked to have been buried in Rochester, but the nation claimed him for Westminster Abbey.

ROMSEY
HAMPSHIRE

This attractive small town lies on the banks of the River Test and has three principal features of interest. **Romsey Abbey**, which has been the parish church since the Dissolution, is an outstanding example of a Norman conventual church that has been altered very little. Dating mostly from the first half of the 11th century, it is built on the foundations of a Saxon nunnery. It contains the tomb of Admiral of the Fleet, Earl Mountbatten of Burma, the Queen's cousin and last Viceroy of India.

Nearby is **King John's hunting box**, a 13th-century merchant's house that contains the original roof timbers and some 14th-century wall graffiti. *Open: Mon–Fri (summer only).*

Broadlands, situated on the edge of the town, is one of the finest examples of English Palladian architecture and was designed by 'Capability' Brown and Henry Holland the younger. The perfect harmony of the rooms is enhanced by the splendid works of art, including paintings by Van Dyck, Lawrence, Reynolds, Romney, Lely and Hoppner. There is an **exhibition of the life of Lord Mountbatten**, whose home it was. *Open: Sat–Thu, Eas–Sep.*

ROUSHAM HOUSE
OXFORDSHIRE
■ OFF THE A423, 12 MILES (19KM) NORTH OF OXFORD ■

A fine country house built by Sir Robert Dormer in 1635, Rousham was remodelled in the Gothic style by William Kent in 1740. Kent also laid out the superb gardens, which were once a place of pilgrimage for students of his work. They represent the first phase of 18th-century English landscape design and remain almost as Kent left them, with pools, classical buildings and statues in a wooded landscape above the River Cherwell. *Open: Wed, Sun and BH, Apr–Sep (house); daily, all year (gardens).*

DON'T MISS

■ The Norman castle (**Rochester**)

■ The irregular arch supporting the roof (**Romsey Abbey**)

■ The Wedgwood room (**Broadlands**)

■ The Roman city of *Verulamium* (St Albans)

RYE
EAST SUSSEX

An enchanting little town, set on a hill, Rye was one of the medieval Cinque Ports, required to furnish the Crown with warships. Once a prosperous port, its trade was destroyed by erosion and attacks by the French. Later it became notorious for smuggling and civil unrest. Most of the houses that line the cobbled streets were built between the 15th and 18th centuries, and range in style from timber-framed and tile-hung cottages to elegant Georgian town houses. The beautiful **parish church** has a clock on which the 'golden quarter boys' come out to strike each quarter-hour. The **Landgate** is the last surviving medieval entrance to the town, and the **Ypres** (pronounced 'wipers') **Tower** was the town's castle. The novelist Henry James lived at **Lamb House**. *Open: Wed and Sat, Eas–Oct (Lamb House, NT).*

ST ALBANS
HERTFORDSHIRE

This attractive market town, the Roman *Verulamium*, derives its modern name from Alban, a Roman soldier and the first English Christian martyr, who was beheaded in AD303 for hiding a priest. To the west of the town lie the extensive remains of the **Roman city**, once the capital of Britain, with its amphitheatre. *Open: daily (except Sun in winter).*

The **cathedral** is predominantly Norman, and constructed largely of Roman bricks. It was built on the site of a Saxon Benedictine abbey by the first Norman abbot. Interesting features include wall paintings on some of the piers in the nave, the rood screen of 1350, a 15th-century painted ceiling in the choir, the shrine of St Alban, and an early 15th-century watching loft.

There is much interest in the town. St Michael's Church is part Saxon and contains the grave of Francis Bacon. The clock tower dates from 1411 and there is a 14th-century moot hall, plus two sets of almshouses.

SCOTNEY CASTLE
KENT

■ OFF THE A21, 10 MILES (16KM) SOUTH-EAST OF TONBRIDGE ■

Scotney Castle is a romantic ruin with a 14th-century tower surrounded by a moat. The rest of the building dates from the 17th century, but was deliberately 'ruined' to harmonise with the tower. The real object of interest, however, are the **gardens**, where a romantic landscape has been created by planting rhododendrons, azaleas and fine forest trees to set off the castle. *Open: Wed–Sun and BH Mon, May–Aug (castle); Wed–Sun and BH Mon, Mar–Nov (gardens), NT.*

■

Above: picturesque Rye, built on a hill beside the River Rother, was once an important port. The sea began to recede in the 16th century, but the town has retained its character. In Mermaid Street there are many old houses, including the Mermaid Inn of 1420

■

■

Below: a romantic, 14th-century moated tower is at the centre of Scotney Castle's gardens, where rhododendrons, azaleas and other flowering shrubs make a wonderful display of colour

■

SELBORNE
HAMPSHIRE

■ ON THE B3006, 5 MILES (8KM) SOUTH OF ALTON ■

Selborne is famous as the home of the naturalist Gilbert White (1720–93). He spent most of his life here, living at 'The Wakes'. Much of his time was spent in the minute observation of nature in the immediate vicinity of Selborne, and in 1788 he published his classic, *The Natural History and Antiquities of Selborne*. Today, 'The Wakes' is home to the **Gilbert White Museum** and the **Oates Museum**. The latter commemorates explorers Frank and Lawrence Oates. *Open: Wed and Sun, Eas–Oct.* Selborne also has a **Romany Folklore Museum and Workshop**. *Open: daily, Eas–Oct.*

SHUTTLEWORTH COLLECTION
BEDFORDSHIRE

■ OFF THE A1, 2 MILES (3KM) WEST OF BIGGLESWADE ■

Located on a small airfield near the charming village of Old Warden, the Shuttleworth Collection contains a remarkable assortment of **historical aircraft** ranging from a 1909 Blériot to a Spitfire of 1941. They are all airworthy, and many of them take part in the regular flying displays held on the airfield. In addition there is a collection of **veteran cars**, including the Panhard in which Edward VII drove to Ascot in 1901. *Open: daily.*

SOUTHAMPTON
HAMPSHIRE

Situated at the head of Southampton Water on the estuary of the River Test, and bounded in the east by the River Itchen, Southampton has one of the finest harbours in England. It also has a double tide. The first comes up the Solent and the second, two hours later, comes via Spithead. There are many parks and open spaces in the town, and some elegant Georgian terraces and squares, as well as several interesting museums.

Southampton has been a port at least since Roman times, and after the Norman Conquest it became a place of considerable importance. Several invasion fleets, from those of the Crusades to those taking part in D-Day, have sailed from Southampton, and the *Mayflower* and the *Speedwell* put in here before sailing to the New World in 1620. In the days of empire, Southampton was the principal English port for the great oceanic liners that plied the seven seas.

The **town walls** were originally built by the Normans and extended for over a mile (1.6km). They are still almost complete on the west side. The 15th-century Arundel Tower in the north-west corner of the wall is nicknamed 'Windwhistle', and the neighbouring tower is 'Catchcold'. Nearby is Bargate, which was once the northern entry to the town. The carefully restored **Tudor House** in Bugle Street contains a fine banqueting hall and is now a museum of domestic life. Behind is an Elizabethan garden, containing a Norman town house known as St John's House. The Wool House at the corner of Town Quay and Bugle Street is a medieval warehouse, now converted into a **maritime museum** that houses relics of the *Titanic* and models of famous ships. **God's House Tower** on Town Quay was part of the 15th-century fortifications, and is now a museum of archaeology. It takes its name as does nearby God's House Gateway, from the 12th-century Hospice of St Julian, popularly known as God's House. *Open: Tue–Sun (Tudor House, Maritime Museum, God's House Tower).*

Other features are the fine **art gallery** in the civic centre, which contains a collection of Old Masters, Impressionist and 20th-century English paintings, and the **Hall of Aviation**, commemorating the work of R J Mitchell, designer of the Spitfire. *Open: daily (art gallery): Tue–Sun and BH Mon (Hall of Aviation).*

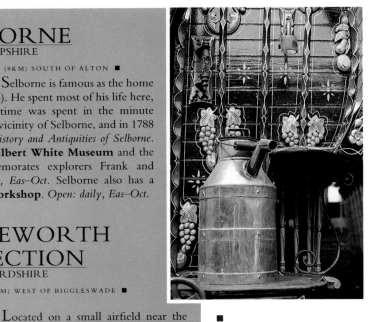

■

Above: the colourful Romany Museum is an unusual attraction at Selborne

■

■

Above: the world's only collection of historic airworthy aeroplanes can be seen at Shuttleworth, where flying days are held regularly. Here a Percival Provost is put through its paces

■

OUT OF DOORS

'Open the book where you will, it takes you out of doors.' Gilbert White's *Natural History and Antiquities of Selborne*, the first great classic of natural history writing in English, came out in 1789. Published almost at the end of its author's life, it has never been out of print since. White was one of 11 children born in the parsonage at Selborne, where his grandfather was rector. Although he became a fellow of Oriel College at Oxford, he spent almost the last 40 years of his life quietly observing the seasonal round, and the life of the fields and beechwoods of his Hampshire parish, with endearing charm, humour and meticulousness.

■

STONOR PARK
OXFORDSHIRE

■ ON THE B480, 5 MILES (8KM) NORTH OF HENLEY-ON-THAMES ■

A stately home set in a beautiful deer park at the foot of the Chilterns, Stonor is as interesting for its history as it is for its architecture. It presents an 18th-century façade which hides parts of a 13th-century aisled hall built by Sir Richard Stonor. In the 14th-century a chapel, in which Mass has been celebrated ever since, was added, and later extensions included a timber-framed hall. Extensive remodelling took place during the Elizabethan and later periods. The Stonors were recusants and suffered fines and imprisonment for their Catholic faith. The Jesuit priest, Edmund Campion (later to be martyred and canonised), was given sanctuary here in the 16th century and established a printing press, making Stonor Park a centre of Catholic learning.

In front of the house there is a small circle of ancient stones. The deer park has interesting views. *Open: Eas–Sep (check exact days with tourist information centre).*

STOWE LANDSCAPE GARDENS
BUCKINGHAMSHIRE

■ OFF THE A413, 3 MILES (5KM) NORTH OF BUCKINGHAM ■

Stowe Landscape Gardens are now owned by the National Trust. They have been described as the largest work of art in Britain, and were originally laid out by Charles Bridgeman, whose work was subsequently modified by William Kent and 'Capability' Brown. Among the many features of interest are several classic temples, a lake with an interesting bridge, a Temple of British Worthies and two grottoes. The Elysian Fields, designed by Kent in the 1730s, was one of the finest examples of the less formal design of garden, in more naturalistic style, a forerunner of the landscape garden. The imposing house is now used as a public school, but was built by Sir John Vanbrugh, followed by Wiliam Kent and Robert Adam, for the Temple family (later Dukes of Buckingham). *Open: school holidays (grounds), NT; occasionally during school holidays (house).*

STRATFIELD SAYE
HAMPSHIRE

■ OFF THE A33, 7 MILES (11KM) SOUTH OF READING ■

The splendid home given by a grateful nation to the Duke of Wellington after the final defeat of Napoleon at the Battle of Waterloo in 1815, Stratfield Saye was built in about 1630. It has subsequently been remodelled, and has had two wings added. It contains an exhibition illustrating the life of the 'Iron Duke', and there are also many personal mementoes, including his state coach, funeral carriage and library.

In the grounds is the grave of Copenhagen, the Duke's mount at Waterloo. *Open: Sat–Thu, Jun–Sep.*

Nearby is **Wellington Country Park**, containing a lake for watersports, nature trails, an adventure playground, a miniature steam railway and the **National Dairy Museum**.

THORPE PARK THEME PARK
SURREY

■ OFF THE A320, 3 MILES (5KM) SOUTH OF STAINES ■

A huge 20th-century pleasure ground, set in 500 acres (200ha) of parkland converted from old gravel workings, Thorpe Park is basically a superior funfair, but with some 'educational' attractions grafted on. Rides include the highest log theme ride in the UK, Loggers Leap, and a variety of other excitements such as Thorpe Farm, Magic Mills and Carousel Kingdom.

It has replicas of a Stone Age cave, as well as of Roman ruins and a galley, and a Saxon hut. The garden has models of famous buildings, such as the Eiffel tower, the Statue of Liberty, the Taj Mahal and Sydney Opera House. There is free transport round the park – either by small train or by water bus. *Open: daily, Eas–Sep, and weekends in Oct.*

■

THE IRON DUKE

The colossal funeral car on which the body of the great Duke of Wellington was borne in solemn state to its final resting place in St Paul's Cathedral in London is now

kept at Stratfield Saye. Black, enormous and unwieldy, it proved difficult to manoeuvre along the processional route on that November day in 1852. Its massive size and splendour, however, were a tribute to the victor of Waterloo. The venerable Iron Duke died quietly at Walmer Castle, at the age of 83. The body lay in state in Chelsea Hospital and was then taken in a procession of unexampled magnificence, by way of Piccadilly and the Strand, to be interred beneath the dome of St Paul's. It was estimated that one and a half million people lined the streets as the cortège passed by. 'No man', Lord Palmerston wrote, 'ever lived or died in the possession of more unanimous love, respect and esteem from his countrymen.'

■

■

DON'T MISS

■ The Museum of Domestic Life (the Tudor House, Southampton)

■ The 14th-century chapel (Stonor Park)

■ The Temple of British Worthies (Stowe)

■ The Wellington Exhibition (Stratford Saye)

■

Above: the Depth Charge, just one of many attractions at Thorpe Park

■

WADDESDON MANOR
BUCKINGHAMSHIRE
■ OFF THE A41, 4 MILES (6KM) WEST OF AYLESBURY ■

The Rothschild family built several great houses in Buckinghamshire, and it is said that they could visit each other without leaving land owned by the family. The Waddesdon estate was bought from the Duke of Richmond in 1874 by Baron Ferdinand de Rothschild, who employed a French architect H A G Destailleur to design a large, French-style chateau. It was constructed at enormous expense and with infinite labour on a wooded hill overlooking the village. The house contains a good collection of Savonnerie carpets, Sèvres porcelain, and Dutch, French, Italian and English Old Masters. The grounds were laid out by Lainé, the famous French landscape artist. *Waddesdon Manor is being refurbished by the National Trust, and is not due to reopen until 1993.*

WEALD & DOWNLAND
OPEN AIR MUSEUM
WEST SUSSEX
■ OFF THE A286 NEAR SINGLETON, 6 MILES (10KM) NORTH OF CHICHESTER ■

This museum contains a collection of old buildings and bygones dating from the 14th to the 19th centuries that have been 'rescued' and removed to this site for preservation. The exhibits include a watermill, a medieval farmhouse and a 17th-century market hall. There is a charcoal-burner's hut, a sawpit, a horse gin, a treadmill and other utilitarian buildings. During the summer months there are demonstrations of weaving, spinning and country crafts. *Open: daily, Eas–Oct; Sun, Wed and BH, rest of year.*

■

Left: Figures in 18th-century costume now occupy the caves at West Wycombe, where Sir Francis Dashwood and other members of the Hellfire Club are reputed to have held orgies

■

■

Below: Whipsnade Zoo specialises in the breeding of a number of animals such as the cheetah. Whipsnade was the first open zoo in the world

■

WEST WYCOMBE
BUCKINGHAMSHIRE

A remarkably interesting village which, except for the church, is wholly owned by the National Trust. It contains a number of pleasing vernacular buildings, but is chiefly famous for its associations with Sir Francis Dashwood (1708–81). Chancellor of the Exchequer, he was a notorious rake and founded the 'Order of the Knights of St Francis', which later changed its name to the Hellfire Club.

The church, situated above the village on the site of an Iron Age hill fort, is a rare example of a medieval parish church that has been classicised. The golden ball on top of the tower was reputedly used by the members of the Hellfire Club for meetings and impious purposes. The roofless mausoleum outside the church contains a number of funerary urns in niches originally intended to hold the hearts of Dashwood's friends.

West Wycombe Park is a fine mid-18th century Palladian mansion, containing frescoes and painted ceilings and set in harmonious grounds, laid out by Humphry Repton in perfect harmony with the house. A number of follies and classical buildings enhance the park.

The extensive **caves**, in which Sir Francis and his profligate friends held orgies, were formed by the extraction of chalk for road-building. *Open: daily, Mar–Oct (caves): Sun–Thu, Jun–Aug (house and grounds, NT).*

WHIPSNADE ZOO
BEDFORDSHIRE

■ ON THE B4540, 4 MILES (6KM) SOUTH-WEST OF DUNSTABLE ■

This, the country branch of the Zoological Society of London, is set in a splendid position high on the Chiltern escarpment. It can be identified several miles away from the north by the large figure of a lion cut in the chalk. Whipsnade contains a collection of larger animals kept, if not in natural surroundings, at least in large paddocks and enclosures rather than cages. A narrow-gauge steam railway puffs its way past some of the paddocks. *Open: daily.*

WINCHESTER
HAMPSHIRE

A fascinating city, full of old churches, pleasing buildings, and interesting nooks and crannies, Winchester was once a prehistoric settlement. It became the Roman town of *Venta Belgarum*, and the Saxon capital of both Wessex and England (a fine statue of King Alfred stands below the guildhall in Broadway). Several kings were crowned here, and Mary Tudor married Philip of Spain in the cathedral.

The present **cathedral** is built on the site of the Roman forum and the Saxon minster, parts of which have been excavated. The exterior of this, the longest medieval cathedral in Europe, is unimposing. The fabric is largely Norman, with later modifications and additions. The nave is Perpendicular in style, and the transepts are Norman. A series of magnificent chantries demonstrates the development of Gothic architecture, and the choir stalls are the oldest in England. The cathedral contains the shrine of St Swithun, some tomb chests of Saxon Kings, and the graves of Izaac Walton and Jane Austen.

Near the cathedral is **Winchester College**, founded by William of Wykeham in 1382 and a model for all English public schools. Parts of the college are open to the public at specified times; there are conducted tours.

At the top of the steep, pedestrianised High Street is **West Gate**, one of two surviving medieval city gates. Close by is the **Great Hall**, all that survives of the castle built by William the Conqueror. On the wall hangs a large painted table, reputedly the round table of King Arthur. It is 18ft (5m) in diameter, and according to radio-carbon tests it dates from the 14th century. *Open: daily (Great Hall).*

One mile (1.6km) to the south of the city centre is the **Hospital of St Cross**, which claims to be the oldest surviving charitable institution in the country. It was founded in 1136 for 13 poor brethren by Bishop Henry, of Blois, who also instituted the wayfarer's dole of beer and bread for 100 poor men. This charity is still dispensed to those who ask for it. Some of the hospital buildings date from the 13th century. *Open: Mon–Sat.*

■

RAIN, RAIN, COME AGAIN

One of Winchester's claims to fame is its connection with St Swithun, who was Bishop of Winchester in the 9th century when the town was the capital of the kings of Wessex. The old tradition is still alive that if it rains on St Swithun's day, 15 July, it will go on raining for the next 40 days and nights. The tradition goes back to 15 July 971, when the monks of Winchester moved the dead bishop's remains to an honoured place in the cathedral. This was in contradiction of the saint's wishes. He had been buried, at his own request, in a humble position outside the west door of the Saxon minster in 862. His removal provoked a formidable rainstorm, which was believed to indicate his severe disapproval. After the Norman Conquest a new cathedral was built and Swithun's body was moved yet again in 1093, to a shrine behind the high altar. The shrine was demolished at the Dissolution but a new shrine was put in place in 1962.

■

■

Below: King Arthur's round table hangs in the Great Hall at Winchester. It bears the names of King Arthur's knights in Gothic script but, alas, it has been proved that the table was made in about 1385, 700 years after Arthur's time

■

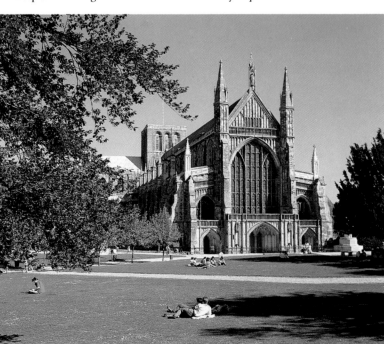

■

Right: Winchester's beautiful cathedral is a blend of several architectural styles. At 556ft (169m) it is the longest medieval cathedral in Europe. It has a charming cathedral close and houses many treasures, including the 13th-century Winchester bible

■

■

DON'T MISS

■ The charcoal-burner's hut (Weald & Downland Open Air Museum)

■ The 12th-century paving tiles (Winchester Cathedral)

■ The wayfarer's dole (Hospital of St Cross, Winchester)

FOR CHILDREN

■ Figures in 18th-century costumes (the Caves, West Wycombe)

WINDSOR
BERKSHIRE

This little town, situated on a chalk hill overlooking the Thames, is deservedly popular with tourists. It still preserves a pleasing 18th-century air and is dominated by the mighty stronghold of **Windsor Castle**, which claims to be the world's largest inhabited fortress.

The castle, which is still a royal residence, was originally constructed in wood by William the Conqueror, but it was later rebuilt in stone by Henry II. It was extensively restored during the reign of George IV to make it more comfortable. Visitors enter the lower ward through Henry VIII's gatehouse. On the right, as the hill ascends, are the residences of the Order of the Military Knights of Windsor, founded in the 14th century by Edward III. The Military Knights are required to deputise for the Knights of the Order of the Garter. On the left is **St George's Chapel**, dedicated to the patron saint of the Order of the Garter and built in the late 15th and early 16th centuries. It rivals King's College Chapel, Cambridge, as the finest flower of Perpendicular architecture. The chapel contains the tombs of several monarchs and the stalls of the Knights of the Garter. Just beyond is the Albert Memorial Chapel, built by Henry III and converted into a shrine to Prince Albert by Queen Victoria. Above the residences of the Military Knights is the splendid Round Tower, to the left of which is the North Terrace. It has good views across the Thames to Eton College.

The **state apartments** are still used for royal functions and are of unparalleled magnificence. The visitor wanders through King Charles II's Diningroom, the King's Drawingroom, containing paintings by Rubens, the State Bedchamber, the Queen's Drawingroom, the Queen's Audience Chamber, the Queen's Presence Chamber and superb St George's Hall. Other delights are the Grand Reception Room, the Throne Room and the Waterloo Room. Not only are these rooms superbly decorated, they also contain numerous outstanding Old Masters, as well as mementoes of some of the great events in British history.

Windsor Castle is also home to **Queen Mary's Dolls' House**, designed by the architect Sir Edwin Lutyens on a scale of 1in to 1ft (2.5cm to 30cm) which more than 1,500 British craftsmen furnished and decorated. The castle is also home to the exhibition of Old Master drawings from the royal collection. *Open: daily (castle); state apartments are closed when the Queen is in residence.*

On the north and east sides of the castle is Home Park, where **Frogmore House** and the mausoleum containing the mortal remains of Queen Victoria and Prince Albert may be found. To the south lies 2,000-acre (810ha) **Windsor Great Park**, which has striking views of the castle. *Open: Wed–Sun, Aug–Sep (Frogmore House): daily (park).*

The town contains several places of interest. At the handsome railway station, on a branch line from Slough that was built specially for Queen Victoria, is the **Royalty and Empire** display, including one of Queen Victoria's railway carriages. *Open: daily.*

Nearby **Windsor Safari Park** is home to many of the world's largest mammals, such as lions, elephants and tigers. One of the first such parks in Britain, there are now many other attractions to fascinate all ages. *Open: daily.*

The small town of **Eton**, a short walk away from Windsor Castle across the Thames, has a quaint old High Street and is home to Eton College, founded in 1440 by King Henry VI.

■

Below: this Victorian paper boy at Windsor station is just one of the realistic figures in a display showing the arrival of Queen Victoria at Windsor, in the Royalty and Empire Exhibition

■

■

HONI SOIT

Windsor Castle has been one of the principal residences of the kings and queens of England since William the Conqueror's time, and is consequently long accustomed to military parades, the clatter of cavalry and guardsmen in scarlet and busbies (below). The castle is the headquarters of England's oldest and most prestigious order of chivalry, the Knights of the Order of the Garter. In St George's Chapel the helms, banners and coats-of-arms of the Knights hang above their seats. There are normally 26 knights, including the sovereign. They gather for a special service at Windsor every year in June, resplendent in plumed hats and mantles of dark blue velvet, each with a Garter star embroidered on his left shoulder.

The most Noble Order of the Garter, with its motto in medieval French – *Honi soit qui mal y pense* ('Evil to him who thinks evil of it') – is the oldest order of chivalry in Europe. It was founded by Edward III and the original knights included his son, the Black Prince, and many formidable paladins.

■

WISLEY GARDENS
SURREY

■ ON THE A3, 7 MILES (11KM) NORTH-EAST OF GUILDFORD ■

These magnificent gardens, covering 300 acres (120ha), are owned and maintained by the Royal Horticultural Society. Throughout the year there is a changing display of the best in flowers, shrubs and trees. The society is in the forefront of horticultural research and has glasshouses and testing-beds for the production of new varieties.

There is an information office where gardeners can obtain advice about horticultural problems, and a shop that sells books, gifts and garden produce. *Open: daily (members and their guests only on Sun).*

WOBURN ABBEY
BEDFORDSHIRE

■ ON THE A5130, 8 MILES (13KM) SOUTH-EAST OF MILTON KEYNES ■

The great house of **Woburn Abbey** is the seat of the Dukes of Bedford. The present elegant mansion, containing magnificent state apartments and an exquisite Chinese Room, was rebuilt in the mid-18th century by Henry Flitcroft. Later additions were made in the 19th century by Henry Holland. It houses one of the world's finest collections of paintings still in private hands, and includes works by Reynolds, Gainsborough, Rembrandt, Canaletto, Cuyp, Teniers, Velázquez and Van Dyck. There are some superb examples of English and French 18th-century furniture, a magnificent Sèvres dinner service presented to the 4th Duke by Louis XV of France, and a sculpture gallery. The 3,000-acre (1,220ha) deer park, surrounded by an enormous wall, was landscaped by Humphry Repton and contains some rare Père David deer, descended from the Imperial Herd of China.

In the **safari park** visitors can drive through the grounds and observe exotic species such as tigers and rhino at close quarters. There are also picnic sites, amusements, shops and a pottery, as well as a 40-shop antiques centre, housed in old shop fronts. *Open: daily, Eas–Oct; weekends, rest of year.*

■

Above: the Wild Animal Kingdom at Woburn Abbey is Britain's biggest drive-through safari park

■

ZOOLOGICAL MUSEUM
HERTFORDSHIRE

■ ON THE A41 AT TRING ■

This museum was built at the end of the 19th century to house the extraordinary collection of rare, exotic, bizarre and extinct specimens collected by Lionel Walter, the 2nd Baron Rothschild (1869–1937). A famous naturalist, he created the largest collection of natural history specimens ever assembled by one man. It contains the largest collection of butterflies and moths in the world, amounting to more than 2 million specimens and many thousands of types. The mammals are superbly displayed in the finest tradition of taxidermy, and there is an extensive range of fish, birds, reptiles, domestic dogs, insects and other invertebrates, collected from all over the world. There is also a well-known collection of dressed fleas.

A newly opened exhibit is **Lord Rothschild's study**, containing information about his life and work. *Open: daily.*

■

DON'T MISS

■ The state apartments and Sèvres dinner service (**Woburn Abbey**)

FOR CHILDREN

■ Queen Mary's Dolls' House (**Windsor Castle**)

■ The collection of butterflies (the **Zoological Museum**, Tring)

CENTRAL ENGLAND
AND
EAST ANGLIA

Vivid moments of history stud the landscape of central England like coloured flags pinned into a map. At Deene Park you can see the head of the horse that led the Charge of the Light Brigade and at Belvoir Castle there is a museum of the 17th/21st Lancers, whose motto was 'Death or Glory': the 17th rode in the charge. 'My kingdom for a horse,' Shakespeare has Richard III cry, going down to a defeat at Bosworth Field that changed the course of English history. What might have followed if victory had gone the other way? No Tudor dynasty, no Reformation, no Dissolution of the Monasteries, no Elizabethan Age, no Civil War, no Cromwell? You can get a glimpse of an earlier England at Laxton, whose medieval open field system has survived. Going back far beyond that, you can descend a shaft at Grime's Graves to explore flint mines worked 4,000 years ago. In Derbyshire at Cromford Mill you can examine a critical later moment of industrial history at the grim factory that gave birth to the Industrial Revolution. Industry in turn created Dudley, where the Black Country Museum has brought the day before yesterday back to life, including mild ale and mushy peas in the pub. Industry created Stoke-on-Trent, where the coolest, most exquisite china – Wedgwood, Minton, Spoke – was manufactured in a nightmare of kilns, furnaces and choking smoke.

Industry and fine scenery are seldom far separated in this part of the country. Cromford Mill stands among the woods and rocks of the lovely Derwent Valley and south of Stoke-on-Trent lie the heathery uplands and secluded war cemeteries of Cannock Chase. To the north-east, the Peak District holds both the bleak moors of Kinder Scout and the deep, secret limestone caverns at Castleton. The flat Norfolk countryside, by contrast, makes a setting of far horizons and enormous cloudscapes for the Broads, where the sails seem to scud across the land and the windmills and church towers point to the towering sky.

The area can fire a heavyweight salvo of cathedrals and churches to match any in the country. At Lincoln the massive church broods on its hill, its spectacular west front the last sight on earth for condemned men hanged on the walls of Lincoln Castle. Ely rides serene above the fen country like a great ship at anchor and Lichfield's triple towers, the 'Ladies of the Vale', soar up above Stowe Pool. The graceful spire and Caen-stone nave of Norwich make a haven from the bustling city's streets, while at Cambridge the fan-vaulting of King's College Chapel is one of the wonders of Europe.

There is another broadside of formidable castles, from Warwick and Kenilworth to Framlingham, Newark and Orford. Derbyshire musters a glowing array of great houses – Chatsworth, Haddon Hall, Hardwick Hall, Kedleston Hall and the deliriously eccentric Calke Abbey – and Norfolk parades the proud Palladian magnificence of Holkham Hall and Houghton Hall. Duxford Airfield and Stanton Hall are nursemaids to the history of flying, the Bass Museum to the history of brewing, Cadbury World to the history of chocolate. Here, history is everywhere.

■

ALTON TOWERS
STAFFORDSHIRE
■ OFF THE B5032, 4 MILES (6KM) EAST OF CHEADLE ■

Between 1814 and 1827, Charles Talbot, 15th Earl of Shrewsbury, created one of the loveliest Chinese gardens in Britain at Alton, out of 600 acres (243ha) of woodland in the Churnet Valley. Remarkably, the gardens and buildings have survived to form the background for Britain's premier leisure park. More than 125 rides, including the Corkscrew, the Dragon, Mini-Apple and Alton Beast roller-coasters, a monorail, cable cars, and the Thunder-Looper are there to tempt adults and children alike. The gaunt shell of the house still gives Alton Towers its historical appeal, while the beauty of the gardens is undeniable. *Open: daily, Mar–Nov (leisure park); daily, all year (grounds).*

BADDESLEY CLINTON
WARWICKSHIRE
■ OFF THE A41, 6 MILES (10KM) WEST OF KENILWORTH ■

The first view of the moated manor house of Baddesley Clinton is one of the most romantic in England. Across the stone bridge the 15th-century battlemented gateway guards the entrance to a small quadrangle of grey stone buildings, capped by deep-red tiled roofs and tall, decorated chimneys. Although Baddesley takes its name from Sir Thomas Clinton, who was the first of his family to live within its moat in 1290, the Ferrers family acquired the estate by marriage in 1517 and held it for 450.

On the ground floor the finest room is the great hall, with its Elizabethan stone chimneypiece and heraldic glass. Above the diningroom is the State Bedroom, which has a magnificent carved wooden overmantel made in 1629. Beyond the chapel is the Great Parlour. *Open: Wed–Sun and BH Mon, end Mar–Oct (NT).*

■

Above: the ceiling of the main banqueting hall at Alton Towers. Britain's top pleasure park can cater for a wide range of requirements, from a fun day out for all the family to a formal banquet or corporate entertaining

■

■

Left: enjoy the thrill of a ride on the Corkscrew roller-coaster at Alton Towers. There are more than 125 rides, and once you pass through the ticket office they are all free, however many times you go on them

■

BASS MUSEUM OF BREWING HISTORY
STAFFORDSHIRE

■ HORNINGLOW STREET, BURTON-UPON-TRENT ■

Since the 18th century, when William Worthington and William Bass moved into Burton-upon-Trent, the town has been the centre of British brewing. In 1875 Bass was the first company to register a trade mark under the Trade Marks Act when it lodged its distinctive red triangle, and Michael Arthur Bass, who became Lord Burton in 1886, gave the town some of its most splendid buildings.

Even today, the smell of hops and malt pervades the town. The Bass Museum of Brewing has audio-visual displays which present the history and technology of the industry, from the discovery by a medieval monk of the properties of the high level of gypsum in the water, which makes it ideal for good ale, to the sophisticated processes of beer-making today. Pride of place is given to the shire horses, their harness and the drays that they used to pull. Horse-drawn tours of the town are still available. *Open: daily.*

BELTON HOUSE
LINCOLNSHIRE

■ OFF THE A607, 3 MILES (5KM) NORTH OF GRANTHAM ■

The home of the Brownlow family, Belton House was built between 1685 and 1688 in Anglo–Dutch style. One of the finest houses of its period, it was, remarkably, built by a master mason, William Stanton, to the design of an amateur architect, William Winde.

Inside, the house is magnificent, with spectacular plaster ceilings by Edward Goudge and delicate wood-carving by craftsmen-followers of Grinling Gibbons. In the Hondecoeter Room, there are early wall paintings, while the Tyrconnel Room has a rare 18th-century painted floor. The old kitchens were separated from the house by a courtyard, and an underground railway that carried food to the diningroom can still be seen.

The grounds range from beautiful formal gardens, with a spectacular orangery, to classical parkland. *Open: Wed–Sun and BH Mon, Apr–Oct (NT).*

BELVOIR CASTLE
LEICESTERSHIRE

■ AT BELVOIR, BETWEEN THE A52 AND THE A607, 7 MILES (11KM) WEST OF GRANTHAM ■

Superbly sited on an outcrop high above the surrounding vale, Belvoir Castle has been the home of the Dukes of Rutland since the early 16th century. The castle was first built shortly after the Norman Conquest, but it has been restored and rebuilt over the centuries. Although its

silhouette is medieval in appearance, with battlemented towers and turret staircases, the interior of the castle is classical. Splendid Gobelins tapestries hang in the house, while the Picture Gallery contains works by Poussin, Van Dyck, Reynolds and Gainsborough. Belvoir – which is confusingly pronounced 'Beever' – also houses the **Museum of the 17th/21st Lancers**, a regiment led by Lord Cardigan in the famous Charge of the Light Brigade.

The gardens are particularly fine, and special events, such as jousting tournaments and rallies of all kinds, are held in the park. *Open: Tue–Sun, Mar–Oct.*

'MANNERS MAKETH MAN'
An appropriate background to today's jousting tournaments, Belvoir Castle (*below right*) owes its romantic mock-medieval appearance to the 5th Duke of Rutland and his Duchess, Elizabeth Howard, who in 1800 decided to remodel the house. When their architect, James Wyatt, died in 1813 the Duchess took over and the castle's appearance today owes much to her and her assistant, the Duke's chaplain, Sir John Thoroton, who was vicar of nearby Bottesford, where generations of the Rutlands lie buried.

The Manners family gained Belvoir and the title of Earl of Rutland by service to Henry VIII. In the next generation they acquired Haddon Hall (which is also open to the public) when a younger son married a Derbyshire heiress, Dorothy Vernon. A distinguished 18th-century member of the family was the Marquess of Granby. This notable general and popular hero is virtually forgotten now, but pubs all over the country are named after him. His son, the 4th Duke of Rutland, was a close friend of William Pitt the Younger and married 'the beautiful duchess', whom Sir Joshua Reynolds loved to paint. Their son, the 5th Duke, appears in Disraeli's novel *Coningsby* as 'the duke'. Their younger son, Lord John Manners, was an ally of Disraeli, a leading member of the House of Commons and a cabinet minister before succeeding his elder brother as 7th Duke. The famous 1920s society beauty Lady Diana Manners, daughter of the 8th Duke, was the model for the character 'Mrs Stitch', who appeared in Evelyn Waugh's novel *Scoop.*

Above: the Daimler bottle car at the Bass Museum of Brewing History in Burton-upon-Trent. Here there are many vintage vehicles that used to carry beer around the country and advertise Bass products

■

■ DON'T MISS _____

■ The splendid gardens (**Alton Towers**)

■ The silver (**Belton House**)

■ The Picture Gallery (**Belvoir Castle**)

FOR CHILDREN

■ The Corkscrew roller-coaster (**Alton Towers**)

■ Shire horses (**Bass Museum of Brewing History**)

■ The underground kitchen railway (**Belton House**)

BIDDULPH GRANGE GARDEN
STAFFORDSHIRE
■ OFF THE A527, 7 MILES (11KM) NORTH OF STOKE-ON-TRENT ■

Laid out on a rocky 15-acre (6ha) site above the River Trent, the garden of Biddulph Grange is one of the most important early Victorian gardens to survive. It was designed and filled with exotic plants over a period of 20 years from 1842 onwards by James Bateman and his wife Maria, and by Edward Cooke, a marine painter. In a remarkably small space, several tableaux evoke different areas of the world: an ornate wooden bridge over a pool, with a Chinese temple and tea-house beyond, introduces visitors to Victorian willow pattern china designs, while a few yards away two pairs of Egyptian sphinxes flank the way to a pharaoh's tomb. *Open: Wed–Sun and BH Mon, May–early Nov; Sat and Sun, Nov and Dec (NT).*

BLICKLING HALL
NORFOLK
■ ON THE A140, 1 MILE (1.6KM) NORTH-WEST OF AYLSHAM ■

Right: Blickling Hall, one of the most romantic of all English country houses. The lovely parterre garden faces the red-brick Jacobean façade of the house with its symmetrical towers, Dutch gables and tall chimneys

The first view of Blickling Hall satisfies all the most romantic conceptions of the English country house. This is the house built between 1619 and 1627 for Sir Henry Hobart, Lord Chief Justice of England, by Robert Lyminge, the architect of Hatfield House.

There is a splendid 17th-century staircase, with its deeply carved balusters and newel post figures. The collection of paintings is also fine, while in the Peter the Great Room there is a tapestry panel depicting the Tsar at the Battle of Poltawa. It was woven in St Petersburg for Catherine the Great. The showpiece of Blickling, however, is the wonderful Long Gallery, which runs 127ft (38m) along the east front. It has a magnificent plaster ceiling dating from the early 17th century.

Beyond the parterre garden and the orangery is the park, with a Tuscan temple attributed to Humphry Repton. In the **church of St Andrew** is a memorial to Anne Boleyn, who spent her childhood in an earlier house on the site. *Open: Tue, Wed, Fri–Sun, BH Mon, end Mar–end Oct (house and garden); daily (park), NT.*

BOSTON
LINCOLNSHIRE

Below: the church of St Botolph in Boston is known throughout the world as 'the Boston Stump'. On top of the tower is a beautiful octagonal lantern, whose beacon light has guided travellers by land and sea for 500 years

On the River Witham, Boston now has the appearance of a conventional market town, but in the early 13th century it was a port second in importance only to London. With the opening up of links with the New World, much of its trade moved to the ports of the west coast, and Boston's importance declined. By that time, however, the great **church of St Botolph** – known as 'the Boston Stump' – had been founded. Constructed between 1309 and 1460 by merchants who had prospered in the wool trade with Flanders, it was given a magnificently embossed roof and choir stalls with misericords. Many buildings speak of Boston's earlier greatness. **Pescod Hall**, a restored merchant's house, stands in Mitre Lane, while South Street has a 15th-century **Guildhall**. Here Brewster and other Pilgrim Fathers were tried and imprisoned in 1607, before they eventually left for Holland and the New World. In the **Market Place** are corporation buildings of 1772 and some early 19th-century assembly rooms.

BOSWORTH BATTLEFIELD
LEICESTERSHIRE

■ OFF THE B585, NEAR MARKET BOSWORTH ■

THE FATAL STONE

Richard III went down to defeat and death at Bosworth (*above*) and many traditions and legends have clustered round this decisive battle. The king moved to his last battlefield from Leicester, and the story goes that he spent the night there at the old White Boar Inn, the white boar being his heraldic badge. Next day he rode out on his white warhorse at the head of his army. The citizens gathered to watch and an old woman cried out that where Richard's foot knocked against a stone as he crossed the bridge over the River Soar, so his head would strike the same stone on his return. Riding over the narrow bridge, Richard's foot happened to touch a stone pillar. When his naked, dishonoured body, flung casually over a horse, was taken back to Leicester after the battle, it was said that the corpse's dangling head struck the same stone.

The Battle of Bosworth in 1485 was an event of crucial significance in the history of England. With it the Wars of the Roses came to an end, and the history of this country as a modern power began.

In an exhibition hall at the **visitor centre**, models, replicas and life-size tableaux bring the events of the late 15th century to life. There are descriptions of the rival claims to the throne made by the Yorkist King Richard III, and by the Lancastrian claimant, Henry Tudor, Earl of Richmond. On 22 August 1485 Henry Tudor was to defeat and kill his rival in battle at Bosworth, thereby becoming King Henry VII of England and founder of the Tudor dynasty.

Maps of the battlefield can be viewed at the centre, but the actual site of the battle is now a park. There are illustrated trail boards showing the disposition of the opposing forces and the location of Lord Stanley's men, whose intervention on Henry's side tilted the balance in Henry's favour. Large flags are frequently flown to mark the positions of the two armies. Visitors can see **King Richard's Well**, and the field in which he was killed. Afterwards, his crown was rescued from a thorn bush, and set on the head of the new king by Lord Stanley. *Open: daily, Apr–Oct (visitor centre); daily all year (park).*

BRESSINGHAM LIVE STEAM MUSEUM AND GARDENS
NORFOLK

■ OFF THE A1066 AT BRESSINGHAM, 4½ MILES (7KM) WEST OF DISS ■

DON'T MISS

■ The Long Gallery (Blickling Hall)

■ Boston Stump (Boston)

FOR CHILDREN

■ Battlefield exhibitions (Bosworth Battlefield Visitor Centre)

■ *The Royal Scot* (Bressingham Live Steam Museum and Gardens)

Bressingham Hall has the most outstanding collection of steam locomotives, tractors and fairground roundabouts in Britain. Housed under cover in extensive sheds are some of the most famous British steam engines, including *The Royal Scot*, the Britannia Class Pacific No.70013 *Oliver Cromwell*, and a 10-ton farm machine called *Bertha*, which was the first to join the collection. The plush interior of a royal coach can be enjoyed, as can a ride on either the narrow-gauge garden and nursery railways, or the Waveney Valley Railway.

The **Norfolk Fire Museum**, a superb collection of fire-fighting equipment from 1882 onwards, is also here, as is a glittering Victorian roundabout, which operates to the sound of a steam engine. The attractions are set in almost 6 acres (10ha) of gardens displaying 5,000 species of hardy plants, including an important collection of alpines. *Open: daily, Apr–Oct (museums); Sun, Thu and BH, Apr–Sep (gardens).*

THE BROADS
SUFFOLK AND NORFOLK

The edges of Broadland form a triangle, its apex at Norwich and its base along the coastline from Sea Palling in the north to Lowestoft in the south. Within this unique area lie 30 Broads, linked together by navigable approach channels, rivers, streams and lakes. The sight of sails seemingly travelling across the ground is common, for the level of the waterways is often well below that of the countryside. The shallow lakes that broaden out like leaves on the stalk of a plant from the main rivers – Yare, Bure, Waveney, and their tributaries, Ant, Thurne and Chet – were created by peat- or turf-digging. Today, reed-cutting for thatching is the main natural industry of the Broads.

The real character of this unique area can best be appreciated by boat. Vessels can be hired at centres such as Wroxham, Potter Heigham or Horning, and visits made, perhaps, to Hickling Broad, noted for the variety of its birdlife.

The Bure and its tributaries link most of the Broads together, while the Yare carries commercial and pleasure craft into the centre of Norwich. The Waveney only connects to the northern Broads through Oulton Broad and Breydon Water. Here all the inland waters collect before debouching into the sea beyond Great Yarmouth. Windmills still work at **Horsey**, **Reedham** and at **How Hill** on the Ant, while at **Herringfleet**, on the Waveney, there is a working smock mill.

On the border of Suffolk and Norfolk is the charming small town of **Beccles**. Towpaths flank the reedy river, a splendid setting for the detached bell-tower of the 14th-century **parish church of St Michael**.

Lowestoft has a long tradition of sea-faring, fishing and resistance to the sea's destructive capabilities. Its lifeboat station was founded in 1801, fully 23 years before the RNLI came into being. Lowestoft Ness is the most easterly point in Britain, and beyond the town's inner harbour is Oulton Broad, the scene of regular motorboat- and yacht-racing. Beyond Fritton Decoy, overlooked by **Burgh Castle** – originally the Roman fortress of *Gariannonum* – is **Berney Arms**, where a late 19th-century windmill drainage pump can be visited. *Open: daily (castle, EH); daily in summer (windmill, EH).*

To the north of **Great Yarmouth**, with its restored Elizabethan Star Hotel and remains of 13th-century Greyfriars Cloisters, are the ruins of **Caister Castle**, built in 1432 by Sir John Fastolf (Shakespeare's Falstaff). Here there is a **veteran and vintage car museum**. *Open: Sun–Fri, May–Sep; Mon–Fri, Oct–Apr (museum).*

Close to where the Bure flows into Ranworth Broad is the **Broadland Conservation Centre**, which has a good exhibition on the ecology of the area, plus bird-watching hides. In the little **parish church of Ranworth**, there is a remarkable 15th-century painted rood screen and the *Sarum Antiphoner*, illuminated by the monks of Langley Abbey in the 14th century. Further north along the Bure is the village of **Horning**, set deep in woodland with inlets from the river leading to private houses and gardens. Two miles (3km) to the west is **Hoveton Great Broad**, a nature reserve administered by English Nature.

At **Potter Heigham**, vessels must still lower their masts to negotiate the medieval hump-backed bridge. Some real working wherries can still be seen, huge masts lowered and sails removed. The Pleasure Boat at **Hickling Staithe** is also a busy sailing centre, while **Hickling Broad** is a National Nature Reserve.

■

Below: a windmill still works at How Hill, on the River Ant in the Broads. The reeds in the foreground are now valued as part of the area's natural industry

■

BURY ST EDMUNDS
SUFFOLK

'Shrine of a king, cradle of the law' is the motto of Bury St Edmunds, the county town of Suffolk. This phrase refers succinctly to two of the most important events in its history. In AD869 Edmund, the last King of East Anglia, was killed by the Danes. His remains were interred in the Saxon abbey of Beodricesworth at modern-day Bury St Edmunds. In 1215 Bury St Edmunds also became a 'cradle of the law' when the barons swore at the altar of the abbey that they would obtain ratification of the Magna Carta from King John.

Today, the town still largely retains the street grid pattern set out around the **abbey** by Abbot Baldwin (EH). The ruins of the abbey are set in gardens of tranquillity and beauty. Immediately to the south of the Norman tower is the **cathedral of St Edmundsbury**, a medieval structure enlarged in the 19th century and given a new chancel by Stephen Dykes Bower in 1960. Beyond the graveyard stands the beautiful 15th-century **church of St Mary**, with a magnificent hammerbeam angel roof over the nave, and a waggon roof to the chancel.

On the south side of Angel Hill is the **Athenaeum**, an 18th-century assembly room where Dickens gave readings. The **Angel Hotel**, of similar date but with 13th-century cellars, figures in *The Pickwick Papers*. Also on Angel Hill is **Angel Corner**, which has a fine collection of clocks and watches given by Frederick Gershom-Parkington. *Open: daily (NT).*

A little below the **Market Cross**, remodelled by Robert Adam in 1774, is **Moyse's Hall**, now a museum of Suffolk history, which was most probably built in the 12th century and is thought to have been a Jewish merchant's house. *Open: daily.*

On Westgate Street is the splendid **Theatre Royal**. Built in 1819 by William Wilkins, architect of the National Gallery in London, it is a rare example of a Regency playhouse, with a fine pit, boxes and gallery. *Open: Mon–Sat (NT).*

Above: clocks and watches of all types are on display at Angel Corner in Bury St Edmunds, which is best visited at noon for special effect

CADBURY WORLD
WEST MIDLANDS
■ AT BOURNEVILLE, SOUTH-WEST BIRMINGHAM ■

Inspired by Quaker idealism, the chocolate manufacturers George and Richard Cadbury employed W A Harvey to lay out a charming village around their factory in the 1890s. Today, this 'factory in a garden' is the setting for Cadbury World, a permanent exhibition devoted entirely to the history of chocolate-making and drinking, and to the part played by Cadbury in this fascinating story. The 'chocolate experience' starts with Central America, where natives of Montezuma's empire worshipped the gods of chocolate, and then tells how chocolate-drinking became popular in 17th- and 18th-century Europe. As well as viewing the famous Cadbury advertising campaigns of the past, visitors can watch chocolate actually being made. A highly sophisticated packaging machine is shown at work processing 15,000 bars of chocolate an hour. *Open: daily in summer; out of season, check with tourist information centres.*

CHOCOLATE CHANGES

The bitter drink which the Aztecs in Mexico called *chocolatl* was made of ground cocoa beans, chillies and honey. Taken to Europe and drunk hot and sweet, it was fashionable and highly expensive. Indeed, the London chocolate houses catered only to the smart set. In the 19th century, however, the import duty was lowered and cocoa became popular and extremely unsmart. Solid eating chocolate came next and then the modern milk-chocolate bar, which was made possible by the invention of condensed milk and was first sold in Britain by Fry's and Cadbury's. Richard Cadbury in the 19th century was the first to design pictorial chocolate boxes and so was the originator of 'chocolate box art'.

Above: one of the old advertisements for Cadbury's Dairy Milk, now on display at Cadbury World.

Left: the natives of Montezuma's empire worshipped the gods of chocolate, as Cadbury World's 'Chocolate Experience' demonstrates

DON'T MISS

■ The Abbey ruins (Bury St Edmunds)

■ The factory in a garden (Cadbury World, Bourneville)

FOR CHILDREN

■ The windmill drainage pump (Berney Arms)

■ The packaging machine (Cadbury World, Bourneville)

CALKE ABBEY
DERBYSHIRE
■ ON THE A514 AT TICKNALL, BETWEEN SWADLINCOTE AND MELBORNE ■

When Calke Abbey passed to the National Trust it was called 'the house where time stood still'. Built by Sir John Harpur between 1701 and 1716, most probably with the help of a Nottingham surveyor, William Johnson, Calke is a handsome, three-storeyed stone house with projecting corner pavilions. Later in the 18th century Sir Henry Harpur, known because of his shyness as the 'isolated Baronet', employed William Wilkins to add the portico and a new suite of reception rooms. The streak of reclusiveness re-emerged in his 20th-century descendant, Sir Vauncey Harpur-Crewe, and nothing was ever disposed of. Rooms when full were simply locked up. It was this 'time capsule' that makes the house so interesting today.

■

Left: Calke Abbey, the 'house where time stood still', standing romantically but rather secretively in the middle of a great park. It remained in the same family for almost 300 years until it was acquired by the National Trust in 1985

■

In place of the more usual Print Room, Calke boasts a caricature room, with satirical cartoons by Rowlandson, Gillray and Cruikshank covering the walls. The greatest treasure of the house is undoubtedly the State Bed, which came to Calke in 1734 on the marriage of Lady Caroline Manners to Sir Henry Harpur. The colours of the Chinese silk hangings remain brilliant even today. *Open: Sat–Wed and BH Mon, end Mar–end Oct (house and garden), NT.*

CANNOCK CHASE
STAFFORDSHIRE
■ OFF THE A460, 1 MILE (1.6KM) SOUTH-WEST OF RUGELEY ■

What is today an oasis of forest and heathland on the edge of the Black Country of south Staffordshire was once a densely forested royal hunting preserve. Now roads cross the 30,000 acres (12,150ha) betweeen Lichfield and Stafford, or run along the edges of the Chase. Tracks offer magnificent walking over the high moorland.

Some majestic oaks still remain in **Brocton Coppice**, where the Chase's large herd of fallow deer run. To the west of the **Sherbrook Valley** heather and gorse take over the hillside, but there is a large variety of bog plants in **Oldacre**. From the hill tops near **Seven Springs** there are long views over the whole Chase, while from the 600ft (183m) **Coppice Hill** the Cley Hills of Shropshire can be seen.

CANONS ASHBY HOUSE
NORTHAMPTONSHIRE
■ ON THE B4525 AT CANONS ASHBY, 6 MILES (10KM) SOUTH-WEST OF NORTHAMPTON ■

In an area noted for its great country houses, the ancestral home of the Drydens may not be the grandest, but it is certainly one of the oldest and most interesting. It derives its name from a priory of Augustinian canons founded in the 12th century, but the present house owes its origins to the marriage of John Dryden to a daughter of Sir John Cope in 1550 and its subsequent additions and embellishments to various of his descendants.

In the Winter Parlour the panels are painted with brightly coloured coats of arms set in strapwork, while in the Spenser Room large-scale murals have been found, depicting scenes of chivalry from Spenser's *The Faerie Queene*. Without any doubt, the finest interior of Canons Ashby is that of the Great Chamber, approached via a splendid processional staircase, built for Sir John Dryden. He enlarged the simple wooden barrel vault of 1590 to create a domed plasterwork ceiling. *Open: Wed–Sun and BH Mon, Apr–Oct (NT).*

■

DON'T MISS

■ The State Bed (Calke Abbey)

■ The Winter Parlour and the Great Chamber (Canons Ashby)

FOR CHILDREN

■ The fallow deer (Cannock Chase)

■ An underground boat ride (Speedwell Cavern, Castleton)

CANAL MUSEUM
NORTHAMPTONSHIRE

■ OFF THE A508 AT STOKE BRUERNE, 4½ MILES (7KM) SOUTH OF NORTHAMPTON ■

At the southern end of the Blisworth Tunnel, on the Grand Union Canal, is the small village of Stoke Bruerne. At the heart of England's canal system, close to the longest tunnel still navigable and above a flight of seven locks, Stoke Bruerne Canal Museum is ideally placed to recall 200 years of canal history and traditions. Stoke Bruerne today is still busy with boats, and the contrast that these holiday craft make with the cramped cabin of the butty boat, *Sunny Valley*, is most marked. *Open: daily, Eas–Oct; Tue–Sun, Nov–Eas.*

CASTLE RISING
NORFOLK

■ OFF THE A149, 2 MILES (3KM) NORTH-EAST OF KING'S LYNN ■

A former port from which the sea has long since departed, Castle Rising is dominated by its great Norman **castle**, built by William de Albini, Earl of Sussex, in 1150. The keep is among the largest in England, and its exterior walls are decorated with rich arcading. *Open: daily, Eas–Sep; Tue–Sun, Oct–Eas (NT).*

Castle Rising **church**, dedicated to St Lawrence, is famous for its Norman west front. On the green to the west side of the church is **Trinity Hospital**, built by Henry Howard, Earl of Northampton, before 1614. One of the sights of Castle Rising is a procession of lady occupants of the almshouse going to church, dressed in red cloaks and tall steeple hats.

CASTLETON
DERBYSHIRE

Castleton is an attractive village with weathered stone houses grouped around a green. Over this idyllic scene glower the ruins of **Peveril Castle**, built by William Peveril on land granted to him by William the Conqueror, and immortalised by Sir Walter Scott in *Peveril of the Peak*. The natural fall of the land offered protection to the castle on three sides, but on the fourth William Peveril constructed a great curtain wall with distinctive herringbone masonry, much of which survives. *Open: daily, Eas–Sep; Tue–Sun, Oct–Eas (NT).*

Below the castle are the four caverns for which Castleton is most famous today. The nearest to the village, and the largest, is **Peak Cavern**, which extends some 2,000ft (610m) beneath the mountain. **Speedwell Cavern**, under Winnats Pass, has to be toured by boat. At the top of Winnats Pass are **Blue John** and **Treak Cliff Caverns**, which are the richest source of Blue John stone (see left). *Open: daily, Eas–end Oct (Peak Cavern): daily (Speedwell, Blue John and Treak Cliff Caverns).*

BLUE JOHN

Found only at Castleton, Blue John was used to make jewellery (above), bowls and ornaments. Some of the biggest and finest pieces came from the Bull Beef working of the Blue John mine. A table top made from it, with its distinctive reddish colouring, can be admired in the Ollerenshaw Collection at Castleton and is part of a choice and fascinating display.

MAGNIFICENT COLLEGE BUILDINGS, CHAPELS

AND GARDENS CONTRAST WITH THE

PEACEFUL RIVER, OVERHUNG WITH TREES,

CAMBRIDGE
CAMBRIDGESHIRE

IN THIS HISTORIC CITY, WHICH REVOLVES

AROUND ITS UNIVERSITY

■

Right: the magnificent gatehouse of King's College, founded by Henry VI in 1441, was designed by William Wilkins in 1828

■

Crowds of students on bicycles, the presence of the tower of the great University Library, narrow, winding streets and numerous bookshops all create a tranquil and scholarly atmosphere in this town on the southern edge of the Fens.

'TOWN AND GOWN'
Cambridge can be said to have begun with the foundation of the first college, **Peterhouse**, in 1284 by Hugh de Balsham, Bishop of Ely. During the next two centuries 11 other colleges were founded, as well as hostels to accommodate the students, who before had had to find their own lodgings. As the university grew in wealth and importance, there were disputes with the townsfolk. These came to a climax during the rebellion of Wat Tyler in 1381, when riots took place, and the phrase 'town and gown' was coined to denote the city's two communities.

KING'S AND QUEENS' COLLEGES
It is impossible to visit Cambridge without exploring its colleges, which are usually open to the public during daylight (although there are certain restrictions during term time). On King's Parade is **King's College**, founded by Henry VI in 1441. The chief glory of King's College is, of course, its chapel, one of the greatest Gothic buildings in Europe, with its wonderfully delicate fan-vaulting and tall windows with outstanding Renaissance glass of 1515. Behind the High Altar stands Rubens' *Adoration of the Magi*.

Almost as old as King's, **Queens' College** was founded by the consorts of Henry VI and Edward IV in 1448 and 1465. The college boasts the picturesque President's Lodging, a half-timbered building of 1540 over the north cloister, as well as the famous Mathematical Bridge over the River Cam. The latter was so-named because it was supposed to have been designed on geometrical principles. It was built in 1749, and when it was taken apart in the 19th century, it could not be put together again without using bolts.

ST JOHN'S AND TRINITY
St John's College, the foundation of Lady Margaret Beaufort in 1509, was established on the site of the early medieval hospital of St John. The College gatehouse bears the image of St John, together with the arms of Lady Margaret, the mother of Henry VII, and the marguerites associated with her name.

The hall has a fine hammerbeam roof, and two bridges span the river – the Kitchen Bridge and the famous Bridge of Sighs. Modelled on the Venetian prison bridge, the Bridge of Sighs has bars in its arcades intended to prevent undergraduates leaving or entering the college at night.

Originally founded as King's Hall by Edward III in 1336, **Trinity College** was refounded and renamed by Henry VIII in 1546. The turreted Great Gate of the earlier foundation was incorporated in the Great Court, with its lovely Renaissance fountain of 1602. The magnificent Library by Sir Christopher Wren has carvings by Grinling Gibbons, a bust of Newton by Roubiliac and an exceptional collection of plate from the 17th century onwards.

CAMBRIDGE CHURCHES
The **church of St Mary the Great** is both the university church and the main parish church of the town. Constructed between 1478 and 1608 it has a fine Tudor roof. The

organ, by 'Father' Willis, was brought from St James's, Piccadilly in 1697. From St Mary's tower all the main colleges can be seen, while opposite is the **Senate House** by James Gibbs, where degree and other university ceremonies take place.

At the end of St John's Street stands the **Round Church**, dating from 1130 and one of only four medieval churches built in this shape in England. Its 15th-century chancel and angel roof in the choir are very fine.

MUSEUMS AND EXHIBITIONS

The **Fitzwilliam Museum** is housed in a building designed by George Basevi and C R Cockerell, to accommodate the collections that Viscount Fitzwilliam left the university in 1816. There are splendid Egyptian, Greek and Roman antiquities, medieval and Renaissance objects, and paintings ranging from early Italian to the pre-Raphaelite and French Impressionists. *Open: Tue–Sun.*

The **Scott Polar Research Institute** was established in Lensfield Road to commemorate the explorer, Captain Scott, and his comrades. *Open: Mon–Sat.*

In Castle Street is the **Cambridge and County Folk Museum**, which portrays the work and everyday life of the people of Cambridge over the last 300 years. The tools of the cobbler, thatcher and brickmaker are shown, and there is a 19th-century kitchen with period equipment. *Open: daily.*

Kettle's Yard, also in Castle Street, contains a permanent display of early 20th-century art collected by the late Jim Ede, whose house it was. Here are drawings and sculptures by Henri Gaudier-Brzeska, Naum Gabo, Joan Míro, Constantin Brancusi and Alfred Wallace, with ceramics and furniture. *Open: Tue–Sun.*

THE BACKS AND BEYOND

College buildings, gardens and parks run down to the river along **the Backs**, creating a peaceful stretch of water for boating. Below Jesus Lock motorboats are permitted; here college rowing competitions, the Lents and the Mays, are held.

Above: punting in the Cambridge style on the Cam. Along the Backs, colleges, gardens and parks meet the River Cam, beautifully overhung with trees

Above: the emblem of St Catherine, St Catherine's College

1   Cambridge and County Folk Museum

2   Kettle's Yard Art Gallery

3   Westminster College & Chestnut College

4   School of Pythagoras

5   Magdalene College

6   Wesley House

7   Triity College

8   Clare College

9   Old Schols

10 Gonville and Caius College

11 Sidney Sussex College

12 Westcott House

13 Christ's College

14 King's College and Chapel

15 Guildhall

16 Lion Yard Shopping Centre

17 Sedgwick Museum of Geology

18 Queen's College

19 St Catharine's College

20 Corpus Christi College

21 Whipple Museum & Museum of Zoology

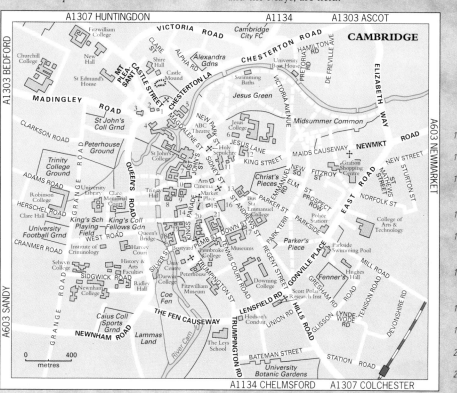

■

Above: looking over the River Derwent to the palatial façade of Chatsworth, one of the great houses of England. The beauty of its setting and gardens is matched by the richness of the interior

■

CHATSWORTH HOUSE
DERBYSHIRE

■ ON THE B6012 AT EDENSOR, 4 MILES (6KM) EAST OF BAKEWELL ■

The home of the Dukes of Devonshire, Chatsworth House is indisputably one of England's greatest houses. It stands above the River Derwent with a steep wooded hillside behind, and is surrounded by spectacular gardens. These were created by George London and Henry Wise in the 17th century, and by Sir Joseph Paxton in the 19th. Viewed from across James Paine's bridge, the classical mansion is an imposing sight. Its construction began in 1687 under the 4th Earl.

The south and east sides of Chatsworth were designed by William Talman, while Thomas Archer was probably responsible for the pedimented west front and the curving entrance side. The north wing was built by Wyatville in the 1820s.

The beauty of Chatsworth and its setting is admirably complemented by the palatial interior. From the Painted Hall, with its wrought ironwork by Jean Tijou and the first of the spectacular painted ceilings by Laguerre, the staircase leads up to the baroque splendours of the state rooms, created in an enfilade along the east front in place of the Elizabethan long gallery. As well as the ceilings by Laguerre and Verrio, depicting mythological scenes, there are paintings by Borzone, Giordano and Sir Peter Lely, furniture by William Kent, Mortlake tapestries and Delftware.

Beyond the Sketch Galleries, which boast an Annigoni of the present Duchess and a fine John Singer Sargent portrait of Duchess Evelyn, a Tintoretto hangs on the west staircase with *Large Interior* by Lucian Freud, commissioned by the present Duke. In the neo-classical dining room there is a splendid group of Van Dyck and Daniel Mytens portraits and silver by Paul Storr, while the Sculpture Gallery has works by Canova and Thorvaldsen, and paintings by Rembrandt and Hals.

One of the outstanding features of the gardens is the 260ft (80m) high Emperor Fountain, created by Paxton in 1844 for the visit of Tsar Nicholas I, and powered only by gravity from an 8-acre (3ha) lake on the moors above the house. This engineering triumph still delights visitors today. It contrasts with the 1st Duke's stepped cascade, designed by the French Huguenot, Grillet, and topped by the little Cascade House by Thomas Archer, with its waterfalls and fountains. Just as remarkable is Paxton's Conservative Wallcase, built to house tender plants. Today a yew maze stands where the Great Conservatory (Paxton's precursor of his own Crystal Palace) once was.

In the summer months, the Chatsworth farm is also open, while woodland walks over part of the 11,000-acre (4,455ha) park, landscaped by 'Capability' Brown and one of the finest in Britain, give an insight into the management of a great estate.
Open: daily, Mar–Oct (house and grounds).

■

DON'T MISS

■ The Conservative Wallcase (Chatsworth)

■ The gatehouse (Coughton Court)

■ The statues of the four seasons (Deene Park)

FOR CHILDREN

■ The farm (Chatsworth)

■ Cotton-spinning machinery (Cromford Mill)

■ The bears (Drayton Manor Park and Zoo)

COUGHTON COURT
WARWICKSHIRE
■ ON THE A435, 2 MILES (3KM) NORTH OF ALCESTER ■

Situated in pleasantly wooded country near to the Forest of Arden, Coughton Court, owned by the National Trust, is famous for its connection with the Gunpowder Plot, as it was owned by the Roman Catholic Throckmorton family since 1409. Once moated, the house today consists of two half-timbered Elizabethan wings flanking an impressive stone gateway. It was in the hall of the gatehouse, with its lovely fan-vaulted ceiling, that the wives of the conspirators awaited the outcome of the Plot. Attacked by both Parliamentary and Royalist forces during the Civil War, and damaged again in the Glorious Revolution of 1688, Coughton Court now contains an interesting collection of Jacobite relics.

The house is in a pleasant setting, with tranquil lake and a riverside walk, while the **parish church** contains the tombs of the Throckmortons. *Open: end Mar–Oct (days vary; check first with the National Trust or tourist information centres), NT.*

CROMFORD
DERBYSHIRE
■ ON THE B5023, 3 MILES (5KM) SOUTH OF MATLOCK ■

It was in the sturdy stone village of Cromford that the Industrial Revolution was born. In 1771, Sir Richard Arkwright built the world's first successful water-powered **textile mill** here, equipping it with the cotton-spinning machinery he had just invented. The original mill now contains an exhibition of cotton-spinning techniques and an audio-visual display, as well as a restaurant and shop. *Open: daily (except BH in winter).*

Arkwright created one of the first industrial villages here by building rows of workers' cottages in **North Street**, as well as a **market place** for the community, the **church of St Mary** and a **lock-up**.

DEENE PARK
NORTHAMPTONSHIRE
■ OFF THE A43, 7 MILES (11KM) NORTH-EAST OF CORBY ■

In the small, limestone village of Deene stands Deene Park, the ancestral home of the Brudenell family since 1514. Built of pale Weldon stone, Deene has grown over six centuries from a medieval manor house with a central courtyard and a battlemented tower to a Georgian mansion.

The elaborate roof of the great hall is made of chestnut, while the parlour is oak-panelled. The ballroom has superb stained glass and a heavy marble fireplace, which was installed in memory of the 7th Earl of Cardigan. He commanded the Light Brigade in the famous charge in 1854 during the Crimean War The exterior is dominated by the great tower with heraldic shields around its top, and the skyline is punctuated by rectangular turrets. The main front looks out over a wooded park and lake. *Open: BH Sun and Mon, Eas, May, Aug; Sun, Jun–Aug.*

DRAYTON MANOR PARK AND ZOO
STAFFORDSHIRE
■ ON THE A4091, 2 MILES (3KM) SOUTH OF TAMWORTH ■

Drayton was the home of the 19th-century Prime Minister, Sir Robert Peel, but his house no longer stands. In the large grounds today is Drayton Manor Park and Zoo. Entertainments include a cruise through the jungle and the Lost World, the Pirate Adventure, Skyflier, the Buffalo Mountain Coaster, the Mississippi Fun House and the Python-Looping Coaster. In the zoo are magnificent lions, leopards and bears, as well as monkeys and birds of paradise. Walks and a nature trail through 40 acres (16ha) of woodland, a farm collection, a nature conservation unit and beautifully laid out gardens cater for visitors with slightly less exuberant tastes. There is also an amusement park and a miniature railway. Aerial cable cars enable visitors to see the whole layout of the park, which covers 160 acres (65ha). *Open: daily, Eas–Oct.*

DUDLEY
WEST MIDLANDS

Dudley is often called the 'Capital of the Black Country' for it was here that, in the 17th century, coal was first used for smelting iron. Situated on an escarpment above the built-up area of Dudley are the ruins of the Norman **castle**. From the barbican and the two drum towers, the views of the surrounding countryside are splendid. An audio-visual presentation describes the castle's important role in history: from medieval fortress to Tudor palace to Royalist garrison during the Civil War.

Below the castle, in its 40-acre (16ha) wooded grounds, is **Dudley Zoo**, with more than 400 species of animals, including rare fish. The zoo is famous for its breeding of rare animals, including the ring-tailed lemur and the silvery marmoset. Both natural and manmade formations have been used to devise an entertaining series of landscaped enclosures for the animals. *Open: daily (castle and zoo).*

Only a short distance from the town centre is the **Black County Museum**. A group of buildings has been reconstructed on the site to show how people lived in the late 19th century. Visitors can ride on an electric tram car across the open-air museum, past the toll house and the tilted cottage, and on to the museum village itself, with its general store, sweet shop, baker's, chemist's and hardware shops. *Open: daily.*

The first glassmakers to arrive in Dudley came from Lorraine in eastern France in the 17th century. The **Broadfield House Glass Museum**, in Barnett Lane, Kingswinford, has a mainly 19th-century collection, which has been enhanced by gifts and loans over the years. *Open: Tue–Sun and BH.*

DUXFORD AIRFIELD
CAMBRIDGESHIRE
■ ON THE A505, 7 MILES (11KM) SOUTH OF CAMBRIDGE ■

A branch of the Imperial War Museum, Duxford Airfield displays the country's largest collection of military and civil aircraft, as well as a great number of tanks, vehicles and guns, and even a lifeboat and midget submarines. First World War hangars are shown, as is a Battle of Britain operations room, while in the 'Wings across the Atlantic' exhibition the latest in inter-active videos illustrate pioneering British and American transatlantic flights.

Duxford is also the largest centre for restoring historic aircraft in Europe, and visitors can watch work in progress. *Open: daily.*

EAST BERGHOLT
SUFFOLK

On 11 June 1776, John Constable, one of Britain's greatest landscape painters, was born in East Bergholt, the son of a

■

Above: a zoo with a view in the grounds below Dudley's Norman castle. Naturally landscaped enclosures like this one have become a feature of the zoo's layout

■

■

Above: like many other buildings nearby, the Victorian chemist's shop in the Black Country Museum at Dudley has been saved from demolition and re-erected on the museum site to recreate the town's past

■

■

Right: restoring one of the exhibits at the Imperial War Museum's Duxford Airfield, which houses the largest collection of old aircraft in the country

■

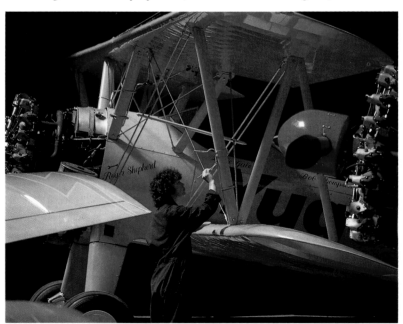

prosperous miller. Loving his native countryside, he once said 'these scenes have made me a painter'. Many can still be traced today. **Willy Lott's Cottage** in *The Hay Wain* is there, as is **Flatford Mill**, now a Field Studies Centre. The subjects of paintings such as *The Valley Farm*, *The Cornfield* and *Flatford Lock* can also still be seen.

In the village is a most unusual church. **St Mary's**, which was begun in 1525, is remarkable for its romantically unfinished tower. Inside the church is a memorial to Constable's wife, Maria, who died in 1829, and a stained-glass window commemorating the painter himself. In the churchyard are the graves of Constable's parents, of John Dunthorne and his wife, and of Willy Lott.

EASTON FARM PARK
SUFFOLK

■ OFF THE A12, 5 MILES (8KM) NORTH OF WOODBRIDGE ■

Close to the charming Suffolk village of Easton is Easton Farm Park. The farm's 100 cows can be seen being milked – a striking contrast with the 'model' dairy built here by the Duke of Hamilton in the 1870s, with its Victorian equipment, floral tiles and fountain. Working animals, such as Suffolk Punch horses, are shown alongside Suffolk carts, old farm implements, and steam engines. There are nature trails to follow through woodland and water meadows and children can enjoy the pet's paddock and the adventure play pit. The Foodchains Exhibition shows how crops of all kinds make their journey from farms to supermarkets. *Open: daily, Eas–Oct.*

ELY CATHEDRAL
CAMBRIDGESHIRE

Rising above the River Ouse on a bluff which was an island until the Fens were drained in the 17th and 18th centuries, Ely still clings to the edges of its great cathedral close. The present church, begun in 1083 by Abbot Simeon, was substantially complete when the nave was finished a century later. The scene of Hereward the Wake's resistance to William the Conqueror, Ely's cathedral has risen like a beacon over the surrounding countryside for about 1,300 years.

Entering the cathedral through the Early English Galilee Porch below a Decorated octagonal tower, visitors pass into the narrow Norman nave with its high clerestory and triforium arcades. In 1322 the central tower fell, but from this disaster sprang Ely's greatest architectural feature. The sacrist, Alan de Walsingham, and his carpenter, most probably William Hurley, created a wonderfully delicate octagon, which takes the whole width of the nave, transepts and choir at its base and rises on four larger and four smaller arches to a wooden lantern, which pours light down into the cathedral. At the east end of the north aisle is the richly carved chantry chapel of Bishop Alcock, built in 1488 in Perpendicular style. The **Lady Chapel**, another creation of Alan de Walsingham, has an amazingly wide vault.

■

Above: the magnificent Norman

west tower of Ely Cathedral is one

of the building's most impressive

features. From any angle it

effortlessly dominates the flat

fenland

■

■

FELBRIGG HALL
NORFOLK

■ OFF THE A148, 2 MILES (3KM) SOUTH-WEST OF CROMER ■

Much of the early history of the National Trust's Felbrigg Hall is written in its charmingly inconsistent exterior. The south range was built in a robust Jacobean style in about 1620 for Thomas Windham, probably using many of the craftsmen who had previously been working at nearby Blickling Hall. In 1675 William Windham employed a local architect, William Samwell, to construct a restrained west wing in brick behind the Jacobean block. In 1749 the second William Windham, freshly returned from his Grand Tour, engaged James Paine to remodel the 17th-century house, and it was during this time that Felbrigg took on its present size and appearance.

The gardens were laid out by Humphry Repton at the beginning of the 19th century; they incorporate an attractive orangery of 1704 and some woodland walks. In the nearby **church** are two rare brasses dating from 1351 and 1380, commemorating Simon de Felbrigg, Roger Felbrigg and their wives. *Open: Sat–Mon, Wed, Thu, end Mar–end Oct (house and gardens); daily (woodland walks), NT.*

FRAMLINGHAM CASTLE
SUFFOLK

■ OFF THE B1119 AT FRAMLINGHAM, 10 MILES (16KM) NORTH OF IPSWICH ■

A frowning silhouette on the banks of the River Ore, Framlingham Castle was one of the earliest to use a surrounding curtain wall with towers at intervals for defence, rather than a central keep. It was probably constructed in the early 13th century by Roger Bigod, 2nd Earl of Norfolk. A stronghold of King John during his struggles with the barons, Framlingham came into royal ownership in the 16th century when the property of the Earl of Norfolk was confiscated. In 1553 Mary Tudor was proclaimed Queen of England here. King James I restored the castle to the Howard family in 1613, but it eventually passed into other hands. *Open: daily, Eas–Sep; Tue–Sun, Oct–Eas (EH).*

THE GARMAN-RYAN COLLECTION
WEST MIDLANDS

■ THE MUSEUM AND ART GALLERY, LICHFIELD STREET, WALSALL ■

Few personal art collections outside London are of such uniformly high quality as this one, assembled by Lady Kathleen Epstein (née Garman), the widow of Sir Jacob Epstein, and the American sculptor, Sally Ryan, from 1959 to 1973. Lady Epstein donated many sculptures by her husband, and it is one of the best collections of his work in this country. Late 19th- and early 20th-century English and French paintings are well represented and displayed by subject matter, rather than by school or chronology. *Open: Mon–Sat.*

■

Below: looking across the rose parterre to magnificent Haddon Hall, one of England's most romantic houses. Legend has it that a daughter of the house, Dorothy Vernon, eloped from here with John Manners in 1567

■

GRIME'S GRAVES
NORFOLK

■ OFF THE A1065, 4 MILES (6KM) NORTH-WEST OF THETFORD ■

The 400 or so holes to be found in the ground just north of Brandon are not graves at all, but the workings of the largest prehistoric flint mines in Europe. Named after the Anglo-Saxon god, Grim, the shafts were sunk by Neolithic man to a depth of 20–40ft (6–12m). Visitors can go down one of the shafts. *Open: daily Apr–Sep; Tue–Sun, Oct–Eas (EH).*

HADDON HALL
DERBYSHIRE

■ ON THE A6, 2 MILES (3KM) SOUTH-EAST OF BAKEWELL ■

The first view of Haddon Hall, high above the Derbyshire Wye, is certain to satisfy every romantic idea of what an English castle should look like. Grey stone walls stand out from the green wooded hill behind, while the sharp silhouette of battlements and towers contrasts with the serene foreground, where an ancient bridge crosses the shallow river.

The estate was first owned by William Peveril, an illegitimate son of William the Conqueror, and parts of the Peveril tower and the chapel still date from that period. One of the remarkable survivals is its late 14th-century banqueting hall. With a dais window and a fine Millefleurs tapestry at the high table end, its minstrels' gallery and a passage to the service area at the other, it still has a strong medieval character.

In the kitchens are ancient water troughs and butchery equipment, while in the parlour is a rare decorated ceiling.

Haddon's greatest treasure is its spectacular Long Gallery, which leads out to the second, higher courtyard. Added by Sir John Manners in the early 17th century, it has wainscot panelling and shimmers with the light that floods in through the irregular panes of old glass. Below the Long Gallery are terraced gardens, bright with roses in early summer. *Open: daily, Apr–Sep.*

■

Above: Hardwick Hall, the most spectacular Elizabethan house in England. More glass than stone, it was built for Bess of Hardwick as a palace, and even the initials 'ES' on top of the towers proclaim her wealth and power

■

HADLEIGH
SUFFOLK

Once an important wool town, Hadleigh's long **High Street** has examples of every kind of Suffolk domestic architecture. Timber-framed houses with either plastered or pargeted decoration rub shoulders with suave Georgian façades. Notable also are the **Guildhall**, **St Mary's Church** and the **Deanery Tower**.

HARDWICK HALL
DERBYSHIRE

■ OFF THE A617, 5 MILES (8KM) NORTH-WEST OF MANSFIELD ■

Set proudly on top of its steep hill, Hardwick Hall is one of the greatest Elizabethan houses in Britain. It was built between 1590 and 1597 by Robert Smythson for the redoubtable Bess of Hardwick, by that time the rich and powerful widow of her fourth husband, the Earl of Shrewsbury. The severity of the façade is softened by the honey-coloured stone, the glittering glass in the great mullioned windows, the Renaissance loggia at the entrance, and Bess's initials at the top of each of the six towers.

Inside, the magnificence of the exterior is continued. The High Great Chamber, perhaps the most beautiful 16th-century room in this country, is decorated above cornice level with a plasterwork frieze modelled by Abraham Smith, depicting Diana hunting in the forest, and below with contemporary tapestries. The Long Gallery runs the whole length of Hardwick's façade and displays – as it did in Bess's day – portraits of the family and their political associates. *Open: Wed–Sun and BH Mon, Mar–Oct, NT.*

HOLKHAM HALL
NORFOLK

■ OFF THE A149, 2 MILES (3KM) WEST OF WELLS-NEXT-THE-SEA ■

Standing in a great park in north Norfolk, Holkham Hall was built for Thomas Coke, 1st Earl of Leicester, to display the treasures that he had acquired on his Grand Tour – and Holkham is still famous for its works of art. This magnificent Palladian house, most probably designed by William Kent, is built of dun-coloured bricks and has a central block of state apartments. The alabaster entrance hall and staircase, modelled on a classical temple, is Kent at his most inspired, while the Saloon, which has a deeply coffered ceiling, and was provided with furniture designed by Kent himself, is one of the most splendid rooms in any great house. The park, with its enormous lake, was landscaped in 1762 by 'Capability' Brown. *Open: Sun–Thu, May–Sep; BH Sun and Mon, Eas, May and Aug (house and park).*

■

DON'T MISS

■ The Long Gallery (Haddon Hall)

■ The High Great Chamber (Hardwick Hall)

■ The medieval lodgings (Holme Pierrepont Hall)

FOR CHILDREN

■ The flint mineshaft (Grime's Graves)

■

BESS OF HARDWICK

The portrait of Bess of Hardwick (below) which hangs in the Long Gallery at Hardwick Hall shows her dressed as a widow. Born Elizabeth Hardwick, the beautiful and forceful daughter of a Derbyshire

squire, she saw off four husbands, made a fortune out of them and gave full rein to her passion for building. She was first married at 14. Her second husband was Sir William Cavendish, who to please her bought the Chatsworth estate. By the time her third husband was buried she was the richest woman in England. Her fourth spouse was the 6th Earl of Shrewsbury, who had been put in charge of Mary, Queen of Scots and so he scarcely knew where to turn between his prisoner and his wife. Bess spent her last years at Hardwick, the terror of her children and grandchildren. She provided herself with an enormous monument in Derby Cathedral, where her Cavendish descendants are buried in respectful attendance upon her.

■

Above: Houghton Hall is one of the greatest Palladian houses. Built for the first Prime Minister, Sir Robert Walpole, it is famous for its sumptuous interiors created by William Kent

HOUGHTON HALL
NORFOLK

■ OFF THE A148, 13 MILES (21KM) EAST OF KING'S LYNN ■

One of the greatest examples of Palladian architecture in England, Houghton Hall was built for Sir Robert Walpole by Colen Campbell and Thomas Ripley between 1721 and 1731. The four corner domes were added by James Paine. In a house noted for the magnificence of its ceilings, the wood-carving in the Common Parlour stands out, as does Kent's splendid four-poster bed in the Green Bedchamber. The hall is faced in beautiful Yorkshire stone and set in a great park, laid out by Charles Bridgeman. *Open: Thu, Sun and BH, Eas Sun–last Sun in Sep.*

ICKWORTH
SUFFOLK

■ ON THE A143, 3 MILES (5KM) SOUTH-WEST OF BURY ST EDMUNDS ■

Probably one of the most eccentric houses in England, Ickworth is an elliptical rotunda, 104ft (32m) high and connected by two curving corridors to flanking wings. The exterior is decorated with two terracotta friezes based on illustrations from Homer by Flaxman, whose marble group, *The Fury of Athamas*, is the centrepiece of the staircase inside. In the sumptuous state rooms there are many fine portraits as well as the famous *Holland House Group* by Hogarth. *Open: end Mar–Oct (days vary; check first with the National Trust – house); daily (park), NT.*

KEDLESTON HALL
DERBYSHIRE

■ OFF THE A52, 4½ MILES (7KM) NORTH-WEST OF DERBY ■

Although the exterior of Robert Adam's Kedleston Hall is grand, it is the interiors that make Kedleston a true masterpiece. The Marble Hall with its 20 tall columns of pink-veined alabaster, Derbyshire stone floor, alcoves with statues and monochrome wall reliefs is one of Europe's most splendid rooms. Behind the south front is the Saloon, a domed rotunda 62ft (19m) high, while on the opposite side of the house from the State Bedchamber is the Dining Room, with a half-domed alcove for the display of silver. Throughout these state rooms the magnificence is sustained by splendid portraits of the Curzon family, and paintings by Van Dyck and Veronese. *Open: Sat–Wed, end Mar–end Oct (house and gardens); daily, Apr–end Oct (park), NT.*

KENILWORTH CASTLE
WARWICKSHIRE

■ OFF THE A452 AT KENILWORTH, 3 MILES (5KM) NORTH OF WARWICK ■

The chief glory of Kenilworth, its castle, founded shortly after 1120, occupies a dramatic position on a grassy mound to the north of the town centre. Kenilworth was granted by Queen Elizabeth I to her favourite, Robert Dudley, whom she created Earl of Leicester. Today the only habitable parts of the castle are Lord Leicester's Buildings, probably created to entertain Queen Elizabeth herself. After its Elizabethan heyday the castle fell into slow decline and suffered dismantling during the Civil War. It achieved literary fame as the subject of Sir Walter Scott's novel, *Kenilworth. Open: daily, Eas–Sep; Tue–Sun, Oct–Eas (EH).*

Above: Ickworth was built from 1794 onwards by Francis Sandys, to designs by the Italian architect Asprucci, for Frederick Hervey, 4th Earl of Bristol and Bishop of Derry. It was originally intended to display the earl's art collection but when Napoleon invaded Italy much was confiscated. The earl died before Ickworth was completed

KING'S LYNN
NORFOLK

The attractive and ancient port of King's Lynn was a walled town of some importance in early medieval times. On the Quay in King's Lynn today stands the **Custom House** (see left). To the south are the **Guildhall**, dating from 1421, and **Thoresby College**, a 15th-century merchant's house. In **King Street**, to the north of the Custom House, the 15th-century **St George's Guildhall**, now used as a theatre. **Lynn Museum** in Market Street has many treasures, including medieval pilgrims' badges, while the **Museum of Social History** in King Street displays some of the glass for which Lynn has always been famous. *Open: Mon–Fri when not in use (St George's Guildhall): Tue–Sat (Museum of Social History): Mon–Sat (Lynn Museum).*

LAVENHAM
SUFFOLK

The most picturesque of Suffolk towns, Lavenham grew prosperous in the wool trade during the later Middle Ages. The **Guildhall** in the market place has been successively an almshouse, a workhouse and a prison. Among the many timber-framed buildings are the **Angel Hotel** and the **Swan Hotel**, now incorporating the old Wool Hall. The **church of SS Peter and Paul**, marvellously sited at the top of the town, was constructed between 1480 and 1520. Another fine building is the **Priory** in Water Street, originally built for Benedictine monks. It has a uniquely designed herb garden. *Open: daily, end Mar– early Nov (Guildhall, NT): daily, Apr–Oct (priory).*

LAXTON
NOTTINGHAMSHIRE

Just off the A1, to the north of Newark-on-Trent, is Laxton, perhaps the last place in the country where the medieval system of strip-farming is still practised. Saxon in origin, the system divided fields into strips and randomly allocated them among the farmers ensuring that all received both good and bad land. They are scheduled as an ancient monument and can be visited.

LICHFIELD
STAFFORDSHIRE

The charming city of Lichfield is dominated by the three tall sandstone spires of its **cathedral**. Inside is the irregularly shaped Chapter House, completed in 1249, which has exquisite arcading. It also contains Lichfield's great treasure, the 7th-century St Chad's Gospels.

In the cobbled market square is the old bookshop which in 1709 was the birthplace of Dr Samuel Johnson, compiler of the first Dictionary of the English Language. It is now the **Samuel Johnson Birthplace Museum**. *Open: daily.*

■ *Above: King's Lynn's elegant Custom House, designed by Henry Bell in 1683, has a statue of Charles II in one of its niches.*

■ *Below: this engraving of Lichfield Cathedral, published in 1819, clearly shows its unique feature: three spires, known locally as the 'Ladies of the Vale'*

■

JOHNSON'S BIRTHDAY

The statue of Dr Johnson in Lichfield market-place honours the city's most distinguished son. He was born there on 18 September 1709, went to the local school and left for London and fame in 1737 with his friend, the actor David Garrick. The two young men could only afford one horse, so they took turns riding and walking all the way. Johnson's birthday is celebrated every year in Lichfield with a civic ceremony; a wreath is laid at the statue and hymns and a special Johnson anthem are sung. At a banquet in the evening the great man's favourite dishes are served – steak and kidney pie, and apple tart with cream.

■

LINCOLN
LINCOLNSHIRE

THE LINCOLN IMP

High up in the soaring Angel Choir of Lincoln Cathedral, the grotesque little figure of the Lincoln Imp has become a symbol – or almost a trademark – of the city and will be found on many Lincoln souvenirs. According to legend, the imp flew mischievously into the

cathedral one day while the Angel Choir was being built and was promptly turned to stone for its presumption. A local jeweller named James Ward Usher secured the right to use the imp on souvenirs and mementoes of Lincoln. He made an ample fortune and when he died in 1921 left his splendid art collection – including a sumptuous array of watches – to the city, together with the money to build the handsome Usher Gallery. So, in its way, the imp has done Lincoln much good.

■

Rising 200ft (61m) above the River Witham, the ancient centre of Lincoln was known as *Lindon* by its Celtic inhabitants. With the arrival of the Romans in AD47, the name was latinised to *Lindum*, and the settlement became a Roman colony, *Lindum Colonia*, 40 years later. They had soon transformed it into an elegant city with colonnaded streets, public baths and a stone-built water-supply and drainage systems, reclaiming the surrounding marshland and creating Fossdyke Canal between the Witham and the Trent.

During the medieval period Lincoln grew rich on the wool trade, but when this declined at the end of the 14th century the city suffered. The domestic architecture of the Middle Ages is admirably represented by the **Jew's House** in The Strait, which dates from about 1170, and the **House of Aaron the Jew**, of similar date. **The Cardinal's Hat**, perhaps named as a compliment to Cardinal Wolsey who was Bishop of Lincoln in 1514, is an attractive timber-framed building leading off The Strait. **Newport Arch**, the north gate of the Roman city, dates probably from the early 2nd century AD. Spanning the ancient Roman road, Ermine Way, it is the only Roman gateway in the country that is still being used by traffic.

Outstanding among English cathedrals, **Lincoln** was first begun in 1072, when Bishop Remigius moved his see from Dorchester to Lincoln. His church was shattered by an earthquake in 1185, and Bishop Hugh (later St Hugh of Lincoln), began its reconstruction in 1192. Above the rich doorway are 11 statues of kings and a weathered frieze of carved panels dating from 1145 illustrate the Old and New Testaments. The central tower, which houses 'Great Tom of Lincoln', rises to a height of 270ft (82m) and was constructed between 1307 and 1311. Inside, the west transepts are famous for their lovely rose windows and original glass. The chief glory of the interior is the Angel Choir, which takes its name from the 30 carved angels in the triforium. The delicacy of the detail, the richness of the bosses and the glorious Purbeck marble make it one of the greatest achievements of Gothic architecture in this country. There is also a fine statue of Alfred, Lord Tennyson in Minster Yard. Tennyson was born in the nearby Lincolnshire Wolds.

The **castle** at Lincoln was a focal point of the struggle between King John and his

■

Below: the west front of Lincoln Cathedral is one of Britain's greatest pieces of medieval architecture, and was said to represent the gateway to heaven

■

barons in the early 13th century, and the cathedral holds one of the four original copies of Magna Carta. The Cobb Hall was added to the castle in the 14th century as a prison. Inside, the iron rings to which prisoners were chained can still be seen in the walls, and the roof of the tower was used as a place of public execution until 1868. *Open: daily, end Mar–end Oct; Mon–Sat, end Oct–end Mar.*

The City and County Museum in Broadgate contains a fine collection of local antiquities, while the **Usher Gallery** in Lindum Road has a distinguished collection of paintings, including watercolours by Peter de Wint and views of the cathedral by J M W Turner. Close to the High Bridge is the **Stonebow**, a fine, 15th-century town gate. The **Museum of Lincolnshire Life** gives an absorbing picture of domestic, agricultural and industrial life in the county from Elizabeth I's reign up until the present day. *Open: daily (City and County, Usher, Lincolnshire Life).*

LONG MELFORD
SUFFOLK

One of Suffolk's loveliest villages, Long Melford derives its name from the length of its High Street, which sweeps for 2 miles (3km) past graceful houses and old shops to the dominating tower of **Holy Trinity Church**. This is a magnificent example of Suffolk craftsmanship, with elaborate flintwork, an immensely long nave and chancel, tall windows and a lofty clerestory.

At the upper end of Melford Green is **Melford Hall**, an early Elizabethan mansion. Little changed since it was built in 1578 by Sir William Cordell, Speaker of the House of Commons, this turreted brick manor house has a panelled great hall and a Regency library. *Open: Sat and Sun, end Mar–Oct (also open at other times; check with the National Trust), NT.*

A little to the north of the village is **Kentwell Hall**, a moated house built 10 years before Melford by the Clopton family. Approached along a 300-year-old lime avenue, Kentwell has a brick-paved Tudor rose maze and an exhibition of Tudor costumes. *Open: Eas–Oct (days vary; check with tourist information centres).*

NATIONAL HORSERACING MUSEUM
SUFFOLK
■ AT 99 HIGH STREET, NEWMARKET ■

The small market town of Newmarket has been the headquarters of British horseracing since the first-recorded meeting in 1619. Alongside the Jockey Club in the High Street is the National Horseracing Museum. Here the history of the sport and its scandals is vividly described, from the reign of King Charles II, who rode in races across Newmarket Heath, to modern times, when jockeys such as Sir Gordon Richards and Lester Piggott have achieved

Above: the stained-glass memorial windows in Long Melford Church date from the late 15th century. They survived a fire that destroyed much of the old church in the 18th century

■

■
Right: silks, from the National Horseracing Museum, show a selection of owners' racing colours. Newmarket has been the centre of British racing since the first meeting in 1619, and exhibits trace the history of all aspects of the sport

international acclaim. The control of horse-breeding and the establishment of the thoroughbred are also discussed. The pedigrees of great racehorses such as Mill Reef and Brigadier Gerard are also traced back through the supreme racehorse of the 18th century, Eclipse to three famous Arab stallions.

The collection of racing art is particularly important. There are fine paintings by Stubbs and Munnings, as well as bronzes of great horses such as Aureole. The Museum organises half-day visits on non-race days to the gallops, to the National Hunt Training Grounds and Tattersalls, to private training establishments and to the National Stud. *Open: Tue–Sat and BH Mon, Apr–Dec; also Mon in Aug.*

■
DON'T MISS

■ The Angel Choir (Lincoln Cathedral)

■ Sporting art (the National Horseracing Museum, Newmarket)

FOR CHILDREN

■ The Lincoln imp (Lincoln Cathedral)

■ Tudor costumes (Kentwell Hall, Long Melford)

■ The skeleton of Eclipse (the National Horseracing Museum, Newmarket)

SWEET LAVENDER

'Buy my sweet lavender' was once a familiar London street-cry and the plant has been valued for its delightful scent for many centuries. The name is derived from Latin *lavare*, 'to wash', and the Romans used to steep the leaves and stems in the water for their baths. They may have introduced the plant to Britain. St Hildegarde of Bingen is credited with inventing lavender water in the 12th century, and it became popular all over Europe; in Tudor and Stuart times many English housewives used to distil it as a matter of course. In Victorian days dried lavender flowers in sachets were placed in clothes chests and cupboards for freshness. Lavender was grown commercially in Lincolnshire and Hertfordshire at one time, as well as in Norfolk, and Mitcham in Surrey was once famous for its lavender.

NATIONAL TRAMWAY MUSEUM
DERBYSHIRE
■ MATLOCK ROAD, CRICH ■

In the Derbyshire village of Crich is one of Britain's most unusual museums. This once-important mining centre is now home to the National Tramway Museum, with more than 40 original vehicles. Steam-driven, horse-drawn, or powered by electricity, the trams have been painstakingly restored by staff and volunteers. The 2-mile (3km) round trip starts in a cobbled street lined with period buildings and then runs through woodland to emerge on a hillside with splendid views over the Derwent Valley. Interestingly, the track-bed now used by the museum was originally a narrow-gauge mineral railway, built by George Stephenson to link the quarry at Crich with the main line at Ambergate.
Open: Sat, Sun and BH, Apr and Oct; Sat–Thu, May–Sep.

NEWARK-ON-TRENT
NOTTINGHAMSHIRE

Known in Saxon times as the 'Key to the North' because it lay between the Rivers Trent and Devon, Newark was also a point of importance on the Fosse Way, although no evidence of Roman remains has been found in the town. Lady Godiva, the wife of Leofric, ruler of Mercia, presented Newark to the monastery of Stow in the 11th century, but for much of the Middle Ages it remained in royal hands.

The **castle**'s greatest days came, however, during the Civil War when, under Lord Bellasis, it survived three sieges by Parliamentary troops and only surrendered at the command of the king. Today all that remains is an impressive shell, with a fine 12th-century gate, a chapel and a beautiful oriel window overlooking the river.

The town's market place has great elegance. The buildings surrounding it include the classical **Town Hall** by John Carr of York, the 18th-century **Royal Victoria Hotel** and the **White Hart**, which has carved and painted woodwork of the 14th century. The **parish church** has a splendid Decorated spire and in the **Markham chantry chapel** two painted panels depict a dance of death.

NEWSTEAD ABBEY
NOTTINGHAMSHIRE
■ OFF THE A60, 10 MILES (16KM) NORTH OF NOTTINGHAM ■

Established by Henry II as an Augustinian priory in 1170, Newstead has been converted by successive members of the Byron family into a comfortable house, but the west façade of the priory church and its cloister have survived virtually intact. The Byrons were raised to the peerage in 1643 for their support of the king during the Civil War, but by the time the poet, the 6th Lord Byron, inherited the property in 1798, it was in a parlous state. He stayed only fitfully at Newstead between 1808 and 1819, when his debts forced him to sell. After restoration by the new owner, Newstead passed to Nottingham City Council, which displays Byron treasures in the house today.

The abbey has 9 acres (4ha) of beautiful gardens, with lakes and waterfalls and a Japanese water garden. Although the poet Byron is buried at **Hucknall Church**, 3 miles (5km) away, there is a huge monument in the grounds of the abbey to his dog, Boatswain. *Open: daily, Eas–Sep (abbey); daily, all year (gardens).*

DON'T MISS

■ The vaulting of the nave and choir (**Norwich Cathedral**)

■ The bosses in the cloister (**Norwich Cathedral**)

■ The teapot collection (**Norwich Castle Museum**)

FOR CHILDREN

■ The Blackpool 59 (**The National Tramway Museum, Crich**)

■ The village sign (**Heacham**)

NORFOLK LAVENDER
NORFOLK

■ CALEY MILL, HEACHAM ■

North Norfolk is justly famous for its lavender-growing industry. During July and early August each year the fields around Heacham are at their radiant best. Caley Mill is the home of the National Collection of Lavenders, and at its visitor centre demonstration beds can be studied and purchases made. Parties are conducted around the fields in season. *Open: daily.*

NORWICH
NORFOLK

Situated in a loop of the river Wensum, Norwich was an important borough trading with the Rhineland in Saxon times. At the Norman Conquest a large motte-and-bailey **castle** was built, and with the creation of the See of Norwich in 1094 Bishop Losinga destroyed much of the Anglo-Saxon borough, to create space for his cathedral, a majestic building, occupying low-lying land near the river. The first phase of building was completed in 1145, and the Norman style can still be seen outside in the great tower and inside in the nave, with its 14 bays of massive columns, aisles and transepts. Bosses on the magnificent lierne vault tell the story of the Bible.

The semi-circular apse at the east end is a French arrangement, quite uncommon in England. Norwich has the only two-storeyed monastic cloister in England, where splendid roof bosses tell stories from the life of Christ and the Book of Revelations.

Norwich Castle was erected by Henry I. It has blank Norman arcading on a stone keep, 70ft (21m) high. It is now a splendid museum with a fine collection of paintings by masters of the Norwich School, as well as displays of local antiquities, such as the Snettisham Iron Age Hoard and the Anglo-Saxon grave goods discovered at Spong Hill. *Open: daily.*

Across Prince's Street is cobbled **Elm Hill**, one of the finest medieval streets in the country. At the top is **St Peter Hungate** with a hammerbeam roof and medieval glass. It is now a museum of church art. **Strangers' Hall** at Charing Cross is a merchant's house with a 15th-century hall standing over an undercroft 200 years older. Once a centre for immigrant weavers, it is now a museum of English domestic life. **St Andrew's** and **Blackfriars Halls** were built between 1440 and 1470, and together constitute the only surviving Dominican church in England. **St Peter Mancroft** is a beautiful Perpendicular church with lofty clerestory windows and a hammerbeam roof. *Open: Mon–Sat (St Peter Hungate, Strangers' Hall).*

■

Below: the Norman tower of Norwich Cathedral received its spire in the 15th century. It is a majestic church on low land, close to the River Wensum

■

■

Below: Norwich Market with the Norman Castle in the background. The Saxon market area was at Tombland before the Normans moved it, and the castle is remarkable for the blank arcading on the stone keep 70ft high

■

■

Below: one of the most beautiful medieval streets in the country, Elm Hill was saved by the Norwich Society and the Civic Trust

■

NOTTINGHAM
NOTTINGHAMSHIRE

Although it is a busy industrial city today, Nottingham has had more than its fair share of disturbances during its long history. The **castle** built here by William Peveril on the orders of the Conqueror, was destroyed twice during the troubled reign of Stephen. It was later rebuilt by Henry II, who presented it to his younger son, John. The cruelties that John perpetrated during the absence of his elder brother, Richard the Lion Heart, on the Crusades, led to the growth of the Robin Hood legends. It was here too that Charles I raised his standard and plunged the country into civil war. Now it is a museum and art gallery with a splendid collection of pictures by Bonington, Richard Wilson, Rossetti and Stanley Spencer, and also the alabaster carvings for which the city was famous during the 14th and 15th centuries. In Castle Boulevard is the **Brewhouse Yard Museum** of everyday life. *Open: daily (castle, museum).*

ALADDIN'S CAVE

Nottingham is famous for its lace – and the industry is still flourishing in the area. The city's own collection can be seen in the Museum of Costume and Textiles, which occupies a row of attractive Georgian terrace houses in Castlegate that narrowly escaped demolition in the brutal 1960s. Lace wedding dresses are on display, with examples of handmade lace from the 16th century up to the modern machine-made variety. Nearby is the area called the Lace Market. The lace industry moved in here in the 19th century and has left some handsome Victorian warehouses behind it. A medieval building in Castle Row is home to the Lace Centre, famed as an 'Aladdin's cave' of lace lingerie and tablecloths, lace curtains and bedspreads, lace mats and panels and lampshades, with working machines and demonstrations. Lace to buy, lace to touch, lace to marvel at.

Beyond Broad Street and Stoney Street is the old **Nottingham Lace Market** with its red-brick warehouses. This area, which has now been restored, recalls the city's industrial past as an important centre of lace- and hosiery-making, which began when the Reverend William Lee introduced a stocking frame in 1589. James Hargreaves came to Nottingham with his spinning-jenny in the 18th century, and Sir Richard Arkwright opened his first cotton mill in the city.

On the eastern edge of the town is Holme Pierrepont Hall, an intriguing house dating from the late 15th century. Behind its entrance front, splendid medieval lodgings for retainers remain unaltered. *Open: Sun, Tue, Thu, Fri, Jun–Aug; also other times (check with tourist information centres).*

ORFORD
SUFFOLK

■ ON THE B1084 AT ORFORD, 8 MILES (13KM) SOUTH OF SAXMUNDHAM ■

Surprisingly for such a small village, the little seaport of Orford is guarded by a massive **castle**. It was built by Henry II in about 1165, but all that remains today is an 18-sided keep with three rectangular towers. Standing 90ft (27m) high, with three towers projecting above the battlements, this glowering structure has survived 800 years of assaults by man and nature. *Open: daily, Eas–Sep; Tue–Sun, Oct–Eas (EH).*

The **church** at Orford saw the first performances of some of Benjamin Britten's compositions, including, especially appropriate for the location, *Noye's Fludde* in 1958 and *Curlew River* in 1964.

OTTER TRUST
SUFFOLK

■ AT EARSHAM, 1 MILE (1.6KM) SOUTH-WEST OF BUNGAY ■

Established by Philip Wayre, the Otter Trust has the world's largest collection of otters in natural enclosures. Here the British otter is bred for reintroduction to the wild, but otters from other parts of the world can also be seen. The Trust is sited in 23 acres (9ha) of grounds on the banks of the beautiful River Waveney and offers **riverside walks**, a picnic area and a gift shop. This is a serene place of river and meadowland, inhabited by night herons and muntjac deer as well as the otters. *Open: daily, Apr–Oct.*

OXBURGH HALL
NORFOLK

■ OFF THE A134, 5 MILES (8KM) SOUTH-EAST OF DOWNHAM MARKET ■

Surrounded by a moat, Oxburgh Hall is one of the most charming country houses in Norfolk. It was begun by Sir Edward Bedingfield in 1487, and his descendants still live in part of the house. Its outstanding feature is the magnificent gatehouse, which rises 80ft (24m) above the moat. When he visited Oxburgh, Henry VII was accommodated on the first floor of the gatehouse in a room which today contains a bed dated 1675. In an adjacent room there are wall hangings with panels worked by Mary, Queen of Scots and Elizabeth, Countess of Shrewsbury ('Bess of Hardwick'). In the grounds beyond the moat, a beautiful French parterre garden was created in the mid-19th century. *Open: Sat–Wed and BH Mon, end Mar–end Sep; Sat and Sun in Oct (house): Sat–Wed, end Mar–end Oct (grounds), NT.*

■

Right: moated Oxburgh Hall was built at the end of the 15th century for Sir Edward Bedingfield, and his descendants still live in part of the house

■

PACKWOOD HOUSE
WARWICKSHIRE

■ ON THE A3400, 11 MILES (18KM) SOUTH-EAST OF BIRMINGHAM ■

Approached from a side road through an old gateway, Packwood House makes a powerful and theatrical impact on the visitor. It is a subtle mixture of Tudor timber-framing and mellow brickwork, and can boast some marvellous period furniture and Jacobean panelling.

But it is the gardens which are outstanding. Symmetrical clipped yews, thought to represent the Sermon on the Mount, are arranged in what is called the Multitude Walk. Weathered brick walls and a gazebo separate the yews from the sunken Carolean Water Garden. *Open: Wed–Sun and BH Mon, end Mar–Oct (NT).*

PETERBOROUGH
CAMBRIDGESHIRE

The first view of the massive Norman **cathedral** at Peterborough, with its triple-arched west front, is breathtaking. The present building was begun in 1117 and was substantially complete by the end of the century. Once through the vast porch with its three tall bays, built at the beginning of the 13th century, the visitor has an uninterrupted view of the rounded apse 480ft (146m) away, beyond a seemingly endless row of Norman pillars. The wooden ceiling is superbly painted with figures of saints, kings and grotesque monsters. By contrast, the apse stands in a square-ended building with delicate fan-vaulting, of 15th-century origin. Catherine of Aragon and Mary, Queen of Scots were both buried in Peterborough.

In Minster Close are the 13th-century **King's Lodgings** and the **Becket Chapel**. **Longthorpe Tower** is a fortified house with rare medieval wall-paintings. *Open: Sat, Sun (tower, EH).*

The **City Museum and Art Gallery** in Priestgate has a collection of Roman remains found in Whittlesey Mere and model ships carved in bone by Napoleonic prisoners-of-war. The **Nene Valley Railway** operates between Wansford and Orton Mere, using both steam and diesel locomotives. *Open: Sat, Sun, Eas–Oct; also Tue–Thu, mid Jun–early Sep (railway): Tue–Sat, BH Mon (museum and gallery).*

■

Below: the painted wooden ceiling of the chancel of Peterborough Cathedral dates from the early 13th century. Figures of saints, kings and grotesque monsters are depicted, but in the apse is the figure of Christ in Majesty

■

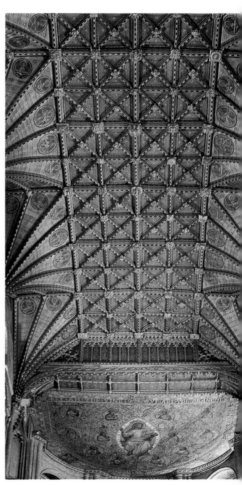

■

DON'T MISS

■ The alabaster carvings (Castle Museum and Art Gallery, Nottingham)

■ The Multitude Walk (Packwood House)

■ The painted ceilings (Peterborough Cathedral)

FOR CHILDREN

■ Otters and deer (the Otter Trust, Earsham)

■ The steam locomotives (Nene Valley Railway, Peterborough)

THE PEAK DISTRICT
DERBYSHIRE

North Derbyshire has some of the most dramatic landscape in Britain. High rocky crags rise out of heather-covered moorland, and, below, rivers have cut deep valleys which are richly pastured and heavily wooded. In the triangle between Derby in the south, Manchester in the north-west and Sheffield in the north-east, some 450 square miles (1,400sq km) of the Peak District National Park make up what for many people is the most magnificent countryside in these islands.

GEOLOGY AND LANDSCAPE

There is no single hill or range of hills known as the Peak. More accurately, the area belongs to what geologists call the 'Derbyshire Dome', a conical rock mass forced up out of the shallow sea that once covered it, the upper level consisting of millstone grit, the lower of Carboniferous limestone. Where the grits have survived, a wild, treeless moorland with peaks over 2,000ft (610m) high, such as Kinder Scout, in the Dark Peak, has been created, fringed with black lines of crag, such as Froggatt Edge. This is splendid 'adventure' country, ideal for walking, scrambling, climbing and pot-holing.

In the White Peak, in the centre and south of the region, the millstone grit has weathered away and the underlying limestone has encouraged green, upland pasture. The fields are divided by stone walls in a seemingly endless chequered pattern. Through this softer rock the Dove, Manifold and Wye rivers have carved their routes, creating the

beautiful Dales – deep wooded ravines, fringed with white cliffs.

MOORS, BRIDGES AND PEAK VILLAGES

Axe Edge Moor, south of Buxton, is a magnificent area of moorland where four of

Derbyshire's rivers – the Wye, Goyt, Manifold and Dove – rise. A grassy track leads over **Axe Edge**, rising to a height of 1,600ft (488m) above sea level. Nearby is **The Travellers' Rest**, at 1,535ft (468m) one of the highest inns in England.

The original village of Goyt's Bridge was submerged by the filling of the Errwood Reservoir in 1967, but the old **packhorse bridge**, which used to be on the route taken by salt smugglers between Cheshire and Derbyshire, has been reconstructed further

Below: Curbar Edge in the Peak District National Park. Froggatt, Curbar and Baslow Edges really form one continuous rocky ridge, fringing the wild, treeless moorland

upstream. During the summer the number of visitors is often so great that vehicular access to the valley is restricted.

Below Abney Moor stands the beautiful village of **Abney**. In the gorge to the south of this stone village is **Abney Grange**, once owned by the Abbots of Welbeck. **Little and Great Hucklow**, south of Abney, are popular gliding centres.

The high trackway over **Eyam Moor** offers distant views of Axe Edge, Mam Tor – the so-called 'shivering mountain' – and Kinder Scout. Nearby is a prehistoric stone circle called **Wet Withins**. In 1665 plague was brought to the village of **Eyam** in an infected box of clothes from London. With great bravery the villagers, led by their rector, cut themselves off from the outside world to prevent the disease spreading. Five out of every six inhabitants died, and in August each year their bravery is commemorated in an open-air service.

EXPLORING THE PEAK DISTRICT

Grindleford, at the eastern end of Hope Valley, offers magnificent moor-

land walking in all directions, while **Long-shaw Park**, 2 miles (3km) north-east, is a National Park estate. Closer to the High Peak is **Edale**, another excellent centre for exploring. Situated on the River Noe, it is surrounded by National Trust land. Gorges lead upwards onto the crags and uplands of the **Kinder Plateau**. A dramatic walk leads west through Upper Booth to Jacob's Ladder, and then passes Edale Cross to reach **Kinder Scout** itself, at 2,088ft (636m) the highest point in the Peak District. The lonely emptiness of the moor is occasionally relieved by waterfalls, such as **Kinder Downfall**, which plunges into a deep gorge below the Plateau.

BUXTON SPA

Although it lies outside the National Park boundary, **Buxton** is the largest and most beautiful town in the region. It stands over 1,000ft (305m) above sea level, but its height did not deter the 5th Duke of Devonshire from constructing The Crescent in 1870 to rival fashionable Bath. This fine architectural composition, as well as the thermal baths and pump room, the pavilion, theatre and concert hall and the Devonshire Royal Hospital gives Buxton a strong individuality, which has enabled it to survive the decline of spa towns in this country.

PLEASUREWOOD HILLS AMERICAN THEME PARK
SUFFOLK

■ OFF THE A12, 3 MILES (5KM) NORTH OF LOWESTOFT ■

Pleasurewood Hills has more than enough entertainment to keep both children and their increasingly exhausted parents busy all day. Once through the ticket gate, all rides are free for the whole day and the choice is seemingly endless. There is the Rattlesnake Coaster, Star Ride Enterprise, Astroglide, Skyleap, Waveswinger and Pirate Ship for the more active, while smaller children can enjoy things to slide down, climb or bounce on. Boating lakes are linked together by a scenic railway and a chairlift, and you can even barbecue your own food before or after you visit the **Haunted Magic Castle**. Take your place in the Cine 180, or in the Big Top to see the Superhuman Circus, which has no animals but, instead, human jugglers, acrobats and the funniest of clowns. *Open: daily, end May–Mid Sep.*

ROCKINGHAM CASTLE
NORTHAMPTONSHIRE

■ ON THE A6116, 1 MILE (1.6KM) NORTH OF CORBY ■

High above the River Welland and a line of thatched cottages stands Rockingham Castle, built on the orders of William the Conqueror. With its commanding views over five counties, Rockingham remained in royal hands, with successive kings refurbishing it, until Queen Elizabeth I gave it to Edward Watson, son-in-law of Lord Chief Justice Montagu, in the hands of whose descendants it remains today.

Although the Norman keep stands in ruins in the garden, the moat can still be seen, and Edward I's gatehouse still survives. Alterations over the centuries have transformed what was a medieval fortress into a comfortable country house. Inside, there are many treasures, including portraits by Reynolds, Zoffany and Angelica Kauffmann, and two ancient chests supposed to have belonged to Kings John and Henry V respectively. The servants' hall and the great kitchen both give visitors a glimpse of life 'below stairs'. In the grounds are ancient yews, a wild garden and a lawn known as the Tilting Ground. *Open: Thu, Sun, BH Mon and Tue, Eas–Sep.*

■

Below: the grounds of Sandringham House in Norfolk are full of surprises, such as this grotesque Buddha. The grounds are open to the public when no member of the royal family is in residence

■

■

Below: looking towards Sandringham House. The estate was purchased in 1862 by Queen Victoria for the Prince of Wales (later Edward VII)

■

SANDRINGHAM
NORFOLK

■ ON THE B1440, 5 MILES (8KM) NORTH-EAST OF KING'S LYNN ■

The country home of the Royal Family, Sandringham estate was purchased in 1862 by Queen Victoria, so that her son, the future King Edward VII, should have a house of his own in which to begin married life. The Prince's architect, A J Humbert, was commissioned to build the Jacobean-style house in 1870. A ballroom was added in 1883, and the upper storey rebuilt after a fire in 1891.

Sandringham is traditionally the place where the Royal Family spends Christmas and the New Year, and it was here that both George V and George VI died. George VI was also born in York Cottage on the estate, and baptised in the **church of St Mary Magdalene**. The church is of considerable interest, and has been embellished over the years by gifts from members of the family. The organ and the exquisite Florentine marble font were given by Edward VII, the communion plate and the oak roof by George V, and an unusual folding lectern by George VI.

The grounds and the well-laid-out routes through them are open to the public when the Royal Family is not in residence and the old stables have been made into a museum. North of the mansion is a colourful flower garden created by George VI, with an 18th-century statue representing Father Time nearby purchased by Queen Mary. The elaborate Norwich Gates, by Thomas Jekyll, were a wedding present from the county of Norfolk to the Prince of Wales in 1863. At **Wolferton**, 2 miles (3km) to the west, the railway station built in 1898 to serve Sandringham is now a museum. *Open: Sun–Fri and BH, Apr–Sep (Wolferton station); Sun–Thu, end Apr–Sep (Sandringham House and grounds; closed when the Royal Family is in residence).*

SHUGBOROUGH HALL
STAFFORDSHIRE

■ OFF THE A513 ON THE NORTHERN EDGE OF CANNOCK CHASE, 2½ MILES (4KM) EAST OF STAFFORD ■

■

Below: the portico façade of Shugborough Hall. The domed bow windows and the handsome neo-classical portico by Samuel Wyatt give the striking white house its character

■

Built originally for the Anson family, latterly Earls of Lichfield, Shugborough stands in a shallow valley in a bend of the River Sow, where it joins the Trent. Between 1745 and 1748 Thomas Anson added flanking pavilions to the house, with domed bow windows designed by Thomas Wright, of Durham. These and the handsome, neo-classical portico by Samuel Wyatt give this white mansion its present-day character.

Inside the house the diningroom has magnificent rococo plasterwork by Vassalli, but the most impressive interior is Wyatt's Red Drawingroom, which has a gently coved ceiling decorated with plasterwork by Joseph Rose. There is much fine furniture and porcelain, as well as paintings. Of particular interest are the canvases by Nicholas Dahl showing the park of Shugborough embellished by the marvellous garden buildings, which were designed by James ('Athenian') Stuart between 1764 and 1771. Among the first examples of Greek Revival structures in England, the Lantern of Demosthenes, the Temple of the Winds, and the Triumphal Arch commemorating Admiral Anson's achievements can be seen between the entrance gate and the house. Stuart's Doric Temple stands in the garden close to the Shepherd's Monument, the Chinese House and Bridge and Thomas Anson's monument to his cat. *Open: daily, Apr–end Sep (NT).*

SOMERLEYTON HALL
SUFFOLK

■ OFF THE B1074, 5 MILES (8KM) NORTH-WEST OF LOWESTOFT ■

A mellowed stone and red-brick mansion standing in 12 acres (5ha) of beautiful gardens, Somerleyton Hall was built for the railway magnate, Sir Samuel Peto, by John Thomas in 1844. Originally a 17th-century manor house, Somerleyton was reconstructed by Thomas in the Italianate style, with a charming campanile on the north side, a Renaissance arcade on the east, and a three-storeyed porch with a decorated oriel window on the west.

Inside, the Oak Parlour is richly panelled, and there is also wood carving in the manner of Grinling Gibbons, pictures by Joseph Wright of Derby, Ferdinand Bol and Clarkson Stansfield. In the gardens there is a maze with a pagoda which stands at the centre. *Open: days vary (check first with local tourist information centres).*

■

DON'T MISS

■ The views from the terrace (Rockingham Castle)

■ The flower garden (Sandringham House)

FOR CHILDREN

■ The Rattlesnake Coaster (Pleasurewood Hills American Theme Park)

■ The great kitchen (Rockingham Castle)

■ The stables museum (Sandringham)

SOUTHWOLD
SUFFOLK

With its harbour at the mouth of the River Blyth and heathland stretching away inland, Southwold is a charming and dignified resort. Victorian terraced houses along North Parade, Gun Hill with its Tudor cannon, colourful cottages, the extensive green and the gleaming white lighthouse in the centre of the town all combine to give the place a distinctive character.

From Norman times, the town was a busy port and its trading links with Holland can be seen in the Dutch gables on some cottages, and on the roof of the **museum**, founded in 1932. It has an interesting local collection, while the **Sailors' Reading Room** has a number of relics and models. Architectural pride of place, however, must be given to the **parish church of St Edmund**, built in the mid-15th century. Under a 100ft (30m) high tower the south porch is decorated with flint and stone patterns. Inside, tall windows allow light to flood down on to the painted and gilded woodwork. The screen of about 1500 is one of the most handsome in England. The carved choir stalls and the hammerbeam roof are also especially fine.

SPALDING
LINCOLNSHIRE

An ancient market-gardening town, Spalding stands on the River Welland in the very heart of the Fens. The flat landscape, criss-crossed by dykes and streams, and the seven bridges that span the river in the centre of the town give the whole area a Dutch flavour. On the eastern edge of Spalding the 25-acre (10ha) **Springfields Gardens**, and the bulbs that are grown there help to reinforce this impression. In early May each year a Flower Parade takes place in the town, followed by a horticultural exhibition. *Open: daily, Apr–Sep (Springfields Gardens).*

Spalding combines old and new buildings with an easy facility. **Ayscoughfee Hall**, dating from the early 15th century, was once the home of Maurice Johnson, who in 1710 founded the Gentlemen's Society of Spalding, a forerunner of the Society of Antiquaries. The **church of St Mary and St Nicholas** has an unusual double aisle and a 160ft (49m) spire. There are also some fine old inns.

■

Above: Burghley House, close to Stamford, was built in the 16th century. It has a remarkable silhouette, made up of turrets, towers and ornate chimneys

■

STAMFORD
LINCOLNSHIRE

The most handsome town of its size in England, Stamford is situated at a convenient crossing-point on the River Welland. One of the five Danelaw towns after the invasions of the 9th century, it acquired a castle in Norman times, and town walls which enclosed the area north of the river. During the Middle Ages no fewer than six religious houses were established here.

■

SAYING IT WITH FLOWERS

At the Flower Parade at Spalding (*above*) early in May every year a dozen or more floats garishly decorated with millions of tulip heads make their way through the streets of the town. The event began in the 1950s and has become an accustomed festivity in the Lincolnshire fenland, where acres of tulips, daffodils and hyacinths bring the fields to a blaze of brilliant colour in the spring. Visitors flock from miles around in special trains and coaches to see the parade on the great day. A different theme is chosen every year and an artist produces designs for the floats, which are built by the same team each year. Each float has a steel frame covered in rye straw mats, to which the tulip heads are attached in their thousands. A local beauty queen rides in the procession with her ladies-in-waiting and the floats are accompanied by bands and entertainers. There are also colourful displays at churches and other locations in Spalding and at the village churches in the surrounding countryside.

■

To the north of Red Lion Square, **All Saints** is mainly Early English with a separate tower and spire of the 15th century. The nearby **church of St John**, dating from the same period, has fine woodwork. **St Mary's**, close to the classical Town Hall and the old theatre where Kean and Sheridan once played, has a 13th-century tower and a fine spire of a century later. Across Town bridge is **St Martin's Church**, late 15th century in origin. It has a memorial to Lord Burghley, Queen Elizabeth I's Lord Treasurer, and to other members of the Cecil family.

Browne's Hospital, built in 1480 by a rich wool merchant and enlarged in the 19th century, is one of the finest examples of a medieval almshouse in the country. **Brasenose Gate**, a pointed arch in the old grammar school wall, recalls the students from Oxford who, in 1333, set up a rival to the older university.

About a mile (1.6km) to the south of Stamford is **Burghley House**, one of the most remarkable of Elizabethan buildings. Its palatial exterior has an exuberant and fantastic silhouette made up of towers, turrets and chimneys, and a multiplicity of Renaissance motifs. Inside, the chapel has an altarpiece by Veronese and carving by Grinling Gibbons. The art collection consists of more than 700 works, among them Delft porcelain and many interesting portraits. *Open: daily, Eas–Oct.*

STANFORD HALL
LEICESTERSHIRE

■ OFF THE B5414 AT SWINFORD, 5 MILES (8KM) NORTH-EAST OF RUGBY ■

Standing in open pastureland on the banks of the River Avon, Stanford Hall is a dignified mansion built by Sir Roger Cave in 1690. The hall remains largely unaltered and has fine furniture, paintings, family costumes and Flemish tapestries.

The stable block now houses an exhibition of old cars and motorcycles, as well as a museum of aviation set up to mark the achievements of Lt P S Pilcher RN, the first man to take to the air in a flying machine, the *Hawk*, in 1898. Unfortunately, Lt Pilcher died the following year when his plane rose 50ft (15m) and travelled 150yds (140m), before crashing during an exhibition flight in the park. The Royal Aeronautical Society has erected a pillar to mark the spot where he died. *Open: Sun, BH Mon and Tue following, Eas–Sep; also Thu, Jul–Aug.*

STOKE-ON-TRENT
STAFFORDSHIRE

The names Wedgwood, Minton, Spode and Copeland are known throughout the world as makers of fine porcelain and pottery. And yet Stoke-on-Trent, Britain's main ceramics centre, was, until the time of the Industrial Revolution, only a village. The present city came into existence when it combined with five adjoining towns: Tunstall, Burslem, Hanley, Fenton and Longton, to form an area known collectively as 'the Potteries'.

Although examples in the **City Museum and Art Gallery** at Hanley make it clear that pottery was made in the district during the Roman occupation, and even earlier, the industry only received real impetus when Josiah Wedgwood opened his factory at Etruria in 1769. The beauty of his pottery, achieved with the help of the neo-classical sculptor and designer, John Flaxman, made Wedgwood's products fashionable throughout the world.

The factories that **Wedgwood** and his fellow potters made famous in the 18th century are now open to the public, and conducted tours give visitors the chance to see traditional skills demonstrated in modern factories and in specially designed centres. The City Museum and Art Gallery has the world's most extensive holdings of English pottery and porcelain. *Open: daily, Eas–Oct; Mon–Sat, Nov–Eas (Wedgwood visitor centre): daily (museum and art gallery).*

Much of the success of the Potteries was due to the proximity of coal supplies needed for firing clay. The **Chatterley Whitfield Mining Museum** at Tunstall offers a fascinating insight into the workings of a coal mine. Guided tours may be taken below ground, and exhibitions on the surface show how the steam-driven machinery and locomotives worked. *Open: daily.*

The environment of Stoke-on-Trent has changed profoundly in the last 10 years. The harsh landscape, once ravaged by industrial development, has been softened by land-reclamation schemes and the removal of most of the great bottle kilns that once dominated the scene. Now parks such as the **1986 National Garden Festival Site** have transformed Stoke's appearance.

■
Above: Stoke-on-Trent City Museum and Art Gallery, in Hanley, has the world's most extensive collection of English pottery and porcelain. These pieces of conservatory furniture exemplify the skilful craftsmanship of the potters
■

■
DON'T MISS

■ The Sailors' Reading Room (Southwold)

■ The Delftware collection (Burghley House)

■ Wedgwood pottery (the City Museum and Art Gallery, Hanley, Stoke-on-Trent)

FOR CHILDREN

■ The memorial to Lt Pilcher, the first man to fly (Stanford Hall)

■ A tour of the coal mine (Chatterley Whitfield Mining Museum)

STRATFORD-UPON-AVON
WARWICKSHIRE

Although it is famous as the place where Shakespeare was born and died, Stratford is a charming market town in its own right. Its half-timbered houses, interspersed with suave Georgian façades, stand on the west bank of the River Avon as it flows gently through lush watermeadows. Gaily painted narrowboats from the canal are moored close to the Royal Shakespeare Theatre, creating an attractive scene that is best explored by walking along the riverbanks and towpaths.

It was through the enthusiasm of the actor, David Garrick, that a Shakespeare Festival was first held in Stratford more than 200 years ago, and now this modest but beautiful town is England's main tourist centre outside London.

Overlooking the river is the red-brick **Royal Shakespeare Theatre**, designed in 1932 by Elizabeth Scott as Britain's first national theatre. The Royal Shakespeare Company (RSC) is famous the world over, and the stage and mechanical equipment were built specifically to perform Shakespeare's plays. The collection of theatrical relics, and memorabilia is remarkable, including the 'Flower Portrait' of Shakespeare. Nearby are two other theatres owned by the RSC, the **Other Place** and the **Swan Theatre**.

Each year more than half a million people visit **Shakespeare's birthplace** in Henley Street. It has been restored as a typical middle-class, timber-framed house of the 16th century, with stone-paved living rooms opening straight on to the street. Upstairs the 'Birthroom' has the names of numerous past visitors scratched on the walls and windows, including Izaac Walton, Sir Walter Scott and Robert Browning. The house contains many treasures associated with Shakespeare, amongst them his school desk, a sword and a ring. *Open: daily.*

Approached along a lime avenue, **Holy Trinity Church** stands in quiet grounds beside the Avon. Inside is the font in which Shakespeare was baptised; the poet's grave is on the north side of the chancel, between those of his wife and daughter.

Timber-framed **Nash's House** was inherited by Shakespeare's grand-daughter, Elizabeth Hall. The garden is planted on the foundations of **New Place**, bought by Shakespeare in 1597. **Hall's Croft** was the home of Dr John Hall and his wife, Shakespeare's daughter Susanna. It houses an exhibition of 16th- and 17th-century medicine. Its walled garden is especially pleasant. *Open: Mon–Sat; also Sun, end Mar–end Oct (Nash's House/New Place, Hall's Croft).*

At Shottery, 2 miles (3km) from Stratford, is **Anne Hathaway's cottage**, an Elizabethan farmhouse. Its 16th-century furniture includes the settle on which Shakespeare is supposed to have courted his bride-to-be. *Open: daily.*

■

Above: the Garrick Inn at Stratford-upon-Avon. It was the enthusiasm of the actor, David Garrick, which led to the first Shakespeare Festival in the town, more than 200 years ago

■

■

Below: Britain's most famous playwright, William Shakespeare, was born in Stratford-upon-Avon in 1564

■

Bottom: the Royal Shakespeare Company is known internationally for its productions – like this one of Henry IV

■

SULGRAVE MANOR
NORTHAMPTONSHIRE

■ OFF THE B4525, 10 MILES (16KM) WEST OF TOWCESTER ■

The ancestral home of George Washington, Sulgrave Manor was rebuilt by his ancestor, Laurence, when he acquired the house in 1539. At that time it was clearly a modest building, but in 1914 a group of British subscribers bought, restored and extended it to mark a century of peace between Britain and America. It was back in 1656 that George Washington's great-grandfather, John, left Sulgrave Manor to settle in America, and because of the association it is a popular place of pilgrimage for Americans.

The house contains many links with George Washington, including an original oil painting of the future President of the USA, in the great hall. Over the porch is carved the family coat of arms, thought, somewhat improbably, to be the origin of the Stars and Stripes. *Open: Thu–Tue, Feb–Dec.*

In the nearby village of Sulgrave the 14th-century parish **church** contains monuments to the Washington family, and there is a pew and a chest in their name.

TATTERSHALL CASTLE
LINCOLNSHIRE

■ ON THE A153, 4 MILES (6KM) SOUTH OF WOODHALL SPA ■

Standing proudly above the surrounding fenland, the massive keep of Tattershall Castle rises to a height of more than 100ft (30m). Built in about 1440 by Ralph, Lord Cromwell, the Lord High Treasurer to Henry VI, it is an interesting example of a fortified house, and one of the best examples of a medieval brick building in the country. Fortified keeps such as Tattershall were built for both defence and comfort in medieval times. However, gunpowder had made castles largely redundant as strongholds during the 15th century and by the 17th Tattershall was left empty and ruinous. It was saved from possible transportation to America and restored by Lord Curzon earlier this century. *Open: daily (NT).*

THE THURSFORD COLLECTION
NORFOLK

■ OFF THE A148 AT THURSFORD GREEN, 6 MILES (10KM) NORTH-EAST OF FAKENHAM ■

With perhaps the best collection of steam engines and musical organs to be found anywhere in the world, the Thursford Collection is a museum with a difference. Each exhibit has been carefully restored, and for the first-time visitor it must be akin to entering Aladdin's cave. All around, old road engines of great beauty and interest, and a large variety of mechanical organs, gleam with gilding and paint and sparkle with rich and exuberant carving. Fairground, cinema and barrel organs are all here in full working condition, but pride of place must be given to the mighty Wurlitzer cinema organ, built by the New York company of Rudolf Wurlitzer for the Paramount cinema in Leeds. In the main museum building there is a **switchback roundabout** with Venetian gondolas, where rides are accompanied by music from the Gavioli organ. *Open: daily, Good Fri–Oct.*

TWYCROSS ZOO
LEICESTERSHIRE

■ OFF THE A444, 6 MILES (10KM) NORTH-EAST OF TAMWORTH ■

Set in 50 acres (20ha) of beautiful parkland, Twycross Zoo specialises in breeding animals which would otherwise be in danger of extinction. Here animals can be observed in attractive surroundings. The zoo has the only group of proboscis monkeys in the country, as well as one of the finest collections of primates in Europe: gorillas, orang-utans, chimpanzees and gibbons, many of them breeding. Many other animals are on display, and flamingos are to be seen on the large lakes. A bird house contains many colourful tropical varieties, and there are also butterfly and reptile houses. *Open: daily.*

DON'T MISS

■ Shakespeare's grave (Holy Trinity Church, Stratford-upon-Avon)

■ Names etched on the window-panes (Shakespeare's Birthplace, Stratford-upon-Avon)

FOR CHILDREN

■ The Wurlitzer (The Thursford Collection)

■ Chimpanzees (Twycross Zoo)

■

ENGLISH BRICK

The great 15th-century keep of Tattershall Castle (*below*) is one of the oldest major brick constructions in the country, and more than 300,000 bricks were needed to build it. The Romans built in brick in Britain, but after they left these islands brick-making mysterioulsy died out and did not start again until the Middle Ages. Large quantities of bricks were imported from the Netherlands in

the 13th century, but gradually English-made bricks were increasingly used. The first really substantial brick building was Holy Trinity Church in Hull, where splendid 14th-century brickwork can be admired today. The nave vault at Beverley Minster was built of brick later that century. In the 15th century handsome buildings of brick went up – among them Eton College and Tattershall itself – setting the stage for the glories of Tudor brickwork.

■

WARWICK
WARWICKSHIRE

One of the least spoilt of country towns in England, Warwick owes the consistency of its present-day appearance to a disastrous fire of 1694 that destroyed over 200 buildings in the centre. There are some notable survivors from the Tudor period still in existence, however, and two of the medieval town gates still survive.

Warwick Castle is one of the finest of all fortified mansions. The mound to the west of the castle buildings is the site of the Norman motte, but the present castle dates from a period of rebuilding undertaken by the Earls of Warwick in the 14th century. Around the turfed Inner Court are Caesar's Tower, with dungeons below, the 12-sided Guy's Tower and the Boar and Clarence Towers. The great hall, dating originally from the 14th century but much restored by Salvin in the 19th, contains arms and armour, a huge medieval cooking-pot, and a bust by Rysbrack of King Charles I. There are also gardens with attractive walks, laid out by 'Capability' Brown in 1753. *Open: daily.*

The chapel and half-timbered buildings of **Lord Leycester's Hospital** make a picturesque group at West Gate. Robert Dudley, Earl of Leicester, in 1571 endowed the hospital to offer asylum for men wounded in the service of the Queen and today it is still a home for ex-servicemen. *Open: Mon–Sat.*

The **church of St Mary** contains one of the most exquisite of medieval tombs, that of Richard Beauchamp, Earl of Warwick, who died in 1439. The **Warwickshire Museum** has exhibitions of the natural history and geology of the area, as well as the Sheldon Tapestry Map of Warwickshire, made in the 17th century, while a branch of the museum is accommodated in the lovely **St John's House**, which is surrounded by beautiful gardens and stands on the site of the medieval Hospital of St John. In Castle Street Oken's House, displays a fascinating collection of antique dolls and toys, gathered together by Mrs Joy Robinson and forming the **Warwick Doll Museum**. *Open: daily, Eas–Sep (doll musuem): Open: Tue–Sat and BH; also Sun, May–Sep (St John's House): Mon–Sat; also Sun, May–Sep (Warwickshire Museum).*

■

Below: the great hall of Warwick Castle was built in the 14th and altered in the 19th century. It houses a collection of arms and armour, including a suit made for the 3-year-old son of Robert Dudley, Earl of Leicester

■

WIGHTWICK MANOR
WEST MIDLANDS

■ ON THE A454 BESIDE THE MERMAID INN, 3 MILES (5KM) WEST OF WOLVERHAMPTON ■

To the casual observer, Wightwick Manor might appear to be Elizabethan, but is, in fact, only just over a century old. Designed by the architect and follower of William Morris, Edward Ould, for the paint manufacturer Theodore Mander between 1887 and 1893, Wightwick is in both appearance and decoration a superb expression of late 19th-century taste.

Inside the house there is much to delight the eye. Fine examples of William Morris wallpapers, wall hangings and tapestries abound. Tiles by William de Morgan, beautiful stained glass by C E Kempe, exquisite carpets and fine furniture all combine to create an air of 19th-century connoisseurship. Wightwick is also rich in Pre-Raphaelite painting, with drawings by Sir Edward Burne-Jones, such as the haunting *Love among the Ruins*, hanging alongside works by Ford Madox Brown, Dante Gabriel Rossetti, John Ruskin, John Everett Millais and George Frederick Watts. It is, indeed, a house conceived, designed and decorated as a whole. *Open: Thu, Sat and BH, Mar–end Dec (NT).*

WIMPOLE HALL
CAMBRIDGESHIRE

■ OFF THE A603 AT NEW WIMPOLE, 8 MILES (11KM) SOUTH-WEST OF CAMBRIDGE ■

The long, low, red-brick façade of Wimpole Hall stands serenely within parkland of great beauty. Alas, the two-mile double avenue of trees leading to the front of the house fell victim to Dutch elm disease and have now been replaced by limes. When these have matured, the view of this, the greatest house in Cambridgeshire, will once again be incomparable.

Wimpole Hall is notable for the many famous architects and gardeners who have worked there. The park was landscaped by Bridgeman, 'Capability' Brown and Repton, and the charming Gothic tower was designed by the gentleman-architect, Sanderson Miller. The central block of the house was designed and built in about 1640 by Sir Thomas Chicheley and enlarged for successive owners by James Gibbs, Henry Flitcroft and Sir John Soane.

Wimpole Home Farm, also built by Soane, has a collection of old farming equipment, while rare breeds of livestock can be seen in the paddocks and grounds. *Open: Sat, Sun, Tue–Thu and BH, end Mar–early Nov (NT).*

WOLSELEY GARDEN PARK
STAFFORDSHIRE

■ ON THE JUNCTION OF THE A51 AND A513 AT WOLSELEY BRIDGE, RUGELEY ■

Created on land owned by the Wolseley family for more than 1,000 years, Wolseley Garden Park occupies a site in a bend of the River Trent where Wolseley Hall once stood. Nothing remained of the Victorian gardens when work began in 1988. Now, in an area of 45 acres (18ha), Swan Lake and Temple Lake form a tranquil setting for the Spring Garden. A walled enclosure has 4,500 roses, tracing the history of the species from medieval varieties to modern hybrids. A scented garden has also been created for the blind and partially sighted. Further on water and bog gardens are encircled by a raised boardwalk. *Open: daily (Sat and Sun only in severe weather).*

WOODBRIDGE TIDE MILL
SUFFOLK

■ TIDE MILL WAY, WOODBRIDGE ■

A favourite subject for artists, the white, clapboarded tide mill stands gaunt beside the River Deben. The first record of a mill powered by the water of the estuary passing under the mill wheel from a tidal pond was in 1176, but the present building dates from 1793. At one time there were 170 such mills around Britain's coasts, but the Woodbridge tide mill was the last of its kind still in operation when a broken main shaft caused it to cease production in 1957. Today, the charming mill can be seen back in working order. *Open: May–Oct (days vary; check first with local tourist information centres).*

WILLIAM MORRIS

The delightful William Morris wallpapers, hangings and fabrics (*below*) at Wightwick Manor are part of the house's rich Pre-Raphaelite heritage. Morris was by a long chalk the most diversely talented of the Pre-Raphaelites. Formidably dynamic and whole-hearted, high-spirited and quick-tempered, he was a craftsman and designer of genius in stained glass, textiles, ceramics and tiles, furniture and carpets, books and typefaces. He was a notable printer. His poetry was considered good enough to make him a possible Poet Laureate in succession to Tennyson. He was a capable administrator and businessman, who ran his own succssful design firm and craft workshop. He was a pioneer conservationist, who founded the Society for the Protection of Ancient Buildings. He was also a Utopian socialist who saw the evils of the Industrial Revolution and the machine age, but was too much of a rebel to fit into the emerging Labour movement of the 1880s. Morris died in 1896, aged 62, and he lies buried in the churchyard of the Cotswold village of Kelmscott, which he so loved.

■

■

Above: red-brick Wimpole Hall stands serenely in parkland of great beauty, devised and planted by no less than four celebrated landscape architects: Charles Bridgeman, 'Capability' Brown, Sanderson Miller and Humphry Repton

■

DON'T MISS

■ Burne-Jones's *Love among the Ruins* (Wightwick Manor)

■ The plunge pool (Wimpole Hall)

FOR CHILDREN

■ The miniature suit of armour (the great hall, Warwick Castle)

■ The dolls (Warwick Doll Museum)

■ Unusual animals (the Rare Breeds Farm, Wimpole)

Wales
AND
The Marches

The sheer physical beauty of Wales – its brooding mountains, its tranquil lakes, its shimmering river estuaries – is matched by the richness of its heritage from the past. If a single view were picked out to demonstrate the point, it might be the prospect from Anglesey looking across the Menai Strait to the mighty battlements of Caernarfon Castle, themselves dwarfed by the towering mountain ramparts of Snowdonia. On a smaller scale, there is another example in South Wales at the Aberdulais Falls, where the river water, tumbling down a deep, wooded gorge, provided the power for the 19th-century tin-plate works whose ruins stand picturesquely there today.

The Romans left less of an imprint on Wales than on England, though the Dolaucothi Gold Mines were worked in Roman days, and on and off until the 1930s. The first outsiders to leave a substantial mark on Wales were Norman warlords. At Chepstow the grim 11th-century keep still stands above a sweeping stretch of the River Wye. The fortress was strengthened in the following century by the great Marcher dynasty of Marshall, which also built the massive stronghold at Pembroke. In the following century Edward I of England constructed a ring of castles to keep Welsh resistance penned in to Snowdonia. Beaumaris, Conwy, Caernarfon, Harlech – all supported by English sea power – stand today as testimony to Edward's iron hand and the skill of his military engineer, James of St George.

Along the border with England meanwhile, order of a rough and ready kind was kept by the Marcher lords, acting almost as independent potentates. They, too, had their stone strongholds, of which Raglan is perhaps the most impressive today. The much more homely Stokesay Castle, which is no more than a fortified manor house, still preserves a remarkably vivid atmosphere of medieval times.

Close to the border is some of Britain's most attractive hill country: the Shropshire Hills of which Housman sang, the Malvern Hills which Elgar loved and the wooded valley of the meandering Wye as it loops past the hallowed ruins of Tintern Abbey. In Wales three national parks protect the noble peaks of the Brecon Beacons, the spectacular cliff and shore scenery of the Pembrokeshire Coast and the soaring summits of Snowdonia (or in Welsh, *Eryri*, 'the High Land').

There could scarcely be a more rewarding quartet of cities to explore than Cardiff, Hereford, Worcester and Shrewsbury, while at Ironbridge the River Severn flows through its gorge below a gigantic modern power station and under the elegant arch of the Iron Bridge itself, the Industrial Revolution's first monument. In Wales the visitor can go deep below ground in a cage to the tunnels where the miner's lamps flicker in the Big Pit colliery, or venture into the subterranean labyrinth of the Llechwedd Slate Caverns. Back on the surface, the titanic ruins of Witley Court and the Indian treasure hoard at Powis Castle speak wistfully of past glory. Engaging oddities appeal for notice, too, from the irritable lobsters in the Anglesey Sea Zoo or the great slate bed of Penrhyn Castle to the gallant Marquess of Anglesey's wooden leg at Plas Newydd.

0   10   20   30   40   50 miles
0   20   40   60   80 kms

Holyhead

Beaumaris
Castle
Bangor
Plas Newydd   Penrhyn Castle
Anglesey Sea Zoo
Caernarfon
North Wales
Quarrying Museum
Snowdonia
Sygun
Copper Mine
Ffestiniog
Railway
Criccieth   Porthmadog
Portmeirion
Harlech Castle
GWYNEDD
Barmouth   Dolgellau   A470
Centre for
Alternative
Technology
Machynlleth
Aberystwyth
New Quay
Cardigan
Pembrokeshire Coast National Park
Fishguard
St David's
Pembrokeshire
Coast
National Park
Haverfordwest
Milford
Haven
Pembroke
Castle   Tenby
Pembrokeshire Coast National Park

Llandudno
Rhuddlan Castle
Conwy
Bodnant   Bodelwyddan
Garden   Castle
Mold
Ruthin
Betws-y-coed
CLWYD
Wrexham
Erddig
Llangollen
Bala   Oswestry
Ellesmere
Lakes
Llechwedd
Slate Caverns
Shrewsbury   Weston Park
Welshpool   **SHROPSHIRE**   Telford   Boscobel
House
Powis Castle   Ironbridge
*Shropshire
Hills*
Newtown   Acton Scott   Severn
Historical Farm   Valley
Railway   Bridgnorth
Clywedog   Stokesay Castle   Kidderminster
Gorge   Bewdley   Harvington
Llangurig   Ludlow   Hall   Bromsgrove
Rhayader   Croft Castle   Berrington Hall   Great Witley
POWYS   Leominster
Llandrindod   **HEREFORD AND**   Worcester
Wells   **WORCESTER**   Spetchley
Lampeter   Builth Wells   Park Gardens
Dolaucothi   Great
Gold Mines   Malvern   Evesham
Llandovery   Hereford   *Malvern
Hills*
Carmarthen   Kilpeck
Llandeilo   *Brecon   Church   Ross-on-Wye
Beacons*   Tretower Court
St Clears   Dan-yr-Ogof   Brecon   and Castle
Showcaves   Abergavenny
Monmouth
Raglan Castle
**WEST   Big Pit
GLAMORGAN**   Aberdulais Falls   Merthyr   Mining   Tintern
Tydfil   Museum   Abbey
Llanelli   Neath   **GWENT**
Rhondda   Cwmbran
Swansea   Heritage Park   Chepstow
Port   Margam
Talbot   Country Park   **MID   Caerphilly Castle   Newport
GLAMORGAN**   Tredegar House
Bridgend   Cardiff
**SOUTH
GLAMORGAN**
Barry

ABERDULAIS FALLS
WEST GLAMORGAN

■ ON THE A465, 3 MILES (5KM) NORTH-EAST OF NEATH ■

This National Trust site shows a combination of great natural beauty and a fascinating history of industrial use. Set within a small, wooded gorge the waters of the Dulais have been harnessed to power a succession of industries, beginning with copper smelting in 1584 and followed by flour and grist mills. The industrial remains seen today are those of a tinplate works which operated from 1830 to 1890. Now, visitors can enjoy a short walk alongside the river, on specially built walkways, on two levels. A number of panels around the site explain the significance of the industries. Nearby, a large water wheel generates power for a lift to help less able visitors to reach the top of the falls. This is part of a long-term programme of conservation and development which may at times limit access to some parts of the site. *Open: daily (NT).*

ACTON SCOTT
HISTORICAL FARM
SHROPSHIRE

■ 1 MILE (1½ KM) EAST OF THE A49,
3 MILES (5KM) SOUTH OF CHURCH STRETTON ■

This branch of the Shropshire County Museum Service covers over 20 acres of the former Home Farm of the Acton Scott Estate. Worked as a mixed farm, using Shire horses and skilled manpower, it demonstrates farming methods of about 1900 and is stocked with a variety of animals typical of those kept here then, including Longhorn and Shorthorn cattle, Tamworth pigs and Shropshire sheep. All are fed in the time-honoured manner, and there are daily demonstrations of hand-milking. Most buildings around the farmyard are late 18th-century, and butter and cheese made in the dairy are for sale to visitors. Throughout the season traditional rural crafts are demonstrated by local people. *Open: Tue–Sun, Apr–Nov.*

ANGLESEY SEA ZOO
GWYNEDD

■ OFF THE A4080 AT BRYNSIENCYN, ANGLESEY, 6 MILES (9½ KM)
SOUTH-WEST OF THE MENAI BRIDGE ■

A complex of modern buildings contains, among other visitor attractions, the largest and most comprehensive aquarium in Wales, housing a huge collection of marine life from the sea around Anglesey. It is not only all under cover but is viewed from below water level, giving a submariner's angle on the world of fish and other underwater life. There is a wave tank, a mullet pool, a wreck to walk through, and touch tanks where sea creatures can be handled. *Open: daily, early Jan–Dec.*

BEAUMARIS CASTLE
GWYNEDD

■ OFF THE A545 ON ANGLESEY, 4 MILES (6½ KM) NORTH-EAST OF THE MENAI BRIDGE ■

Now a World Heritage listed site, in care of Cadw, Beaumaris was the last of the castles built by Edward I to contain the Welsh. Its French name Beau Mareys, meaning 'beautiful marsh', describes the virgin site overlooking the Menai Strait where building started in 1295. Much of Beaumaris was built in the next 10 years, continuing spasmodically afterwards, but the castle was never completed.

An enormous amount of money was spent to create what is probably the most sophisticated example of medieval military architecture in Britain, the ultimate in 'concentric' design, unified in a near-perfect geometry, and for its time unbelievably palatial, although it is the fortress aspect of Beaumaris which dominates.

In Beaumaris itself the **Gaol and Courthouse** is a vivid reminder of 19th-century punishments, and, on a more cheerful note, the **Museum of Childhood** illustrates the life and interests of children over 150 years. *Open: daily (castle, Cadw): daily, Eas, end-May–Sep (gaol): daily, mid-Mar–mid-Jan (museum).*

■
Above: for over 300 years Aberdulais Falls provided the energy to drive the wheels which powered a succession of industries. It has been a favourite subject for many artists, including Turner
■

■
Below: subjects on this window symbolise the colour and marine beauty experienced in dry comfort in the 'Big Fish Forest' at Anglesey Sea Zoo
■

PRISON BARS

Stone walls may not a prison make, nor iron bars a cage, but they can do a powerful atmospheric job, as visitors to Beaumaris Gaol may agree. The prison was built in 1829 to the plans of J A Hansom, who left his name to the Hansom cab, and was designed to introduce greater efficiency and humanity into the prison system. You can see the grim stone cells, the treadwheel that the convicts trod to work the running water system, the pitch-dark and soundproof punishment cell and the condemned cell. Two murderers were hanged here, William Griffiths in 1830 and Richard Rowlands in 1862. Women prisoners did the laundry and sewing, and a slit in the ceiling of their workroom was apparently for a rope, attached to the babies' cradles in the room above, so that the women could rock their babies while they worked. The prison was closed in 1878 and is now a museum.

Left: the Seaward Gate in the outer curtain wall at Beaumaris Castle used to guard a 'cut' where the moat meets the sea. A tidal dock adjoining it allowed vessels up to 40 tons to sail close to the gatehouse

BERRINGTON HALL
HEREFORD AND WORCESTER
■ OFF THE A49, 3 MILES (5KM) NORTH OF LEOMINSTER ■

This elegant house was designed by Henry Holland for Thomas Harley, third son of the 3rd Earl of Oxford, and built between 1778 and 1781, the year in which his second daughter, Anne, married Admiral Lord Rodney's eldest son. By the time of Harley's death in 1804, Anne's husband had succeeded his father as Lord Rodney, and Berrington was for most of the last century the principal home of the Rodney family. In 1901 it was sold to Frederick Cawley MP, who became a peer in 1918. In 1957 the 3rd Lord Cawley surrendered the house, park and 'pool' to the Treasury, who then transferred it to the National Trust.

The main rooms have scarcely altered, with beautifully decorated ceilings, much fine furniture, and, among the many paintings, four great naval scenes illustrating Admiral Rodney's battles. Visitors can see the nursery, a Victorian laundry and an attractively tiled Georgian dairy. Berrington's modest size contributes to the friendly atmosphere of a much-loved family home.

Henry Holland's father-in-law, 'Capability' Brown, planned the layout of the grounds, including the construction of a 14-acre (5.6ha) lake (the 'pool') with an island, on which is a heronry. Views from the house steps embrace a vast panorama extending south-westwards to the Welsh hills and mountains. A recent addition to the grounds is a historic apple orchard planted inside a walled garden. *Open: Wed–Sun, May–Sep; Sat, Sun, Apr and Oct (NT).*

BEWDLEY
HEREFORD AND WORCESTER
■ ON THE A456, 3 MILES (5KM) WEST OF KIDDERMINSTER ■

A new bypass and river bridge to the south has allowed this charming small Georgian town to breathe more quietly again. Industry, too, has largely passed it by, as did the Staffordshire and Worcester Canal, in 1770. The nucleus of the old town lay up the hill west of the river, along what is still High Street, but the building of the first bridge in 1447 changed the street pattern, with Load Street continuing the line of the bridge and providing a wide market area.

Bewdley prospered in Elizabethan and Stuart times, mainly on its woollen trade, but also as a busy port on the river. A wide range of goods was brought on the Severn from Bristol, unloaded at Bewdley and carried by packhorse to Midland towns. Worn stone wharves line a river now empty of commercial craft, but the view from Telford's stone bridge of 1798 shows one of the finest river frontages in England. Bewdley's three main streets – Load Street, High Street and Severnside – contain outstanding houses, inns, hotels and public buildings of most periods and styles – half-timbered, Georgian, Victorian, but predominantly brick. **Bewdley Museum**, set in an 18th-century row of butchers' shops in Load Street called The Shambles, illustrates local crafts and trades, often with demonstrations and working models. *Open: daily, Mar–Nov.*

DON'T MISS

■ Diningroom chimneypiece, tiled Georgian dairy and walled garden (Berrington Hall)

■ Names of inns (Bewdley)

■ Turbine house and Visitor Interpretation Centre (Aberdulais Falls)

FOR CHILDREN

■ Touch tanks, radio-controlled boats and adventure trail (Anglesey Sea Zoo)

BIG PIT MINING MUSEUM
GWENT

■ ON THE B4248, 1 MILE (1½KM) WEST OF BLAENAFON ■

Big Pit closed as a working colliery in 1980, after exactly a century of coal mining, and is now a museum where visitors can experience something of the conditions in which South Wales miners lived and worked. The mine's workshops and pithead baths are open to the public; there is a reconstruction of a typical miner's cottage as well as a display of various aspects of the area's industrial history, which also included ironstone mining.

Undoubtedly the highlight of a visit to Big Pit is the 300ft (90m) descent, by cage, of the mine shaft. Kitted out with safety helmet, cap lamp and 'self-rescuer' as miners would have been, visitors are guided by ex-miners along underground roadways to coalfaces. Relics of working days are seen and explained, including haulage engines and stables for the pit ponies. The underground tour lasts about an hour. *Open: daily, Mar–Oct.*

BODELWYDDAN CASTLE
CLWYD

■ OFF THE A55, 3 MILES (5KM) WEST OF ST ASAPH ■

In its parkland south of the main road Bodelwyddan Castle is an authentically restored Victorian mansion recently chosen as an outstation of the National Portrait Gallery for a collection of portraits and photographs. A former owner, Sir John Hay Williams, added impressive castellations soon after 1830, and the interior has been refurbished to reflect design styles from various periods of the 19th century.

Furniture from the Victoria and Albert Museum and sculptures from the Royal Academy complement the architecture to provide a perfect setting for the collection of over 200 works of art, illustrating all aspects of portraiture and photography from the last century. Major paintings by G F Watts, William Holman Hunt, Sargeant, Landseer, and Sir Thomas Lawrence are displayed.

Extensive formal gardens have been restored and a half-mile woodland walk has been created, while a maze and aviary are additional attractions. For children there are adventure play areas.

On the opposite side of the main road, the 200ft (60m) spire of the 'marble church' – it is actually very white limestone which looks superb in sunlight – is a landmark for miles. Built between 1856 and 60 by John Ginson for the Dowager Lady Willoughby de Broke in memory of her husband, the church has a lavish, ornate interior, that oozes expense and quality, but may not be to everyone's taste. *Open: Sat–Thur, Eas–Jun and Sep–end Oct; daily, Jul–Aug.*

■

Below: beneath the terraces in Bodnant Garden is this formal canal, with the historic Pin Mill, a garden house built in 1730 and brought from its original Gloucestershire site to Bodnant about 200 years later

■

BODNANT GARDEN
GWYNEDD
■ ON THE A470, 8 MILES (13KM) SOUTH OF LLANDUDNO ■

In a splendid position above the Conwy Valley, with distant views to the mountains of Snowdonia, Bodnant is one of the most renowned gardens in Britain. Started in 1875, it is a family creation now superintended by the present Lord Aberconway whose father gave it to the National Trust in 1949. A carefully designed series of terraces, connected by flights of steps, balustrading and pergolas, leads down a hillside to a paved rose walk, below which is a formal canal focused on the Pin Mill. Well-kept hedges contain the garden which elsewhere spreads more informally. Magnificent collections of rhododendrons, azaleas, camellias, magnolias, and other shrubs and trees ensure attractive interest through spring and summer. In the dell at the bottom, conifers include sequoias and wellingtonias, seen against rocky outcrops and heard against sounds of rushing water. Many plants from the southern hemisphere thrive here. Bodnant is an important centre for plant breeding, and hybrids of many genera have been raised. *Open: daily, mid-Mar–Oct (NT).*

BOSCOBEL HOUSE
SHROPSHIRE
■ 8 MILES (13KM) NORTH-WEST OF WOLVERHAMPTON ■

Remotely situated in what was dense woodland in the 17th century, Boscobel House, built about 1630, enjoyed one brief hour of fame in the events which followed the Civil War. After the rout of his army at the Battle of Worcester in September 1651 the future Charles II, aiming to escape to Wales, found temporary shelter and safety at Boscobel House before continuing to nearby Moseley Hall. He subsequently reached Bristol and the West Country before sailing from Sussex to the Continent on 15 October 1651 and remained in exile until 1660.

Boscobel is a modest, early Jacobean house, with changes made in the 19th century by the Evans family. Many rooms retain their panelling, and some contain secret places and priest's holes, including that in which Charles is said to have stayed. Adjoining the house is a small garden with an unusual mount in a corner, from which there is a good view of the house.

An oak tree in a railed enclosure 150 yards to the south-west is a successor to the original oak, which had probably vanished by the end of the 18th century. *Open: daily, Apr–Sep; Tue–Sun, Oct–Mar.*

BRECON
POWYS
■ JUST NORTH OF THE A40, WHICH BYPASSES THE TOWN ■

In its beautiful setting in the valley of the Usk this historic small town looks south to a skyline dominated by the peaks of the Brecon Beacons. In Norman times a **castle** was built above the confluence of the Honddu and Usk rivers, and the town then developed under its protection. An early charter of 1246 makes Brecon one of the oldest of Welsh towns.

Closely grouped streets around **St Mary's Church** mark the town's busy heart, with a fascinating assortment of medieval, Tudor, Jacobean and Georgian buildings, most with ground floors converted into shops. Timber gables, occasional bow-windows, barley-sugar columns, and colour-washed fronts provide a lively variety, although too much wirescape remains. The actress Sarah Siddons was born in the High Street inn now named after her.

North of the town centre is the imposing **priory church of St John**, dating mainly from the 13th and 14th centuries and raised to cathedral status for the newly formed diocese of Swansea and Brecon in 1923. Side chapels are dedicated to various local trades – tailoring, weaving, shoe-making and fulling – pointers to Brecon's past, while the South Wales Borderers are commemorated in the Havard Chapel. The **Museum of the South Wales Borderers** in The Watton includes a Zulu War Room. In Glamorgan Street the **Brecknock Museum** displays an interesting collection of local history artefacts, and across the river **Christ's College** is the older of two recognised public schools in Wales. *Open: Mon–Sat, Apr–Sep, Mon–Fri, Oct–Mar (South Wales Borderers museum): daily, Apr–Sep; Mon–Sat, Oct–Mar (Brecknock museum).*

■
THE ROYAL OAK

One of the most popular inn signs in the country is the Royal Oak, showing a tree with the youthful Charles II (*below*) hiding in it. Sometimes the royal presence is symbolised by a crown among the branches. The tree is the famous Boscobel Oak, in which the future king and one of his officers, Major William Careless, spent the whole day on Saturday, 6 September 1651, while Roundhead soldiers searched for them. The fugitives had taken bread, cheese and beer

with them for provisions, but they found their refuge desperately uncomfortable. In the evening they climbed cautiously down and went to the house, where Charles had a dish of chicken for his supper. That night he slept in a cramped hidey-hole in the house, which can still be seen through a trap door at the top of the stairs to the attic. He left Boscobel the following evening. King Charles's birthday on 29 May is still remembered as Oak Apple Day, but the original tree at Boscobel was long ago destroyed by souvenir hunters.
■

■
Below: Welsh love spoons on display in the Brecknock Museum, Brecon. Carved, mainly in Welsh farms, from the 17th to the end of the 19th centuries, these were commonly used as symbols of betrothal. Their acceptance by a girl indicated that courtship could proceed
■

■
DON'T MISS

■ Borders of gentians and the long laburnum walk near the south lawn (**Bodnant Garden**)

■ The largest known cresset stone and the rood loft doors (**Brecon Cathedral**)

■ Annual Jazz Festival in August (**Brecon**)

FOR CHILDREN

■ Adventure woodland play area and maze (**Bodelwyddan Castle**)

BRECON BEACONS NATURAL PARK

BRECON BEACONS NATIONAL PARK

MAINLY IN POWYS

Designated in 1957, this national park covers 519 square miles (1344 km²) of mainly hill country in South Wales. The triple, shapely peaks of the Beacons themselves command the skyline south of Brecon and, reaching 2,906ft (886m) at Pen-y-fan, are at the heart of the mountain mass that forms four blocks, with Fforest Fawr to the west and the Black Mountain beyond (not to be confused with the Black Mountains to the east). Roughly equidistant main roads cross the uplands north to south, giving good views of the spacious, hilly landscapes and pastoral valleys, and linking small grey towns and cradled villages, but they don't reach the secret places where rare birds of prey soar and swoop in windy skies. Nor do they hint at the spectacular waterfalls and limestone gorges and caves of the upper Tawe Valley, in the Ystradfelte area, above Merthyr Tydfil, and near Crickhowell.

National parks were created to conserve areas of fine landscape and to encourage people to enjoy their peace and beauty through walking, climbing, riding, trekking, canoeing, sailing and caving, and the Brecon Beacons offers all these in abundance. For walkers, in particular, the choice is endless and varies from the most demanding challenges on the highest hills to low-level walks through quiet farming country, and the towpath of the Monmouthshire and Brecon Canal. The National Park Service runs guided walks, discovery days and craft demonstrations, with many special opportunities for children. Around 35,000 people live within the Park area, all of which is a 'working' landscape based mainly on pastoral farming.

Fish are plentiful in many waters, and **Llangorse** is the largest natural lake in South Wales offering many types of water sports. Reservoirs among the hills reflect changing skies; the small-gauge **Brecon Mountain Railway** takes passengers on a steam-hauled 2-mile (3km) journey from above Merthyr, and the **Brecon Beacons Mountain Centre** at Libanus, near Brecon, is the ideal starting point for visitors wanting to know more about the National Park, to explore its varied beauties and experience its rich historical legacy, which includes Roman roads, medieval castles and churches, and beautiful **Llanthony Priory**. *Open: daily, Eas, May–early Sep (railway): daily (mountain centre): free access all year (priory, Cadw).*

■

Below: Ystradfelte is one of the four main caving areas in Brecon Beacons National Park. Here, a group of visitors is standing in front of one of the largest cave entrances in Wales – Porth-yr-Ogof

■

■

Below: tiny St Mary's Church at Capel-y-ffin in the Honddu Valley at the heart of the Black Mountains, whose bare crests are seen (bottom) across a pattern of fields and hedgerows in this view from Mynydd Llangattock, south of Crickhowell

■

BRIDGNORTH
SHROPSHIRE
■ ON THE A442 BETWEEN TELFORD AND KIDDERMINSTER ■

High Town, the main part of Bridgnorth,
occupies a high sandstone ridge above the Severn, with Low Town on the opposite
bank, across a six-arched road bridge of 1823. Flights of stone steps, a steep narrow
lane, and England's only inland cliff railway also link the two. Meagre remains of
Bridgnorth's 12th-century **castle**, in a public park at the southern end of High
Town, include the keep, which has been leaning at an angle of 17 degrees for nearly
three centuries. Weekly markets are held in High Street, dominated by the open-
arched Town Hall, built immediately after the Civil War. High Street has many
half-timbered and 18th-century buildings, but East Castle Street, in the castle's outer
bailey, was laid out in 1786, with fine, well-proportioned brick houses, and curves
gently to **St Mary Magdalene's Church**, built by Telford in 1792. Until 1786
Cartway was the only route for wheeled traffic from High Town to Low Town.
Last century Bridgnorth's work folk lived there. At its foot **Bishop Percy's House**
is the town's finest Elizabethan building.

CAERNARFON
GWYNEDD
■ ON THE A487, 8 MILES (13KM) SOUTH-WEST OF BANGOR ■

Begun in 1283 **Caernarfon Castle** was
never completed. Nine towers and two gatehouses break the circuit of walls
honeycombed with passages and stairways, and in all it covers an area of almost 3
acres (1ha), The triple-turreted Eagle Tower houses an exhibition and audio-visual
programme; in the Queen's Tower is the **Regimental Museum of the Royal
Welsh Fusiliers**. Since 1911 the castle has been the venue for investitures of the
Princes of Wales, and it is now designated a World Heritage Site.

Caernarfon's town walls survive as an unbroken circuit of 800 yards and include
eight towers and two gateways. A lively Saturday market is held in Castle Square.
Open: daily (castle, Cadw).

CAERPHILLY CASTLE
MID-GLAMORGAN
■ IN CAERPHILLY, BY THE A468 AND THE A469 ■

This enormous fortress, second in size to
Windsor among British castles, was built by Earl Gilbert de Clare, 1268–71, to
control all exits from valleys to the north. It represented the climax of European
castle construction, with concentric defences, water, an outer ring and an inner heart
– virtually impregnable to medieval attack. Its 'leaning tower' is the result of ground
subsidence following the draining of adjoining lakes. Caerphilly cheese is still made
in the town. *Open: daily (Cadw).*

CARDIFF
SOUTH GLAMORGAN

Welsh capital since 1955, Cardiff's origins go back to Roman times. It became a Norman borough and probably remained a small port and market town until the late 18th century. The South Wales iron and coal industries brought great change, and, recognising Cardiff's potential as a port, the 2nd Marquess of Bute built the first dock in 1839. The Taff Valley Railway linked Merthyr to Cardiff in 1841, and branch lines followed. More docks were opened over the next 60 years, and the population rose dramatically.

Now the nearest mines are 10 miles (16km) away, and 2,700 acres (1,090ha) of the former port are the site of a huge redevelopment aiming to re-establish Cardiff internationally as a superb maritime city. In the **Welsh Industrial and Maritime Museum** working exhibits show how Welsh industries were powered. There is also an outdoor transport display and, at nearby Bute Road Station, a **railway gallery**. **Techniquest** is a unique, 'hands-on' science experience. *Open: Tue–Sun, all year, also Mon, school hols (museum, railway gallery and Techniquest).*

Cardiff is proud of its past, for which the **castle**, close to the city centre, is the starting point. The site was occupied continuously from Norman times on the remains of the Roman fort, and the current building is a fantasy in stone, conceived by the Marquess of Bute and created by William Burges in medieval magnificence between 1865 and 1880. Within the great ramparts, a section of Roman wall is shown, together with the **Museums of the Welsh Regiment and the 1st Queen's Dragoon Guards**. The shell keep of the Norman castle crowns a high motte, with panoramic views from its tower. *Open: daily (castle).*

East of the castle, Cardiff's **Civic Centre**, one of many fine buildings in Portland stone built around the turn of the century, is set in parkland with wide avenues. The **National Museum of Wales** illustrates Welsh history, and houses an outstanding collection of modern European paintings and sculptures. *Open: Tue–Sun (museum).*

The city's commercial and shopping centre, largely pedestrianised, includes fine department stores, speciality shops, and new shopping malls contrasting with seven Victorian and Edwardian shopping arcades, plus several theatres and the new **St David's Hall**, Wales's national concert hall, and the **National Stadium** at Cardiff Arms Park is the home of Welsh rugby.

Outside the city but within easy reach, **Llandaff Cathedral**, beautifully restored in the 1950s after suffering bomb damage, survives in a quiet oasis of green. Epstein's awesome statue of Christ in Majesty dominates the nave. The **Welsh National Folk Museum** at St Fagans needs a whole day to explore thoroughly. **Castell Coch**, north of the city, is another fairy tale created by Burges and Lord Bute in 1875. *Open: daily, Apr–Oct; Mon–Sat, Nov–Mar (museum): daily (Castell Coch, Cadw).*

Above: at Cardiff Castle in the Herbert Tower, dating from 1876, the beautiful Arab Room, a favourite of Lord Bute's, has walls lined with cedarwood and marble. This remarkable ceiling with golden stalactites, emphasises its Islamic character

Right: the Clocktower of Cardiff Castle was started in 1876 and was designed as a suite of bachelor apartments, one room above another, for the Lord of the Castle. Inlaid tiles, murals and a gallery must make this a remarkable Summer Smoking Room

CHIVALRY REBORN

William Burges was one of the most original and eccentric talents of the 19th century. He was the architect of both Cardiff Castle and the smaller, Prisoner-of-Zenda-style Castell Coch (*below*). Born in 1827, he grew up a passionate enthusiast for the Middle Ages, equipped with a profound scholarly knowledge of medieval buildings and art. He took drugs to stimulate his inspiration and long before Long John Silver had been thought of, he used to go about with a parrot on his shoulder. In the 3rd Marquess of Bute, who was 20 years younger and on the verge of conversion to Roman Catholicism, Burges found a patron with almost unlimited resoruces. Bute had been one of the richest men in Britain since succeeding to his title as a baby and he shared Burges's romantic admiration for medieval Christian chivalry. Together they employed an army of craftsmen to cover their castles with a spirited exuberance of murals, carvings, tiles, inscriptions, blazing heraldry and bulging chimneypieces. They never completed either building, and Burges died in London in 1881 when he was 53. Bute lived on until 1900.

CENTRE FOR ALTERNATIVE TECHNOLOGY
POWYS

■ OFF THE A487, 2 MILES (3KM) NORTH OF MACHYNLLETH ■

This unique and predominantly 'green' visitor attraction, set up in 1974 in an old slate quarry, demonstrates various methods of generating, using and conserving energy, including water power, wind power, solar power, bio-gas, wood-gas and insulation techniques. The Centre is a working community which shows how alternative technology overlaps into environmental conservation, as well as methods of food production such as organic vegetables, smallholding, forestry and fish culture. There is a blacksmith's forge, electric vehicles, a small railway, and a water-operated cliff railway to take visitors to the site. Some staff and their families live and work on site. Although there is not complete self-sufficiency, the aim is to show that an acceptable life-style can be achieved on far less electric power or other resources than is normal. *Open: daily.*

CHEPSTOW
GWENT

On the rising Welsh bank within an embracing loop of the River Wye, Chepstow is a splendidly historic gateway to South Wales. Limestone cliffs above the river were a natural site for the Norman **castle**, whose four courtyards are dominated by a 40ft (12m) high keep surrounded by walls with flanking towers, gatehouse and barbican. Successive building stages are evident; alterations were made to meet domestic needs in Tudor times, and there was some re-modelling after the Civil War. West of the castle a 1,200yd (1,100m) wall, built in the late 13th century, protected the small town. The **Town Gate** at the top of High Street leads to narrow, steep streets whose buildings cover a range of centuries, and the graceful **iron bridge** across the Wye was built in 1814. North of the town **Chepstow Racecourse** has regular National Hunt and Flat race meetings. *Open: daily (castle, Cadw).*

CLYWEDOG GORGE
POWYS

■ OFF THE B4518, 4 MILES (6½KM) NORTH-WEST OF LLANIDLOES ■

Clywedog Reservoir, built between 1964 and 1967, is a 'regulating' reservoir at the head of the River Severn system. The area round it was carefully landscaped with visitor amenities in mind. A 2½-mile (4km) scenic trail passes through woodland, by the water's edge and on open upland, always with good views and much wildlife interest. A second trail, below the massive dam, is much shorter but steeper and covers the former workings of the Bryn Tail Lead Mine, dating mainly from the mid-19th century.

CONWY
GWYNEDD

■ ON THE A55, SOUTH OF LLANDUDNO ■

In its setting between the wide Conwy Estuary and Snowdonia's foothills, Conwy merits all the superlatives. One of the best-preserved of all medieval walled towns, it also has the most attractive of all Edward I's castles in North Wales, which is itself a masterpiece of military architecture, justifiably a World Heritage Site. Raised hurriedly between 1283 and 1287 **Conwy Castle** shows all the genius of James of St George, master mason and Master of the King's Works in Wales, in being a functional, symbolic fortress, linear rather than concentric, with eight massive towers springing out of the rock.

The ancient walls, with 21 semi-circular towers and three gateways, enclose the old town, where **St Mary's Church** occupies the site of Aberconwy Abbey. **Aberconwy House**, dating from 1300, has an exhibition of Conwy's history, and there is an **aquarium** near the busy harbour. Telford's **suspension bridge**, constructed in 1826 and another National Trust property, replaced a ferry; Stephenson's tubular railway bridge came in 1848, and the 1958 road bridge is now supplemented by a tunnel carrying the A55 beneath the Conwy estuary. *Open: daily (castle, Cadw); Wed–Mon, Apr–Oct (house, NT).*

■

Above: on the quay at Conwy is the smallest house in Britain, 6ft (2m) wide and 10ft (3m) high, with its two rooms linked by a near-vertical stairway

■

■

DON'T MISS

■ Chapel Royal, on the first floor of Chapel Tower (**Conwy Castle**)

CRICCIETH
GWYNEDD

■ ON THE A497, 4 MILES (6½KM) WEST OF PORTHMADOG ■

Ruins of Criccieth's 13th-century **castle** dramatically crown a rocky headland which separates two south-facing sandy bays. Sea-bathing in Victorian times revitalised the little town, which retains its medieval character around the market place below the castle. Buildings still occupy original burgage plots, 75ft × 60ft (23m × 18m), and in the Victorian resort quarter by the harbour, a cottage named Hen Felin is on the site of the town's former corn mill. In nearby Llanystumdwy the Lloyd George Memorial Museum gives a picture of the life and times of the Liberal Prime Minister, who grew up in the village. *Open: daily (castle, Cadw): daily, Eas–Sep (museum).*

CROFT CASTLE
HEREFORD AND WORCESTER

■ OFF THE B4362, 5 MILES (8KM) NORTH-WEST OF LEOMINSTER ■

Apart from the period 1750–1923, the Croft family has been here since the time of *Domesday Book*. Four round corner towers date from the late 14th or early 15th century, but the quadrangular building was subsequently modified between 1750 and 1760, principally in the new Gothick taste, and most internal decoration is from that time. Up the hill behind the house and part of the large estate is **Croft Ambrey**, a spectacular Iron Age hill fort. Its panoramic views are a reward for the mile-long (1½km) walk and easy climb. Nearer the house are fine avenues of Spanish chestnut, oak, beech and lime. *Open: Wed–Sun, May–Sep; Sat, Sun, Apr, Oct (NT).*

■

Above: the great Welsh politician and prime minister, David Lloyd George, spent much of his boyhood in this humble terraced cottage at Llanystumdwy, near Criccieth. His grave is by the banks of the nearby River Dwyfor

■

DAN-YR-OGOF SHOWCAVES
POWYS

■ BY THE A4067, MIDWAY BETWEEN BRECON AND SWANSEA ■

The Dan-yr-Ogof cave complex extends over 9 miles (14½km) – the Half-mile Showcave is the largest British cave open to the public, and the Cathedral Showcave contains the largest single chamber. The Bone Cave gives an insight into cave archaeology, and the whole tour is an awesome experience of underground waters and limestone wonders, where lights illuminate stalactites, stalagmites and other strange rock formations. *Open: daily, Apr–Oct.*

■

Below: in the award-winning Dan-yr-Ogof Showcave complex, the Cathedral Showcave, with its shallow lake, waterfalls and beautiful rock formations, reaches an awe-inspiring climax at the 'Dome of St Paul's', which is the largest single chamber in any British showcave

■

■

DON'T MISS

■ Disused sundial on wall near gate of parish church (**Criccieth**)

FOR CHILDREN

■ The Dinosaur Park above the visitor centre (**Dan-yr-Ogof Showcaves**)

DOLAUCOTHI GOLD MINES
DYFED

■ OFF THE A482, NORTH-WEST OF LLANWRDA, NEAR LLANDOVERY ■

Set amid wooded hillsides above the Cothi Valley, within a 2,600 acre (1,050ha) estate given to the National Trust in the 1940s, these gold mines were worked intermittently over 2,000 years, finally closing in 1938. This is in fact the only place in Britain where the Romans mined gold. Pre-war mining equipment from elsewhere in Wales has been installed to help re-create the environment of its last working years. A visitor centre explains the history and exploitation of the mines. A self-guided surface trail, the Miners' Way, passes the main features of the area, involves some steep little climbs and takes about an hour. During the summer guided tours are arranged through the cave-like underground workings, and an additional fee is charged for these. Helmets with lights are provided, strong footwear is advised, and children under five are not allowed. The hour-long tour is a fascinating and memorable experience. *Open: daily, Apr–Oct. Underground tours: late May–mid-Sep.*

ELLESMERE LAKES
SHROPSHIRE

■ NEAR THE A528 AND THE A495, EAST OF ELLESMERE ■

A group of lakes or meres formed during the last Ice Age, some are designated as Sites of Special Scientific Interest. Largest is **The Mere** in Ellesmere, its 116 acres (47ha) used for pleasure boating in summer. Bird life is plentiful and many species of wild duck and geese like to roost on the artificial islands. The meres are also fine examples of the succession of plant life from open water to oak woodland. Sailing is permitted on **White Mere** and **Colemere**, and much of the latter is accessible by public footpath. The Llangollen branch of the **Shropshire Union Canal** passes the edge of Colemere and Blakemere, and its towpath offers a convenient linking walk.

ERDDIG
CLWYD

■ OFF THE A525 OR THE A483, 2 MILES (3KM) SOUTH OF WREXHAM ■

This huge, nine-bay house of 1684–7, added to in the 1720s and refronted 50 years later, is probably more important for its contents and furnishings than for its architecture. Simon Yorke inherited the property in 1733, and it passed through successive generations until, in 1973, the last

squire, Philip Yorke, gave it and 2,000 acres (810ha) of land to the National Trust. Erddig's most outstanding quality is the family atmosphere built up over the years, lovingly preserved and recorded, through portraits of family and servants and collections of items accumulated by the Yorkes, who had antiquarian interests. The original furnishings include a magnificent state bed in Chinese silk and some splendid gilt and silver furniture.

Throughout, staterooms and domestic offices show the social history of a country house, and this picture of a family home for nearly two and a half centuries is completed by the extensive range of outbuildings round a series of yards where the essential activities of a large estate were carried out. The large garden has been restored to its 18th-century formal design, based on a long central axis leading to the canal. *Open: Sat–Wed, Apr–Sep (NT).*

■

DOMESTIC GALLERY

By the 1960s, before the house and garden were given to the National Trust, Erddig was close to total dereliction. Subsidence as a result of coal mining had opened gaping cracks in the walls. Much of the furniture was broken, Bowls and a chamber pot stood in a row on the great state bed to catch the water dripping through its canopy from the decaying ceiling above. The Trust was inspired to undertake the most ambitious restoration programme in its history to that time because the estate preserved the complete workings of a country house of the 18th and 19th centuries. Outside, all the service buildings had survived – the sawpit, the smithy, the laundries, the bakehouse. Inside were portraits, not only of the family but of generations of the servants, starting in the 18th century with the gamekeeper, the carpenter, the blacksmith, the black coachboy and the 'spider brusher' who had been in service in the house for more than 70 years. The portraits carried on into the 20th century, with cooks and nannies, maids and gardeners, footmen and woodmen, immortalised in a unique gallery of domestic service.

■

■

Left: this bicycle collection, in one of the stableyard buildings at Erddig, contains Philip Yorke II's 19th-century 'bone-shaker' and some earlier penny-farthings acquired by Philip Yorke III this century. One of these was bought for a shilling at an Aberystwyth scrapyard

■

■
HIDING PLACES

Concealed behind the walls and under the floors of Harvington Hall is the country's best collection of priest's holes. Some of them were designed by Nicholas Owen, a specialist master craftsman in the art of constructing hides, which he installed in many Roman Catholic houses. At one place in the house, in a particularly cunning example, a heavy timber beam swings on a pivot to reveal a narrow entry to a hiding place, so ingeniously disguised that it was not discovered until 1894. Another room has a false fireplace and two of the steps of the main staircase lift up to allow entry to another hide. Poor Nicholas Owen was caught in 1606 and tortured to death in a vain attempt to make him reveal details of the priest's holes he had built.

■

FFESTINIOG RAILWAY
GWYNEDD
■ PORTMADOG (A497) TO BLAENAU FFESTINIOG (A470) ■

The longest of Wales's famous narrow-gauge railways runs from Portmadog on the coast to Blaenau Ffestiniog, 700ft (210m) above sea-level and $13\frac{1}{2}$ miles (22km) away. Most trains are steam hauled and carriages have buffet and observation facilities. The route winds along hillsides above the beautiful Vale of Ffestiniog, through forests and tunnels, past lakes and waterfalls, with stops at intermediate stations. The journey takes 65 minutes. *Open: daily service, late Mar–Early Nov; reduced in winter.*

GREAT WITLEY
HEREFORD AND WORCESTER
■ ON THE A443, 10 MILES (16KM) NORTH-WEST OF WORCESTER ■

Only a shell remains of one of Europe's grandest mansions, **Witley Court**, devastated by fire in 1935. Built by Lord Dudley in 1838 on to a Jacobean manor, which had already been enlarged in the early 18th century, its scenes of splendour are now a memory. A local campaign in 1967 saved further vandalism and robbery, and the ruins are now secure.

Adjoining the ruins is the sumptuous, finest baroque **church** in Britain, with gilded plasterwork and ceiling panels painted by Bellucci for the chapel of Canons, Edgware, and bought at auction by Lord Foley in 1747 for Witley. *Open: daily (ruins, EH).*

HARLECH CASTLE
GWYNEDD
■ OFF THE A496, 10 MILES (16KM) NORTH OF BARMOUTH ■

Another of Edward I's chain of fortresses, built between 1283 and 1289 to contain the Welsh in their mountain fastness of Snowdonia, Harlech Castle is dramatically situated on a high crag, once at the sea's edge but now half-a-mile inland, with a golf course between castle and beach. Tremendous views of Snowdonia and across Tremadog Bay are the reward for walking the battlements, and an exhibition in the gatehouse shows the life of a castle and its people. *Open: daily (Cadw).*

■

Above: opened in 1836 for the carriage of slate, the Ffestiniog Railway pioneered the use of steam traction in 1863 on its remarkable 2ft (61cm) gauge track. One of the old engines still draws passenger coaches along the original picturesque route

■

HARVINGTON HALL
HEREFORD AND WORCESTER
■ NEAR THE A448 AND THE A450, 3 MILES (5KM) SOUTH-EAST OF KIDDERMINSTER ■

This moated brick house has remained largely unchanged since it was built by Humphrey Pakington about 1580, and many of its rooms retain their original Elizabethan wall-paintings. An unusual number of hiding places adds a touch of intrigue. The Throckmortons inherited Harvington in 1696 and demolished part of the courtyard. They replaced the domestic chapel with a garden one in 1743, and in 1825 this was used as a village school. The chapel has recently been restored with the addition of a Georgian altar and chamber organ. In 1923 Harvington was acquired by the Roman Catholic Archdiocese of Birmingham, which restored the building. *Open: daily, Mar–Oct.*

■

Above: the great gatehouse of Harlech Castle was built as a fortified domestic residence with a degree of comfort, but in 1404 the castle fell to Owain Glyndwr, who made it his campaign base. It was retaken by the future Henry V four years later

■

HEREFORD
HEREFORD AND WORCESTER

Although Hereford began as a stronghold on the Welsh border about AD700, the modern city has grown with the prosperity of its surrounding countryside into an important trading centre whose rural flavour is most apparent on Wednesdays, when its cattle and sheep market brings in farmers and their families from all around. A busy administrative, commercial and shopping centre, it has kept its few industries at arm's length. Its riverside situation coupled with its status as a cathedral city make Hereford a popular place both to live in and to visit.

Hereford first acquired a **cathedral** around 792. This was replaced by a stone building in 1020, and the present structure, started about 1080, shows architectural styles of every century up to the present – all in warm pink sandstone, medieval in character and modestly beautiful. Of its many treasures the Mappa Mundi is a unique map of the world drawn about 1300, and the Chained Library is the finest in existence. Hereford has a second chained library, in **All Saints' Church**, whose soaring, slightly crooked spire is a prominent landmark near the city centre. *Open: Mon–Sat, Eas–Oct (cathedral treasury and chained library).*

Left: built in 1490, Wye Bridge at Hereford has been repaired many times and was widened in 1826. A new road bridge to the west now carries through-traffic and provides a fine viewpoint for the older structure with the cathedral beyond

Above: Bulmer's have been making cider in Hereford since 1887, and the Cider Museum tells the story of cider-making from the 17th-century to the mass-production methods introduced in the 1920s

The medieval street pattern, easily explored on foot, lies north of the cathedral, between it and the modern ring road, which loops in a semi-circle, roughly following the line of the medieval walls.

High Town, now traffic-free, represents the commercial and shopping centre, with the attractive, timber-framed **Old House** of 1621, the sole survivor of Butchers' Row, at its eastern end. It is now a museum and the interior is furnished in Jacobean style. Between High Town and the cathedral, Church Street is the most satisfying of Hereford's streets and medieval in character. Broad Street to the west is spaciously Victorian, while the city's Georgian face is shown in St Owen's Street, St Ethelbert Street and Castle Street. Between these and the river the great motte of an early Norman castle is now a public park. *Open: daily (Old House).*

Eighteen groups of almshouses make a special contribution to Hereford's townscape. Aubrey's Almshouses (1630) in Berrington Street are the most picturesque, but **Coningsby's Hospital** (1618) north of the city wall is the most famous, with the unique 14th-century Blackfriars Preaching Cross nearby. Eight museums display a wide range of items, from archaeology and natural history to steam engines and cider. Personalities associated with Hereford include the actor David Garrick, who was born here in 1716, Roger Kemble, born in 1720, and his daughter Sarah (Siddons), who acted here. Nell Gwynne is said to have been born in Hereford in 1650, while Sir Edward Elgar lived here from 1904 to 1912, when he composed some of his greatest works. *Open: Tue–Thu, Sat, Sun, Eas–Sep (Coningsby's Hospital).*

Hereford is at the heart of the Wye Valley, surrounded by gentle hills with pastoral landscapes, orchards, hop-fields and meadows. Charming villages nearby include Eardisland, Pembridge and Weobley, famous for their wealth of black-and-white, timber-framed buildings. Fine houses and gardens abound, many of which are open to the public, and there is a wide variety of places of interest within easy reach of the city. The Wye and its tributaries are famous for their fishing, and walkers have a wide choice of riverside, field and woodland paths.

DON'T MISS

■ The treasury (Hereford Cathedral)

■ The chained libraries in the cathedral and All Saints' Church (Hereford)

■ Three Choirs Festival, every three years in August, 1994, 1997, 2000 (Hereford)

IRONBRIDGE
SHROPSHIRE
■ ON THE A4169, 4 MILES SOUTH OF TELFORD TOWN CENTRE ■

The Ironbridge Gorge was the scene of the remarkable breakthrough which saw Britain become the first industrial nation, soon the workshop of the world. Here in 1709 the Quaker ironmaster, Abraham Darby, pioneered the use of coke instead of charcoal for smelting iron, thus paving the way for the first iron wheels, iron rails, iron cylinders for steam engines, and the first high-pressure steam locomotives. Seventy years later Abraham Darby's grandson cast the world's first iron bridge across the Severn. The small town of Ironbridge developed on the river's north bank and is today a compact place of late Georgian and Victorian brick terraces and other buildings.

Iron foundries sprang up in the area, followed by other industries using local resources. The river became Europe's busiest waterway. But from early this century there was industrial decline. In 1967 the Ironbridge Gorge Museum Trust was formed, derelict areas were cleared, old furnaces excavated and new projects initiated to create a prestigious museum complex located in sites spread over six miles.

The **Museum Visitor Centre** in the Severn Warehouse provides an introduction and includes a superb, detailed model of the Severn Gorge. The **Iron Bridge and Tollhouse** downriver form a dramatic focal point. In Coalbrookdale, the **Musem of Iron** illustrates the history of iron-making and the story of the Coalbrookdale Company. Well worth a visit is the restored **Old Furnace** nearby. Two miles away **Blist's Hill Open-Air Museum**, set in 50 acres (20ha), takes visitors back to a living and working community of the 1890s and needs a half-day visit to be fully appreciated. Back near the river the **Jackfield Tile Museum** and the **Coalport China Museum** show manufacturing techniques and products. A museum 'passport' covers admission to all the sites. *Open: daily.*

KILPECK CHURCH
HEREFORD AND WORCESTER
■ OFF THE A465, 8 MILES (13KM) SOUTH-WEST OF HEREFORD ■

This, the most perfectly preserved small Norman church in England – a simple plan of nave, chancel and apse – is decorated with carvings attributed to the great Hereford school of masons working in Herefordshire and Gloucestershire in the mid-12th century. In particular, the corbel-table beneath the eaves is riotously glorious, an almost comic-strip assemblage of mainly non-Christian features, which so offended Victorians, but, in vividly depicting various sins, were fearful to the medieval mind. In complete contrast, the calm interior has some wonderful carving, particularly on the chancel arch, where figures of saints have faces suggesting serenity and spirituality.

LLANDUDNO
GWYNEDD
■ OFF THE A55 ■

In the mid-19th century Llandudno developed from a small fishing and copper mining settlement into a Victorian seaside resort. Robert Stephenson had brought his railway line along the North Wales coast in the 1840s, by which time sea-bathing had become popular. A Liverpool surveyor, Owen Williams, recognised the potential of flat land behind a sandy bay between two limestone headlands. The local Mostyn family sold land for development on a spacious layout. Broad streets behind the curving promenade were built, with the finest hotels and other residences in an elegant Crescent, and Mostyn Street behind forming the main commercial and shopping centre.

In spite of some expansion southwards, Llandudno retains a pleasantly Victorian individuality with little brashness. **Great Orme** towers above, separating the town's two superb beaches. As well as a road or public footpaths, an Edwardian tramway and a cable railway are alternative ways to its summit. As a designated Country Park and Nature Reserve, with a complex of modern buildings at its summit, it offers nature trails, archaeology, industrial history, all the usual visitor facilities, plus panoramic views. A toll road, the Marine Drive, circuits the foot of Great Orme, passing on the hill's northern slopes the ancient **church of St Tudno**, from which the town derives its name. Above the town, on the lower slopes of the Orme, the **Happy Valley Rock Gardens** have rare plants, shrubs and trees.

■
Below: unveiled by Lloyd George in 1933, this White Rabbit Memorial commemorates Lewis Carroll's many walks along Llandudno's nearby West Shore with Alice Liddell, the inspiration for his children's story Alice in Wonderland
■

LLANGOLLEN
CLWYD
■ ON THE A5, 30 MILES (48KM) NORTH-WEST OF SHREWSBURY ■

This unpretentious, friendly little town by the River Dee is essentially Victorian in appearance and character except in July when the International Eisteddfod brings it a lively, colourful, cosmopolitan atmosphere. The surrounding countryside of lovely hills, with dramatic limestone scenery to the north at Eglwyseg and the charming valley of the Dee, make Llangollen a popular tourist centre, as it has been for two centuries. In 1780, Lady Eleanor Butler and Miss Sarah Ponsonby set up home at **Plas Newydd**, a cottage above the town. They enlarged and 'gothicized' it, and were visited by important public figures of the day, who journeyed by coach along the Holyhead road which passed through Llangollen. The half-timbered house is open to the public. *Open: daily, Apr–Oct.*

Early last century the town became the terminus of the Llangollen branch of the Shropshire Canal, now a favourite leisure waterway, offering easy towpath walking or a **horse-drawn boat trip**. An **exhibition centre** illustrates the heyday of canals in Britain. Nearby, a 3½-mile stretch of the **Vale of Llangollen Railway** has been restored westwards, while above the town the hill-top fortress of **Dinas Bran**, reached by a steep lane, is a famous viewpoint. Of easier access are the **Horseshoe Falls** and the ruins of the Cistercian abbey of **Valle Crucis**, in a deep, narrow valley north-west of Llangollen. Substantial remains of the church, founded in 1201, can be seen and there are some beautifully carved grave slabs. *Open: daily, Jul–Aug; Sat, Sun, Apr–Jun, Sep–Oct (Horse-drawn Boats and Canal Exhibition centre): daily (abbey).*

■
Below: three miles east of Llangollen, Telford's Pontcysyllte Aqueduct is one of the greatest engineering achievements of all time. Completed in 1805, it carries the canal 120ft (37m) above the River Dee in a cast-iron trough 1007ft (307m) long
■

LLECHWEDD SLATE CAVERNS
GWYNEDD
■ BY THE A470, NORTH OF BLAENAU FFESTINIOG ■

Two underground rides take visitors into this time capsule from the Victorian slate miners' world. The miners' tramway passes a series of vast caverns, where tableaux illustrate and guides explain old mining techniques. On the deep mine tour, Britain's steepest inclined passenger railway descends several hundred feet into the lowest accessible levels, where a miner-guide accompanies visitors through more huge caverns, past an underground lake, and the past is again re-created by a colourful sequence of sound-and-light presentations. Back on the surface there are demonstrations of slate-splitting, a craft workship and exhibitions, as well as a small restored miners' village with shops, pub and bank. *Open: daily.*

■
DON'T MISS

■ Llangollen International Musical Eisteddfod, held in early July (**Llangollen**)

LUDLOW
SHROPSHIRE

One of Britain's most beautiful small towns, Ludlow stands on high ground above the River Teme, its nine centuries of history preserved in its buildings and streets. From Norman foundations through the troubled Middle Ages to Tudor prosperity based on wool and cloth, Ludlow became increasingly important as a political and administrative capital, its castle being the seat of the Council of the Marches for 200 years. In Georgian and early Victorian times the town became a fashionable social centre for nobility and gentry of the surrounding countryside. Today its role is that of a market town, with some, mainly light, industries, but it is increasingly important as a service and tourist centre.

Ludlow's huge Norman **castle** was the largest of a chain of castles along the border between England and Wales. A regular pattern of intersecting streets represents an unchanged 12th-century town plan, parts of whose medieval walls still stand, with Broad Gate the only surviving gateway. Broad Street, one of the finest streets in England, has Georgian houses and timber-framed buildings, with the elegant **Butter Cross** at the top. Behind this, and largely hidden in the near view, **St Lawrence's Church**, late 15th-century, is large and light, with fine carvings and a superb view from the churchyard. The **Reader's House** nearby and buildings around the Bull Ring, including **The Feathers**, typify the town's wealth of half-timbering with exuberant carving. Neatly lettered blue plaques mark buildings of particular historic interest and add to the delights of a stroll through Ludlow's streets. *Open: daily, Feb–Nov (castle).*

MALVERN HILLS
HEREFORD AND WORCESTER

Always satisfying to look at, and even more rewarding to be on, the Malvern Hills form a distinctive narrow range 9 miles (14½km) long of mostly common land under the jurisdiction of the Malvern Hills Conservators. This body, established in 1884, follows a policy of keeping the land open and unbuilt on, for the benefit of the public, who appreciate the miles of paths and bridleways. The Worcestershire Beacon at the northern end is the highest point at 1,394ft (425m), and Herefordshire Beacon, at 1,111ft (339m), to the south has an Iron Age hill fort known as British Camp.

William Langland, one of our earliest poets, is said to have dreamed his *Vision of Piers Plowman* on the Malvern Hills, and the composer, Sir Edward Elgar lived in Malvern from 1891 to 1904, when he wrote the *'Enigma' Variations* and *The Dream of Gerontius*. There is little doubt that he derived great inspiration from the hills.

Great Malvern is the largest of six Malvern settlements along the foot of the eastern flanks. Its hilly streets, terraces and buildings reflect Malvern's Victorian development as a spa town based on its spring waters, but Malvern Priory is its prized possession. Rebuilt in the 15th century on the site of a Norman monastic church, its grace and beauty are a counterpoint to the hills that form an immediate backdrop.

MARGAM COUNTRY PARK
WEST GLAMORGAN

■ OFF THE M4 AT EXIT 38, ON THE A48, 8 MILES (13KM) SOUTH-EAST OF NEATH ■

The greatest 16th-century landed estate in Glamorgan has been owned and managed since 1973 by West Glamorgan County Council as an outstanding visitor attraction. The enormous early Victorian mansion, now largely an empty shell, is the hub and houses in its outbuildings a visitor centre, theatre, shop, and other facilities. A large herd of fallow deer graze some of the park's 800 acres (325ha), and there is ample space for walks, boating and fishing lakes, a field study centre, nature reserve, showground and farm trail. The superb 18th-century orangery is used for social functions, and its gardens contain ruins of a 12th-century Cistercian abbey, a Gardener's Museum, a putting green and a maze. *Open: daily, Apr–Sep; Wed–Sun, Oct–Mar.*

MONMOUTH
GWENT

Monmouth is an attractive historic town at the confluence of the Rivers Wye and Usk. At the hub of a network of good roads, with beautiful countryside all round, it has added tourism to its importance as a market centre. Recent excavations in Monmow Street have revealed more of its Roman past. Its easily defended position was recognised by the Normans, and the 13th-century Monmow Gate is the only complete fortified bridge structure in the country.

Agincourt Square is the charming centre of the town, partly cobbled and flanked by 17th- and 18th-century buildings, including coaching inns, which are flower-garlanded during the summer. Radiating streets are fronted by modest houses and shops, mainly with colour-washed fronts. In Castle Street the 17th-century Great Castle House is now headquarters of the Royal Monmouthshire Militia, with the **Castle and Regimental Museum** in the west wing. **Monmouth Museum** in Priory Street now houses the Nelson Collection of items about the admiral's life, while overlooking Monmouth is **The Kymin** (NT), an 800ft (240m) high hill with the late 18th-century **Round House** and **Naval Temple** on it summit – a fine viewpoint. *Open: daily (both museums).*

NORTH WALES QUARRYING MUSEUM
GWYNEDD

■ OFF THE A4086, NEAR LLANBERIS ■

On the edge of Llyn Padarn Country Park this museum occupies the former central workshops of Dinorvic Quarry and reflects the life and labour of the slate industry centred on Llanberis. The workshops, built in 1870, closed in 1969, but much of the original machinery remains intact, including the foundry, smithies, pattern and woodworking shops, and the locomotive shed. A 50ft (15m) diameter water wheel, the main power source for the workshop from 1875 to 1925, is on view, and there are demonstrations of slate splitting and trimming. *Open: daily, Eas–Sep (Cadw).*

PEMBROKE CASTLE
DYFED

■ IN PEMBROKE, BY THE A477 ■

Perched on limestone rock at the western edge of a ridge carrying the Norman-planned town's single street, Pembroke Castle has cliffs on three sides. The present castle, dating from 1189 to 1245, is mainly the creation of the great marcher lord William Marshall and his sons, and is dominated by its circular Great Keep, one of the mightiest in Europe, with 100ft (30m) high walls. Entrance is from the town side by the Barbican Gate, restored in 1885, and the Bygate Tower. Nearby the Henry VII Tower is the supposed birthplace of the founder of the Tudor dynasty. Other towers protect the curtain walls. In the Civil War Pembroke was a Parliamentary stronghold. It later declared for the king, but was besieged by Cromwell for 48 days, when much damage was done. *Open: daily, Mar–Oct; Mon–Sat, Nov–Feb.*

■

CHARLES STEWART ROLLS

The statue of C S Rolls (*below*) in Agincourt Square, Monmouth, is by Sir William Goscombe John. The engineer and aviator was born in 1877 at the nearby estate of The Hendre, a younger son of Lord Llangattock. A keen cyclist, he won a half blue for cycling at Cambridge. He developed an enthusiasm for the newfangled motorcars, raced them and set up his own company to make them. In

1904 he joined another engineer, F H Royce, to found the firm of Rolls-Royce Ltd. The firm went on to make the finest cars in the world, while the daredevil Rolls turned to flying and racing aeroplanes. Tragically, he was killed at the age of 32, in an air crash at Bournemouth in 1910.

■

DON'T MISS

■ The screen walls of the chancel, faced with 1,200 15th-century wall tiles in 90 different patterns

(Malvern Priory, Great Malvern)

PEMBROKESHIRE COAST
DYFED

Britain's only maritime national park, designated in 1952, covers 225 square miles (580 km²) of the sunny south-west corner of Wales. The area embraces long, narrow strips of coastline, hinged at St David's Head and extending north-eastwards to St Dogmaels at the mouth of the Teifi, near Cardigan, and southwards and eastwards to Amroth beyond Tenby. It includes a number of islands, much of the estuary of Milford Haven, the estuarine valleys of the twin Cleddau rivers near Haverfordwest and the moors of the Preseli Hills. It is a varied countryside, patterned by hedged fields, with sparkling streams, clear rivers and wooded valleys. The 180-mile (290km) Pembrokeshire Coast Path, a National Trail, follows the whole length of a spectacular coastline where impressive cliffs, especially in the north and west, alternate with secluded coves and sandy beaches. A coastal road runs too far inland to give more than distant views of the sea, but minor roads lead down to the small villages.

Each of the three faces of the Pembrokeshire peninsula is different. The northern coast, from St David's Head to the Teifi, is dramatic and rugged, with few sandy stretches. The few access roads lead to some little gems, however, such as Abermawr, Abercastle, Porthgain and Abereiddy, while Newport is a tiny town with a Norman castle and a market. Rocky outcrops rise above the plain, prehistoric remains are thick on the ground, particularly at Dinas Head, Strumble Head and the St David's peninsula.

Once the hinge is turned, St Bride's Bay reveals its vast sweeping curve, with Ramsey Island beyond its northern tip and Skomer Island to the south. Solva has a superb, fjord-like harbour, and there are coves at Notton Haven and Little Haven and safe sandy beaches at Newgale, Druidston and Broad Haven. The Marloes peninsula has colourful, sandstone cliffs and fine beaches, while St Ann's Head, guarding the Milford Haven Estuary, shelters some favourite yachting waters near Dale.

Limestone cliffs introduce the south Pembrokeshire coast, with remarkable rock formations near St Govan's Head. Bosherston is most famous for its beautiful lily pools, and Stackpole Quay is one of many places on the coast now safeguarded by

Below: walkers on the Pembrokeshire Coast Path enjoy this westward view as they follow the cliffs above Marloes Sands, which sweep invitingly round towards the small island of Gateholm in the distance

the National Trust. Beyond the popular Freshwater Bay to the east, Manorbier has a 12th-century castle, birthplace in 1146 of the great Welsh traveller and scholar, Giraldus Cambrensis. Skrinkle Haven has sandstone clifs, but limestone returns at Lydstep. Tenby has a superb setting and slightly Italian air, while more sandy beaches to Saundersfoot and beyond ensure that this is the popular holiday part of the Pembrokeshire coast.

Spring comes early to this corner of Wales with its mild climate, and wildlife is rich and varied, especially along the coast with its wild-flowered splendour and the sights and sounds of sea birds and grey seals.

PENRHYN CASTLE
GWYNEDD

■ OFF THE A5, 1 MILE (1½ KM) EAST OF BANGOR ■

HOME FOR FALLEN BUILDINGS
Sir Clough Williams-Ellis died in 1978 at the age of 95, secure in the knowledge that what he called his 'home for fallen buildings' at Portmeirion was an acknowledged success. He rescued its ingredients from all over the place: an 18th-century colonnade from Bristol, the upper half of a Cheshire fireplace, a 17th-century barrel-vaulted ballroom from Emral Hall in Flintshire which he turned into his town hall, and a statue of Venus from Stowe. He also added oddities of his own devising, such as a stone boat to create one of the oddest and most delightful villages in Britain. Sunlight of a summer evening highlights the Mediterranean character of the domed Pantheon (*below*).

Dramatically situated between Snowdonia and the Menai Strait and looking convincingly Norman, this huge structure was built between 1827 and 1847 by the 2nd Lord Penrhyn, probably to symbolise his status as owner of the profitable Bethesda slate quarries. Its picturesque outline suggests real solidarity – details are remarkable – but it remains essentially early Victorian, with profuse ornamentation, an aura of opulence and a rare degree of comfort. Furnishings are appropriately ostentatious, including the great bed of slate made for a visit by Queen Victoria. She preferred something more conventional. Guided tours of the keep and roof may be made by prior arrangement.

Housed in the old stables is Britain's only museum dedicated to industrial locomotives and rolling stock. The **Penrhyn Railway Collection** contains exhibits from the Bethesda quarries, including many steam engines, and a second section houses locomotives from a variety of other industries. There are also model engines and a collection of railway signs. *Open: Wed–Mon, Apr–Oct (NT).*

Above: the great slate bed at Penrhyn Castle may represent a high point of the mason's skill, but although it was made for Queen Victoria's visit, she preferred something more comfortably familiar

PLAS NEWYDD
GWYNEDD

■ ON ANGLESEY, ON THE A4080, 1 MILE (1½ KM) SOUTH-WEST OF LLANFAIR PG ■

It would be difficult to imagine a finer setting for a stately mansion, with the Menai Strait below, and the mountains of Snowdonia across the water. Built around 1800 by James Wyatt and his assistant Joseph Potter for the 1st Marquess of Anglesey, the house is largely in the Gothick style which was then fashionable. Of its many fine rooms the Diningroom is most memorable for its 1930s decorations. Rex Whistler's large murals manage to be imaginative, beautiful and even witty. Among many treasures displayed in the house are the 1st Marquess's boot, ruined trousers and wooden leg – trophies, so to speak, of his cavalry command at Waterloo, when he was shot in the right leg near the battle's end. The house is surrounded by lawns and parkland. *Open: Sun–Fri, Apr–Sep; Fri, Sun, Oct (NT).*

PORTMEIRION
GWYNEDD

■ OFF THE A487, 1 MILE (1½ KM) SOUTH-EAST OF PORTHMADOG ■

Portmeirion proves that in the 20th century picturesque perfection can be planned. Clough Williams-Ellis was a talented if conventional cottage builder. From 1925 onwards he set out to show that a beautiful site could be developed without spoiling it. It took over 40 years to create this eye-catching, highly original, if derivative village. Here architecture raises a smile, gives pleasure, yet is practical. Slender towers and spires harmonise with pastel-coloured cottages (all let as holiday accommodation). Turrets, domes and walls are reflected across the bay against a woodland background, all stunningly theatrical yet gloriously real. It is deliberately Italianate and therefore needs sunlight to reveal its subtleties.

Seventy acres (280ha) of subtropical woodland gardens are famous for their displays of azaleas, rhododendrons and hydrangeas and are at their best in May and June. Miles of paths network the estate and lead down to Whitesands Bay. Hotels, restaurants and shops cater for all tastes in this unique community, and there are picnic areas and a children's playground. *Open: daily.*

DON'T MISS

■ The two-storey hall and main staircase decoration; the figure with six toes on one foot in a stained-glass window of the upstairs chapel (**Penrhyn Castle**)

POWIS CASTLE
POWYS
■ BY THE A483, 1 MILE (1½ KM) SOUTH OF WELSHPOOL ■

Commanding the upper reaches of the Severn Valley and surrounded by oak-rich parkland, Powis was designed to guard the Welsh Marches. Unlike other great 13th-century fortresses it never fell into ruins, so its architectural continuity spans seven centuries, during which successive generations adapted it to meet different needs. From Welsh baronial ownership it was bought by Sir Edward Herbert in 1587, and the family, now Earls of Powis, have lived there ever since.

First remodelled in the late 16th century, the house was extensively altered in the late 17th and late 19th centuries, and the interior, with its sumptuous furniture, tapestries and pictures, represents three centuries of craftsmanship and the fine arts. One of the Herbert heiresses early last century married the son of Clive of India, and he was created Earl of Powis in 1804. Powis Castle now houses a glittering collection of Indian treasures representing a broad spectrum of Indian art from 1680 to 1800.

Powis's hanging gardens – four 200yd (180m) terraces with statuary, balustrades, shrubs and plants above wide lawns – are the only formal gardens in Britain still existing in their late 17th-century form. They are a memorable sight against the red sandstone splendour of the castle. *Open: Wed–Sun, Apr–Jun, Sep–Oct; Tue–Sun, Jul–Aug (NT).*

RAGLAN CASTLE
GWENT
■ OFF THE A40, 7 MILES (11KM) SOUTH-WEST OF MONMOUTH ■

This is the most exotic, and one of the most recent, of Welsh castles, yet it was neither royal nor baronial. Begun about 1435 by the chief steward of the Duke of York's Welsh estates, whose hexagonal Yellow Tower of Gwent is a self-contained fortress, Raglan was added to in a palatial manner in the 1460s by William Herbert, 1st Earl of Pembroke, and gained courtyards, service rooms and machiolated towers. Between 1549 and 1589 the Somersets, Earls of Worcester, built those Elizabethan essentials, a splendid great hall and an elegant Long Gallery. Within another century Raglan suffered under a Civil War siege, was deliberately damaged by Cromwell's men and its days of glory were over; but it continues to stand, proudly handsome, with memorable façades and details. An excellent exhibition illustrates Raglan's history. *Open: daily (Cadw).*

RHONDDA HERITAGE PARK
MID GLAMORGAN
■ ON THE A4058, 2½ MILES (4KM) WEST OF PONTYPRIDD ■

The Rhondda Valley, wooded and peaceful beneath wild moorlands in the early 19th century, became the Black Klondyke in the second half of the century. By the early 1920s about 180,000 people were crammed into this tiny area of a few square miles, a unique, vibrant, close-knit community. Welsh steam-coal supplied power to the world. In 1986 the last coal was brought to the surface.

Today, the Rhondda Heritage Park presents a complete picture of life, work and culture in this famous mining valley, in the pithead buildings of the Lewis Merthyr Colliery. Multi-media presentations with many special effects and tableaux evoke with an almost breathtaking intensity the days of a working pit. *Open: daily.*

RHUDDLAN CASTLE
CLWYD
■ OFF THE A525, ON THE WESTERN EDGE OF RHUDDLAN ■

Another of Edward I's castles in North Wales, Rhuddlan was started in 1277, completed three years later, and was the first for which James of St George – Master James, the future Master of the King's Works – was architect. A new channel for the River Clwyd was dug, and the castle was designed on the concentric plan with two parallel lines of defence. Within today's empty interior would have been a range of workshops, granaries and stables in the outer ward. Nearby is the Twthill, a high, earthen motte of the original Norman castle. *Due to reopen by summer 1993, then open daily (Cadw).*

■

Above: baroque dancing figures of shepherds and shepherdesses, probably by John van Nost around 1675, grace the long balustrade of one of the four formal terraces below the south front of Powis Castle

■

■

Above: the massive, twin-towered west gatehouse of Rhuddlan Castle overlooks the River Clwyd. In 1284, after Llywelyn's war with Edward I, the Great Statute of Wales was issued from Rhuddlan, a settlement for the country that lasted until the 1536 Act of Union

■

ST DAVID'S
DYFED

■ ON THE A487, 16 MILES (26KM) NORTH-WEST OF HAVERFORDWEST ■

St David founded a monastery here in the 6th century, far from the haunts of men. By the Norman Conquest it had become a bishopric, whose prelates in medieval times controlled vast estates in this the largest of four Welsh dioceses and owed allegiance only to the Crown. They built a great palace, and successive bishops over 350 years created the noble cathedral admired today. In the first view of the **cathedral**, on approaching from the village square, all but the top of the tower is hidden. Today's impressive ruins are all that remain of the **Bishop's Palace**. Descending a long flight of steps (known as the 39 Articles) reveals the full splendour of the church in weathered, purplish stone. Inside it is both charming and beautiful, with Romanesque pillars, pointed arcades, later chapels and much fine 15th-century woodwork, particularly the roof in the choir and presbytery where a shrine to St David dates from 1275 and contains a richly decorated casket. *Open: daily (palace, Cadw).*

Villagers claim the cathedral gives city status, making St David's Britain's smallest city, the only one in a national park. The rocky, windswept peninsula has other memorials to the patron saint and his mother, including **St Non's Well**, near the coast path at St Non's Bay.

Whitesands Bay has the best bathing and surfing beach, and the coast path gives exciting views of superb cliffs, secret coves, soaring sea birds and the surge and sweep of restless waves. St David must have loved it.

Above: Substantial ruins of the Bishop's Palace, with St David's Cathedral beyond to the east, make this one of the most satisfying groups of medieval buildings in Britain. The size of the palace is indicative of the power of the bishops

SEVERN VALLEY RAILWAY
SHROPSHIRE AND HEREFORD AND WORCESTER

This country branch line originally ran from Shrewsbury to Hartlebury, near Worcester. Opened in 1862, it was taken over by the Great Western Railway during the 1870s, with a link from Bewdley to Kidderminster added soon after. Most of it closed in 1963, to be reborn through the efforts of enthusiasts of the Severn Valley Railway Society in 1965. Enormous amounts of restoration work enabled re-use of the line in 1970. The Society became a limited company, and by 1984 steam-hauled passenger trains were operating a daily service from May to September, with weekend trains March to October plus a few winter specials, between Kidderminster, Bewdley and Bridgnorth with stops at intermediate stations.

Its route through the lovely Severn Valley makes it a popular tourist attraction, and at busy periods 300 voluntary staff are needed to run it. There is also a growing team of paid staff in administration and maintenance.

Frequently used in location filming of all kinds, the Railway has won many awards for the quality of its restoration work. It houses one of the largest British collections of working steam locomotives, railway coaches and wagons. At Victoria Bridge near Upper Arley, a 200ft (60m) span iron bridge, cast at Coalbrookdale, carries the railway over the Severn. There are riverside paths throughout this stretch of valley, but no accompanying roads. *Open: daily, mid-May–early Oct; Sat, Sun, end-Nov–mid-Dec.*

■

DON'T MISS

■ Rhosson farm, a huge, round Flemish chimney (**St David's**)

■ St Justinian's Chapel, above the lifeboat station (**St David's**)

■ Carn Llidi, a superb viewpoint (two miles north of **St David's**)

SHREWSBURY
SHROPSHIRE

Within a huge horseshoe loop of the River Severn Shrewsbury has been an important town since Norman times, when a **castle** was built to command the approach from the north. Thomas Telford made modifications to the structure in 1790, and it now houses the **Shropshire Regimental Museum**. The street pattern was established in early medieval times and is scarcely changed today, although the shopping focus has shifted slightly from the old Square, High Street and Butcher Row to the traffic-free Pride Hill with modern malls neatly hidden behind earlier frontages. *Open: daily, Eas–Oct; Mon–Sat, Nov–Eas (castle, Regimental Museum).*

Rowley's House is an impressive timber-framed late 16th-century building, of which there are many in the town, and houses a museum of local history and archaeology. An 18th-century house occupied by Clive of India whilst he was mayor is now the **Clive House Museum** and contains outstanding collections of Coalport and Caughley porcelain. Shrewsbury's progress as an administrative, social and fashionable centre is illustrated in its Queen Anne, Georgian and early Victorian houses. The town's charm lies in its narrow, cobbled streets and passages known as 'shuts', with historic names such as Grope Lane, Gullet Passage and Plough Shut. *Open: daily, Eas–mid-Sep; Mon–Sat, mid-Sep–Eas (Rowley's House): Mon–Sat (Clive House Museum).*

Occupying a wide area between town and river, **Quarry Gardens** has been a public open space since medieval times. Impressive floral displays at its centre, the Dingle, were designed by Shrewsbury's horticulturist, Percy Thrower. Charles Darwin, Lord Clive and Sir Philip Sidney are all associated with the town, while the fictitious Brother Cadfael, a medieval monk at **Shrewsbury Abbey**, has brought renewed interest to that lovely, red sandstone church. **St Mary's** and **St Alkmund's** have soaring spires, classical **St Chad's** a circular nave.

Nearby places of interest include, to the east, **Wroxeter Roman Town** and **Haughmond Abbey**, and **Attingham Park**. *Open: daily, Apr–Sep; Tue–Sun, Oct–Mar (Wroxeter, Haughmond, EH): Sat–Wed, BH, mid-Apr– early Sep (Attingham, NT).*

SHROPSHIRE HILLS
SHROPSHIRE

Designated in 1958 as an Area of Outstanding Natural Beauty covering 300 square miles (775km²), the Shropshire Hills embrace wild uplands, moors, valleys and woodlands. Castles, churches, villages and small towns add dimensions of history and humanity to superb landscapes.

The A49 running north–south through the Stretton Valley roughly bisects the area, and the attractive little town of Church Stretton is its obvious centre. To the east are Caer Caradoc, Lawley, the Cardington hills, Wenlock Edge, and the twin Clee Hills rising to over 1,700ft (520m). Westwards is the whaleback of Long Mynd (NT), its steep-sided eastern face broken by narrow valleys called 'batches'. Closer to the Welsh border, the rocky crest of Stiperstones exerts its special magic and holds memories of lead mining. In Shropshire's south-western corner the rounded hills of Clun Forest generate quick streams and rivers. Offa's Dyke marks the boundary of ancient kingdoms and is the line of a National Trail. Iron Age hill forts are thick on the ground. Small ruined castles hint at a troubled medieval past in this Marches land. Larger houses followed in more peaceful times, when prosperity came from sheep – still the commonest living things in these lonely, lovely landscapes.

SPETCHLEY PARK GARDENS
HEREFORD AND WORCESTER

■ ON THE A422 2 MILES (3KM) EAST OF WORCESTER ■

Spetchley is the territory of the historic Berkeley family, and the 30 acres (12ha) of formal gardens here were designed by Rose Berkeley and her sister, the great gardener, Ellen Willmott, late last century. In spring they are a riot of flowers. Plants, shrubs and trees maintain the interest, especially in the adjoining park which was laid out in the mid-17th century and is grazed by herds of red and fallow deer. The whole place is a plantsman's delight, with views across the lake to the dignified Regency house (not open). *Open: Sun–Fri, late Mar–Sep.*

STOKESAY CASTLE
SHROPSHIRE

■ ON THE A49, 8 MILES (13KM) NORTH OF LUDLOW ■

Although called a castle, Stokesay is in fact a fortified 13th-century manor house, the oldest and best-preserved example of its kind in England. Begun about 1240 by a member of the Say family, it was bought 40 years later by the wealthy wool merchant Lawrence of Ludlow. Building operations continued from 1285 until 1305, although Lawrence died in 1294. His descendants lived at Stokesay for almost three centuries, after which it passed

Above: in the wide valley of the River Onny and set against gentle, wooded hills, Stokesay Castle and its neat little gatehouse nowadays present a peaceful scene. In medieval days the Welsh Marches was a troubled region

through other owners' hands. It is now cared for by English Heritage.

At its heart is the great hall, famous for its roof structure, its central hearth and the original 13th-century wooden staircase leading to upper floors in the north tower, which overlooks the moat. The polygonal south tower has three storeys, a look-out turret and twin cylindrical chimneys – a rare 13th-century survival. Another special feature is the solar with 17th-century panelling. The charming timber-framed gatehouse replaced an earlier stone one in late Elizabethan times. *Open: Wed–Mon, Mar–Oct (EH).*

SYGUN COPPER MINE
GWYNEDD

■ ON THE A498 1 MILE (1½km) NORTH-EAST OF BEDDGELERT ■

Copper mining was widespread in North Wales, particularly on Anglesey and in Snowdonia, where it was centred on Beddgelert. Sygun Mine prospered last century and since 1986 has revealed its secrets to the general public. Guided tours of the underground workings, on foot, take visitors along winding tunnels and into large chambers, where veins of ore can be seen as well as magnificent stalactites and stalagmites. The tour lasts about 40 minutes, a hard-hat job, and involves climbing and descending a number of stairways. Special lighting and sound effects help to provide a fascinating glimpse into the working conditions of Victorian miners. *Open: daily.*

■

DON'T MISS

■ The Devil's Chair on Stiperstones (**Shropshire Hills**)

■ The Solar, a private, family room, with its elaborate Flemish overmantel and two peepholes in the north wall (**Stokesay Castle**)

SNOWDONIA
GWYNEDD

The Snowdonia National Park covers 845 square miles (2,190km²) in North Wales, extending almost 50 miles (80km) from Conwy in the north to Machynlleth in the south, and from the coast inland to Betws-y-coed and Bala. Of all Britain's national parks Snowdonia has the greatest variety of landscape, embracing mountains, moorlands, lakes and the coast, with large areas of planted coniferous forest. Blaenau Ffestiniog near the centre and several coastal towns are not in the National Park area.

SNOWDON AND THE NORTH
The Snowdon area forms only a part of the National Park. At 3,560ft (1,085m) Snowdon is unchallenged as the highest mountain in England and Wales. Its elemental character is matched by the Carneddau, a range to the north only 100ft (30m) lower, with Tryfan and the Glyders in-between. Their harsh crags are beloved by climbers and were used as a training ground by members of the first successful Everest expedition, whose names are on the ceiling of the Pen-y-Gwryd Hotel between Capel Curig and Beddgelert. These last two are the best climbing centres for mountains of the Snowdon massif. Three roads running north-west from them to Bangor and Caernarfon give motorists

splendid views of the peaks, particularly from Llanberis Pass (A4086) which runs down to Llyn Padarn, and the A5 from Capel Curig along Telford's superbly engineered route of early last century, past Llyn Ogwen and the Nant Ffrancon Pass to Bethesda.

DOLGELLAU AND THE SOUTH
At the head of the beautiful Mawddach estuary, Dolgellau is the largest town and a popular centre for the central and southern parts of the National Park. To the south lies the bulk of Cader Idris, whose modest 2,927ft (892m) belies the dramatic force of its ridges, crags and summit views, but it is not too demanding to climb.

Good scenic roads radiate from Dolgellau, south to Machynlleth, east to Mallwyd, north-east to Bala, west to the coast, north to Ffestiniog. Between the coast and the A470 the Rhinogs are a strange, remote area where no roads penetrate the heather moors and their skyline of rocky summits. Almost as remote are the Aran and Arenig ranges between Dolgellau and Bala, although a few tempting minor roads cross these lovely hills, where the bleating of sheep and bird calls emphasise the solitude. Lonely, white-washed farms are far more common than colourful cagoules in the southern half of the National Park.

■

Below: morning sunlight glances across the mighty Snowdon range, with the shapely peaks of Y Lliwedd, Snowdon and Crib Goch reflected in the tranquil waters of Llyn Mymbyr near Capel Curig, with the A4086 on the right

■

Left: the dramatic rock scenery of Snowdonia's mountains shown here on the Glyders above Cwm Idwal, looking northwards down to Llyn Idwal, with Nant Ffrancon Pass beyond carrying the A5 to Bethesda

WILDLIFE OF THE PARK

Snowdonia's wide range of habitats is reflected by the existence of 16 National Nature Reserves. These include mountain habitats such as Cwm Idwal, Cwm Glas Crafnant, and parts of Snowdon, Cader Idris and the Rhinogs, as well as areas of broad-leaved woodland like Coed Camlyn and Coeddydd Maentrog in the Vale of Ffestiniog. There are two coastal reserves at Morfa Dyffryn and Morfa Harlech.

Below: the Snowdon Mountain Railway, opened in 1896, is unique in Britain, being mainly steam-hauled with rack-and-pinion traction.

Engines always push their coaches (one per engine) uphill, reversing this to act as a brake on the way down. The journey takes about an hour

Acidic soil cover on the uplands yields a vegetation which consists of rough grassland, heather and peat bogs. However, among high cliffs and crags occasional limey soils encourage an 'arctic alpine' flora, including various saxifrages, holly-fern, mountain avens, moss campion, and the very rare Snowdon lily in its only British site. These high crags also provide nest sites for buzzards, ravens and a few peregrine falcons. Among mammals, pine martins are the rarest, but polecats are relatively common on bare hillsides and in the woodlands below.

OPENING UP THE FORESTS

With 12 per cent of the land area, the Forestry Commission is the largest single landowner in the Snowdonia National Park.

The two main forests are Coed-y-Brenin, north of Dolgellau near the heart of the National Park, and Gwydyr, around Betws-y-coed. Since the 1970s the Commission has succeeded in opening up its forests for public recreational use, with car parks, visitor centres, picnic sites, woodland trails and waymarked paths. These help to absorb people in a controlled way, and introduce them to favourite beauty spots such as the Swallow Falls, and the Gwydyr Walk above Llanrwyst.

SLATE QUARRIES AND NARROW-GAUGE RAILWAYS

Although mineral extraction in Snowdonia dates back to Roman and medieval times, farming has always been the main occupation. Slate quarrying developed from the late 18th century onwards, peaking about 1900. The inter-war years saw a rapid decline and only a handful of slate quarries now operate. Old ones at **Ffestiniog**, **Llanberis** and **Harlech** have become industrial museums, as has the **Sygun Copper Mine**. *Open: Mon–Fri, Eas–Oct; Sun–Fri, mid-Jul–Aug (Gloddfa Ganol Slate Mine, Blaenau Ffestiniog): daily (Welsh Slate Museum, Llanberis): daily, Eas–mid-Oct (Hen Llanfair Slate Caverns, Harlech). See separate entries for Llechwedd Slate Caverns and Sygun Copper Mine.*

Narrow-gauge railways were built to link quarries to the ports, and many of the 'Great Little Trains of Wales' now carry passengers instead of slate, along lines at **Tal-y-llyn**, **Bala**, **Llanberis** and **Ffestiniog** (see separate entry), but the **Snowdon Mountain Railway** was always intended to provide the easiest way up the mountain. *Open: daily, Apr–Oct (Tal-y-llyn Railway): Tue–Thu, Sat, Sun, late Mar-Sep (Bala Lake Railway): Sun–Fri, Eas–Oct (Llanberis Lake Railway): daily, mid-Mar–Oct (Snowdon Mountain Railway).*

Above: Llanberis Pass offers motorists travelling between Capel Curig and Llanberis a spectacular journey. Climbers know it as a popular start, from Pen-y-Pass, for a variety of routes up Snowdon, whose range is to the left in this view

TENBY
DYFED
■ ON THE A478, SOUTH PEMBROKESHIRE COAST ■

Right: sparse ruins of a 13th-century castle on a rocky headland overlook Tenby's sheltered harbour and good beaches. High tide and late afternoon sunlight on colour-washed houses complete the picture of this popular little resort

■

From a small fishing centre Tenby developed in Regency and Victorian times as a fashionable resort. Medieval walls with round towers enclose narrow streets and lanes centred on Tudor Square. On Quay Hill, the **Tudor Merchant's House** is a late 15th-century house in the traditional style of south-west Wales, and **St Mary's**, Wales's largest parish church, reflects the town's 15th-century prosperity. Caldey Island, owned and farmed by Cistercian monks, is a short boat trip away. *Open: Sun–Fri, Apr–Oct (Merchant's house, NT).*

TINTERN ABBEY
GWENT
■ ON THE A466, 6 MILES (9½KM) NORTH OF CHEPSTOW ■

Tourists have been visiting Tintern for over 200 years. It inspired one of Wordsworth's greatest poems. Turner and other artists have painted it. Surrounded by wooded hills of the lovely Wye Valley, the ruins of the late 13th-century church are awesomely beautiful. The abbey was founded by Cistercian monks in 1131 and survived until the Dissolution of 1536. *Open: daily (Cadw).*

TREDEGAR HOUSE
GWENT
■ OFF THE M4 EXIT 28, AND THE A48, 2 MILES (3KM) WEST OF NEWPORT ■

Set in fine parkland, the ancestral home of the Morgans, later Lords of Tredegar, is essentially a late 17th-century mansion of warm red brick with stone dressings. The palatial interior is even richer than the exterior, with all main rooms panelled from floor to ceiling. There is sumptuous plasterwork, lavish decoration and splendid carving. *Open: Wed–Sun, Eas–Sep.*

TRETOWER COURT AND CASTLE
POWYS
■ OFF THE A40 AND THE A479, 3 MILES (5KM) NORTH-WEST OF CRICKHOWELL ■

The round keep of the 13th-century castle announces its presence first, from behind farm buildings. Nearby, to the south-east standsTretower Court, the fortified manor house that replaced it as a domestic residence. Work started on the Court around 1300. From about 1450 Sir Roger Vaughan and his son Sir Thomas created the exquisite range of buildings round a square courtyard. These were re-modelled in the 1630s and new windows were inserted in the west range. No changes have been made since then, and Tretower Court today is one of the loveliest late medieval houses in Wales. A 'medieval' garden is being created to the south-west of the courtyard. *Open: daily (Cadw).*

■
DON'T MISS

■ Worcester Woods Country Park, on the eastern edge of the city, A422 (**Worcester**)

FOR CHILDREN

■ Oakwood Adventure and Leisure Park (**Tenby**)

■ Mr Morgan's Adventure and Play Farm (**Tredegar House**)

■ Pets' Corner (**Weston Park**)

WESTON PARK
SHROPSHIRE
■ ON THE A5, 8 MILES (13KM) EAST OF TELFORD ■

Below: the Dyson Perrins Museum has the finest and most comprehensive collection of Worcester porcelain. From its beginnings in the early 18th century, the Worcester Porcelain Factory nearby has specialised in tableware and ornamental vases. Examples are on show from services made for the Royal Family and European aristocracy

Situated in nearly 1,000 acres (405ha) of mature parkland and the home of successive Earls of Bradford, this elegant, brick Renaissance house was built in 1671 by Lady Wilbraham. Since 1961 an extensive series of improvements and decorations, revealing many Victorian alterations, has restored it much nearer to its 17th-century original. Its contents include superb furniture, Gobelin tapestries and an outstanding collection of paintings including 17th- and 18th-century portraits in a series of beautiful rooms.

The park includes many architectural features and woodland walks, as well as fallow deer and rare sheep breeds. *Open: Sat, Sun, BH, mid-Apr–mid-Jun, Sep; Tue–Thu, Sat, Sun, mid-Jun–Jul, daily, Aug.*

WORCESTER
HEREFORD AND WORCESTER

Much of Worcester's historic character has been ravaged by insensitive modern development. Nevertheless, isolated examples survive of medieval and Georgian buildings to hint at its former glory. The **cathedral** takes pride of place, and the early Norman crypt of St Wulfstan's original structure is the largest in England. Elsewhere, the building shows work from all periods, and the circular Chapter House, dating from 1120, is especially notable. There is also a memorial window to Sir Edward Elgar and a statue of him outside. To the south College Green leads by Edgar Tower to Severn Street, where the **Dyson Perrins Museum** has a superb collection of Worcester's famous porcelain. At Diglis Basin the Worcester and Birmingham Canal joins the River Severn, and a busy marina occupies the old wharf area. *Open: Mon–Sat (museum).*

In High Street the flamboyantly baroque **Guildhall**, with its statues of Charles I and II and Queen Anne, looks down on busy modern shops. Arcades connect High Street to the Shambles, but the few half-timbered survivals from the city's past have to be sought, mainly in New Street and Friar Street with its antique shops. **Nash House** in New Street is a three-storeyed 16th-century town house. **The Greyfriars** was built a century earlier on the site of a Franciscan friary and has a charming garden, while the **Tudor House** is a museum of household utensils and agricultural implements. **The Commandery**, by the canal, has a wonderful hammerbeam roof and was the royalist headquarters of the Battle of Worcester in 1651. The accessible banks of the Severn offer quieter views of Worcester's skyline, whose most unusual symbol is the **Glover's Needle**, the former spire of St Andrew's Church, but best of all views is that across the county cricket ground. *Open: Wed, Thu, BH Mon, Apr–Oct (Greyfriars, NT): Mon–Wed, Fri, Sat (Tudor House): daily (Commandery).*

Worcester is the start of the Elgar Trail and **Elgar's Birthplace Museum** is three miles away at Lower Broadheath. *Open: Thu–Tue, all year.*

WITH A DASH

Apart from its china, Worcester's best-known product is Worcester Sauce. It was first made by a Mr Lea and a Mr Perrins, who were quietly running a chemist's shop in Broad Street when an official named Sandys, returning to England from governing Bengal, brought them an Indian recipe to make up for him. They made some extra for themselves, but when they tasted it, it was revolting. They left it for a while and tasted it again before throwing it away. It had matured meantime and was delicious. They soon gave up the chemist's shop and opened a successful sauce factory, where the secret of the recipe has been guarded for more than 150 years.

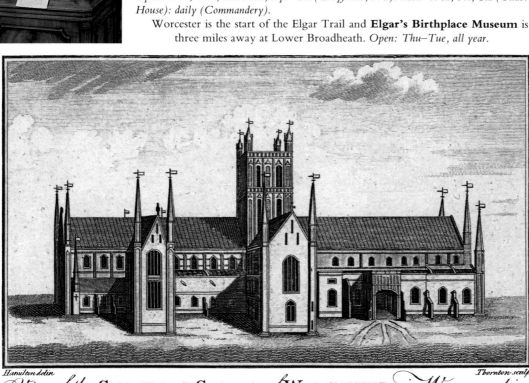

Hamilton delin.   *Thornton sculp.*
View of the CATHEDRAL CHURCH of WORCESTER, in Worcestershire.
Published by Alexr Hogg Nº 16, Paternoster Row.

THE NORTH COUNTRY

Any area of the country that contains Malham Cove and Gaping Gill, Durham Cathedral, the Settle–Carlisle railway line and Hadrian's Wall is not short of spectacular and historic things to see. Some of Britain's most satisfying scenery can be enjoyed in the North, from the snow-capped peaks of the Lake District across to the hump-backed Cheviots in Northumberland, where the distant bleating of sheep drifts gently over the wind-stirred turf. Further south lie the bare heights of the Forest of Bowland, the green valleys and drystone walls of the Yorkshire Dales and a tossing ocean of purple heather on the North York Moors. There is a splendour of cliff scenery on the Yorkshire coast, while the North Sea beats on the sandy Northumbrian beaches where Lindisfarne was the cradle of Christianity in the North.

Centuries before the monks settled on Lindisfarne, the Romans had raised Hadrian's Wall across the country from sea to sea. All these centuries later, it keeps its power to impress. Castles stand as stern reminders of another time when the peace was kept by main force: Bamburgh, Brougham, Carlisle, Conisbrough, Middleham, Raby, Richmond, Warkworth. Ruined abbeys bear gentler witness to spiritual values in a harsh world – Fountains, Rievaulx, Jervaulx, Byland, Kirkstall and Roche. The crypts of Saxon churches survive at Ripon and Hexham. Stone crosses dot the North York Moors as waymarkers and symbols of divine protection.

A list of the North's famous people and places could start with Wordsworth and Ruskin in the Lake District and proceed by way of the Brontës at Haworth in the direction of the Sitwells in Scarborough and the Beatles in Liverpool. Industrial archaeology is naturally one of this area's strengths, explorable in museums in Manchester and Sheffield, Leeds and Bradford. Antiquated machinery has clattered back into action with gusto at Quarry Bank Mill and the Stott Park Bobbin Mill, the giant wheel is turning again at Killhope on the Durham hills and another in Trencherfield Mill at Wigan Pier. There, and in the North of England Open Air Museum and the York Castle Museum, whole regiments of bygones are on parade.

As well as a treasure of industry there is a glory of art in the magnificent collections of the Walker Art Gallery in Liverpool, the City Art Gallery in Manchester, the Lady Lever Art Gallery, the Oriental Museum in Durham and the Bowes Museum at Barnard Castle. From the vast baroque grandeur of Castle Howard by way of elegant Harewood House and graceful Newby Hall you can reach the Edwardian richness of Sledmere House and Cragside House, while at Little Moreton Hall and Rufford Old Hall black-and-white half-timbering runs wonderful riot.

Special collections include rude seaside postcards in Holmfirth, glass in St Helens, steam yachts at Windermere. You can nervously follow the Dracula Trail in Whitby, watch the falcons fly at Leighton Hall, eye the wild white cattle at Chillingham Castle, smell the toffee in Halifax, hear the skirl of the pipes in Morpeth or the curfew horn blow at Ripon. A touch of the unusual adds spice to the day.

∎

0   10   20   30   40   50 miles
0   20   40   60   80 kms

Berwick-upon-Tweed
Lindisfarne
Bamburgh
Chillingham Castle
Alnwick
Northumberland
Cragside House
Warkworth Castle
NORTHUMBERLAND
National
Wallington
Morpeth Bagpipe Museum
Ashington
Hexham
Newcastle upon Tyne
Seaton Delaval Hall
Tynemouth
South Shields
TYNE AND WEAR
Hadrian's Wall
Carlisle
North of England Open Air Museum
Consett
Sunderland
Killhope Wheel
Durham
DURHAM
Bishop Auckland
Cockermouth
Penrith
Brougham Castle
Raby Castle
CLEVELAND
Workington
Lake
Keswick
Stockton-on-Tees
Middlesbrough
Whitby
CUMBRIA
Brough
Barnard Castle
Darlington
Dove Cottage
Rydal Mount
Scotch Corner
North York Moors National Park
District
Richmond
Muncaster Castle
Brantwood
Windermere
Bolton Castle
Rievaulx Abbey
Scarborough
Kendal
Jervaulx Abbey
NORTH
Thirsk
Flamingo Land
Stott Park Bobbin Mill
Sizergh Castle
Levens Hall
Yorkshire Dales
Lightwater Valley Theme Park
YORKSHIRE
Castle Howard
Holker Hall
Kirkby Lonsdale
Leighton Hall
National
Ripon
Newby Hall
Sewerby Hall
Barrow-in-Furness
Steamtown Railway Museum
Park
Fountains Abbey
Sledmere House
Bridlington
Morecambe
Lancaster
Skipton
York
HUMBERSIDE
Fleetwood
Forest of Bowland
Harrogate
Beverley
Burton Constable Hall
LANCASHIRE
Clitheroe
Wetherby
Kingston upon Hull
Blackpool
Haworth
Harewood House
Preston
Burnley
Bradford
Leeds
Lotherton Hall
Selby
Blackburn
WEST YORKSHIRE
Goole
Rufford Old Hall
Halifax
Wakefield
Carlton Towers
Southport
Camelot Theme Park
Rochdale
Huddersfield
Nostell Priory
Scunthorpe
Skelmersdale
Wigan Pier
Bolton
Oldham
Holmfirth
Barnsley
Grimsby
GREATER MANCHESTER
Manchester
SOUTH YORKSHIRE
Doncaster
MERSEYSIDE
St Helens
Pilkington Glass Museum
Conisbrough Castle
Bootle
Stockport
Rotherham
Birkenhead
Liverpool
Warrington
Sheffield
Roche Abbey
Lady Lever Art Gallery
Runcorn
Catalyst Chemical Museum
Tatton Park
Quarry Bank Mill
Lyme Park
Ness Gardens
Boat Museum
Macclesfield Silk Museum
Chester
Jodrell Bank
CHESHIRE
Little Moreton Hall
Nantwich

ALNWICK
NORTHUMBERLAND

■ ON THE A1 19 MILES (30KM) NORTH OF MORPETH ■

The Duke of Northumberland owns possibly the grimmest front door in England at **Alnwick Castle**. The lion badge of the Percy family surmounts the 15th-century gateway and on the menacing battlements life-sized figures of warriors stand ready to resist assault. The castle, from which generations of Percys kept such peace as was possible on the Border, was restored in romantic style by Anthony Salvin in the 19th century. Inside are magnificent 19th-century state rooms with paintings by Titian, Tintoretto, Claude and Turner, and a celebrated collection of Meissen china. The castle dominates the pleasant old town of Alnwick, with its medieval gatehouse and lively market. *Open: daily, Jun–Aug; Sun–Fri, May, Sep (castle).*

BAMBURGH
NORTHUMBERLAND

■ ON THE B3140 5 MILES (8KM) EAST OF BELFORD ■

The grey Norman keep of **Bamburgh Castle** stands dramatically on a crag above the sea. Long a royal fortress, it was restored in the 19th century by Lord Armstrong, the armaments magnate. The village church is dedicated to St Aidan, who died at Bamburgh. In the churchyard is the grave of Grace Darling, the local lifeboat heroine, and the **Grace Darling Museum** is nearby. Offshore are the Farne Islands, now a bird sanctuary. *Open: daily, Eas–Oct (castle): daily, Apr–Oct (museum).*

BARNARD CASTLE
CO. DURHAM

■ ON THE A67 16 MILES (26KM) WEST OF DARLINGTON ■

This bleak but nonetheless attractive town on the River Tees is home to one of the finest art galleries in the country. The **Bowes Museum** houses the collection of the 19th-century coal magnate John Bowes and his wife in a specially built imitation French château. Besides paintings by El Greco and Goya, there are marvellous French decorative art and treasures of porcelain, glass, jewellery and furniture. Ruined **Barnard Castle** glowers out over the Tees. *Open: daily (museum): daily (castle, EH).*

BERWICK-UPON-TWEED
NORTHUMBERLAND

■ ON THE A1 29 MILES (47KM) NORTH OF ALNWICK ■

A hotly disputed town for centuries, standing at the mouth of the River Tweed on the border between England and Scotland, Berwick is guarded by the oldest barracks in Britain and some of the finest town walls. Not much is left of the town's medieval fortifications, but early in Elizabeth I's reign in the 16th century formidable walls were built to protect

■

Below: looking across the beach to the stern bulk of Bamburgh Castle, crouched on its high rock. The fortress is the legendary 'Joyous Garde', stronghold of Sir Lancelot of the Lake, the noblest champion of the Round Table in the stories of King Arthur and his heroic knights

■

■

GRACE DARLING

This popular heroine of Victorian England was born at Bamburgh in 1815. Her father was keeper of the Longstone Light in the Farne Islands. One wild night in 1838, when Grace was 22, the steamer *Forfarshire* struck a rock in the early hours of the morning. She sank, drowning 43 of those on board, but nine struggled on to the rock. Grace and her father rowed out to them, took five safely back to the lighthouse and then rowed back to the rock a second time to rescue the other four. The exploit caused a sensation, but poor Grace only lived four more years to enjoy it. The lifeboat and other mementoes can be seen in the museum at Bamburgh.

■

Berwick against artillery fire. **Ravensdowne Barracks**, possibly designed by Vanbrugh and completed in 1721, is today home to the **Museum of the King's Own Scottish Borderers** and the **town museum**. Berwick also boasts notable bridges over the Tweed, including the 17th-century Old Bridge and Stephenson's railway bridge of 1850. *Open: daily, Eas–Sep; Tue–Sun, Oct–Eas (barracks, EH): daily (regimental museum): daily, Eas–Sep; Tue–Sun, Oct–Eas (town museum).*

BEVERLEY
HUMBERSIDE

■ ON THE A164 8 MILES (13KM) NORTH OF HULL ■

A landmark for miles around, the twin towers of **Beverley Minster** rise above the flat landscape of the old East Riding of Yorkshire. The church is one of the loveliest in Britain, big enough to be a cathedral and a treasure of medieval architecture and art. The beautiful Percy tomb, the misericords and the Saxon Frith stool are among the highlights. The church of St Mary is also unmissable, with a wealth of stone carvings including a rabbit which is thought to have been the model for the White Rabbit in *Alice in Wonderland*. The **Museum of Army Transport** is much livelier than it may sound, with a legion of land, sea and air vehicles to explore. There are also local bygones in the **Art Gallery and Museum**. *Open: daily (Army Transport): Mon–Tues (Art Gallery and Museum).*

■

Above: Beverley Minster was raised above the tomb of St John of Beverley, who died at the monastery here early in the 8th century. The church was rebuilt in soaring Gothic in the 13th and 14th centuries, the twin towers were added in the 15th century and the interior was handsomely refurnished in the 18th century

■

BLACKPOOL
LANCASHIRE

When the awesome illuminations are switched on in September, around 400,000 light bulbs blaze and sparkle along Blackpool promenade to bring the nights to glittering life. The archetypal North

■

Right: the most recognisable seafront landmark in Britain, Blackpool Tower rises to a height of 518ft (158m). Inspired by the Eiffel Tower in Paris, it was put up in the 1890s and for a good many years it was the tallest construction in the country. At the bottom is the famous Tower Ballroom, renowned for its magnificent Wurlitzer organ and recently restored

■

Country seaside resort has been packing the visitors in since the 1840s, when the arrival of the railways made it possible for the people of the teeming northern industrial towns to go to the seaside. Here they would find 7 miles (11km) of sandy beach, three piers, a bristling army of landladies and a host of good-humoured attractions. These nowadays include an 'indoor seaside' in case of rain and countless discos, shows and amusement centres. On the central pier is Europe's biggest **Ferris wheel**, 180ft (55m) high. The seafront trams are a delight, while quieter attractions include **Stanley Park**, the **Grundy Art Gallery** and **Blackpool Zoo**. *Open: Mon–Sat (art gallery): daily (zoo).*

THE BOAT MUSEUM
CHESHIRE

■ IN ELLESMERE PORT, OFF THE M53 7 MILES (11KM) NORTH OF CHESTER ■

Boat trips and canal art are among the attractions of the Boat Museum, which is imprisoned in one of the dreariest towns in England, at the point where the Shropshire Union Canal joins the Manchester Ship Canal. There is a collection of narrowboats, steam engines, warehouses, workshops, dockhands' cottages and material on life along the canal. *Open: daily, Apr–Sep; Sat–Thu, Oct–Mar.*

■

DON'T MISS

■ The Meissen china services (Alnwick Castle)

■ Grace Darling's lifeboat (Bamburgh)

■ French luxury and extravagance (Bowes Museum, Barnard Castle)

■ The Percy tomb carvings (Beverley Minster)

FOR CHILDREN

■ The silver swan automaton swallowing a fish (Bowes Museum, Barnard Castle)

■ The 'white rabbit' carving (Beverley Minster)

■ The flight simulator (Museum of Army Transport, Beverley)

■ The narrowboat trip (Boat Museum, Ellesmere Port)

BOLTON CASTLE
NORTH YORKSHIRE

■ AT CASTLE BOLTON, ON A MINOR ROAD 5 MILES (8KM) WEST OF LEYBURN ■

Mary, Queen of Scots was held prisoner in the 1560s in this isolated Wensleydale fastness, described at the time as 'very strong, very fair and very stately'. Still one of the best preserved medieval fortresses in England, it has recently been refurbished inside, with armour, tapestries and historical tableaux. *Open: daily, Mar–Oct.*

BRADFORD
WEST YORKSHIRE

Once the archetypal Yorkshire wool town, Bradford has preserved much of its character despite the efforts of its post-war planners. The city hall's 200ft (60m) Italian-style clocktower is a symbol of its rivalry with Leeds. One of the big Victorian warehouses is home to a collection of contemporary art guaranteed to raise eyebrows in **Treadwell's Art Mill**. The city's other attractions are more decorous. The **National Museum of Photography, Film and Television (NMPFT)** has hands-on exhibits which attract children in hordes and shows white-knuckle films on a screen three storeys high. The intriguing **Colour Museum** investigates our perception and use of colours, there is good Victorian and Edwardian art in the purpose-built **Cartwright Hall Art Gallery** and the **Industrial Museum** includes a 'working horse' section. Imperially magnificent Manningham Mill still has a wool shop. The dead have the best view of Bradford – from the Victorian **Undercliffe Cemetery**. *Open: daily (art mill): Tue–Sun, BH Mon (museums and art gallery): daily (cemetery).*

BRANTWOOD
CUMBRIA

■ ON A MINOR ROAD 2½ MILES (4KM) SOUTH-EAST OF CONISTON ■

Purple prose is inadequate to describe the situation of John Ruskin's house on a hillside, looking across Coniston Water to the peak called the Old Man of Coniston. The views are an enchantment. The critic and philosopher enjoyed them from 1872 until his death in 1900 and the house contains many mementoes of Ruskin and his friends. *Open: daily, mid-Mar–mid-Nov; Wed–Sun, mid-Nov–mid-Mar.*

BROUGHAM CASTLE
CUMBRIA

■ OFF THE A66 1½ MILES (2.4KM) EAST OF PENRITH ■

In an idyllic spot by the River Eamont, the ruined fortress once guarded the main route between England and Scotland in the north-west. Built in the 12th century and enlarged by its Clifford lords, it was

■

JOHN RUSKIN

One of the most eminent of eminent Victorians, John Ruskin was born in London in 1819. The idolised son of a rich wine merchant, who was the agent for Pedro Domecq sherry, he never needed to work for a living and devoted his considerable talents to art criticism and later to social reform. He was in his fifties and a famous figure when he bought Brantwood and began to enlarge it, first adding the turret on the south-west corner of the house with its Elysian view of Coniston Water and the fells, and then laying out paths in the woods behind the house, where there is now a nature walk. Many of his own watercolours and drawings can be seen, together with his boat and other personal relics.

■

■

Right: time-worn and mellow now, the ruins of the Clifford stronghold of Brougham Castle stand by the bridge over the quiet River Eamont. The castle was built to block any Scots invading force that passed Carlisle and came south down the Eden Valley. A Roman fort stood at the same site centuries before

■

■

Above: an important collection of heraldic stained glass is one of the points of interest at Bolling Hall, on the south-eastern outskirts of Bradford, along with a ghost room and many items of Yorkshire life over the centuries. The house goes back to the 15th century and the Georgian wing was remodelled by John Carr of York

■

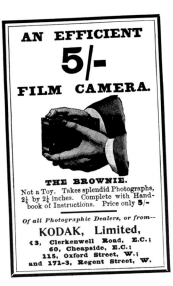
■

SAY CHEESE

A Kodak advertisement of 1900
(above) is part of the Kodak
Museum, which is included in the
National Museum of Photography,
Film and Television at Bradford.
Opened in 1983, one of the
Museum's principal themes is the
way in which photography, which
was one of the marvels of the age
when it was first invented in the
1830s and 1840s, has developed to
the point where in Britain more
than a billion photographs are
taken each year. Exhibits show the
early cameras of the pioneering
days when those who wanted their
pictures taken had to stand rigidly
still for uncomfortable lengths of
time, hence the characteristic
stuffed look of the period: a far cry
from today's instant 'snapshots'.

■

■

Right: Bulky and menacing,
Carlisle Castle has a long and grim
history as the main English bastion
against the Scots in the north-
west. Edward I used it as a base for
his attempt to conquer Scotland
and later the Lord Wardens of the
West March had their headquarters
here

■

restored by the redoubtable Lady Anne Clifford, who died here in 1676. About
half a mile (0.8km) to the east along the A66 is the Countess's Pillar, an unusual
monument with family crests and sundials which she erected 20 years before.
Open: daily, Eas–Sep; Tue–Sun, Oct–Mar (EH).

BURTON CONSTABLE HALL
HUMBERSIDE
■ OFF THE B1238 7 MILES (11KM) NORTH-EAST OF HULL ■

The stately Tudor house was built by the
Constable family in the 16th century. It was remodelled in the 18th century by
Cuthbert Constable with advice from 'Capability' Brown, who also redesigned
the parkland. Cuthbert's son William was a scientist and Fellow of the Royal
Society, and there is a collection of his scientific equipment, as well as family
portraits, Chippendale furniture and carriages. *Open: BH; Sun, Jun, Jul; Sun–
Thur, late Jul–Aug; check with local tourist information centres.*

CAMELOT THEME PARK
LANCASHIRE
■ OFF THE M6 (BETWEEN JUNCTIONS 27 AND 28) AT CHARNOCK RICHARD ■

Drawing more than half a million visitors
a year, the park is based on the magic world of the Athurian legends. It includes a
roller-coaster that rises to 100ft (30m) and then hurls itself headlong into the Tower
of Terror, and other white-knuckle rides as well as jousting and live entertainment,
falconry displays and Merlin's magic show. *Open: daily, May–Aug; check with local
tourist information centres for other opening times.*

CARLISLE
CUMBRIA

Scotch Street runs out of Carlisle market-
place to the north and English Street to the south in the city which was for centuries
the principal fortress town between England and Scotland in the North-West.
There were periods when the Scots held Carlisle and many occasions when they
attacked it. Ironically, it may have been the Scots who built the stern stone keep of
Carlisle Castle. The castle was later enlarged and strengthened on many occasions.
In some of the keep's rooms are wall carvings by prisoners whiling away their
captivity. The stronghold is also home to the Border Regiment Museum. *Open:
daily (castle, EH, and museum).*
Earlier, Carlisle was the main Roman base at the western end of Hadrian's Wall,
and the **Tullie House Museum** has an excellent Roman collection and much
material on local history, presented in almost alarmingly lively style. **Carlisle
Cathedral**, built of the local crumbly red stone, was almost collapsing when
restored in the 1850s. Don't miss the wooden Brougham Triptych altarpiece. *Open:
daily (museum).*

■

DON'T MISS

■ The colour tests (**Colour
Museum, Bradford**)
■ The lake views (**Brantwood**)
■ 18th-century scientific
instruments (**Burton Contable Hall**)
■ Prisoner's carvings (**Carlisle
Castle**)
FOR CHILDREN
■ White-knuckle films (**NMPFT
Bradford**)
■ Make your own TV show
(**NMPFT, Bradford**)
■ Rides and thrills (**Camelot
Theme Park**)

CARLTON TOWERS
NORTH YORKSHIRE
■ OFF THE A1041 6 MILES (10KM) WEST OF GOOLE ■

The strange black clocktower of this wonderfully eccentric mansion can be seen rising hauntingly above the trees and hedges for miles around. The house never reached the immense size planned for it – the money ran out – but is remarkable enough as it is. It was remodelled in the 1870s for the 9th Lord Beaumont, a rich Roman Catholic peer who traced his descent from the last Christian king of Jerusalem. His architect was Edward Welby Pugin and the older house, of the 17th and 18th centuries, was transformed with battlements, turrets, gargoyles and heraldic devices. Inside, a set of colossal rooms was decorated by John Francis Bentley, the architect of Westminster Cathedral in London, in a splendour of marble and gold, bronze and ormolu, marquetry and plush. The high point is the Venetian drawingroom, glittering in golden magnificence. Fine panelling, pictures, tiles by William de Morgan and gorgeous chandeliers complete the effect. The house now belongs to the Duke of Norfolk. *Open: Thu, Sun, BH, May–Sep.*

CASTLE HOWARD
NORTH YORKSHIRE
■ OFF THE A64, 6 MILES (10KM) WEST OF MALTON ■

The vast domed bulk of Castle Howard was one of the 'heavy loads' which Sir John Vanbrugh laid upon the earth. If possible, approach from the north by the minor roads from Malton or Slingsby, to get the magical view across the Great Lake. Castle Howard became a television star in its own right as the setting for many scenes in *Brideshead Revisited*. It was built for the 3rd Earl of Carlisle, designed in sumptuous baroque style by Vanbrugh and Nicholas Hawksmoor, and was still unfinished when Vanbrugh died in 1726. The interiors are appropriately magnificent, with the main hall, the centrepiece of the building, rising 70ft (21m) high in an ornate splendour of Corinthian pillars, soaring arches, murals, massive marble chimneypieces, statues and beautiful ironwork. Elsewhere are treasures of furniture, porcelain, paintings and Burne-Jones stained glass, as well as a notable costume collection.

The house is placed in a romantically beautiful landscape. The main entrance is through Vanbrugh's huge gatehouse and past an obelisk 100ft (30m) high. The south front faces on to formal gardens and a spectacular fountain. The Temple of the Four Winds is designed by Vanbrugh and the noble Mausoleum is by Hawksmoor. *Open: daily Mar–Oct; check with local tourist information centres.*

CATALYST CHEMICAL MUSEUM
CHESHIRE
■ IN WIDNES, ON THE A561 7 MILES (11KM) WEST OF WARRINGTON ■

The new museum is being developed in a building, dating from 1860, on Spike Island. The displays focus on the chemical industry's influence on all our lives, with items from salt and paint tins to toiletries, medicines, fungicides and plastics. There are fragrance identifying tests and reminiscences of the past can be heard on telephones. Marvellous views over the Mersey and the industrial scene are a bonus. *Open: Tue–Sun, BH.*

CHESTER
CHESHIRE

The best way to see Chester is to walk around it on top of the city wall, which has been strengthened and kept in repair ever since Roman times. The town grew up round a major Roman military base, the headquarters of the 20th Legion, and the cruciform Roman street plan underlies the modern city. The military base stood on a ridge beside the River Dee, which has since changed its course. The Roman harbour was where the racecourse now is, on the open space called the Roodee. The remains of the Roman amphitheatre are outside the wall, near Newgate.

Chester remained an important town and military base all through the medieval period, whose principal legacy to the city is **the Rows**. These are the two-decker shopping streets in the centre, which provide a pleasantly sheltered window-shopping walk along covered wooden galleries at the first-floor level, with more shops on the ground floor beneath. The arrangement beats today's pedestrian shopping precincts hollow.

The city is also famous for its glittering display of half-timbered buildings, all spick and span in gleaming black and white. A few of these are genuinely old, dating from Tudor times, but most are Victorian creations and none the less enjoyable for that. In Watergate Street, for instance, God's Providence House and Bishop Lloyd's House, both originally of 17th-century date, were splendidly rebuilt and restored in the 19th century. For a dramatic example of Victorian skill and confidence, look at the east side of St Werburgh Street, designed by the local architect John Douglas.

The man behind the Victorian rebuilding of Chester was the 1st Duke of Westminster, head of the Grosvenor family, which has played a leading role in the city's affairs for centuries. Their old town house, the Falcon, is in Lower Bridge Street, not far from the spectacular Bear and Billet Inn, which has more than 1,600 panes of glass in its leaded windows.

Another largely Victorian creation is **Chester Cathedral**, which goes back to Norman times, but was crumbling away to ruin by the 1860s and 1870s, when it was drastically restored by Sir George Gilbert Scott. Inside is wonderful 14th-century woodwork in the carved choir stalls, misericords and bench ends. Outside, an unusual addition is a 1970s bell tower, designed by George Pace.

Another local architect, Thomas Meakin Lockwood, designed the **Grosvenor Museum**, in Grosvenor Street, in the 1880s. It has a particularly good Roman collection, with tombstones and carved stones, whose inscriptions bring the legionaries and their families vividly to life. There is much other material on local history, as well as an art gallery, displays of Chester silver and an entire Georgian house. The history of the Cheshire Regiment is admirably displayed in the **Cheshire Military Museum** and just to the north of the city, at Upton, is **Chester Zoo**.

Open: daily (museums and zoo).

■

Right: the Rows are one of Chester's great delights, with shops on two storeys – some on the ground floor and others opening off the gallery which runs along the floor above. This feature, which goes back ultimately to medieval times, allows shoppers to stroll pleasantly along, safe from both traffic and rain. The scene here is in Bridge Street

■

■

Above: the town crier in full traditional rig stands in front of one of the spectacular examples of black-and-white half-timbered architecture for which Chester is well known. Most of it dates from Victorian days. The city's history goes far back to Roman times, however, and the modern focus of the town is at the central point of the Roman miltary base here

■

CHILLINGHAM CASTLE
NORTHUMBERLAND
■ OFF THE A697 5 MILES (8KM) EAST OF WOOLER ■

Set in attractive grounds, the castle was for generations the home of the Earls of Tankerville. Furniture, armour and tapestries can be admired in the house and in the **parish church** is the impressive 15th-century tomb of Sir Ralph Gray and his wife.

Chillingham is better known, however, for the wild white cattle which have lived in the park since early medieval times. Trapped in the park when the wall was built in the 13th century and never crossbred outside the herd, they are the nearest thing to prehistoric oxen to be seen today. White with black muzzles, reddish ears and wicked horns, they are ruled by their king bull. Binoculars are recommended for a close view. At the far side of the park, there are rewarding views from the hill fort of **Ros Castle**, which is owned by the National Trust. *Open: Wed–Mon, May–Sep (castle): Wed–Mon, Apr–Oct (park).*

CONISBROUGH CASTLE
SOUTH YORKSHIRE
■ OFF THE A630 4 MILES (6KM) SOUTH-WEST OF DONCASTER ■

Surrounded by a grim landscape of coal mining and heavy industry between Doncaster and Rotherham, the massive white Norman keep of Conisbrough is the oldest circular keep in England and possibly the finest of its kind in the country. Rearing up 90ft (27m) above the River Don, it was built in the 1180s, with the curtain walls and their round towers added in the following century. The castle is featured in Sir Walter Scott's novel, *Ivanhoe. Open: daily (EH).*

CRAGSIDE HOUSE
NORTHUMBERLAND
■ ON THE B6341 OUTSIDE ROTHBURY ■

Born in Newcastle in 1810, the 1st Lord Armstrong was an inventor and businessman of genius who made a fortune in the armaments trade (he was the founder of Armstrong Vickers). In 1869 he engaged the architect Richard Norman Shaw to transform his country house at Rothbury into what was described at the time as 'the palace of a modern magician'. Shaw's exterior is a picturesque 'Old English' creation in stone and half-timbering, with tall chimneys and spacious bay windows. The interiors combine ostentation, comfort and the products of Armstrong's engineering expertise. Cragside was the first house in the world lit by water-powered electricity. Internal telephones were another of its owner's innovations and both the main lift and the kitchen spit were hydraulically driven.

The house stands on a steep hillside in 900 acres (365ha) of grounds which Armstrong planned and beautified, with trees and shrubs by the million, artificial lakes and miles of underground pipes for his hydro-electric system. A scenic drive winds its way through the grounds. In the Visitor Centre is the Armstrong Energy Centre.

A recent acquisition by the National Trust is Cragside Garden, with the notable Orchard House, ferneries, rose loggia and Italian garden. *Open: Tue–Sun, BH Mon, Apr–Oct (house): daily, Apr–Oct; Sat, Sun, Nov–Mar (park) (NT).*

Above: the drawingroom of Cragside House is on a monumental scale; it has a curved glass roof and a 10-ton marble-lined inglenook, designed to soak up the heat of peat fires. Apart from the house and the park, visitors can also enjoy the Armstrong Energy Centre (contact local tourist information centres for opening times)

DOVE COTTAGE
CUMBRIA
■ AT GRASMERE, ON THE A591 3 MILES (5KM) NORTH-WEST OF AMBLESIDE ■

William Wordsworth wrote some of his best-loved poetry while living at Dove Cottage, which is kept today as it was in his time (between 1799 and 1808). The poet lived here with his wife, sister and children, until it became too cramped. The Wordsworth Museum in a former barn has manuscripts and mementoes of the great man. After the Wordsworths left the cottage, Thomas De Quincey, author of the *Confessions of an English Opium Eater*, was the tenant for more than 20 years. The Wordsworths are buried in Grasmere churchyard. *Open: daily, mid-Feb–mid-Jan.*

THE POWER CIRCUIT

William George Armstrong was among other things a hydraulic engineer of formidable brilliance. An exhibition at the Visitor Centre at Cragside illustrates his achievements. Starting from there, an enjoyable walk called 'the Power Circuit' takes the visitor through the grounds on the trail of Armstrong's ingenious hydro-electric system. Tumbleton Lake was made by damming the Debdon Burn and, at the foot of the dam, the Ram House is the pump house where a hydraulic engine, now restored, drove a pair of plunger pumps. The walk goes on to Armstrong's fine steel bridge, made in the 1870s and one of the earliest of its kind in the world. Passing the pinetum, there's a stop valve which controls the water supply to the greenhouses, where fruit trees growing in huge pots were turned by hydraulic power so that the whole tree got the sun. Further on is the power house which, until 1945, supplied electricity to the main house. A cable enclosed in a wooden conduit above ground carried the current to the main house, the stables, the laundry and the tenants' cottages.

DON'T MISS

■ The wild white cattle (**Chillingham Castle**)

■ The Turkish bath and opulent interiors (**Cragside House**)

■ St Cuthbert's coffin and relics (**Durham Cathedral**)

■ The bed made for a 19th-century Chinese opium dealer (**Oriental Museum, Durham**)

DURHAM
CO. DURHAM

Oneof England's most spectacular sights is the titanic Norman bulk of **Durham Cathedral** standing on top of its high cliff above a horseshoe bend of the River Wear. There are particularly fine views of it from the railway station, Framwelgate Bridge and the riverside walk.

In the year 995 the coffin containing the remains of St Cuthbert, which had been removed from Lindisfarne for fear of Viking raids more than 100 years before, came at last to the end of its peregrinations in the north and was interred on top of the rock at Durham. A small church was built over it, which was replaced after the Norman Conquest by the present cathedral with its massive Romanesque pillars. The towers were added later in the Middle Ages.

Attempts were made to build a lady chapel to the Virgin Mary at the east end, not far from St Cuthbert's shrine, but the stones kept falling down. It was decided that the saint must dislike women, so a black line was drawn across the floor of the church at the west end and women were not allowed to go further in. The line can still be seen. Also of special interest are the tomb of the Venerable Bede, the miners' memorial and the 17th-century woodwork in the choir. In the treasury are the fragments of St Cuthbert's coffin as well as the finest of the cathedral's vestments and plate.

Until the 1830s the prince-bishops of Durham, who were great potentates in the North, lived in the Norman **castle**, close to the cathedral. Largely rebuilt in the 18th and 19th centuries, it is now part of Durham University. The university's attractive 18-acre (7ha) **botanic garden** is also rewarding, and a 'must' for any visitor to the city is the **Oriental Museum**, where row upon row of fabulous treasures from India, China and Japan inhabit a specially constructed gallery. Among them is one of the world's finest collections of Chinese jade, as well as numerous Buddhas, metalwork and lacquerware, and antiquities from ancient Egypt and Palestine. *Open: daily, Apr–Sep; Mon, Wed, Sat, Oct–Mar (castle): daily (botanic garden): daily (Oriental Museum).*

The other museum of exceptional interest in the city is the **Durham Light Infantry Museum and Arts Centre**, with a most effectively displayed collection of weapons, uniforms, medals and objects related to the history of one of Britain's most famous regiments. *Open: Tue–Sat, BH Mon.*

■

Bottom: the cathedral, which towers up in majesty above the River Wear, is generally regarded as the finest example of Norman architecture in the country. The building on the river is the old fulling mill

■

Below: the famous bronze door-knocker was used by those claiming sanctuary at Durham Cathedral: this is a replica of the 12th-century original now in the cathedral treasury

■

■

Below: an imaginary portrait of St Cuthbert in a medieval wall-painting at Durham. Cuthbert was the most admired and revered saint of the north of England and Durham Cathedral was built over his grave. The pectoral cross and portable altar from his coffin are among the cathedral's treasures

■

FLAMINGO LAND
NORTH YORKSHIRE
■ OFF THE A169 3 MILES (5KM) SOUTH OF PICKERING ■

One of Yorkshire's most popular visitor attractions, the zoo and 'family funpark' at Flamingo Land offers rides, slides, shows and exotic animals. In getting on for 400 acres (160ha) there are elephants, polar bears, tigers, monkeys and baboons, crocodiles and alligators, as well as performing chimps, dolphins and sealions. There are also roller-coasters and white-knuckle rides with names like the 'Corkscrew' and the 'Flying Carpet', and undercover amusements in case of rain. *Open: daily, Eas–Sep; Sat, Sun, Oct.*

FOREST OF BOWLAND
LANCASHIRE

There is no longer any forest in the Forest of Bowland; the ranks of trees which once sheltered deer in this former royal hunting ground disappeared long ago. All the same, this Area of Outstanding Natural Beauty is still one of the wildest and least accessible districts in the north. Walkers can explore the high, rolling moors and deep, secluded valleys, called 'cloughs'. For drivers a single scenic road goes through the heart of the area from Lancaster to Dunsop Bridge. The **Beacon Fell Country Park** in the south-west, near Preston, organises guided walks in Bowland in the summertime.

FOUNTAINS ABBEY
AND STUDLEY ROYAL
NORTH YORKSHIRE
■ OFF THE B6265 2 MILES (3KM) WEST OF RIPON ■

Two attractions in one bring together the most famous of Yorkshire's ruined abbeys and one of the most satisfying landscape gardens in England. The combination is no accident. The Aislabie family who created the Studley Royal gardens in the 18th century, bought Fountains Abbey to make the romantic ruins their principal eye-catcher.

The **abbey** was founded in the 1130s on the bank of the River Skell, in what was then a desolate wilderness. The Cistercian monks tamed the wilderness and turned Fountains into the richest of their English houses, the owner of vast flocks of profitable sheep. The abbey buildings, constructed over the next 400 years, fully reflect its wealth and today there are substantial remains of the church and the buildings where the monks lived, ate, slept and worked, until the foundation was closed down at the Reformation. Nearby is **Fountains Hall**, built in the 17th century with stone from the crumbling abbey. An entrancing walk leads along the Skell into the landscape of **Studley Royal Gardens**, sumptuously equipped with artificial lakes, classical temples and vantage points – as well as a 19th-century **church** by William Burges – in a beautiful Arcadian harmony of elegance and due proportion. *Open: daily (abbey, hall, gardens, NT: church, NT, EH).*

Right: a Ferris wheel called the Starship Enterprise is one of more than 50 rides in Flamingo Land's large-scale family adventure playground. More than 1,000 animals on show in the zoo range in size from two Indian elephants at one end of the scale to tiny weaver birds at the other

Below: silent now under the blue sky lie the ruins of Fountains Abbey, where generations of Cistercian monks prayed and toiled. Besides the abbey church, visitors can explore the dormitories, the infirmaries for the sick and the refectories where the monks and lay brothers ate their meals. Apart from the kitchens, the warming room is the only room in the whole monastery that was heated

■

DON'T MISS

■ The high fells (**Bowland**)

■ The 'surprise view' of **Fountains Abbey** from the gardens (**Studley Royal**)

■ The surviving stretches of fortification (**Hadrian's Wall**)

FOR CHILDREN

■ Rides, slides and animals (**Flamingo Land**)

■ The Roman wall reconstruction (**Vindolanda Fort, Hadrian's Wall**)

HADRIAN'S WALL
NORTHUMBERLAND (AND CUMBRIA)

Even after 19 centuries of the relentless depredations of time, weather and mankind, the wall remains the most impressive legacy of Roman rule in Britain. For much of its active life the Wall was the northernmost frontier of the Roman Empire and it ran originally right across England from the North Sea to the Solway Firth. Roughly 75 miles (120km) long – 80 Roman miles – standing perhaps 15ft (4.5m) high and varying between 8 and 10ft (2.5 and 3m) thick, it contained something like a million cubic yards (750,000m³) of stone, and an idea of its original awesome proportions can be gained by looking at the modern reconstruction at *Vindolanda*. Much of the wall has disappeared over the centuries, but the central part of it, swooping over crags in dramatic scenery, is an abiding testimony to the power and energy that built it. For motorists, the best stretches can be seen along the B6318. English Heritage has charge of most of the sites and museums, including the **military base at Corbridge** and, going westwards, **Chesters Fort and Museum**, the **Temple of Mithras** at Carrawburgh and **Vindolanda Fort**. English Heritage and the National Trust jointly run **Housesteads Roman Fort**. *Open: daily (all, EH; Housesteads, EH and NT).*

HALIFAX
WEST YORKSHIRE

■ ON THE A58 7 MILES (11KM) WEST OF BRADFORD ■

Both toffee and cat's eyes (for roads) came from Halifax, but the town's prosperity in its palmy days was based on the cloth trade. The handsome **Piece Hall** was built in the 1770s for merchants to buy the local weavers' 'pieces', or products. Splendidly restored two centuries later, it is now home to shops, a market and an art gallery. Close by, in the **Calderdale Industrial Museum** you can see the textile machinery and sniff the odour of boiling toffee. **Bankfield Museum and Art Gallery**, strong on military art and history, contains the museum of the Duke of Wellington's Regiment and the **Shibden Hall Folk Museum of West Yorkshire** has a good collection. *Open: Tues–Sat, BH Mon (Calderdale/Bankfield museums): daily, Mar–Nov; Sun, Feb (Shibden Hall).*

■

Below: Hadrian's Wall, rising and swooping over the Northumberland fells on its way from Cuddy's Crag to Housesteads Crag. The wall was constructed by the Roman army with extraordinary skill and speed on the orders of the Emperor Hadrian, who visited Britain in AD122, as a barrier against the tribes to the north.

■

■

A THIN TOWN

Life for the 10,000 or more soldiers who garrisoned Hadrian's Wall must have been largely monotonous, and bleak in the cold and wet of Northumbrian winters. The garrison was made up not from Roman legionaries, but auxiliary troops, mainly German and Celts from France, and from Britain itself. Regiments which stayed on the wall for generations settled in and made themselves at home. At Housesteads Fort there was a civilised bath-house and latrines flushed with running water, with long-handled sponges doing duty for toilet paper. Civilian settlements grew up, where there were inns and home comforts to compensate for years of tedium. In *Puck of Pook's Hill* Rudyard Kipling called Hadrian's Wall 'a thin town eighty miles long .

■

HAREWOOD HOUSE
WEST YORKSHIRE

■ ON THE A61 8 MILES (13KM) NORTH OF LEEDS ■

The home of the Lascelles family (Earls of Harewood) is one of the noblest houses in England. Designed by John Carr of York and Robert Adam in the mid-18th century and enlarged by Sir Charles Barry in the 1840s, it rejoices in superbly elegant Adam interiors, sumptuous plasterwork and ceilings, Chippendale furniture, fine paintings and porcelain. There are many memories of the Princess Royal, daughter of King George V and Queen Mary, and wife of the 6th Earl. The grounds were landscaped by 'Capability' Brown and there is a huge walk-through aviary and tropical houses alive with the birds and plants of a rain forest. *Open: daily, Eas–Oct.*

HARROGATE
NORTH YORKSHIRE

■ ON THE A61 15 MILES (24KM) NORTH OF LEEDS ■

Once the North's leading spa, Harrogate is known for its gracious atmosphere, tree-lined streets, smart shops, green open spaces and colourful flower gardens. The original (and pungently odorous) medical sulphur spring was discovered in 1571 and is now inside the **Royal Pump Room Museum**, where those courageous enough can still taste the water. In the western outskirts, the impressive **Harlow Carr Botanical Gardens** include the trial grounds of the Northern Horticultural Society. *Open: daily (museum and gardens).*

HAWORTH
WEST YORKSHIRE

■ ON THE A629 2 MILES (3KM) SOUTH-WEST OF KEIGHLEY ■

Crowded by tourists and literary pilgrims, this small and unpreposessing town high up in the moors outside Bradford is visited for its associations with the Brontë sisters. They grew up in the parsonage, now the **Brontë Parsonage Museum**, quite a sizeable 17th-century house which is much as it was in their day. Mementoes of the gifted and tragic family include Charlotte's wedding bonnet, Emily's writing desk and the sofa in the dining room on which, it is believed, Emily died. Copies of family portraits include the one of Anne, Emily and Charlotte by their ne'er-do-well brother Branwell. Charlotte died in the main bedroom in 1855. The house is fascinating and remarkably atmospheric, though so uncomfortably crowded with sightseers. Memorials to the family are in the parish church which, apart from the tower, has been completely rebuilt since

■

Left: the grim gritstone village of Haworth developed as a weaving centre before the Industrial Revolution, which passed it by. It still has the cobbled streets which originally gave horses' hooves a better purchase on the steep slopes. In the Brontës' time, in the 1840s, the average age of death in the village was 26 and more than 40 per cent of the children died before they reached the age of six. Today Haworth flourishes as a tourist honeypot

■

their time. *Open: daily, early Feb–late Jan (museum).*

Walks in the surrounding moorland follow in the sisters' footsteps to places such as the ruined farmhouse of Top Withens, possibly the original 'Wuthering Heights'. There is a 9-mile (14km) Brontë Way footpath from Haworth to Wycoller Country Park which passes this and other Brontë sites. Haworth is also the headquarters of the **Keighley and Worth Valley Railway**, which runs steam and diesel-hauled trains on 5 miles (8km) of line between Keighley and Oxenhope through charming local stations. *Open: Sat, Sun, BH, all year; daily, Jul–Aug.*

HEXHAM
NORTHUMBERLAND

■ OFF THE A69 20 MILES (32KM) WEST OF NEWCASTLE ■

Ensconced on the bank of the River Tyne, south of Hadrian's Wall, Hexham survived the attentions of marauding armies and Border raiders for many centuries. It still has an embattled air. **Hexham Abbey** stands where a monastery was founded by St Wilfrid in the 7th century. It was repeatedly sacked by the Vikings, but the crypt of the original church remains largely unaltered below the medieval priory church, with its Victorian additions and Edwardian nave. Things to look out for inside include the dashing Roman tombstone of Flavinus, the standard-bearer, the Saxon bishop's seat called the Frith Stool, the dance of death panels and the worn stairs used by the sleepy canons dutifully making their way down into the church for night-time services. In the town the turbulent past is recalled in the **Border History Museum**. *Open: daily, Spring BH–Sep; Mon–Sat, Eas–Spring BH and Oct; Mon, Tue, Sat, Feb–Eas and Nov.*

HOLKER HALL
CUMBRIA

■ ON THE B5278 OUTSIDE CARK-IN-CARTMEL ■

Once the favourite home of the 7th Duke of Devonshire, the house (pronounced 'Hooker') blends opulent Victorian comfort with delicious views of the gardens, the deer park and Morecambe Bay. Largely rebuilt after a fire in 1871, it has splendid paintings, furniture and panelling, and a warmly 'lived-in' atmosphere. A motor museum, a craft and countryside museum, a baby-animal farm, an exhibition of kitchens, garden walks, balloon rides and other events all go to make a pleasurable family day out. *Open: Sun–Fri, Eas–Oct.*

"DO YOU KEEP STATIONERY, MISS?"
"NO, I ER···WRIGGLE A BIT!"

HOLMFIRTH
WEST YORKSHIRE

■ ON THE A635 6 MILES (10KM) SOUTH OF HUDDERSFIELD ■

This pleasant, homely textile town on the River Holme, set in gorgeous Pennine countryside, has become a tourist magnet as the setting for the *Last of the Summer Wine* television series. Fans may be surprised to see how different some of the familiar locations on the screen look in real life. The town centre is by the bridge over the river, and markers and plaques show the remarkable heights to which the Holme has sometimes flooded. Narrow alleys, known here as 'ginnels', climb up the steep hillside to rows of weavers' gritstone cottages. The **Holmfirth Postcard Museum** has a nostalgic and rib-tickling display of postcards made by the local firm of Bamforth & Co. *Open: daily.*

■

*Above: towering topiary in the
formal gardens of Holker Hall. The
grounds were laid out on the
advice of Sir Joseph Paxton, head
gardener to the 6th Duke of
Devonshire, and included one of
the first monkey-puzzle trees in
England, grown from seeds
brought back from Chille in 1844*

■

HULL
HUMBERSIDE

Still a flourishing port on the Humber, Hull (officially Kingston upon Hull) is a far more entertaining place to visit than is often realised. The old docks are being rescued from decay and the town's whaling and trawling past is brought vividly to life in the **Town Docks Museum**. The singing of the leviathans of the deep echoes hauntingly through the whaling galleries while you wince at the vicious implements used to butcher them. One of the best collections of scrimshaw, or art on whalebone, is on display here. *Open: daily.*

The **Ferens Art Gallery**'s striking collection is strong in marine paintings by the local school of artists as well as modern British paintings and sculpture. The **University of Hull Art Collection** specialises in British art from 1890 to 1940. The 16th-century **Old Grammar School** is being developed as a museum of local life. William Wilberforce, the anti-slavery campaigner, was born in 1759, in **Wilberforce House**, now a museum to him containing material on the horrors of the slave trade. The tall column of the Wilberforce Monument is nearby. The **Hull and East Riding Museum** has exceptionally good archaeology displays and the old **Spurn Lightship** can be inspected in the Hull Marina. *Open: daily (Ferens Art Gallery): Mon–Fri during term time (University Art Collection): daily (school museum, Wilberforce House and East Riding Museum): daily, Eas–Oct; Wed–Sun, Nov–Mar (lightship).*

JERVAULX ABBEY
NORTH YORKSHIRE
■ ON THE A6108 5 MILES (8KM) SOUTH-EAST OF LEYBURN ■

The name is pronounced 'Jervo' and this Cistercian monastery was founded in the 12th century. The romantically crumbling ruins stand in an idyllic setting above the bank of the River Ure and include the remains of the church, chapter house and kitchen. According to tradition, this is where Wensleydale cheese was first made. *Open: daily.*

JODRELL BANK
CHESHIRE
■ ON THE A535 3 MILES (5KM) NORTH-EAST OF HOLMES CHAPEL ■

Amidst the gentle Cheshire countryside the University of Manchester's observatory looks as if it has landed from another planet. Its giant Lovell Radio Telescope is as big as the dome of St Paul's Cathedral. Beneath it, the Science Centre explains the technicalities and the planetarium takes visitors on 'a whistle-stop tour of the galaxy'. Back on the ground, there is a beautiful 35-acre (14ha) arboretum to explore. *Open: daily, Eas–Oct;Sat, Sun, Nov–Mar.*

■

Below: storm clouds build up over the giant radio telescope at Jodrell Bank. The vast dish is painted white to keep it cool by reflecting as much of the sun's heat as possible. Radio astronomy works by detecting and analysing radio emissions from the sun, the planets, galaxies, pulsars and quasars

■

■

'The moot point', Herman Melville wrote in *Moby Dick*, 'is whether Leviathan can long endure so wide a chase and so remorselessly a havoc; whether he must not at least be exterminated from the waters …' The armoury of harpoons, blubber hooks and flensing knives in the Town Docks Museum in Hull testifies to both the cruelty and the fierce excitement of whaling in the days when six-man crews in 28ft (9m) boats dwarfed by their prey hurled a barbed harpoon to stick in its flesh. Attached to the harpoon was a long rope and the whale would run until exhausted, dragging the boat with it, until it surfaced to be killed with a long lance. The invention of the harpoon gun in the 19th century made the chase even deadlier; the 'remorseless havoc' has still not been ended.

■

KENDAL
CUMBRIA

■ ON THE A6 20 MILES (32KM) NORTH OF LANCASTER ■

The old grey town on the River Kent is a good base for visiting the southern Lake District and its speciality, Kendal mint cake, is good for mountaineers. The parish church is Cumbria's largest. The famous fell-walker Alfred Wainwright once ran **Kendal Museum**. **Abbot Hall Art Gallery** shows off English paintings and furniture in a Georgian mansion attributed to John Carr of York. Across the yard, the **Abbot Hall Museum of Lakeland Life and Industry** has a section on Arthur Ransome. *Open: daily (all).*

KILLHOPE WHEEL LEAD MINING CENTRE
CO. DURHAM

■ ON THE A689 8 MILES (13KM) EAST OF ALSTON ■

High up in Weardale in the North Pennines, the great 18-ton wheel, 33ft (10m) in diameter, that powered the crushing mill here is turning again. The painstakingly restored site gives a vivid insight into the life and working conditions of lead miners in the 1870s, with the miners' living and sleeping quarters, the smithy and stables, the mine shop and office. Visitors can go panning for lead and work some of the machinery, and there is a woodland trail through the old workings. *Open: daily, Eas–Oct; Sun, Nov–Mar.*

LADY LEVER ART GALLERY
MERSEYSIDE

■ AT PORT SUNLIGHT, OFF THE A41 3 MILES (5KM) SOUTH-EAST OF BIRKENHEAD ■

Ravishing Pre-Raphaelite paintings and Wedgwood pottery greet the visitor to this beautiful purpose-built gallery, opened in 1922, as well as French sculpture, Chinese porcelain and English furniture. The gallery was founded by the 1st Lord Leverhulme, the soap king – he made his money by manufacturing detergents. The garden village he built for his employees here is well worth exploring, starting from the **Port Sunlight Heritage Centre**. *Open: daily (gallery): daily, Eas–Oct; Mon–Fri, Nov–Mar; (heritage centre).*

■
DON'T MISS

■ The whaling galleries (Town Docks Museum, Hull)

■ Roman mosaics (Hull and East Riding Museum, Hull)

■ The tranquil ruins (Jervaulx Abbey)

■ Pre-Raphaelite art (Lady Lever Art Gallery)

FOR CHILDREN

■ The whistle-stop tour of the galaxy (Jodrell Bank)

■ Panning for lead (Killhope Wheel Lead Mining Centre)

THE LAKE DISTRICT
CUMBRIA

Below: the Lake District's enchantment is captured in this view of Derwent Water, with the leaves of autumn gleaming bronze against the snowy panorama of the distant fells. This lake is often rated as the most attractive of them all

The Lake District is quite a small area, but crammed into it is the finest mountain scenery in England. The mountains are not particularly high in cold figures, but they look tremendously impressive because the scale and proportion of the landscape is so exactly right. The highest of them is Scafell Pike, whose summit at 3,210ft (978m) is the highest spot in England. Other notable peaks include Scafell itself, Helvellyn rearing up above Ullswater, Skiddaw looming in the north above Bassenthwaite Lake, and the splendid barrier of the Langdale Pikes towering above the fertile green valley of Great Langdale. Altogether there are more than 60 summits above 2,500ft (762m).

SHIMMERING LAKES

At the foot of the mountains are the lakes themselves, which were scooped out by Ice Age glaciers and are mostly called 'waters' or 'meres'. Beautiful, island-studded Derwent Water is widely regarded as the loveliest of them all and from its southern shore the valley of Borrowdale leads up to the heights of Great Gable and Scafell Pike. Buttermere and Grasmere are also especially entrancing. Wast Water, the deepest lake in England, hemmed in by grim mountains and scree slopes, is often rated as the most sombre of the lakes, and long and snaky Ullswater the most spectacular. Steamers cruise on Ullswater in the season and the National Trust's restored Victorian steam yacht *Gondola* puffs opulently on the 5-mile (8km) length of Coniston Water. *Open: daily, Eas–Oct (weather permitting, NT).*

Much the busiest lake is Windermere, which is also the biggest at $10\frac{1}{2}$ miles (17km) long. The towns of Windermere and Bowness on the eastern shore are packed with visitors in summertime and the **Windermere Steamboat Museum** has an agreeable array of Victorian and Edwardian vessels which have done yeoman service on the lake. To the north, at Brockhole, the **Lake District National Park Visitor Centre** provides a good introduction to the area. *Open: daily, Eas–Oct (museum): daily, Apr–Oct (visitor centre).*

LEISURE PURSUITS

Fell walking, rock climbing, pony trekking, fishing and touring are major Lake District activities, besides watersports. Spring and autumn are the best times to visit the area, which can become uncomfortably crowded in summer. It was not until the 18th century that the beauty of the Lake District began to be fully appreciated and not until the arrival of the railways in the 19th that tourists in large numbers came to visit it.

ILLUSTRIOUS RESIDENTS AND VISITORS

One of the first to urge protection for the area was William Wordsworth, a long-time resident who was also, paradoxically, the greatest single influence on its popularity. **Wordsworth House** in Cockermouth, where he was born in 1770, belongs to the National Trust. The school he attended at Hawkshead is still there and two of the houses he lived in, **Dove Cottage** and **Rydal Mount**, are open to visitors (see separate entries). *Open: daily, Eas–Oct (Wordsworth House, NT).*

Many other authors and artists stoked the fires of public interest in the Lake District. Gainsborough, Constable and Turner all painted it, while the great critic John Ruskin lived at **Brantwood** (see separate entry) beside Coniston Water. Memories of Tennyson cling to **Mirehouse** on Bassenthwaite Lake. Sir Hugh Walpole lived near Derwent Water and set his 'Herries' historical novels in the area, and Arthur Ransome set *Swallows and Amazons* there. Beatrix Potter's home at **Hill Top**, near Sawrey, is intriguing but desperately crowded in summer. *Open: Wed, Sun, BH Mon, Apr–Oct (Mirehouse): Sat–Wed, Eas–Oct (Hill Top, NT).*

OTHER ATTRACTIONS

The main base for exploring the northern part of Lakeland is Keswick, at the head of Derwent Water. Its industry before tourists came was the manufacture of lead pencils and the **Pencil Museum** preserves the memory. There is also the **Cars of the Stars Motor Museum** of celebrity film and TV vehicles. The town **Museum and Art Gallery** has material on local history. *Open: daily (Pencil Museum): daily, Mar–Dec (Motor Museum): Mon–Sat, Apr–Oct (museum and art gallery).*

Near Keswick is the **Castlerigg Stone Circle**, one of the most impressive prehistoric monuments in the country. **Hardknott Roman Fort**, built early in the 2nd century in a dramatic situation, once controlled the road between Ambleside and Ravenglass,

where the remains of the **Roman Bath House** still stand. *Open: daily (all, EH).*

Here on the Lake District's western flank the **Ravenglass and Eskdale Railway** runs steam trains through delectable scenery in Eskdale. They pass **Muncaster Mill**, which is still busy grinding flour and oatmeal. **Muncaster Castle** is also nearby (see separate entry). *Open: daily, Eas–Oct; check with local tourist information centres for other times (railway): Sun–Fri, Apr–Oct (mill).*

Millom Folk Museum illustrates everyday life in the past. **Townend** at Troutbeck was the home of a well-to-do Lakeland farming family for three centuries. *Open: Eas; Mon–Sat, May–mid-Sep (museum): Tue–Fri, Sun, BH Mon, Eas–Oct (Townend, NT). (See separate entries for: Hooker Hall; Kendal; Leighton Hall; Levens Hall; Sizergh Castle; Stott Park Bobbin Mill.)*

Above: Dove Cottage at Grasmere was the home of William Wordsworth and his family from 1799 to 1808. The poet wrote one of the first Lake District guidebooks, intended as 'a Guide and Companion for the Minds of Persons of Taste' published in 1810

Left: fell walkers high above Grasmere. Climbing the Lake District peaks was enjoyed by pioneer visitors to the area like John Keats, who ascended Skiddaw, and Charles Dickens, who went up Carrick Fell in 1851. The modern sport of rock climbing developed in the Lake District in the 1880s

Below: the Lady of the Lake on Ullswater, which at 7¼ miles (12km) is second only to Windermere in length. Many visitors enjoy taking the boat along the lake in one direction and then walking back again along the shore

LANCASTER
LANCASHIRE

High above the city in baroque grandeur rises the **Ashton Memorial**, completed in 1909 for Lord Ashton, the linoleum tycoon, as a monument to his family. They were the Williamsons, Lancaster's largest employers. The memorial stands in Williamson Park, with a splendid butterfly house nearby. Surviving from a much earlier period is the medieval **priory church**, with beautiful oak woodwork and a fine view over the River Lune. Close by is **Lancaster Castle**, on the medieval site, but largely rebuilt in the 18th century. The town's long history as a port is recorded in the **Maritime Museum** and the **City Museum** is in the old town hall. The **Judges' Lodging Museum** concentrates on Gillow furniture and on childhood, and has a noted collection of dolls. *Open: daily (memorial): daily, Eas–Oct, subject to court requirements (castle): daily (Maritime Museum): Mon–Sat (City Museum): daily, Eas–Oct (Judges' Lodging Museum).*

LEEDS
WEST YORKSHIRE

Yorkshire's commercial capital is a confusing town, which seems to have little clear identity, but its magnificent 1858 town hall, in classical style by the local architect Cuthbert Brodrick, is one of the finest in the country. Brodrick also designed the Corn Exchange and the Leeds Institute. The 17th-century church of St John is famous for its woodwork. In full armour on horseback, a 30ft (9m) statue of the Black Prince bestrides City Square, surrounded by engaging art nouveau nymphs by Alfred Drury, who also did the statue of Circe in Park Square.

The **City Art Gallery** houses a treasure of Victorian and 20th-century art and the **City Museum** has wide-ranging archaeology and natural history exhibits. A trail runs from the Black Prince statue along the canal through the Aire Valley to historic sites and museums, including the **Leeds Industrial Museum** in a gigantic former woollen mill and the ruins of medieval **Kirkstall Abbey**, with a folk museum in which you can stroll through three full-sized streets. **Temple Newsam House** in the south-eastern outskirts offers Chippendale furniture, gardens and a home farm with rare breeds. *Open: daily (art gallery): Tue–Sun (City Museum and Leeds Industrial Museum): daily (Kirkstall Abbey): Tue–Sun, BH Mon (Temple Newsam House).*

LEIGHTON HALL
LANCASHIRE
■ OFF THE A6 3 MILES (5KM) NORTH OF CARNFORTH ■

The strange white 'Gothick' house of the Gillow furniture dynasty stands in a delectable natural amphitheatre with a stunning view of the Lake District fells. Richard Gillow moved in with his wife and 16 children in 1822, and in 1870 the tower and the cross-wing were added to make an intentionally asymmetrical effect. A family home of real charm, it contains many examples of Gillow furniture. An especially enjoyable treat is the flying of eagles, falcons and owls on fine afternoons; the birds seem to enjoy it as much as the visitors. *Open: Sun, Tue–Fri, BH Mon.*

LEVENS HALL
CUMBRIA
■ ON THE A6 5 MILES (8KM) SOUTH OF KENDAL ■

If a small black dog bounds up the stairs ahead of you, it is probably one of the ghosts that linger here – as any sensible ghost would. The Elizabethan mansion grew up around a medieval pele tower and passed to Colonel James Grahme, who allegedly won it gambling, on the turn of the ace of hearts. Its warm and welcoming atmosphere is a compound of time and much-loved family belongings, oak panelling and carved chimneypieces, paintings and clocks. It was Colonel Grahme who had the elaborate 17th-century topiary garden laid out, which has been preserved ever since and for which Levens Hall is celebrated. There is also a deer park and a collection of model steam engines and traction engines. *Open: Sun–Thu, Eas–Sep.*

Above: the flamboyant County Arcade in Leeds was designed by Frank Matcham and opened in 1898. Matcham was the leading theatre architect of his time – he designed both the Coliseum and the Palladium in London – and he created here a theatrical extravaganza in opulent contrast to today's benighted shopping precincts

■

A DEVIL OF A TABLE

There is a story that Richard Gillow once quoted a nobleman so high a price for a table that the flabbergasted peer exclaimed, 'It's a devil of a price!' To which Gillow replied, 'It's a devil of a table' and the aristocrat paid up. The family firm was founded by a Lancaster joiner named Robert Gillow, who also doubled as an undertaker and dealer in rum and other spirits. His son Richard joined him as a partner in the 1750s and they were so successful that they opened a branch in London. Richard Gillow made the first billiard table and invented the first telescopic dining table. His son was the procreative Richard Gillow who bought Leighton Hall and his son in turn was the 'Old Squire' of Leighton, Richard Thomas Gillow, who owned the estate from 1849. After he was 70 he felt he had little time left and refused to make repairs because things would see him out. As he lived on to be 99, the house was badly run down when he died in 1906.

■

■
DON'T MISS

■ The Ashton Memorial (Lancaster)

■ Gillow furniture (**Leighton Hall**)

■ Topiary (**Levens Hall**)

■ Tranquillity and peace (Lindisfarne)

FOR CHILDREN

■ The folk museum (**Kirkstall Abbey**, Leeds)

■ Flying falcons (**Leighton Hall**)

■ Roller-coasters (**Lightwater Valley Theme Park**)

LIGHTWATER VALLEY
THEME PARK
NORTH YORKSHIRE

■ ON THE A6108 3 MILES (5KM) NORTH OF RIPON ■

The boxer, Frank Bruno, formally launched 'The Ultimate', the world's biggest roller-coaster, here in 1991. It covers 44 acres (18ha) of ground and makes two drops of over 100ft (30m). Other white-knuckle rides include a swingboat that rises to 60ft (18m) in the air and something called 'The Rat' which hurtles through underground 'sewers'. Gentler pursuits include a children's farm and train and steamboat rides. *Open: daily, Jul–Aug; Sat, Sun, BH, May, Jun, Sep; most school holidays – check with tourist information centres.*

LINDISFARNE
NORTHUMBERLAND

■ REACHED BY CAUSEWAY 2 MILES (3KM) OFF THE A1, NEAR BEAL ■

Arrived at and left again only around low tide, when the causeway is clear of water, this is a special place off the Northumberland coast, also known by its older name of Holy Island. Much of the island is a nature reserve, visited by bird watchers and naturalists as well as seals, Brent geese and multitudes of wintering wildfowl. The monastery founded here in the 7th century was home to St Aidan and St Cuthbert, produced the Lindisfarne Gospels and carried Christianity to much of the North. The Danes looted the island in 793 and slaughtered many of the monks. The ruins on the site today are those of the medieval **Lindisfarne Priory** and its church. **Lindisfarne Castle**, which was built in the 16th century to protect Holy Island's harbour, was restored by Sir Edwin Lutyens in 1903. *Open: daily, Eas–Sep; Tue–Sun, Oct–Mar (priory, EH): daily, Eas–Sep; Wed, Sat, Sun, Oct (castle, NT).*

Below: perched theatrically on its outcrop of rock, Lindisfarne Castle is a 20th-century creation inside a 16th-century skin. It was in a dilapidated state in 1902 when it was bought by Edward Hudson, the founder of Country Life magazine, and enchantingly restored by Sir Edwin Lutyens

LITTLE MORETON HALL
CHESHIRE

■ ON THE A34 4 MILES (6KM) SOUTH OF CONGLETON ■

Looking like a mad, tumble-down dolls' house that might at any moment fall into its attendant moat, Little Moreton Hall has in fact been standing solid and unperturbed since the 16th century, when the Moreton family built it. Inside it has vast beams and acres of panelling. There are 16th-century wall paintings in the chapel and a secret chamber underneath the moat. *Open: Wed–Mon, Apr–Sep; Sat, Sun, BH, Mar, Oct (NT).*

Below: top-heavy, riotously half-timbered and leaning precariously in all directions, Little Moreton Hall dates from the 16th century and is one of the most startling sights in England. Cheshire had plenty of woodland and until the Industrial Revolution timber was still used for many sizeable buildings

LIVERPOOL
MERSEYSIDE

One of England's liveliest and most interesting cities to visit, Liverpool is seen at its most impressive from the Mersey on an approaching ferry. It was in the 19th century that Liverpool supplanted Bristol as England's leading west-coast seaport and the three buildings behind the Pier Head embody the Edwardian grandeur of the city's palmy days in the years leading up to the First World War. The Royal Liver Building of 1910, with its clocktowers rising to 295ft (90m), was Britain's first skyscraper on a reinforced concrete frame. On top of each tower is one of the mythical 'liver' birds (pronounced to rhyme with 'diver') from which the city is supposed to take its name. Next to it is the former headquarters of the Cunard Company, which ran its great ocean liners from here to America, and the third building is the domed baroque office of the Mersey Docks and Harbour Board, set up to run the docks in 1858.

To the south, the handsome 1840s brick warehouses of the restored **Albert Dock** are now stocked with smart shops, craft galleries and cafés. Here too is **The Beatles Story**, where the city's most famous musical group is celebrated and the sounds (and even smells) of the swinging sixties are throbbingly recreated. Less vivacious, the austere chambers of the **Tate Gallery Liverpool** house modern sculpture and paintings from the London gallery's collection. The **Merseyside Maritime Museum** traces the Port of Liverpool's history. There is a marvellous gallery of model ships and a section on emigration from Liverpool docks in the days when thousands of families took ship here for new lives in America, Australia or

Above: seen reflected in the water of the dock, the buildings at the Pier Head themselves reflect Liverpool's thriving prosperity in Edwardian days as a major Atlantic seaport. The dome belongs to the offices of the Mersey Docks and Harbour Board and one of the Royal Liver Building's clocktowers can also be seen

New Zealand. *Open: daily (Beatles Story, Maritime Museum): Tue–Sun (Tate).*

Looming up majestically, set back from the waterfront, is the huge bulk of the **Church of England Cathedral**. The largest church in Britain, it was designed by Sir Giles Gilbert Scott and completed in 1978. He made it up more or less as he went along and it is a masterpiece, like a vast hall tunnelled out of the local red sandstone. Also a 'must' for the visitor, in its much more aggressively modernistic style, is the **Roman Catholic Cathedral**, with its circular nave, central altar and 'crown-roast-of-lamb' lantern, 290ft (88m) high, known locally as 'Paddy's wigwam'.

Over in William Brown Street, the statue of the great Duke of Wellington looks out from a 130ft (40m) column over a townscape of the utmost grandeur. The centrepiece is St George's Hall, with its soaring Corinthian columns, opened in 1854 and one of the finest neo-classical buildings in Britain. Outside stand some of Liverpool's superlative collection of statues, and down the road is one of its beautifully preserved Edwardian pubs, 'The Vines'.

There are more statues, including remarkable works by the Liverpool sculptor John Gibson, in the **Walker Art Gallery**, which houses one of the best collections in the country outside London, especially strong in early Italian and Flemish paintings and in Victorian art. You could spend days happily exploring the **Liverpool Museum**, which has everything from dinosaur footprints to today's space technology, and there is another fascinating art collection in the **Sudley Art Gallery**, out from the centre in Mossley Hill. *Open: daily (museum and galleries).*

A walk along the Mersey bank leads to the pleasure gardens originally created on a derelict site in 1984. Further on stand the National Trust's **Speke Hall**, an

Elizabethan symphony of a house in black–and–white half-timbering, with a notable great hall and a number of priest's holes. *Open: Tue–Sun, BH Mon, Eas–Oct; Sat, Sun, Nov–mid-Dec (NT).*

Liverpool Football Club has a museum at the famous **Anfield** ground, and exotic animals happily roam the **Knowsley Safari Park** out in Prescot. In **Croxteth Hall**, the former seat of the Molyneux family, Earls of Sefton, room settings and character figures create the illusion of a grand Edwardian house party, while outdoors there is a farm with rare breed animals and a miniature railway in the park. *Open: Mon–Fri (Anfield): daily, Mar–Oct (safari park): daily in summer season, contact local tourist information centres for details (hall and farm).*

LOTHERTON HALL
WEST YORKSHIRE
■ ON THE B1217 10 MILES (16KM) EAST OF LEEDS ■

A charming Edwardian mansion, built round an older one of the 18th century, the house centres on a strange 'flying' staircase, which seems to shoot off in all directions. The family home of the Gascoignes, it was given to the city of Leeds in 1968 and contains a splendid collection of paintings and porcelain, with silver racing trophies and some spectacular high-Victorian furniture. There is also a gallery of oriental art and outside are the delightful Edwardian gardens, a deer park and bird garden. *Open: Tue–Sun, BH Mon.*

LYME PARK
CHESHIRE
■ OFF THE A6 7 MILES (11KM) SOUTH-EAST OF STOCKPORT ■

Guides dressed up as the great house's domestic staff in Edwardian days greet visitors to the noble mansion of the Legh family. On the edge of the Peak District, it is set in an ample park, 9 miles (14km) round, with red and fallow deer and acres of Victorian gardens. The original Elizabethan house was remodelled in the grand Palladian manner by Giacomo Leoni in the 18th century. There are splendid ceilings and tapestries as well as triumphs of wood carving. It was here that the famous Lyme mastiffs were bred, once prized all over Europe. *Open: Tue–Thu, Sat, Sun, BH Mon, Eas–Sep (house); daily (grounds). (NT, but members* are *charged for admission.)*

MACCLESFIELD SILK MUSEUM
CHESHIRE
■ MACCLESFIELD IS ON A523 10 MILES SOUTH OF STOCKPORT ■

From the cocoon to the loom, the Silk Museum and Heritage Centre follows the history of what was once Macclesfield's main industry. Housed in the old Sunday School building of 1813, it includes costume displays. Not far away, the **Paradise Mill Silk Museum** with its Jacquard looms is in the town's last handloom mill, which closed in 1981. Silk industry bygones can also be found in **West Park Museum**, with Egyptian antiquities and work by local artists, including the great bird artist C F Tunnicliffe. *Open: Tue–Sun, BH Mon (all three museums).*

MANCHESTER
GREATER MANCHESTER

Manchester began life as the Roman fort of *Mancunium*, which is why its citizens are called Mancunians. Later, a sizeable market town developed, which the Industrial Revolution transformed into Cottonopolis, the capital of the booming Lancashire textile industry. Visitors went to Manchester in the 19th century to gaze in awe at a noisy, cramped, dirty city of atrocious slums and factory chimneys belching smoke, which seemed to be the shape of the future. Today the city has lost such coherence and visitors are drawn by its individual attractions.

One of the most popular is the **Granada Studios Tour**, which takes you backstage into the world of television, cinema and fantasy. Nearby in the Castlefield area is the huge and steadily developing **Museum of Science and Industry**, with galleries on themes including air and space, electricity, textiles, gas, machine tools, printing and cameras, as well as Manchester's history. There are countless working machines and hands-on exhibits. The world's oldest passenger railway station is here and working steam locomotives are on display. *Open: Tue–Sun, Apr–Dec; Wed–Sun, Jan–Mar (studio tours): daily (museum).*

The site of the original Roman fort is close to the museum; part of it has been reconstructed by a quiet canal basin sheltering among a titanic tangle of Victorian railway viaducts. The Bridgewater Canal, which opened in 1761, was Britain's first major canal and inaugurated the 'Canal Age'. The **John Rylands University Library** is internationally renowned for its medieval manuscripts and jewel-bound books. *Open: Mon–Sat, except BH.*

From Victorian viaducts to Victorian art; the **City Art Gallery** is famous for its superb and splendidly displayed collection of 19th-century paintings, including a gorgeous array of Pre-Raphaelites. Attendant upon them are sculpture, furniture, porcelain, glass and silver in one of the most satisfying galleries in the country. It occupies a Greek Revival building by Sir Charles Barry, with an extension in another Barry building next door. *Open: daily.*

A short walk from here takes you to Albert Square to admire the stupendous triangular town hall with its 280ft (85m) clock-tower, designed by the Manchester-trained architect Alfred Waterhouse. Another fine 19th-century edifice, the **Free Trade Hall**, is the home of Manchester's famous Hallé Orchestra. Waterhouse designed the building of the university, where the **Manchester Museum** is known for its Egyptian mummies and its archery collection. Down the road is the **Whitworth Art Gallery**, with an excellent collection of British watercolours, prints, textiles, wallpapers and contemporary art. *Open: Mon–Sat (museum and gallery).*

Manchester Cathedral, the former parish church, has fine 15th-century choir stalls. The city is home to a flourishing Chinatown and also to Britain's largest Jewish community outside London; the English branch of Rothschild's Bank started here. The history is most endearingly told in the **Manchester Jewish Museum**, housed in a former synagogue. The new and developing **National Museum of Labour History** covers another interesting subject, and football enthusiasts will certainly not want to miss the **Manchester United Museum** at Old Trafford, the first purpose-built British football museum. *Open: Sun–Thu (Jewish Museum): Wed–Sun (Museum of Labour History): Sun–Fri (Old Trafford).*

Above: the Air and Space Hall is one of the rooms in the Museum of Science and Industry, which is claimed to be the biggest industrial museum in Europe. Many hours can be spent happily here among ponderous mill machinery, steam locomotives, trams, veteran cars and do-it-yourself exhibits

■

■

Below: statues of Mr Gladstone, John Bright and other worthies stand in Albert Square, outside Manchester's splendid Victorian Gothic town hall. In the background rise the spire and pinnacles of the memorial to the Prince Consort, designed by Thomas Worthington, with a statue by Matthew Noble, unveiled in 1867

■

BANNERS BRIGHT

Manchester's National Museum of Labour History has a good collection of trade union banners, which colourfully and nostalgically express the history and ideals of the labour movement. From the 1840s on, the banner was normally a silk panel, up to 16ft (5m) high and 12ft (4m) wide, illustrated with appropriate scenes, figures, symbols and inscriptions. No march or rally was complete without them and at May Day parades a century ago banners in their hundreds flew proudly in procession.

■

■

Right: visitors to Granada studios in Manchester can stroll along the hallowed cobbles of Coronation Street for a glass of something in the Rovers Return, as part of a tour which goes behind the scenes of some of Britain's most popular television programmes

■

MORPETH BAGPIPE MUSEUM
NORTHUMBERLAND

■ MORPETH IS OFF THE A1 16 MILES (26KM) NORTH OF NEWCASTLE ■

One of the strangest museums in the country lurks in Morpeth's 13th-century Chantry. It has one of the world's most extensive collections of bag-pipes and a special sound system which enables visitors to appreciate the subtle differences between them. The emphasis is on Northumbrian pipes, but there are instruments from Scotland, Ireland and from continental Europe as well. **Morpeth parish church** has medieval stained glass and in the churchyard is the tomb of Emily Wilding Davidson, the suffragette who was killed when she threw herself under the horses at the 1913 Derby, and a shelter of 1813 built for the watchers who guarded the graveyard against body snatchers. *Open: Mon–Sat except BH (museum).*

■

Above: a rare Northumbrian six-drone small pipe. Although bagpipes are linked with Scotland in most people's minds, there is an old tradition of Northumbrian piping. Contests for Northumbrian, Border and Highland pipes are among the competitions at the three-day Northumbrian Gathering held at Morpeth every year after Easter

■

MUNCASTER CASTLE
CUMBRIA

■ ON THE A595 1 MILE (1.6KM) EAST OF RAVENGLASS ■

This is a great place for owls, since it is the headquarters of the 'British Owl Breeding and Release Scheme'. The house, the home of the Pennington family for generations, goes back to a 14th-century pele tower. The other tower was built by Anthony Salvin, who modernised the castle in the 1860s and designed the sumptuous library. There is a wealth of fine furniture, porcelain, tapestries and family portraits and belongings, including a portrait of the 17th-century household fool, Thomas Skelton, from whom the word 'tomfool' is said to derive. The gardens command marvellous views of Eskdale and are famous for their rhododendrons and azaleas. There is also a commando course for children. *Open: Tue–Sun, BH Mon, Eas–Oct (castle): daily (grounds and owl centre).*

NESS GARDENS
CHESHIRE

■ OFF THE A540 9 MILES (14KM) NORTH-WEST OF CHESTER ■

These are the botanic gardens of Liverpool University, boasting the finest show of rhododendrons and azaleas in the north-west of England, with stately trees and spreading lawns. Ness Gardens were formerly owned by A K Bulley, who sent George Forrest and other plant hunters abroad to collect specimens. The original *Pieris formosa forrestii* and many Asiatic primulas brought back by Forrest are still here, along with a superlative heather garden, rock garden, rose garden, water garden, herb garden and herbaceous borders, topped off with fine views across the River Dee to North Wales. *Open: daily.*

NEWBY HALL
NORTH YORKSHIRE

■ OFF THE B6265 3 MILES (5KM) SOUTH-EAST OF RIPON ■

The house is a dream come true, a William-and-Mary country home in soft red brick with stone facings and balustrade, nestling idyllically among its woods and gardens by the River Ure. Not content with the magical charm of its exterior, it has interiors by Robert Adam and a church by William Burges in the grounds. It was built in the 1690s and in the following century John Carr of York added two wings while Robert Adam designed the entrance hall, the tapestry room (with its Gobelins tapestries on the theme of 'the loves of the gods' and Chippendale furniture) and the sculpture galleries where the Barberini Venus and other classical pieces pose in elegant splendour. In an entirely different style are the ample Victorian billiards room and the church of Christ the Consoler, which Burges designed as a memorial to a son of the house who was kidnapped and murdered by bandits in Turkey in 1870. The gardens are delightful and there are miniature train rides beside the river. *Open: Tue–Sun, BH Mon, Eas–Sep.*

■

DON'T MISS

■ Victorian art (**City Art Gallery, Manchester**)

■ Bagpipes (**Morpeth**)

■ Robert Adam elegance (**Newby Hall**)

FOR CHILDREN

■ The TV tour (**Granada Studios, Manchester**)

■ Interactive exhibits (**Museum of Science and Industry, Manchester**)

■ Owls (**Muncaster Castle**)

NEWCASTLE UPON TYNE
TYNE & WEAR

Once a Roman frontier station at the eastern end of Hadrian's Wall, later a medieval fortress town – the 'new castle' was built in 1080 – the city was subsequently a leading coal port (hence 'coals to Newcastle') and heavy industry centre. It boasts a proud set of bridges over the Tyne, set close together, among them the high-arched iron 1920s Tyne Bridge and Robert Stephenson's 1840s High Level Bridge carrying the railway line, with the road suspended beneath it. The builders of the railway casually cut the remains of the castle in two. Today the **Castle Keep Museum** covers the history of the site. *Open: Tue–Sun.*

Curving, classical Gray Street leading up to the 135ft (41m) pillar of the Gray Monument is the 1830s showpiece of the local architect John Dobson, who also designed the imposing Central Station, opened in 1849. The **cathedral**, the former parish church of St Nicholas, is known for its majestic crown spire, and the **Laing Art Gallery** for its array of British art from the 18th century on: from Reynolds to Landseer, Burne-Jones and Stanley Spencer, with a special collection of pictures by John Martin. The **Museum of Antiquities** has an exceptional Roman collection with material from Hadrian's Wall and the **Hancock Museum** has one of Britain's finest natural history collections. Also well worth seeing are the **John George Joicey Museum** of local life and the **Museum of Science and Engineering**, *Open: Tue–Sun (art gallery): Mon–Sat (Museum of Antiquities): daily (Hancock Museum): Tue–Sat, BH (Joicey Museum and Museum of Science and Engineering).*

Right: visitors can ride around the North of England Open Air Museum enjoyably in a veteran electric tramcar. The museum's transport collection also includes a 100-ton 1930s steam navvy and a steamroller, a steam traction engine and a variety of horse-drawn vehicles as well as steam railway locomotives

NORTH OF ENGLAND OPEN AIR MUSEUM
CO. DURHAM

■ AT BEAMISH, OFF THE A693 3 MILES (5KM) WEST OF CHESTER-LE-STREET ■

The entrance to the museum's spacious 200 acres (80ha) of grounds is guarded by a huge 70-ton steam hammer of 1883, fondly known as 'Tiny Tim'. The museum set itself the task of recreating life in the North-East in the late years of the 19th century and the early years of the 20th, and it has done so with a thoroughness and inspired verisimilitude that have won it awards by the sackload. Buildings have been brought here to make the nucleus of a small town, with a delightful working pub – the Sun Inn from Bishop Auckland – a park with a Victorian bandstand, a Co-op shop and tearoom, and a terrace of houses from Gateshead. The terrace includes a dentist's homely surgery with its handsome dental chair, and also his family's comfortable home of the 1920s.

Elsewhere there is a country railway station with oil lamps, North Eastern Railway platform seats and steam locomotives puffing to and fro. The working farm with its farmhouse, stables and midden yard, its pigs and poultry, also has a herd of Durham Shorthorn cattle. There's a colliery dating from about 1913 and a drift mine with an underground tunnel to be explored. A row of typical pit cottages has been furnished in different styles from the 1890s to the 1930s. With events as diverse as leek shows and whippet racing, this is a thoroughly enjoyable place for a family day out. *Open: daily, Eas–Oct; Tue–Sun, Nov–Mar.*

■
DON'T MISS

■ The natural history displays (Hancock Museum, Newcastle)

■ A drink in the Sun Inn (North of England Open Air Museum)

■ Lonely moors and green tracks (Northumberland National Park)

FOR CHILDREN

■ The home farm (North of England Open Air Museum)

NORTHUMBERLAND NATIONAL PARK
NORTHUMBERLAND

From the high Cheviots on the Scottish border the park extends 40 miles (64km) to the south, down to Hadrian's Wall (see separate entry). The main road across it is the A68, running through Redesdale, with the A697 skirting the park's north-eastern edge. Much of the area, however, is walking and riding country, miles from any roads, forming some of the most remote and least visited countryside in England. This is particularly true in the north, where the grassy, whale-backed Cheviots rise to 2,676ft (816m) in The Cheviot itself. Further south there are extensive conifer forests. The Pennine Way runs all the way through the park from Kirk Yetholm down to Hadrian's Wall. Rock climbing, pony trekking, angling and bird watching are favourite pursuits here, but above all it is walker's territory.

The park's area is just under 400 square miles (1,000km²), with a resident population of only some 2,000 people (who mostly live by farming and are vastly outnumbered by sheep). Close to the border with Scotland, this was lawless and fought-over ground for centuries, as the battlefields of Flodden and Otterburn testify – as do the pele towers and bastles (fortified houses) into which people retreated when danger approached. Green tracks through the hills were once used by swift raiders and later by cattle drovers and whisky smugglers.

Surviving from far earlier days are prehistoric stone circles and standing stones, and there are mysterious rock carvings at Lordenshaws, near Rothbury. Of the many Iron Age hill forts, the biggest and most impressive is **Yeavering Bell**, in the north above the B6351. The old church at **Kirknewton** nearby, incidentally, has a great curiosity – a carving which seems to show the Three Wise Men wearing Scottish kilts.

The park's boundaries were deliberately drawn to exclude towns and villages as far as possible, but Bellingham on the B6320 is a useful base for the southern part of the park and for **Kielder Water**, the huge manmade reservoir within the Border Forest Park. Further north, **Elsdon** is a particularly attractive village of stone houses round a green, with a medieval church and pele tower. Rothbury is a pleasant town, with **Cragside House** outside it (see separate entry). West from Rothbury, a minor road follows the valley of the Coquet through Harbottle to peter out high on the lonely moors.

The Breamish Valley, with its path to the Linhope Spout waterfall, is the most visited of the Cheviot dales. Not far away, the old market town of Wooler is a good base for the park's northern reaches, close to the Flodden Memorial and **Chillingham Castle** (see separate entry). At Ford is the **Lady Waterford Hall**, with 19th-century murals by the Marchioness of Waterford and nearby are the remains of **Etal Castle**. *Open: daily (hall and castle, EH).*

Above: the curlew, flying with wings outstretched and giving mournful cry over the solitary moors, was chosen as a suitable emblem of the Northumberland National Park when it was established in 1956

Below: Kielder Water, the biggest manmade lake in western Europe, is on the western edge of the national park. From the huge reservoir, with its sailing and boating, canoeing, water skiing and fishing, the North Tyne runs across the park to Bellingham through a valley once notorious for Border raiding, cattle rustling, feuding and violence

NORTH YORK MOORS NATIONAL PARK
NORTH YORKSHIRE

Designated in 1952 and covering some 550 square miles (1,400km²) of the old North Riding of Yorkshire, the park extends from spectacular cliff scenery along the North Sea shore on the eastern edge, across high moorland – a rolling sea of purple heather as the summer moves towards autumn – to the Cleveland Hills and the Hambleton Hills in the west. Intersecting the moors are the farming dales, green and peaceful with their stone villages and churches, and the landscape has a particularly enticing combination of the natural and the manmade.

Some 25,000 people live in the park and the principal occupation is sheep farming. Substantial areas of moorland are also used for breeding grouse. Most of the central area is penetrated only by minor roads, but there are more than 1,200 miles (2,000km) of paths for walking, riding and cycling.

STRANGE ROCK FORMATIONS

Among the scenic splendours is the Hole of Horcum, in the Tabular Hills north of Lockton, a vast natural amphitheatre which, according to legend, was created by a local giant in a rage, when he scooped up a huge handful of earth to throw at his wife. She dodged and the mis-

sile landed a mile or so away to form the 875ft (265m) cone of Blakey Topping. Over to the east are the strange shapes of the **Bridestones**, weathered rock-formations now cared for by the National Trust. Other strange shapes are the manmade 'randomes' of the Early Warning Station on Fylingdales Moor, which could be the giant's golf balls. Hard by, **Lilla Cross**, erected in the 7th century, is one of the oldest Christian monuments in northern Europe.

Doyen of the park's waterfalls is **Mallyan Spout**, near Goathland, where the water of the West Beck drops 70ft (20m). On the western edge of the park in the Hambleton Hills, Sutton Bank commands a marvellous panorama of the Vale of York with a view of more than 90 miles (140km) on a clear day. There is a sweeping view, too, from the summit of Roseberry Topping on the park's northern rim and from the nearby monument on Easby Moor to Captain Cook, erected in the explorer's honour in 1827. **Captain Cook's Schoolroom Museum** at Great Ayton is in the building where he learned his letters. *Open: daily, Apr–Oct.*

The Cleveland Way path, some 90 miles (140km) long altogether, follows an ancient trackway from Helmsley to Sutton Bank and then through the park's western and northern hills to the coast, while the much-trodden Lyke Wake Walk runs across from Osmoth-

Below: in the Bridestones Nature Reserve, on the rolling moors north-west of Scarborough, sandstone rocks have, over the ages, been carved into strange shapes by wind and weather. The lower strata, softer than the upper ones, have been worn away to create a mushroom-like effect. The area is now owned by the National Trust

Below: a stretch of Roman road running over Wheeldale Moor, south-west of Goathland, was uncovered with its flagstones and gutters intact early in this century by a local gamekeeper and is now protected by English Heritage. The road, which became known as Wade's Causeway, probably ran between York and the coast

erley to the sea. For motorists, the Dalby Forest Drive winds its 9-mile (14km) course through the Forestry Commission's plantations. The national park's visitor centre is at Danby, in the valley of the Esk. *Open: daily, Apr–Oct; check with local tourist information centres for other times.*

OTHER ATTRACTIONS

Deep in the heart of the park, the wild daffodils nod to the spring breezes on the banks of the River Dove in Farndale. This is north of the pretty village of Hutton-le-Hole, where the **Ryedale Folk Museum** has a collection of rescued buildings, which include a medieval longhouse and an Elizabethan manor house. At Pickering, the **Beck Isle Museum of Rural Life** has a large collection illuminating local life over the last two centuries. *Open: daily, Eas–Oct (folk museum): daily, Apr–Oct (museum of rural life).*

Pickering is the headquarters of the **North Yorkshire Moors Railway** which runs steam trains over 18 miles (29km) of scenic line to Goathland and Grosmont. There are attractive walks from stations and halts along the way. English Heritage has charge of the ruined keep and towers of **Pickering Castle**, where Richard II was held prisoner, and of **Helmsley Castle** with its immense earthworks. **Duncombe Park**, by contrast, exhibits all the splendour of the 1890s. *Open: Sun, Jan–Mar; daily, Eas–Oct (railway): daily, Eas–Sep; Tue–Sun, Oct–Eas (both castles, EH); Sun–Thu, Eas–Sep (house).*

SIGNS OF THE PAST

Ruined abbeys are something of a North York Moors speciality. The star of them is generally reckoned to be **Rievaulx** (see separate entry), but **Mount Grace Priory**, near Osmotherley, has many admirers. **Byland Abbey** is a beautiful Cistercian house further south, below the Hambleton Hills. Stone crosses are another speciality.

Mostly of medieval or later date and put, often by the monks, as waymarkers, they have such names as 'Fat Betty', 'Margery' and 'Young Ralph' (the national park's symbol). *Open: daily, Eas–Sep; Tue–Sun, Oct–Mar (priory and abbey, EH).*

Surprising as it seems, iron mining once flourished in the area, but fewer than a handful of mines survived into this century. Rosedale was once a thriving iron district and remains of workings can be seen today.

Kilburn owes its more recent fame to Robert Thompson, the great wood craftsman, whose trademark was a mouse; some of his work can be admired in the village church. There is a path to the **Kilburn White Horse** on the hillside, made in 1857. **Shandy Hall** at Coxwold is the delightful medieval house where Lawrence Sterne wrote *Tristram Shandy*. Nearby **Newburgh Priory** claims to have the body of Oliver Cromwell. **Nunnington Hall** on the River Rye has fine panelling and a collection of miniature rooms. *Open: Wed, Sun, Jun–Sep (Shandy Hall): Wed, Sun, May–Aug (Priory): Sat, Sun, Eas–Apr; Tue–Thu, Sat, Sun, May–Oct (Nunnington Hall, NT).*

The National Trust also protects large areas of the precipitous cliffs and coastline, including the 600ft (180m) headland of Ravenscar with views of Robin Hood's Bay and the picturesque fishing village of the same name. Further north is the old fishing and whaling port of Whitby (see separate entry). Sandsend and Runswick have sandy beaches and Staithes is another old fishing port of character. Boulby Head towers up to 660ft (200m), the highest cliff on England's east coast.

Below: the national park includes an impressive stretch of the Yorkshire coast; one of the gems is the fishing harbour of Staithes, a village always easier to reach from the sea than by land. In isolation it developed its own quirks, including a characteristic style of ladies' bonnet. The artist Dame Laura Knight lived and painted here for many years

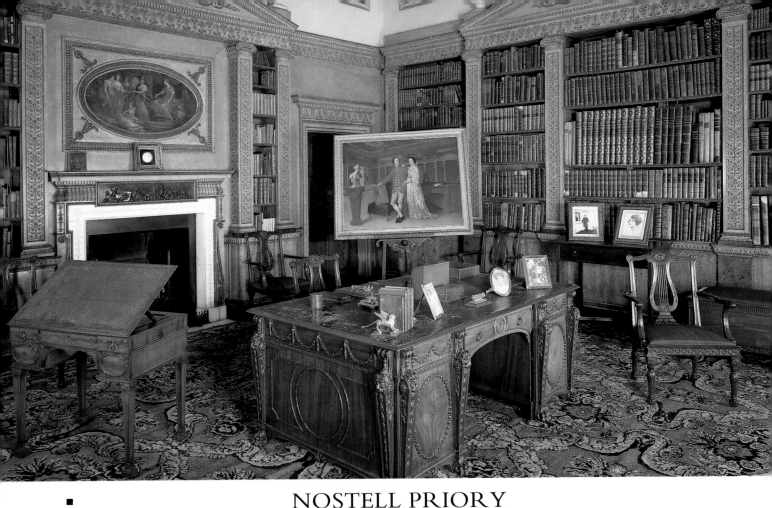

NOSTELL PRIORY
WEST YORKSHIRE
■ OFF THE A683 6 MILES (10KM) SOUTH-EAST OF WAKEFIELD ■

After the priory had been closed down the estate at Nostell was acquired by a rich Londoner, Rowland Winn. His 18th-century descendant, Sir Rowland Winn, hired the architect James Paine to build him a new house here, but after Winn's death in 1765 the next Sir Rowland engaged Robert Adam to complete the work. Paine and Adam between them designed the superb interiors for which the house is noted today, with painted walls and ceilings by Antonio Zucchi and Angelica Kauffman, plasterwork by Joseph Rose and wonderful Chippendale furniture. *Open: Sat–Thu, Jul–Aug; Sat, Sun, Apr–Jun, Sep–Oct (NT).*

PILKINGTON GLASS MUSEUM
MERSEYSIDE
■ IN ST HELENS, ON THE A58 10 MILES (16KM) EAST OF LIVERPOOL ■

The sprawling industrial town of St Helens has been a glass-making centre for more than 200 years. The museum in the Pilkington factory covers 4,000 years of glass-making history with objects both beautiful and strange. There are drinking glasses, bottles, glass ornaments, stained glass windows, glass sculptures, mirrors, holograms and glass fountains. There is glass plain and coloured, clear and opaque, plain and patterned. The collection shows how techniques have developed and illustrates the many uses of glass, from windows to telescopes, in a lively and enjoyable display. *Open: daily.*

QUARRY BANK MILL
CHESHIRE
■ AT STYAL, ON THE B5166 11 MILES (18KM) SOUTH OF MANCHESTER ■

Something of the tough, noisy life of a factory community in the early days of the Industrial Revolution can be experienced at Quarry Bank, with the looms clattering in the cotton mill founded (1784) and owned by the Greg dynasty. Standing beside the little River Bollin, the mill is powered by the largest working water wheel in England. Real cloth is made here and is on sale to visitors. It is not only the mill and the machinery that have survived, but a complete company village – the cottages which the Gregs built for their workers, the school, shop and chapels. The Gregs employed pauper children as hands; they worked 13 hours a day, six days a week, and you can see the Apprentice House where they lived in the 1830s. They were well cared for and taught their lessons, and an eye was kept on their health. In the garden grow rare fruit, vegetables and herbs, and there are pleasant walks along the river and in the woods, for the mill's iron routines had a pleasant rural setting.

RABY CASTLE
CO. DURHAM
■ OFF THE A688 AT STAINDROP, 5 MILES (8KM) NORTH-EAST OF BARNARD CASTLE ■

Even today the sight of Raby Castle crouched in its deer park like a savage watchdog ready to spring can send a shiver or two down the spine, for all the efforts of its 18th- and 19th-century inhabitants to civilise it. Dating basically from the 14th century, with nine towers rising up to 80ft (25m) high, it was the fortress of the Nevilles – one of the leading families in the wild North – who rose to the summit of political power in the person of Warwick the Kingmaker during the Wars of the Roses. The Nevilles lost their estates in Elizabeth I's time, when they plotted to put Mary, Queen of Scots on the English throne and from 1626 the castle belonged to the Vanes. There were substantial alterations in the 1760s and 1840s.

The castle is ranged round a central courtyard, with an immensely impressive medieval hall, a gigantic medieval kitchen and a handsome Victorian drawingroom to admire. There are family portraits, fine furniture and ceramics, and a collection of carriages and horse-drawn fire-engines. Impressive Neville and Vane tombs can be seen in **Staindrop Church**. *Open: Eas; Wed, Sun, BH Mon, May–Jun; Sun–Fri, Jul–Sep (castle).*

RICHMOND
NORTH YORKSHIRE
■ ON THE A6108 12 MILES (19KM) SOUTH-WEST OF DARLINGTON ■

Poised high and dramatically above the River Swale, the castle and town of Richmond enjoy one of the finest situations in all England. The spacious cobbled market-place is surrounded by Georgian and Victorian buildings, including the 18th-century town hall. The former church of Holy Trinity, which Sir Nikolaus Pevsner's *Buildings of England* series described as 'the queerest ecclesiastical building one can imagine', now houses the **Green Howards Museum**, which tells the story of the famous Yorkshire regiment. It first saw service in 1690 when it fought at the Battle of the Boyne, and in the museum today are 18 Victoria Crosses won by its soldiers. Besides medals, uniforms and weapons, there is superb regimental silver and some of Richmond's civic plate on view. One room has furniture made by the famous Robert Thompson of Kilburn, with his mouse craft mark. *Open: Mon–Fri, Feb; Mon–Sat, Mar; daily, Apr–Oct; Mon–Sat, Nov.*

The delightful **Georgian Theatre Royal**, built in 1788, is one of the oldest theatres in the country and is claimed to be the oldest still surviving in its original form. Its museum proudly displays Britain's oldest complete set of painted scenery, dating from 1836, as well as playbills, model theatres and thespian photographs. Frances I'Anson, the 'sweet lass of Richmond Hill' of the famous song, grew up in Richmond, at Hill House in Pottergate, and left her name to I'Anson Road. The **Richmondshire Museum** traces the history of the town since the 11th century, with many bygones. *Open: daily, Eas–Oct (theatre and museum).*

The town grew up in the shelter of its formidable Norman **castle**, which rears up on its cliff above the Swale, and which is now cared for by English Heritage. Begun in 1071, it has seen little action. The huge keep, just over 100ft (30m) high, was built in the 12th century above the original gatehouse, an unusual position. King William the Lion of Scotland was held here after being taken prisoner in 1174. The great hall, or Scolland's Hall, which dates from about 1080, is one of the earliest buildings of its kind. *Open: daily, Eas–Sep; Tue–Sun, Oct–Mar (EH).*

Richmond Castle is one of the places where, according to legend, King Arthur and his heroic knights of the Round Table sleep until their country needs them. There is also a story of a secret passage leading from the castle to **Easby Abbey**, whose ruins stand on the banks of the river below. *Open: daily, Eas–Sep; Tue–Sun, Oct–Mar (EH).*

■

Above: from glass art to a lighthouse optic, the collection in the Pilkington Glass Museum illustrates the history and techniques of glass-making from Ancient Egyptian times to the present day

■

■

Above: full-dress officer's uniform, in the Green Howards Museum in Richmond. The name was originally the regiment's nickname, based on the green facings to its uniform, but became official in 1920. Its battle honours go back to Malplaquet in the 18th century

■

DON'T MISS

■ The Chippendale furniture (Nostell Priory)

■ Rare and beautiful glass (Pilkington Glass Museum)

■ The octagon drawingroom (Raby Castle)

■ The Georgian theatre (Richmond)

FOR CHILDREN

■ The views through a submarine periscope (Pilkington Glass Museum)

■ The Apprentice House (Quarry Bank Mill)

RIEVAULX ABBEY
NORTH YORKSHIRE
■ OFF THE B1257 2 MILES (3KM) NORTH-WEST OF HELMSLEY ■

Above: quiet among sweetly wooded hills in Ryedale, the ruined abbey church and monastery of Rievaulx have stood untenanted and decaying for four centuries since the last Cistercian monks were expelled and the foundation closed down in 1538. At one time this silent, peaceful place swarmed with monks and lay brothers, 'like a hive of bees' it was said

Only 22 monks were left at Rievaulx (pronounced 'Reevo') in 1538, when the abbey was closed. Founded in 1131 as a Cistercian mission centre, it became a prosperous foundation, rich in sheep. The abbey was built on a slope above the River Rye, on a site which forced the monks to orientate their church north/south instead of the customary east/west. The ruined 13th-century choir is particularly lovely and around the church are the remains of the chapter house and other monastic buidings, today in the charge of English Heritage. Overlooking the abbey, and owned by the National Trust, is **Rievaulx Terrace**, which was built in the 18th century to command the delectable view. *Open: daily, Eas–Sep; Tue–Sun, Oct–Mar (abbey, EH): daily, Eas–Oct (terrace, NT).*

RIPON
NORTH YORKSHIRE
■ ON THE A61 11 MILES (18KM) NORTH OF HARROGATE ■

Curfew still sounds in this charming little cathedral city at 9 o'clock every evening, when the 'wakeman's' (or watchman's) horn is blown. In the market-place the town hall of 1801, by James Wyatt, bears the civic motto: 'Except Ye Lord Keep Ye Cittie, Ye Wakeman Waketh In Vain.' The 90ft (27m) obelisk was raised in honour of William Aislabie, who owned the magnificent landscape gardens at Studley Royal nearby. Ripon Cathedral stands on the site where St Wilfrid built a church in the 7th century and beneath it is the saint's original crypt. The cathedral itself dates mainly from the 12th century to the 16th, and the 15th-century choir stalls are especially fine. **Ripon Prison and Police Museum** follows the history of local crime and punishment in what was once the town gaol and later the police station. *Open: daily, Eas–Oct.*

ROCHE ABBEY
SOUTH YORKSHIRE
■ OFF THE A634 2 MILES (3KM) SOUTH-EAST OF MALTBY ■

Another melancholy ruined Cistercian abbey stands in a wooded valley below a limestone cliff in a setting enhanced by 'Capability' Brown, who landscaped it for the Earl of Scarborough in the 18th century. Founded in 1147, the abbey was closed down in 1538 and promptly plundered: 'every person bent himself to filch and spoil what he could', a local clergyman wrote at the time. *Open: daily, Eas–Sep; Sat, Sun, Oct–Mar (EH).*

■
DON'T MISS

■ The view of Rievaulx Abbey (**Rievaulx Terrace**)

■ The sounding of the curfew horn (**Ripon**)

■ The Saxon crypt (**Ripon Cathedral**)

■ Wordsworth's garden hut and view (**Rydal Mount**)

■ Pre-Raphaelite art treasures (**St Martin's, Scarborough**)

RUFFORD OLD HALL
LANCASHIRE

■ ON THE A59 6 MILES (10KM) NORTH OF ORMSKIRK ■

The house presents a remarkable contrast between the spectacular black-and-white great hall and the plain and simple 17th-century wing in brick. It was built by the Hesketh family and the late 15th-century great hall has a tremendous hammerbeam roof and a huge wooden screen, elaborately carved. There is also some fine oak furniture as well as tapestries and an arms and armour collection. *Open: Sat–Thur, Eas–Oct (NT).*

RYDAL MOUNT
CUMBRIA

■ OFF THE A591 2 MILES (3KM) NORTH OF AMBLESIDE ■

Five years after leaving Dove Cottage, the Wordsworths moved into this plain, lime-washed house with its beautiful view over Rydal Water in 1813. The great poet lived here for the rest of his long life, until his death in 1850, and the house has a delightful atmosphere, and many family possessions. Wordsworth himself designed the garden. *Open: daily, Mar–Oct; Wed–Mon, Nov–mid-Jan, Feb–Mar.*

SCARBOROUGH
NORTH YORKSHIRE

■ ON THE A64 38 MILES (61KM) NORTH-EAST OF YORK ■

Scarborough was a smart spa in the 17th century and in the 18th became a fashionable seaside resort. The headland on which the ruins of the castle stand was inhabited far back in prehistoric times and was used for a signal station by the Romans. The sprawling Norman castle, now in the charge of English Heritage, was bombarded by a German battleship in 1914. *Open: daily, Eas–Sep; Tue–Sun, Oct–Mar (EH).*

The town is known for its sandy beaches and luxuriant gardens. Pre-Raphaelite enthusiasts should not miss the 1860s church of St Martin on the Hill, with marvellous work by Rossetti, Burne-Jones and Morris. The architect was GF Bodley. Anne Brontë is buried in St Mary's churchyard. There is a Sitwell collection at **Wood End Museum** in the family's Scarborough house. **Scarborough Art Gallery** has work by Lord Leighton and others, and by local artists and the **Rotunda Museum** is an unusual example of a purpose-built museum opened as early as 1829, with its original display cases and material on local history. *Open: daily, Apr–Sep; Tue–Sat, Oct–Mar (museums and gallery).*

■

THE GREAT MAN

Already in Wordsworth's own time trippers used to come to Rydal Mount and hang about outside in the lane – as many as a hundred a day in the summer – hoping to catch a glimpse of the great man as he walked in his garden. If they did see him, he usually looked more like a Cumbrian shepherd than a distinguished man of letters and Poet Laureate, dressed in rough trousers and a frock coat with a straw hat on his head and a black kerchief knotted round his throat.

■

■

Below: beyond the harbour and its brightly painted fishing boats, the battlements of Scarborough Castle lie like a sleeping lion on the headland. A fishing settlement since far back in prehistoric times, Scarborough turned into Britain's first seaside resort in the 18th century

■

■

Above: originally a 16th-century farmer's cottage, Rydal Mount was Wordsworth's home for close to 40 years – almost half his life. It was a lively affectionate household, not overawed by the distinguished visitors who came to see the poet, from William Wilberforce, the anti-slavery campaigner with 18 of his family and servants, to Sir Walter Scott, Thomas De Quincey and Dr Arnold of Rugby

■

SEATON DELAVAL HALL
NORTHUMBERLAND
■ ON THE A190 4 MILES (6KM) NORTH OF WHITLEY BAY ■

The great grim mansion of the Delavals, with its imposing classical portico, was designed by Sir John Vanbrugh for Admiral George Delaval, who urged him to spare no expense on it. Completed in 1729, the house has been described as combining the maximum of dignity with the minimum of accommodation. In its unlucky history it has suffered several serious fires. There are state rooms in the west wing, a mausoleum and a handsome stable block, and a Norman church in the grounds. The rakish and talented 'gay Delavals' traced their lineage back to the Norman Conquest, but their fortune was made on the discovery of coal beneath their land, and they built the harbour of Seaton Sluice to export it. *Open: Wed, Sun, BH, May–Sep.*

SEWERBY HALL
HUMBERSIDE
■ OFF THE B1255 2 MILES (3KM) NORTH-EAST OF BRIDLINGTON ■

Up on the cliffs above Bridlington Bay, the Georgian house was built by John Greame and completed in 1720, with additions in the following century. The town bought it in the 1930s and it is now used as an art gallery and museum of archaeology and local and natural history. One room has mementoes of Amy Johnson, the Hull-born pioneer aviatrix, who formally opened the estate to the public in 1936. She was killed during the Second World War, five years later. There is a small zoo and aviary in the 50 acres (20ha) of grounds. Nearby Bridlington is a seaside resort with sandy beaches, a bustling harbour and a medieval priory church. *Open: daily, Eas–late Sep (house): daily (grounds).*

SHEFFIELD
SOUTH YORKSHIRE

Known for cutlery, steel and some remarkable post-war housing developments, Sheffield stands at the edge of the Pennines, in the district once known as Hallamshire, where the River Don is joined by the Sheaf. Local iron ore deposits supported an iron industry here from early in the Middle Ages and Sheffield became the unrivalled queen of the English cutlery trade. The Don Valley coalfield enabled the town to take full advantage of the introduction of steam power. Iron and steel works spread all along the river from Rotherham to Sheffield and in the 19th century Sheffield was England's premier steel town, its products known all over Europe. By 1911 it had become the largest town in Yorkshire.

Standing in due dignity and majesty near the centre of the city is the Cutlers' Hall of 1832, in Greek Revival style, where the cutlers hold annual revel. The 1890s town hall has a figure of Vulcan, the Roman god of smiths, on top of its tower. The more restrained city hall was completed in

THE BEST OF ITS KIND

John Ruskin wrote of Sheffield cutlery as 'the best of its kind, done by English hands, unsurpassable'. Already in the 14th century, the miller in Chaucer's *Canterbury Tales* carries a 'Sheffield knife' in his stocking, which suggests that the town was by then well-known for its cutlery. The miller's knife would be for both eating and self-defence. Inns did not provide table cutlery in those days and travellers carried their own with them. By 1500 Sheffield was a leading producer of cutlery and edged implements and in 1682 the master craftsmen of the Company of Cutlers of Hallamshire included 1,562 knife makers, 137 shears and sickle makers, 284 scissor makers, 33 scythe makers, 221 file smiths and 17 awl-blade smiths. Sheffield had a virtual monopoly of the English cutlery industry.

Below: the 18th and 19th centuries saw the transformation of Sheffield, in its beautiful setting on the eastern rim of the Pennines, into a powerhouse of the Industrial Revolution. Benjamin Huntsman's discovery in the 1740s of how to make crucible steel stimulated what became its principal industry. At the same time, also in Sheffield, Thomas Boulsover successfully fused silver and copper to create Sheffield plate. He used it to make buttons, but the process was soon applied to other articles and spread far beyond Sheffield. The original 'Old Sheffield Plate' is now rare and valuable

the 1930s. The **cathedral** is the 15th-century parish church of St Peter and St Paul, extensively restored in Victorian times and enlarged in this century. Castle Market stands on the site where Sheffield Castle once stood, above the Don. Mary, Queen of Scots was held captive there and the tomb of her warder, the Earl of Shrewsbury, is in the cathedral.

Among Sheffield's attractions are its art galleries. The **Graves Art Gallery** has European and British art of the 20th century as well as African, Islamic and oriental collections. The **Mappin Art Gallery** has a fine display of 18th-century and Victorian British paintings and sculpture. The delightful **Ruskin Gallery** displays the collection assembled by John Ruskin for the benefit of the Sheffield working class. *Open: Mon–Sat (Graves): Tue–Sun (Mappin): Mon–Sat (Ruskin).*

On the industrial side, the **Sheffield Industrial Museum** at Kelham Island gives a lively depiction of four centuries of the city's past, with cutlery craftsmen and machinery at work. The tilt-hammers can be seen pounding at **Abbeydale Industrial Hamlet**, an 18th-century scythe factory and there are treasures of Sheffield cutlery and plate in the **City Museum**. The Victorian **Sheffield Botanic Gardens** are a treat. *Open: Wed–Sat, BH Mon (Industrial Museum): Wed–Sat (Industrial Hamlet): Tue–Sun, BH Mon (City Museum): daily (Botanic Gardens).*

SIZERGH CASTLE
CUMBRIA
■ OFF THE A591 3½ MILES (6KM) SOUTH OF KENDAL ■

A bulky 14th-century pele tower 60ft (18m) high, built for protection against marauding Scots, is the nucleus of the house, which was later enlarged and made comfortable by one of the leading families of the district, the Stricklands. Inside are portraits of the Stricklands – a long-nosed, determined-looking dynasty – and particularly fine Elizabethan carved chimney-pieces, panelling, furniture, paintings and china. Outside there is a lake with swans and a rose garden, while paths wind through a large rock garden among pleasant pools and trickling rills. *Open: Sun–Thu, Eas–Oct (NT).*

SLEDMERE HOUSE
HUMBERSIDE
■ ON THE B1252 7 MILES (11KM) NORTH-WEST OF DRIFFIELD ■

The noble Georgian mansion of the Sykes family in its 'Capability' Brown park was gutted by fire in 1911. It was then splendidly reconstructed by the York architect Walter Brierley to the 18th-century designs – but on a grander Edwardian scale – for Sir Mark Sykes. In the beautiful staircase hall, in green and white with marble pillars, the Joseph Rose plasterwork was restored from the original moulds. Much of the furniture and paintings survived. The horse room, where the business affairs of the Sledmere stud were conducted, has a portrait of Sir Tatton Sykes, the great 19th-century sportsman and racehorse breeder, who used to ride all the way to Epsom every year to watch the Derby. The Turkish room was designed for Sir Mark by an Armenian artist. The attractive church was largely rebuilt in the 1890s. In the village there is a fascinating monument to the Waggoners Reserve, which Sir Mark raised locally in the First World War. *Open: Tue–Thu, Sat–Sun, mid-Apr–Sep.*

■

Below: at work in the engine shed at Steamtown. A locomotive depot was built at Carnforth in 1942, with Italian prisoners of war supplying the labour. Closed by British Rail in the 1960s, it was saved from demolition by steam railway enthusiasts, who opened Steamtown to the public in 1969

■

STEAMTOWN
RAILWAY CENTRE
LANCASHIRE
■ IN CARNFORTH, OFF THE A6 6 MILES (10KM) NORTH OF LANCASTER ■

In a desolate wilderness of sidings outside Carnforth station a large collection of veteran steam locomotives rescued from the scrap heap live out their days in dignity. Pre-eminent among them is the *Flying Scotsman*, though she is often away on trips. Others include the sleekly streamlined *Sir Nigel Gresley* and the Merchant Navy class *Canadian Pacific*. There are numerous industrial locomotives, workshops, a coaling plant, and an exhibition of railway paraphernalia, as well as a model railway and a miniature railway for the children. *Open: daily.*

DON'T MISS

■ The Amy Johnson room (**Sewerby Hall**)

■ Ruskin's collection (**Ruskin Gallery, Sheffield**)

■ Cutlery and plate (**Sheffield City Museum**)

■ The delicious staircase hall (**Sledmere House**)

STOTT PARK BOBBIN MILL
CUMBRIA
■ OFF THE A590 2 MILES (3KM) NORTH OF NEWBY BRIDGE ■

Enormous numbers of bobbins were required by the Lancashire textile factories in the 19th century. One of the places where they were made was the Stott Park mill, where the local tree trunks were turned into bobbins all under one roof. Watching the machinery at work today, belts flapping and sawdust flying while a guide explains the processes is a stunning experience in every sense of the term. The mill eventually closed down in 1971, but it was built in 1835 and remains fundamentally Victorian. It is admirably run by English Heritage and no visitor to the Lake District should miss it. *Open: daily, Eas–Sep (EH).*

TATTON PARK
CHESHIRE
■ OFF THE A50 2 MILES (3KM) NORTH OF KNUTSFORD ■

Set grandly in 1,000 acres (400ha) of rolling deer park, the stately Georgian mansion of the Egertons was left to the National Trust in 1958 by the last Lord Egerton. His big-game trophies are now one of the sights of Tatton Hall, along with the handsome state rooms. Outside, the grounds were landscaped successively by Humphry Repton and Sir Joseph Paxton. The home farm is kept as it was in the 1930s, there is a Japanese garden, meres with wildfowl and the original medieval Old Hall, as well as facilities for swimming, sailing and fishing. *Open: Tue–Sun, BH Mon, Apr–Sep (hall, NT): Tue–Sun (park, NT).*

WALLINGTON
NORTHUMBERLAND
■ ON THE B6342 1 MILE (1.6KM) SOUTH OF CAMBO ■

A house packed with history, Wallington was built in the 17th century, remodelled in the 18th and altered again in the 19th, when it was the home of Sir Walter and Lady Trevelyan, who entertained Ruskin, Swinburne and many of the Pre-Raphaelites. Ruskin helped to decorate the central hall. There is a late Victorian nursery, and displays of model soldiers and dolls' houses, as well as fine plasterwork, portraits, furniture and porcelain. Outside, besides a handsome walled garden and conservatory, the spacious park has lakes, woods and an 18th-century bridge by James Paine. *Open: daily, Eas–Oct (house, NT): daily (grounds, NT).*

WARKWORTH CASTLE
NORTHUMBERLAND
■ ON THE A1068 7 MILES (11KM) SOUTH OF ALNWICK ■

Towering above the River Coquet, the grim keep of Warkworth was one of the Percy dynasty's bastions against marauding Scots. A Norman stronghold originally, it was strengthened in subsequent centuries. The keep, in the shape of a Greek cross, was built in the 1400s and partly restored by Anthony Salvin in the 19th century. It is now kept by English Heritage. In summer visitors can take a boat trip up the river to the old hermitage. *Open: daily, Eas–Sep; Tue–Sat, Oct–Mar (EH).*

■

Below: one of the stone griffin's heads, originally brought north from London's Bishopsgate in 1760, which guard the east lawn of Wallington House. The simple mansion was the centre of a vivid intellectual and artistic life when owned by the Trevelyan family

■

■

DON'T MISS

■ The machines at work (**Stott Park Bobbin Mill**)

■ The big-game trophies (**Tatton Park**)

■ Jet ornaments and Captain Cook memories (**Whitby**)

■ The giant mill engine (**Wigan Pier**)

FOR CHILDREN

■ The home farm (**Tatton Park**)

■ The nursery and model soldiers (**Wallington**)

■ The schoolroom (**Wigan Pier**)

■

Left: the scene is peaceful enough today, with the River Coquet running smoothly towards the sea, but Warkworth Castle was originally a bastion against the Scots, who set siege to it more than once, and in 1405 Henry IV of England brought an army against it

■

WHITBY
NORTH YORKSHIRE

■ ON THE A171 20 MILES (32KM) NORTH-WEST OF SCARBOROUGH ■

An old fishing and sometime whaling port, Whitby has links with characters as diverse as Captain Cook and Count Dracula. It was an important religious centre in Anglo-Saxon times and the ruins of medieval **Whitby Abbey** 200ft (60m) up on the headland above the town, stand on the site where St Hilda founded a community of monks and nuns in the 7th century. The poet Caedmon was a monk here and in 664 the Synod of Whitby, held here, settled the differences between Roman Catholic and Celtic Christianity in favour of the Roman tradition. St Hilda's abbey was destroyed 200 years later by the Vikings and a Benedictine monastery was built soon after the Norman Conquest. The ruins, which in 1914 were shelled by a German battleship, are in the charge of English Heritage. *Open: daily, Eas–Sep; Tue-Sat, Oct–Mar (EH).*

Also on the headland, reached by a climb of 199 steps from the town, is the parish church of St Mary, which escaped Victorian restoration with its 18th-century interior of box pews and three-decker pulpit intact. The churchyard commands a splendid sea view. The houses of the town fall away down to the bustling harbour. The one in which the young James Cook lived as an apprentice is now the **Captain Cook Memorial Museum**, with displays relating to the great explorer's career. **Whitby Museum** also has Cook material and displays on local whaling and ship-building, as well as the jet ornaments for which the town is celebrated. A statue of Captain Cook stands high on the West Cliff. *Open: daily, May–Oct (Cook Museum): daily (Whitby Museum).*

WIGAN PIER
GREATER MANCHESTER

■ ON THE A49 IN CENTRAL WIGAN ■

From music hall joke to one of the most successful attractions in the North is a long step, but Wigan Pier has taken it. There is no pier, of course – Wigan is miles inland – but the warehouses on the Leeds and Liverpool Canal have been transformed into a vivid pageant of life as it was in this area around 1900. The most popular attraction of all is the schoolroom, where lessons of the period are conducted by actors, but there are also workshops, a coalface, a market and displays that create a picture of 'The Way We Were'. Waterbuses ply on the canal, a hall stages concerts ranging from classical music to jazz, and the ranks of machines in Trencherfield Mill tell the story of cotton spinning in the heyday of industrial Lancashire. They include what is possibly the largest working mill steam engine in the world. Several festivals are held here each year. *Open: daily.*

■

Below: tending the machines in Trencherfield Mill at Wigan Pier; in the background is part of the drum of the mammoth mill flywheel, over 26ft (8m) high, installed and 'christened' here in 1908. It is set working, with much hissing and rumbling, every half hour and is a vastly impressive spectacle

■

■

ON THE VAMPIRE'S TRAIL

Whitby's Dracula Trail caters for students of one of the great supernatural monsters of fiction, Bram Stoker's chilling nobleman with the ice-cold hands, gleaming red eyes and no reflection in a mirror. He was introduced to a quaking public in *Dracula* in 1897, in which he has himself shipped from Transylvania to Whitby in a box of his native earth and spends some time prowling St Mary's churchyard, where at one point he is seen hovering like a great black vampire bat over the motionless form of one of the story's heroines. The trail begins at the Bram Stoker Memorial Seat on the West Cliff – and you can follow the Whitby part of the tale from there.

■

YORK
NORTH YORKSHIRE

Until the coming of the Industrial Revolution, which largely passed it by, York was the first city of the north of England. As *Eboracum*, it was the principal Roman base in the North; Roman engineers chose the site at the furthest navigable point on the River Ouse. Wharves were built and a town grew up on the bank. After the Roman withdrawal the town became a Saxon settlement as *Eoforwic*, an important Christian missionary base in the North, a centre of learning and eventually the capital of the kingdom of Northumbria. As *Jorvik* in the 9th century, the town was the capital of a Viking kingdom, which lasted until the last king, Eric Bloodaxe, was driven out in 954. Later the Normans took York and built two castles, and in medieval times the city grew rich on the wool trade.

THE WALLS AND THE MINSTER

A walk along the top of the medieval town walls, which were restored in the 19th century, provides a striking and traffic-free prospect of the town. At intervals the walls are broken by fortified gates, called 'bars'. The formidable **Micklegate Bar** to the west was the city's principal entry and **Bootham Bar** was the gateway to the north.

Above: the emblem on the city's sign is the white rose of the house of York. This younger branch of the Plantagenet dynasty was descended from Edmund of Langley, son of King Edward III, who was Duke of York. By long tradition, the title is now conferred on the second son of the reigning sovereign

York Minster stands on the site of the Roman military headquarters, and on the very spot where the first little wooden church was built in the 7th century. It was later rebuilt in stone and then replaced in Norman times. Today's massive church dates mainly from the 13th, 14th and 15th centur-

Above: the twin west towers of York Minster, with part of Bootham Bar in the left foreground. The immense church is England's largest medieval cathedral and the Archbishops of York hold sway over the Church of England in the North. The massive central tower, which can be seen in the background, stands 198ft (60m) high and weighs some 16,000 tons

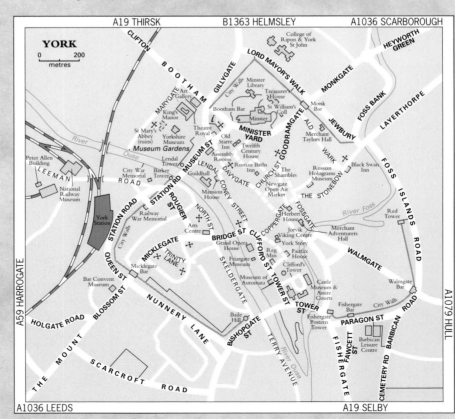

Above: narrow old streets in York ultimately go back to the Middle Ages, and the city today is a pleasure to stroll and shop in. This is the Shambles, where the butchers once plied their trade. One of the houses was the home of St Margaret Clitherow, a butcher's wife, who in 1586 was pressed to death with heavy stones for being a Roman Catholic

■

ies. It has survived several catastrophic fires, including one in 1984, and is famed especially for its magical stained glass. A window near the west end contains 12th-century glass which may be the oldest in the country. The immense 15th-century east window, the size of a tennis court, holds the largest expanse of medieval stained glass in the world.

Descending below ground into the undercroft, you can see the giant concrete foundations reinforced with miles of steel rods which have been put in since 1967 to support the crushing weight of the great central tower. You are also burrowing about in the Roman headquarters; there are Roman finds on display and you can see the Norman cathedral's foundations.

SAXON AND MEDIEVAL YORK

Little has survived from the Saxon period, but the very popular **Jorvik Viking Centre** carries visitors in 'time cars' through a vivid recreation of York as a thriving port and trading centre under its Danish kings, with the sights, sounds and even smells of the period. Thousands of objects found during archaeological work on the site are on display. For the archaeologically minded, the **ARC**, or **Archaeology Resource Centre**, in St Saviour's Church provides all sorts of lively hands-on experiences. *Open: daily (Jorvik Viking Centre): daily, Apr–Oct; Mon–Fri, Nov–Mar (ARC).*

The half-timbered **Merchant Adventurers' Hall** on the bank of the little River Foss was built in the 14th century by the most powerful of the city's merchant guilds.

Beneath the hall is the hospital provided for the guild's pensioners. There is still a row of 14th-century houses in Goodramgate and in gardens beside the Ouse are the remains of medieval **St Mary's Abbey**. The medieval York mystery plays are performed here every four years. The **Yorkshire Museum**, close by, has Roman, Saxon and Viking collections, including an impressive head of Constantine the Great, who was in York when he was proclaimed emperor in AD306. *Open: daily, end Mar–early Nov; Mon-Sat, early Nov–end Mar (hall): daily (museum).*

YORK'S MUSEUMS

Housed in the 18th-century women's prison and debtors' prison, the **York Castle Museum** is one of the best in the country, with an astonishing array of bygones, a walk-through Victorian shopping street and the condemned cell where the highwayman Dick Turpin spent his last night. In the 19th century York became a major railway centre and the **National Railway Museum** has the finest collection of rolling stock and railway memorabilia in the country, not to be missed by anyone remotely interested in steam trains. A newer venture is the **Museum of Automata**, which covers the subject from ancient articulated figures all the way to present-day robots. **Friargate Museum**, meanwhile, brings the past to life with waxworks. *Open: daily (all).*

John Carr, the great York architect of the 18th century, designed elegant **Fairfax House**, which was rescued by the York Civic Trust in 1983. With fine plaster ceilings, it is now stocked with the furniture, paintings, clocks and porcelain of the Terry Collection. Terry's were rivals of Rowntree's and Craven's, the other famous York chocolate firms. Close to the minster, the 17th-century **Treasurer's House** has a fine collection of furniture and, just outside the western walls, the Georgian **Bar Convent** has an interesting museum of Christian history in the North. *Open: Sat–Thur, late Feb–Dec (Fairfax House): daily, Eas–Oct (Treasurer's House, NT): Tue–Sat, Feb–Dec (Bar Convent).*

A statue of the painter William Etty, who was born in York (so were Guy Fawkes and W H Auden), stands in front of the **City Art Gallery**, which has an enjoyable collection of European paintings from the 14th century on, including some delightful portraits by Etty of his York friends. There is fine pottery, too. Next door is **King's Manor**, originally the house of the abbots of St Mary's and later the headquarters of the Lords President of the Council of the North. *Open: daily (gallery): daily (courtyards); check with porter for opening times of other rooms.*

■

Below: York's handsome, curving railway station dates from the 1870s. The architect, Thomas Prosser, also designed the magnificent Royal York Hotel next door, with its fine ironwork

■

■

Above: Victorian York is vividly recalled in a lifesize reconstructed street in the York Castle Museum. The museum's enthralling collection of bygones was founded by a local country doctor named John Kirk, who collected oddments on his rounds in the 1890s and after

■

YORKSHIRE DALES NATIONAL PARK
NORTH YORKSHIRE

Stretching from the Pennines in the west to the Vale of York in the east, the 680 square miles (1,760km²) of the national park offer some of the country's most appealing scenery. Much of it is the preserve of walkers, climbers and pot-holers, as well as the soaring larks, the hovering hawks and the inescapable sheep. Dales and their rivers run east, or at least most do: the Swale, the Ure, the Wharfe and their smaller sisters

eventually empty into the North Sea. There is also the Ribble, which heads south through the park, but then perversely turns west to make for Preston and out into the Irish Sea.

WALKING IN THE DALES
The Pennine Way tramps north through some of the best of the limestone scenery by Malham Cove, and pushes on to Hawes, and across the Swale to leave the park near the Tan Hill Inn, possibly England's highest pub, at 1,732ft (528m). The second major footpath is the Dales Way which runs all the way up Wharfedale to cross the Pennine Way, follow the River Dee to Sedbergh and disappear towards the Lake District. Many lesser walking routes and old green tracks and 'corpse roads' explore the countryside, making up more than 1,000 miles (1,600km) of public rights of way.

THE NORTHERN DALES
In the park's northernmost reaches, Arkengarthdale and Swaledale are the wildest of the valleys. Abandoned lead mines crumble on the sheep-nibbled slopes. At Reeth the **Swaledale Folk Museum** tells the story of the past with particular emphasis on lead mining

and sheep farming. Lovers of the vets' adventures in *All Creatures Great and Small* on television will recognise some of the scenery here and around Langthwaite. A scenic road leads through the Buttertubs Pass. The Buttertubs are deep holes in the limestone, as much as 65ft (20m) deep, where villagers on their way to market are said to have hung their butter to keep cool while they paused for a rest. *Open: daily, Eas–Oct (museum).*

This road leads to Hawes, a picturesque market town of Wensleydale, which is the valley of the Ure. Its old railway station houses a national park information centre as part of the **Dales Countryside Museum** with its collection of local artefacts and curiosities. It includes displays formed by two remarkable local historians. Outside Hawes is a famous 90ft (27m) waterfall, **Hardraw Force**, where you can walk behind the cascade, between the water and the cliff. *Open: daily, Apr–Oct; Sat, Sun, Nov–Mar, check with local tourist information centres for details (museum).*

The A684 follows Wensleydale eastwards to Aysgarth, where the Ure swirls down three sets of falls. An old mill that once made red shirts for Garibaldi's army is now the **Yorkshire Carriage Museum**. The **National Park Centre** provides maps, organised walks and information. To the north is **Bolton Castle** (see separate entry) and to the east, just outside the park, are the impressive remains of **Middleham Castle**, childhood home of Richard III. Nearby is **Jervaulx Abbey** (see separate entry). *Open: daily, Eas–Oct (museum): daily, Eas–Oct; Nov–Mar, check with tourist information centres for details (National Park Centre): daily, Eas–Sep; Tue–Sun, Oct–Mar (castle, EH).*

WHARFEDALE AND THE SOUTHERN DALES
Further south lie the beauties of Wharfedale. Many of the place names are Norse and reflect Viking settlement of the area in the 9th and 10th centuries. Kilnsey Crag poses a considerable challenge to rock climbers, while further south Grassington has a cobbled square and a **National Park Centre**. The gardens at **Parcevall Hall** command delectable views and close by is the limestone gorge of Troller's Gill. The Wharfe's loveliest stretch flows through a murderous cataract called the **Strid**, which has claimed

■

Above: Middle Force, one of the three waterfalls on the River Ure at Aysgarth in Wensleydale. Yore Bridge and the old mill are further upstream, towards High Force. Wensleydale, unusually, is not named after its river, but takes its name from the village of Wensley, lying east of Aysgarth, near Leyburn

■

Left: looking north over Swaledale to the high moors. The valley was for centuries a thinly populated and isolated backwater with hardly a church to its name, so that pall bearers had to carry the dead long distances to bury them in consecrated ground. Then came lead mining and, after its demise, the tourist industry

Above: wild flowers stud a traditional hay meadow at Muker. The rich soil of the valley floors was used for growing hay and the fields were lively with buttercups and herbs, which were left to seed before the hay was cut and stored as winter feed for the farm livestock

Above: knowledgeable eyes assess the sheep for sale at an auction in Hawes. Sheep farming has been the mainstay of Dales agriculture for many centuries. The old horned and black-faced Swaledales have been crossed with Scottish blackfaces to produce the new Dalesbreed strain. Farmers also cross these hill breeds with the Wensleydales to produce Mashams, with their crinkly fleeces

many lives in its time, to the ruins of **Bolton Priory** which stand in tranquillity in one of the most beautiful settings in England. *Open: daily, Eas–Oct; Nov–Mar, check with tourist information offices for details (National Park Centre): daily, Eas–Oct (hall): daily (priory).*

Outside the park, Pateley Bridge lies at the heart of Nidderdale, where the **Nidderdale Museum** of local life occupies the Victorian workhouse. At **Brimham Rocks** the National Trust protects the weathered outcrops of stone in their fantastic shapes high on the moor. *Open: daily, Spring BH–Sep; Sun, Oct–Eas; Sat, Sun, Eas–Spring BH (museum): Eas; Sat, Sun, BH Mon, Eas–Spring BH; daily, Spring BH–Oct (Brimham Rocks information centre, NT).*

To the south of the park, the town of Skipton is the capital of the Craven district. **Skipton Castle**, the stronghold of the Clifford family, was restored in the 17th century and there are fine Clifford tombs in the nearby parish church. The **Craven Museum** illuminates local history, while the **Yorkshire Dales Railway** runs steam trains on a short stretch of line between Skipton and Embsay. *Open: daily (castle): Wed–Mon, Apr–Sep; Mon, Wed–Sat, Oct–Mar (museum): Sun, all year; Tue, Sat, Sun, Jul; Tue–Thu, Sat, Sun, Aug (railway).*

GEOLOGICAL ODDITIES

Skipton is a gateway to the spectacular limestone formations of the Craven area in the south-west of the National Park. The **National Park** at Malham introduces the weird geology of this region. Malham Cove is a towering 300ft (90m) cliff with a cracked and fissured limestone 'pavement' on top. The National Trust owns Malham Tarn, the moorland lake which inspired Charles Kingsley's *The Water Babies. Open: daily, Apr–Oct; Nov–Mar, check with local tourist information centres for details (National Park Centre).*

Going on north-west, the ground is riddled with caves, pot-holes and underground rivers. The abyss of **Gaping Gill** is deep enough to swallow York Minster (descents are organised for visitors on some Bank Holidays). Stalactites and stalagmites glisten in vast, cathedral-like subterranean caverns, like the **White Scar Caves**. *Open: daily (White Scar).*

This strange landscape is explained at the **National Park Centre** at Clapham and the **Museum of North Craven Life**. This is in Settle, a market town on the Ribble which is at one end of the Settle to Carlisle railway line, an astonishing triumph of Victorian engineering which runs through wild upland scenery over a succession of heroic viaducts. *Open: daily, Apr–Oct (National Park Centre): Sat, Sun, May–Jun; Tue–Sun, Jul–Sep; Sat, Oct–Apr (museum).*

Close to the north-western corner of the national park is Sedbergh, which is officially in Cumbria. It is the biggest town in the park and there is another **National Park Centre** here. The quiet, rounded Howgill Fells here are richly rewarding to explore. *Open: daily, Apr–Nov.*

SCOTLAND

∎

Inquisitive visitors to Abbotsford, the house Sir Walter Scott built for himself in his beloved Border country, can see a lock of Bonnie Prince Charlie's hair, a purse that belonged to Rob Roy and a drinking glass that felt the grip of Robert Burns's hand, as well many other curios and a strange painting depicting the head of Mary, Queen of Scots, the day after it had been removed from her shoulders. Within easy reach of Abbotsford, the same inquisitive visitors can admire the melancholy ruins of Melrose Abbey, where in some unknown spot the heart of Robert Bruce lies buried, and climb the shapely Eildon Hills, where in legend Thomas the Rhymer met the beautiful Queen of Faerie and was taken away to her magic realm to be her lover. Sir Walter Scott himself once said he could stand on the Eildons and point out 43 places famous in war and verse.

This blend of scenic beauty, romantic legends and a violent past is what draws many visitors to Scotland. In a country which is roughly three-fifths the size of England, there is a rewarding wealth of hill, water and mountain scenery, much of it of surpassing loveliness. Loch Lomond is famed in song and it was Scott's poetry that first drew tourists to the rugged mountains and sparkling lochs of the Trossachs. Further north brood the grim defile of Glencoe and the wild, snow-capped barrier of the Cairngorms. North again, across the Great Glen, lie the graceful Seven Sisters of Kintail, the black and jagged Cuillins of Skye and the sublime peaks and sea-lochs of Wester Ross.

Across the landscape stand the relics and memorials of Scotland's turbulent past. On the island of Iona in the western sea St Columba founded a monastery for the Christianising of the country. Caerlaverock stood siege by Edward I in 1300. Mary, Queen of Scots, was born at Linlithgow and spent happy hours at Falkland. The Glenfinnan Monument at the head of Loch Shiel marks the spot where Bonnie Prince Charlie raised his banner with high hopes in 1745 – and the battlefield of Culloden is where those hopes were bloodily broken. Historic and impregnable fastnesses, planted on unclimbable crags at Stirling and Edinburgh, are the veterans of centuries of warfare and siege. Blair Castle still has its own private army, while fairy fortresses like Craigievar and Crathes could fittingly shelter Sleeping Beauty. Other castles, products of a more peaceful age, are stately residences bulging with treasures and informed by cultivated taste: Culzean and Drumlanrig, Fyvie and Floors.

Cities and towns, too, have an inimitable flavour. Edinburgh, 'the Athens of the North', is a city of the utmost distinction, admirably equipped with museums and galleries, statues and monuments, and the 18th-century elegance of the New Town. Glasgow boasts some of the best Victorian architecture in Britain, the fabulous Burrell Collection and an art school by Charles Rennie Mackintosh. In Dumfries there are memories of Robert Burns. St Andrews is the capital of golf and Dufftown of whisky, while Aberdeen brings the history of the land up to today as the supply base for the North Sea oil rigs.

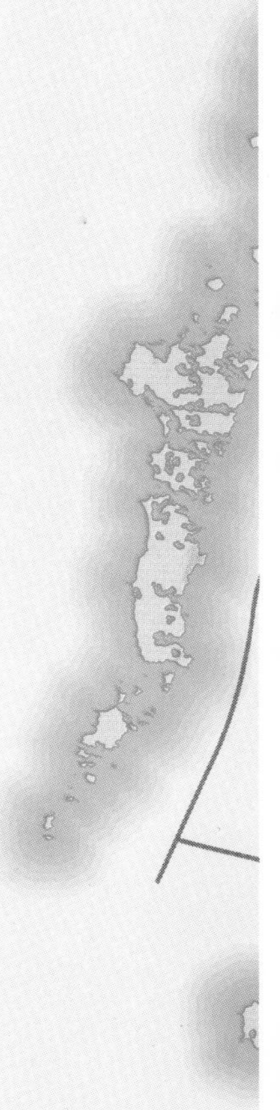

∎

WESTERN ISLES

Isle
of
Skye

Thurso

Wick

Dunrobin
Castle

Ullapool

Inverewe
Gardens

Dornoch

Wester ROSS

Fraserburgh

Dingwall

Elgin

Fyvie
Castle

Peterhead

Cawdor
Castle

Dufftown

Haddo
House

Inverness

Culloden
Battlefield

HIGHLAND

GRAMPIAN

Kintail

Grantown-
on-Spey

Craigievar
Castle

Aberdeen

Aviemore

The
Cairngorms

Fort Augustus

Highland
Wildlife Park

Ballater

Crathes
Castle

Balmoral
Castle

Glenfinnan
Monument

Blair
Castle

Fort William

Pitlochry

Montrose

Tobermory

Glencoe

TAYSIDE

Angus Folk
Museum

Cruachan
Power
Station

Dundee

Iona

Oban

Perth

St. Andrews

Inveraray
Castle

CENTRAL

Callander

FIFE

The Trossachs

Loch
Lomond

Falkland
Palace

Stirling

Hill
House

Culross

Kirkcaldy

Kyles of
Bute

Bo'ness &
Kinneil Railway

Hopetoun House

Dunoon

Greenock

Dumbarton

Linlithgow
Palace

Dalmeny
House

Edinburgh

Rothesay

Glasgow

LOTHIAN

Largs

STRATHCLYDE

Lanark

Peebles

Mellerstain
House

Kilmarnock

New Lanark

Galashiels

Melrose
Abbey

Floors
Castle

Traquair
House

Abbotsford
House

Selkirk

Jedburgh

Campbeltown

Ayr

BORDERS

Burns Cottage

Sanquhar

Moffat

Culzean
Castle

Drumlanrig
Castle

Girvan

DUMFRIES AND
GALLOWAY

New Galloway

Dumfries

Stranraer

Gatehouse
of Fleet

Sweetheart
Abbey

Caerlaverock
Castle

Logan
Botanic
Gardens

ABBOTSFORD HOUSE
BORDERS (ROXBURGHSHIRE)
■ OFF THE A7, 2 MILES (3KM) SOUTH-EAST OF GALASHIELS ■

This romantic, rambling mansion was built between 1817 and 1822 by the famous Scottish novelist, Sir Walter Scott. It remains very much as in Scott's day, strongly atmospheric, with dark wooden panelling, ornate carvings, armour, firearms and trophies almost lending it the air of a Gothic horror movie setting. Scott's extraordinary collection of artefacts breathes life into the story of Scotland's past: Prince Charlie's *quaich* (drinking vessel); Bonnie Dundee's pistol; a glass on which Robert Burns scratched some verses. Take time to study the curiosities – but avoid the crowds at high season. *Open: Mar–Oct.*

ABERDEEN
GRAMPIAN (ABERDEENSHIRE)

Aberdeen is Scotland's third and most northerly city. Its silver granite buildings sparkle in the sun – or cast an austere grey pall if it rains. Before oil became its main industry, Aberdeen seemed like an overgrown market town, servicing a prosperous agricultural hinterland. For the last two decades it has been the oil capital of Europe, and now the city bustles. Office blocks and edge-of-town industrial estates have all but banished its sleepy air. Conscious that first-time visitors might otherwise find Aberdeen cold and northerly, the city authorities have placed great emphasis on floral decoration. In Aberdeen, flowers do not just grow in neat parks (of which the city has several). Instead, they have escaped into every public space, colourfully defying outsiders' expectations – from the sheets of daffodils splashed all around the main A92 southern approaches, to the numerous displays of roses that brighten the ringroad for most of the summer. Though tough granite is not a material normally associated with exuberant building styles, the city's **Marischal College** is notable among many fine civic buildings. With a façade halfway between a cathedral and a wedding cake, this is the second-largest granite building in the world. A much-admired trio is that of **St Mark's Church**, Aberdeen's **main library** and **His Majesty's Theatre** – an architectural grouping known locally as 'Salvation, Education and Damnation'. Elsewhere, the city offers an outstanding **art gallery**, a range of **museums**, one offering an appropriate maritime theme, as well as children's wet-weather attractions, notably the **Satrosphere**, a 'hands-on' science discovery centre, **James Dun's House** with its changing programme of family-orientated exhibitions and also Jonah's Journey, an activity-based learning centre with biblical themes. Also worth exploring are the university precincts of **King's College** in **Old Aberdeen**, (note the fine Georgian town house and also the converted artisans' cottages, now housing academic staff), **St Machar's Cathedral** and, beyond, the picturesque 14th-century Brig o' Balgownie spanning the River Don. Aberdeen is the gateway to Royal Deeside; to the very finest of Scotland's castles in the Gordon District Castle Trail; and to some of Britain's finest unspoilt coastline in Banff and Buchan.
Open: daily (art gallery, Satrosphere): Mon–Sat (James Dun's House).

SIR WALTER SCOTT

Sir Walter Scott was the greatest single influence on the modern image of 'romantic Scotland' – the Scotland of clans and pipes, heather and the fiery cross. Scott was born in Edinburgh in 1771, the son of a lawyer. He was one of the great Border family of Scott, and as a boy he spent time poring over ballads and annals of Border history, with their tales of feuds and raids, heroism, treachery and sudden death. He later brought them vividly to life in poems and novels, which were best-sellers in their day.

Above: Sir Walter Scott's study at Abbotsford still contains his desk, in which two secret drawers were found as recently as 1935. These contained previously unknown letters to his wife, both before and after marriage

Below: the Winter Gardens in Aberdeen's Duthie Park are mainly modern glasshouses with a range of floral themes. As well as tropical hothouses, there is a cactus house and conservatories with major collections of ferns, alpines and other exotic plants. The Winter Gardens are claimed to be one of Scotland's top free attractions

ANGUS FOLK MUSEUM
TAYSIDE (ANGUS)
■ OFF THE A94 AT GLAMIS, 5 MILES (8KM) SOUTH-WEST OF FORFAR ■

In Kirk Wynd, within the attractive little village of Glamis near the famous castle of the same name, the National Trust for Scotland has created a museum which displays various aspects of rural life (mainly 19th-century) in the county of Angus. A row of early 19th-century terraced cottages with unusual stone slabbed roofs has been converted into a series of display areas, linked by a passage. Each room has a different theme, ranging from schooldays to leisure and pastimes. A whole variety of artefacts, from specialist farming tools to everyday domestic equipment, is on display both in cases and forming room tableaux. *Open: Eas and May–Sep (NTS).*

BALMORAL CASTLE
GRAMPIAN (ABERDEENSHIRE)
■ OFF THE A93, 8 MILES (13KM) WEST OF BALLATER ■

The Royal Family's association with Deeside, the river valley adjoining Aberdeen, came about because Prince Albert and Queen Victoria experienced incessant rainfall in western Scotland when they were looking for a holiday home. They later heard that the son of the Queen's doctor had enjoyed brilliant sunshine on Deeside, in the east, at the same time. The Prince investigated the rainfall statistics of the area and made his decision accordingly, acquiring the lease for the Balmoral estate in 1848 and building a new castle there by 1855. It was built in the Scottish baronial style by Aberdeen's city architect, William Smith. Queen Victoria subsequently visited Balmoral each year, until the death of Prince Albert in 1861. These holidays were probably the happiest times of her life. So special was Balmoral's magic that in the last decades of the 19th century she spent up to one-third of each year there – which did not please her ministers. After her death the castle and grounds became the personal property of each succeeding monarch, providing a private home and retreat from the rigours of high office for both members of the Royal Family and heads of state from home and abroad.

Visitors can enjoy walking in the grounds, down by the River Dee, and can follow trails high into the ancient pinewoods and hills. There are also herbaceous borders, conservatories and a water garden. The ballroom is the only part of the castle which is open to the public. It offers an annual exhibition of paintings, works of art and photographs from the Queen's own collections. Be warned: Balmoral has two distinct personalities, one public, one intensely private. For three months of the year visitors are free to wander in the grounds. At other times, this gentle, peaceful place is transformed into a high security establishment, and visitors are *not* welcome. *Open: Mon–Sat, May–Jul.*

BLAIR CASTLE
TAYSIDE (PERTHSHIRE)
■ OFF THE A9, 6 MILES (10KM) NORTH-WEST OF PITLOCHRY ■

The ancient seat of the Dukes of Atholl, this impressive and rambling castle stands on a site of former strategic importance, controlling the main route into the central Highlands. Although the castle has altered greatly in appearance, due to damage in warfare and the structural changes made over the years by its owners, Cumming's Tower, the oldest part of the present structure, dates from the 13th century. During its 700-year history, the castle has been associated with many well-known figures and events. Mary, Queen of Scots was entertained here and taken on a grand hunt, in which five wolves and 360 deer were said to have been killed. The Atholl estates today are still very extensive. Blair Castle was also the last fortress in Britain to be besieged. This was during the 1745–6 Jacobite uprising, when General George Murray, one of the Jacobite leaders, attempted to regain control of Blair. At the time it was controlled by the government (and was therefore in Hanoverian hands). A framed portion of flooring marked by red-hot shot can be seen today as a reminder of the incident – just one of many curiosities on display in the 30 or so rooms open to the public. With so many to stroll through, a visit may easily become blurred into a recollection of Chippendale cabinets, Sheraton chairs, and sumptuous tapestries. The impressive mixture of historical pieces on display is truly a grand collection, assembled over the centuries by a powerful family close to the centre of Scotland's political life. *Open: Apr–Oct.*

■

Below: Balmoral Castle was built in Scottish baronial style by Aberdeen's city architect, William Smith. It was later a model for another building which in part resembles it externally, though at the other end of the social spectrum – Aberdeen's Salvation Army Citadel

■

■

Below: the Duke of Atholl is unique amongst the Scottish aristocracy in that he is permitted to keep his own private army. The Atholl Highlanders are seen here on parade in the castle grounds. Their function these days is purely ceremonial. Many of them are actually estate workers

■

■

DON'T MISS ___

■ The maze (Hazlehead Park, Aberdeen)

■ The Rose Hill in August (Duthie Park, Aberdeen)

■ Historical Scottish artefacts (the library, Abbotsford)

BO'NESS & KINNEIL RAILWAY
LOTHIAN (WEST LOTHIAN)
■ OFF THE M9 (JUNCTION 3), 3 MILES NORTH OF LINLITHGOW ■

The Scottish Railway Preservation Society has re-created a typical Scottish branch line out of dereliction. It runs from a station on the foreshore at Bo'ness, west to the former colliery at Kinneil, then up a wooded valley past the former Birkhill Clay Mine (opportunities to visit), eventually reaching Manuel Junction on the main Edinburgh–Glasgow line. Bo'ness station is of particular interest. There are, of course, steam-hauled services, and the star of the show is *Maude*, a Holmes 0-6-0 (class J36) from the Victorian era.
Open: weekends only (extended during the summer season), all year.

BURNS COTTAGE
STRATHCLYDE (AYRSHIRE)
■ ON THE B7024 AT ALLOWAY, 2 MILES (3KM) SOUTH OF AYR ■

Scotland's national poet, Robert Burns, was born in this small thatched cottage in 1759, and lived here until 1766. Restored and furnished as it was in the poet's time, the cottage, along with the next-door **museum** of Burnsiana, is an important attraction. Other local places with Burns associations include the **Land o' Burns Centre**, **Alloway Kirk**, the **Burns Monument** and the **Brig o' Doune**. *Open: daily, Apr–Oct; Mon–Sat, Nov–Mar.*

CAERLAVEROCK CASTLE AND NATURE RESERVE
DUMFRIES AND GALLOWAY (DUMFRIESSHIRE)
■ OFF THE B725, 9 MILES (14KM) SOUTH OF DUMFRIES ■

Though ruined, this 13th-century moated frontier fortress, constructed in warm red sandstone, remains very impressive. Its builder, whose name does not survive, employed a most unusual triangular design with round corner towers. The castle was much altered during the years of Anglo–Scottish warfare. The castle defences were restored by Lord Maxwell in the 15th and 16th centuries. His armorial can be seen above the main gateway. Also relating to the Maxwell family are the carved pediments to be seen in the later eastern range – the mansion-like Nithsdale's Building of 1639.

Nearby is **Caerlaverock National Nature Reserve**, 13,600 acres (5,500ha) of marsh and mudflats enjoyed by wildfowl. The entire Spitzbergen population of barnacle geese also overwinters here. The Wildfowl Trust's (centrally heated) observatory offers the visitor deluxe bird-watching. *Open: daily (castle, HS and nature reserve).*

THE PLOUGHMAN POET

Robert Burns, Scotland's greatest poet, grew up on a succession of impoverished farms where his father struggled to scratch a living from the soil. In his teens he was his father's principal labourer, leading a life which he afterwards described as combining 'the cheerless gloom of a hermit and the unceasing toil of a galley-slave'. His father died when the poet was 24 and the young man thought of emigrating to Jamaica, but his life was changed by the tremendous success of his first volume of verse, published at Kilmarnock in 1786, when he was 27. His lyrics and songs, composed while he walked behind the plough or by candlelight in his room of a cold night, struck an immediate chord everywhere in Scotland. Burns was summoned to Edinburgh to be lauded and lionised, and his career was made. He farmed for a time, married his great love, Jean Armour, and in 1791 obtained a post as a customs officer at Dumfries, where he spent the rest of his life and where today the Robert Burns Centre honours his memory.

Above: Robert Burns is sometimes known as 'the ploughman poet'. His humble origins are evident from his birthplace (left). Burns was, in fact, well educated for his time. He is still remembered with great fondness by Scots today, and the annual Burns Night celebrations give him unique status among British poets

THE CAIRNGORMS
GRAMPIAN/HIGHLAND
(ABERDEENSHIRE/BANFFSHIRE/INVERNESS-SHIRE)

■

Above: Loch Morlich, below the Cairngorms plateau, was once a long walk from Aviemore. Now, because of an access road built for skiers, its sense of unspoilt remoteness has gone for ever. Today the loch plays its part in the leisure industry which threatens the mountain habitat

■

The great mountainous plateau of the Cairngorms forms the most extensive area of land in Britain above 3,500ft (1,067m). The highest top is **Ben Macdhui**, at 4,296ft (1,310m) second only to **Ben Nevis** in Lochaber, while **Braeriach** and **Cairn Toul** on the western section of the plateau, as well as **Cairn Gorm** itself, are among other high tops above the 4,000ft (1,220m) contour. The Cairngorms are a designated National Nature Reserve of over 64,000 acres (25,920ha) – the largest in Britain. However, this status has not made them immune to the pressures of a leisure-orientated age: ski developers nibble at the wild corries (steep glacial valleys) and aspire to open up additional runs, while chair lifts now whisk not just skiers, but also tourists and walkers throughout the year, to heights that were unreachable 30 years ago except by going on a day-long hike. Sadly, the delicate, tundra-like landscape of the central plateau, the habitat of a wide variety of fauna and flora, is becoming increasingly scarred by paths and litter.

Fortunately there are still some remote sections where the exposed, frost-shattered pink granite forms a habitat for arctic-alpine plants, such as creeping azalea or dwarf willow; and there are also concealed places, where the ptarmigan, snow bunting and dotterel (a wading bird of extraordinary tameness, with a penchant for high, domed mountain tops) can all breed in relative peace. Also in these high, bouldery, windswept places a few Cairngorm stones can still be found – gemstones which are actually yellow or brown quartz crystals, formed in cavities of cooling granite long ages ago. Away from the searing exposure of the plateau, in the more sheltered corries, there is a wider variety of flora and fauna (including golden eagle and wildcats). The pinewoods of the lower slopes also add a softer theme to the Cairngorms experience. There the great red-limbed trees, with their high carpet of juniper and rank heather, are an attractive habitat for all manner of birds such as the elusive capercaillie, as well as several other northern species, like the crossbill and the crested tit.

The Lairig Ghru is the main pass which dissects the plateau, an old-established through-route between Speyside and Deeside. To the west of it lie **Braeriach** and **Cairn Toul**, perhaps the least spoilt parts of the plateau. The pinewoods of **Rothiemurchus** lie to the north, where fragments of the ancient wood of Caledon can still be found, particularly around **Loch an Eilein**. Another speciality are reindeer, reintroduced to the area in 1954, about 800 years after extinction. As in the mountains of Scandinavia, the high tundra provides them with their basic food, reindeer moss, a primitive lichen. The **Rothiemurchus Estate Visitor Centre** offers a variety of experiences, from Landrover safaris to estate tours, while another centre at **Loch an Eilein** portrays the diversity of this unique part of Scotland's heritage. The main (southern) gateway to the Cairngorms is at **Aviemore** on Speyside. Here there is a brutally modern tourist centre, offering a wide range of attractions, and accommodation.

■

DON'T MISS

■ Wintering barnacle geese (Caerlaverock National Nature Reserve)

■ The walk round Loch an Eilein (Cairngorms)

CAWDOR CASTLE
HIGHLAND (NAIRN)

■ OFF THE B9090, 5 MILES (8KM) SOUTH-WEST OF NAIRN ■

A 14th-century tower, 15th-century fortifications and a 16th-century range of buildings, later remodelled, form the structure of Cawdor Castle. As a bonus there are beautiful gardens and interesting nature trails. But its highlight is that, perhaps uniquely among Scottish stately homes, it displays a sense of humour. Nowhere else in Scotland is the usually stuffy air of faded grandeur punctuated and refreshed by gusts of laughter, yet visitors to Cawdor who take the trouble to read the captions and notes in each room are invariably amused. There are fine tapestries, ornate pieces of furniture, ancient artefacts, plus all the paraphernalia of a 600-year-old family home. There is also all the romance and tragedy of Shakespeare's *Macbeth* (the Thane of Cawdor). But the sense of fun which lightens the gloom is what you will remember. *Open: May–Sep.*

CRAIGIEVAR CASTLE
GRAMPIAN (ABERDEENSHIRE)

■ OFF THE A980, 6 MILES (10KM) SOUTH OF ALFORD ■

Craigievar is sometimes described as the most perfect of the castles of Mar, that part of the old county of Aberdeenshire which has such a wealth of castellated architecture. Craigievar was completed in Scottish baronial style in 1626 for a merchant, William Forbes (sometimes also known as 'Danzig Willie', because he traded with the Baltic). The castle reflects not just the confidence and prosperity of a successful 17th-century businessman, but also the relative peacefulness of the age. Now in the care of the National Trust for Scotland, the building still stands much as Willie knew it, a slender, airy edifice with turrets, cupolas and corbelling, like a picture in a fairytale. Inside there is exceptionally fine plasterwork, notably in the great hall, which has barely altered in over 350 years. There is also some beautifully worked wooden panelling, particularly in the Withdrawing Room. *Open: late Apr–Sep (NTS).*

CRATHES CASTLE
GRAMPIAN (KINCARDINESHIRE)

■ OFF THE A93, 3 MILES (5KM) EAST OF BANCHORY ■

This L-plan towerhouse was built by the Burnett family between 1593 and 1596, during a wave of castle-building in the north-east at that time. Perhaps the most notable feature of the interior is its painted ceilings. The most noted artefact on display is the Horn of Leys, said to have been presented to the Burnett family by King Robert the Bruce, along with lands, in 1323. There is some fine furniture on display, including chairs and beds from the 16th-century Aberdeen school of woodworking. Another important attraction is the series of eight linked gardens, each bounded by yew hedges and dating from c.1702. *Open: Apr–Oct (castle); daily (grounds).*

CRUACHAN POWER STATION
STRATHCLYDE (ARGYLL)

■ OFF THE A85, 18 MILES (29KM) EAST OF OBAN ■

After travelling by minibus down a tunnel more than half a mile (800m) long, bored into Ben Cruachan, visitors can see the turbines and associated machinery of Scottish Power's 400,000kW pumped storage scheme. This uses water from a dammed reservoir high on Ben Cruachan to generate power. The water flows into Loch Awe, and is then pumped back up to the reservoir when demand is low. The impressive process is explained in a visitor centre on the shores of Loch Awe. *Open: late Mar–Oct.*

CULLODEN BATTLEFIELD
HIGHLAND (INVERNESSSHIRE/ NAIRN)

■ OFF THE B9006, 5 MILES (8KM) EAST OF INVERNESS ■

The Battle of Culloden was the decisive conflict in a civil war between the Jacobite Roman Catholic and Episcopalian supporters of the exiled Stuart dynasty and the Protestant Hanoverians, defending the government and the status quo. Prince Charles Edward Stuart ('Bonnie Prince Charlie') raised only about one-sixth of an estimated 30,000 fighting clansmen in the Highlands for his rebel forces. In the fierce fighting that took place on 16 April 1746, the government's forces, under General (later 'Butcher') Cumberland used their superior power to blow away the rebel lines. They then carried out the worst atrocities in the history of the British Army. Today Culloden is one of the most sombre spots in the Highlands. *Open: daily (visitor centre Feb–Dec), NTS.*

CULROSS
FIFE

■ OFF THE A985, 7 MILES (11KM) WEST OF DUNFERMLINE ■

Culross is a remarkable survivor – a little Scottish town that was bypassed by the Industrial Revolution, and has so escaped development. In consequence, when much of the townscape was saved for restoration by the National Trust for Scotland, it still included many fine examples of 17th- and 18th-century domestic architecture. Though it looks like a filmset, Culross remains a living community.

Below: although it is often portrayed as a Scots versus English conflict, Culloden was the last battle in a civil war which divided political and religious loyalties, irrespective of nationality. Many Highland chiefs forbade their men to join Bonnie Prince Charlie (inset), considering him mad and dangerous

The defeat at Culloden ended any prospect of a Stuart restoration. Prince Charles Edward escaped from the battlefield and for five months was hunted through the Highlands. Though there was a price of £30,000 on his head, he was never given away, and many took desperate risks to help him. Among them was the famous Flora Macdonald, who took the prince, disguised as her maid, in a rowing boat from Benbecula 'over the sea to Skye'.

CULZEAN CASTLE
STRATHCLYDE (AYRSHIRE)
■ OFF THE A719, 12 MILES (19KM) SOUTH-WEST OF AYR ■

Dating mostly from 1777 and for generations the home of the Kennedys, the Earls of Cassillis, Culzean is considered to be one of Robert Adam's finest designs, with outstanding plasterwork and a magnificent staircase. It also has a connection with General Eisenhower, the Supreme Commander of the Allied Forces in Europe during the Second World War. He was given a flat within the castle by the Scottish nation as a token of gratitude. In addition to the treasures of the house, the 560-acre (226ha) landscape park and wooded grounds are now known as **Culzean Country Park**. They have their own reception and interpretation centre. Castle and grounds are in the care of the National Trust for Scotland. They are their most popular attraction, with almost 400,000 visitors annually. About a quarter of these visit the castle. *Open: Apr–Oct, daily (castle, NTS); daily (grounds).*

DALMENY HOUSE
LOTHIAN (WEST LOTHIAN)
■ OFF THE A90, 7 MILES (11KM) WEST OF EDINBURGH ■

Although the Earls of Rosebery have lived on this site for 300 years, the present house, in Tudor Gothic style, dates from 1815. Originally the family lived in Barnbougle Castle, still on the estate but beside the shore of the Firth of Clyde. This pile was much neglected during the 18th century – the 3rd Earl was once drenched by a wave that came through the dining-room window! His son, the 4th Earl, built Dalmeny House. Today its contents are sumptuous, including French furniture, tapestries and porcelain from the Rothschild Mentmore collection. *Open: Sun–Thu, May–Sep.*

DRUMLANRIG CASTLE
DUMFRIES AND GALLOWAY (DUMFRIESSHIRE)

■ OFF THE A76, 3 MILES (5KM) NORTH OF THORNHILL ■

This opulent example of 17th-century Renaissance architecture is the perfect setting for a store of treasures, including many extremely valuable paintings, gathered from various aristocratic residences. *Open: Sun–Fri, May–Aug (castle); daily, May–Sep (grounds).*

DUFFTOWN
GRAMPIAN (BANFFSHIRE)

■ ON THE A941, 17 MILES (27KM) SOUTH-WEST OF ELGIN ■

James Duff, the 4th Earl of Fife, founded Dufftown (originally called Balvenie), to create employment for soldiers returning from the Napoleonic Wars. His plan was to build a cross-shaped settlement with a battlemented clocktower at its centre. This building was originally the town jail and it later became the burgh chambers (town hall). Dufftown is at the centre of the local whisky distilling industry. There are at least seven distilleries in and around the town; the best-known is **Glenfiddich**, with its important visitor centre. Other attractions within the town include **Balvenie Castle**, a ruined courtyard castle dating from the 13th century; and **Mortlach Parish Church**, one of the oldest places of worship in Scotland, founded in the 6th century. Close to the town is the dramatic hilltop castle of **Auchindoun**. *Open: daily, Apr–mid-Oct; Mon–Fri, mid-Oct–Mar (Glenfiddich visitor centre): daily Apr–Sep (castle, HS).*

DUMFRIES
DUMFRIES AND GALLOWAY (DUMFRIESSHIRE)

This ancient burgh is sometimes called 'The Queen of the South' – a reminder of its importance as the largest town in the modern administrative region of Dumfries and Galloway. Originally a village settlement on the Roman road through Nithsdale, it was the seat of a Galloway sub-king by c.1160. King William the Lion had gained control of the area by c.1185, and the burgh's first charter was granted soon afterwards. (A royal burgh is a Scottish town with trading and administrative rights granted by the monarch.) The long-vanished Greyfriars Monastery was the setting for the fatal stabbing of John Comyn, Earl of Badenoch (the 'Red Comyn') by his rival, Robert the Bruce, in 1306, an incident which precipitated the Scottish Wars of Independence. Robert Burns is also strongly associated with Dumfries, writing *Tam o' Shanter* while at Ellisland, a farm to the north. Later he moved into the town, and the house that he occupied for three years prior to his death has Burnsiana on display. His elaborate mausoleum is in St Michael's Churchyard, also in the town. However, Dumfries' main Burns attraction is probably the **Robert Burns Centre**. Close by is **Dumfries Old Bridge** (also known as 'Devorgilla's Bridge'), one of the oldest multiple-arch bridges in Scotland. Local museums include **Dumfries Museum**, housed in a former 18th-century windmill and featuring a camera obscura. *Open: daily, Apr–Sep; Tue–Sat, Oct–Mar (Robert Burns Centre): daily, Apr–Sep; Tue–Sat, Oct–Mar (museum).*

DUNROBIN CASTLE
HIGHLAND (SUTHERLAND)

■ OFF THE A9, 12 MILES (19KM) NORTH-EAST OF DORNOCH ■

The largest house in the Scottish Highlands, Dunrobin is a monument to five Dukes of Sutherland. The 1st Duke of Sutherland gained his title when, as 2nd Marquess of Stafford and probably the richest man in Britain, he married Elizabeth, Countess of Sutherland in 1785. An English grandee without a word of Gaelic, he thus became a Highland laird, initiating a policy of philanthropic improvements known as the Sutherland Clearances. His giant statue dominates the skyline to the south of the nearby town of Golspie. No longer regularly lived in, the large Franco-Scottish-style palace which surrounds the 14th-century keep of Dunrobin has been a hospital and a school in the present century. Its rooms have the cold and slightly bogus air of having been arranged as theatrical sets to display only lumber and trophies. Extreme care should be taken on the steep steps and pathways of the attractive terraced gardens that lie between the castle and the sea. *Open: May–Sep (not daily in May).*

■

Above: four cherubs adorn the fountain at the corner of High Street and English Street, Dunfermline. The fountain was installed in 1851 to celebrate the arrival of clean piped water to the town – a development prompted by several cholera epidemics, the last in 1848

■

■

Above: much of Dunrobin Castle as we know it today was built by Sir Charles Barry, the architect of the Houses of Parliament. Dunrobin suffered severe fire damage in 1915 while serving as a hospital, and was afterwards extensively renewed by Sir Robert Lorimer

■

■
DON'T MISS

■ The view across the Firth of Clyde (Culzean Castle)

■ Old masters and family portraits (Drumlanrig Castle)

■ The Robert Burns Centre (Dumfries)

■ The bottling plant (Glenfiddich)

WITH ONE OF THE MOST DISTINCTIVE URBAN

SETTINGS OF ANY OF EUROPE'S CITIES

SCOTLAND'S CAPITAL OFFERS AN EXCITING

EDINBURGH

CITY EXPERIENCE, WITH OLD TOWN HISTORY

AND NEW TOWN GEORGIAN ELEGANCE

Right: the famous Edinburgh Military Tattoo enjoys a spectacular setting on the Esplanade of Edinburgh Castle. It usually overlaps with the Edinburgh International Festival

With its floodlit castle and the crags of Arthur's Seat beyond the Palace of Holyroodhouse, Scotland's capital can sometimes feel like a stage-set. Edinburgh is certainly designed to impress. The theatricality of the cityscape is enhanced by an annual bout of artistic overkill: the **Edinburgh International Festival** and **the Fringe**, plus other festivals parading in their wake, on themes such as television, books or jazz. Every year for three weeks or more, Edinburgh is transformed from a *douce* (Scots for gentle, almost smug) community of locals preoccupied with going to the right school or golf club, into a cosmopolitan capital with fine music and theatre.

THE STORY OF THE CITY

The **Castle** flags the city centre from every compass point. The effect of geography on the city's development can easily be read, simply by standing on Castle Esplanade and looking north over Princes Street Gardens, to the New Town of Edinburgh beyond Princes Street. An eastward-moving glacier originally created the castle crag on which the ancient fortress stands. It swept round the tough rock, forming a ramp of debris, rather like the tail of a comet. While the head became the castle site, the ramp became the **Royal Mile** running down to **Arthur's Seat**. *Open: daily (castle, HS).*

Edinburgh's earliest inhabitants were sheltering on a defended rock by at least 800BC. A fort followed in the Dark Ages. In

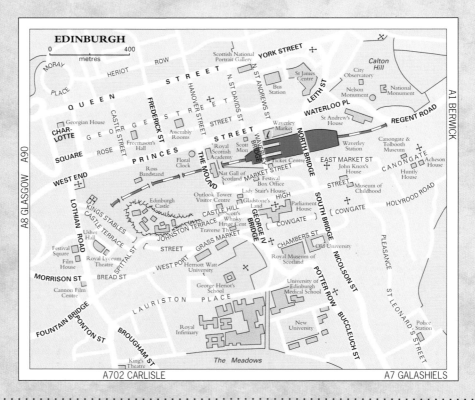

EDINBURGH

the 11th century the southern Saxon Queen Margaret persuaded her Celtic husband, King Malcolm Canmore, to move his court from Dunfermline to the Lothians, then under the influence of the Saxon Northumbrians. She built the oldest surviving building in Edinburgh, **St Margaret's Chapel**, high on the castle ramparts.

As centuries passed, the settlement in the shadow of the rocky fortress gradually extended further down the Royal Mile, protected by the town walls. Invading armies left their mark, the guesthouse of the Abbey of Hollyrood rose to become the **Palace of Holyroodhouse** and the houses on the Royal Mile were eventually built in stone, not wood, with overhanging galleries. One of the earliest surviving examples is **John Knox House** in the High Street, which has associations with the fiery 16th-century reformer. Later, the Old Town dwellings rose ever taller. Among them were great tenements with forestairs (like the National Trust for Scotland's Gladstone's Land. *Open: daily, Apr–Oct; Mon–Sat, Jan–Mar (Holyrood House): Mon–Sat, all year (John Knox House): daily, Apr–Oct (Gladstone's Land, NTS).*

OLD AND NEW TOWNS
After Scotland lost her independence in 1707, the nation and its capital – by now a cramped, noisy and smelly town – were seized by a desire to move forward into a new and scientific age. This was the 'Age of Enlightenment', an academic and social movement that became the basis for Edinburgh's academic reputation today. Among its wide-ranging collections, the **Royal Museum of Scotland** in Chambers Street has many displays recalling this exciting time. One aspect of this progressive mood was the creation of a **New Town** with wide streets, strongly influenced by the order and symmetry of classical architecture. There was also a need to escape from the confines of the Old Town, perched on its narrow hill. This New Town started to appear in the latter half of the 18th century. Charlotte Square is typical: its palace-fronted north side was designed by Robert Adam in the last decade of the 18th century. Visitors can see what life was like then by vising the **Georgian House** in Charlotte Square. *Open: daily (Royal museum): daily, Apr–Oct (Georgian House, NTS).*

The oldest part of the New Town (the symmetrical portion centred on George Street, with Princes Street at its southern extremity), was conceived as a residential area, but commerce quickly arrived. Today, **Princes Street** has as many High Street stores as any other British city. Only a few blocks northwards, though, are leafy avenues, private gardens and symmetrical circuses, little changed since the days of sedan chairs.

'THE ATHENS OF THE NORTH'
Edinburgh's finest civic buildings, which helped earn it the title 'The Athens of the North', sprang from this neo-classical inspiration. Visit the **National Gallery of Scotland** to view one of the most distinguished smaller art galleries in Europe; and take in the **Scottish National Portrait Gallery** to see Scotland's story from the 16th century to the present day. Twentieth-century paintings and sculpture are on view at the **Scottish National Gallery of Modern Art**. *All open daily.*

Among the city's many museums is **Huntly House**, which has important collections of silver, glass and pottery, all with local associations. A museum opposite houses **The People's Story**, showing the lives and work of ordinary folk of the city from 18th century to the present day. *Open: Mon–Sat (Huntly House): Mon–Sat, May–Oct (People's Story).*

Out of doors there is the **Royal Botanic Garden**, of world class and with major collections, notably of alpines and rhododendrons. **Edinburgh Zoo** is a traditional attraction which has updated itself to regain popular appeal. *Both open daily.*

ON THE FRINGE
An appealing aspect of Edinburgh is its village life. Beyond Arthur's Seat is Duddingston, once a brewing community and in an attractive setting. Further out lie the whitewashed, thatched cottages of Swanston, with its Robert Louis Stevenson connections, while closer to hand are attractive shopping areas such as Bruntsfield and Morningside – a reminder that beyond the immediate city centre there is still plenty to explore in Scotland's capital.

ELGIN
GRAMPIAN (MORAYSHIRE)

This former county town, now the administrative headquarters of Moray District, is an ancient royal burgh which once had both a castle and a cathedral. A fragment of the castle on top of Ladyhill, near the west end of the main street, has survived. It has excellent views. Look out for the hilltop column dated 1839, commemorating the Duke of Gordon. The **cathedral** is now a poignant ruin in Cooper Park. Known as 'The Lantern of the North', it is thought to have been the most beautiful of Scotland's cathedrals. It was founded in 1224 and burned in 1390 by the Wolf of Badenoch (the illegitimate son of King Robert II, and a notorious terrorist), although it was subsequently rebuilt and used at least until the Reformation. *Open: daily (HS).*

Elgin's medieval street plan can still be made out, although the townscape has been altered by successive rebuilding. A few buildings, particularly those at the east end of the main street, still have the arched façades that were characteristic of the town in the 18th century. **Pann's Port** is an archway fragment from the defensive walls that once surrounded the cathedral, and Little Cross at the east end of the High Street dates from 1703 and replaced an earlier cross of 1402. Other attractions in the town include Johnston's of Elgin, a working woollen mill, and Old Mills, a fully restored and working watermill. Elgin has an excellent museum, housed in an attractive, 19th-century Italianate building. Its contents are presented in exciting displays. Among them are finds from ancient fossil beds to the north of the town, where some of the oldest fossils in Britain have been discovered. *Open: Tue–Sat, Apr–Sep.*

FALKLAND PALACE
FIFE
■ IN FALKLAND ON THE A912, 11 MILES (18KM) NORTH OF KIRKCALDY ■

The attractive, Renaissance-style façade of this former hunting seat of the Stuart monarchs dominates the main street of the village of Falkland. King James V died here in 1542, and his daughter, Mary, Queen of Scots, was a frequent visitor. The palace buildings date from between 1501 and 1541. As well as boasting attractively laid-out gardens, the palace has a royal tennis court, built in 1539 and still in use. *Open: daily, Apr—Oct (NTS).*

FLOORS CASTLE
BORDERS (ROXBURGHSHIRE))
■ OFF THE B6089, 2 MILES (3KM) NORTH-WEST OF KELSO ■

Sometimes described as the largest occupied building in Scotland, this grand mansion was built by William Adam in 1721. Later additions were made to it by William Playfair in the 1830s. *Open: Eas; Sun–Thu, Apr–Jun and Sep; daily, Jul–Aug; Sun, Wed, Oct.*

FORT WILLIAM AND THE GREAT GLEN
HIGHLAND (INVERNESS-SHIRE)

At the southern gateway to the Great Glen, Fort William cannot be described as the most attractive of Highland towns. Nevertheless, it attracts large numbers of visitors. This is due to its comprehensive range of shops and its setting, within easy reach of the natural attractions of the West Highlands. These include Ben Nevis, whose rounded bulk rises 4,406ft (1,343m) above the town, the summit hidden beyond its broad shoulders.

Fort William's name recalls its role as a former garrison town. Founded in 1690, it was named after the Protestant Prince of Orange (King William III), who ruled Britain jointly with his wife Mary, until her death in 1694. Next to nothing of the actual fort remains today. The walls survived until the 1880s, when they were demolished to make way for the arrival of the railway.

Besides shops, Fort William has several attractions. These include the **West Highland Museum**, noted for its Jacobite relics – among them some early tartans and a secret portrait of Bonnie Prince Charlie. To the west of the town is Glen Nevis with its spectacular alp-like scenery. It is often overlooked by visitors with limited

■

Below: one of many decorative coats-of-arms which stud the façade of Renaissance-style Falkland Palace

■

■

Above: built on a terrace overlooking the River Tweed, Floors Castle was a fairly plain Georgian mansion until the architect Playfair added flamboyance with his 1838 remodelling. He designed castellated parapets, ornate waterspouts, pepperpots and many other details

■

■

Above: the highest mountain in Britain, Ben Nevis dominates the skyline above Fort William, its steep crags hidden to the north.

■

Right: the Gallery at Fyvie Castle

■

time, intent on exploring the Edinburgh–Inverness–Fort William triangle. The Great Glen itself is part of this 'tourist route', closely following the line of the Caledonian Canal. The canal, which was completed in 1822 as part of an early government job-creation scheme, took advantage of three natural waterways (Loch Lochy, Loch Oich and Loch Ness), which lie in the great trench created by a giant fault, running coast to coast. Another dramatic example of natural forces at work can be found in Glen Roy, about 18 miles (29km) north of Fort William. During the last Ice Age, a mere 10,000 years ago, a glacier filled the Great Glen, blocking the Glen Roy exit. As it melted, the glacier created a loch, which filled Glen Roy and was released in stages. Now known as the Parallel Roads, the old loch shorelines are still plainly visible on the sides of the glen. *Open: Mon–Sat (museum).*

FYVIE CASTLE
GRAMPIAN (ABERDEENSHIRE)

■ OFF THE A947, 8 MILES (13KM) SOUTH-EAST OF TURRIFF ■

In this great, rambling five-towered castle can be traced at least 500 years of Scottish history, as well as the story of the five great families which have owned the property. The castle is now in the care of the National Trust for Scotland. It has an outstanding collection of paintings, as well as the hallmarks of Edwardian opulence created by the 1st Lord Leith of Fyvie. *Open: daily, Eas–Sep; weekends in October (castle); daily (grounds), NTS.*

■

DON'T MISS

■ The secret portrait of Bonnie Prince Charlie (West Highland Museum, Fort William)

■ A spectacular trip by steam train (Fort William to Mallaig)

■ The Parallel Roads (Glen Roy)

SCOTLAND'S LARGEST CITY IS LIVELY AND

SOPHISTICATED, WITH EXUBERANT

VICTORIAN ARCHITECTURE, VIBRANT

GLASGOW

NIGHTLIFE AND A WIDE RANGE OF PLACES TO

VISIT.

Few places in Britain have undergone such a change in style and image in recent years as Glasgow. Scotland's largest city in the 1980s shook off its image of industrial decline and urban decay. Instead, it now flaunts its outstanding Victorian architecture, its sparkling cultural life and the best choice of shops in Scotland, to the consternation of Edinburgh, its rival in the east. Best of all, from the visitor's point of view, in downtown Glasgow the locals believe in their new image: visitor attractions, restaurants and pubs have a decidedly jaunty air.

THE MERCANT CITY

Glasgow's origins go back to the time when it was a small settlement on the sluggish River Clyde. St Ninian, the city's patron saint, is said to have built a church on the site of the present cathedral which achieved its status in 1125. In the Middle Ages the development of the city's trade was hindered by the shallow, silty river. Only after the Reformation, and with the later construction of the first wharf around 1688, did the mercantile activities which were to underpin the city's development really get underway. After 1707 (when Scotland gained access to England's colonies in the Americas), trade began to flourish with the export of manufactured goods like hats, shoes and linen. The imported rum, cotton and tobacco were the concern of a powerful group of merchants, the 'Tobacco Lords', who brought great wealth to the rapidly expanding city.

Their work is recalled today in the name of the Merchant City, part of the revitalised heart of Glasgow (south and west of George Square), which is now home to specialist and exclusive shops and businesses. This area developed as the city expanded westwards, away from its old medieval centre. The Victorians added to Glasgow's wealth of public and commercial architecture, building in the exuberant style which gives such a lively feel to the city today.

Above: Charles Rennie Mackintosh's Willow Tea Rooms display his plant themes on both the structure and the furniture

Above: the City Chambers, one of the most exuberant and ornate Victorian buildings in Glasgow

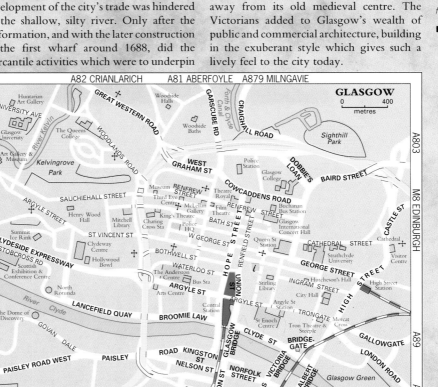

CIVIC BUILDINGS

Notable in the cityscape are splendid edifices such as the **City Chambers**, dating from the 1870s and built in Italianate style. It has an ornate marble stairway as well as many interesting interior features. **Hutchesons' Hall** (1802–5), the **Trades House** (1791), with its Adam façade, and **Stirling Library** (1827), are just a few other period buildings nearby.

Places of interest from earlier stages in the city's development include **Glasgow Cathedral**. Dating mainly from the 13th century, it is regarded as one of the finest early Gothic churches in Scotland, with its upper and lower church one above the other. The mercantile symbols of a royal burgh, the **Tolbooth** (or, more accurately, its steeple of 1626), and the **Mercat Cross** (a modern replica of the original), can be seen today at Glasgow Cross in the centre of the old city. There are many other civic buildings of note, and the city is best viewed on foot, keeping your eyes at least some of the time above shop-window level.

MUSEUMS AND GALLERIES

Glasgow also has a wealth of museums, the most down-to-earth of which is the **People's Palace**. This tells the tale of ordinary city folk, with fascinating displays on both the workplaces and the entertainments of the city, as well as social and political trends, such as the suffragettes or the temperance movement. Attached to the museum building are the **Winter Gardens**, where the steamy breath of the tropics defies the sometimes damp westerly climate. Yet another reminder of everyday life in Glasgow is the very popular **Tenement House**. Here, in a typical red sandstone tenement building, the National Trust for Scotland cares for a perfectly preserved flat, filled with furniture and fittings as well as the accumulated ephemera of 50 years of 20th-century family life. *Open: Mon–Sat (People's Palace): daily, Apr–Nov; Sat, Sun, Nov–Mar (Tenement House, NTS).*

Victorian Glasgow's cultural aspirations were symbolised in the construction of the grand **Kelvingrove Art Gallery and Museum** near the university. Here visitors can enjoy one of the nation's finest municipal art collections, including works by the Impressionists, Old Masters and some famous British painters, as well as sculpture. The museum contains a wide-ranging collection of archaeological, ethnological and historical material. Further discoveries can be made at the **Hunterian Museum** nearby. Like the **Hunterian Art Gallery** (an art collection including works by Charles Rennie Mackintosh – see below), it stands within the precincts of Glasgow University. *Open: daily (Kelvingrove): Mon–Sat (Hunterian Museum and Art Gallery).*

Across the road from the Kelvingrove Art Gallery and Museum is Glasgow's **Museum of Transport**, housed in a roomy building in a part of Kelvin Hall. There is plenty of space for railway locomotives, Scottish-built cars and a reconstructed Glasgow street scene of the 1930s. *Open: daily.*

OF ART AND ARCHITECTURE

Among Glasgow's extraordinary wealth of places to visit is its flagship, the **Burrell Collection**. This breathtaking private collection of *objets d'art*, housed in a custom-made building, has drawn the crowds since 1983. Among other reminders of Glasgow's intellectual life is the **Mitchell Library**, the largest public reference library in Europe. *Open: daily (Burrell).*

The Scottish architect Charles Rennie Mackintosh is widely celebrated in the city and visitors should take the **Charles Rennie Mackintosh Society** as their starting point. It is housed in a former church, built to his design between 1897 and 1899 at Queen's Cross. The society can give full details of the buildings in the city which show Mackintosh's distinctive style. Glasgow has also embraced modern architecture – as visitors can see in the **St Enoch Centre** and **Princes Square**, in the city's main shopping area. As an antidote to exclusive shopping, a visit to **The Barras** is essential – a wildly extrovert weekend fleamarket.

THE 'DEAR GREEN PLACE'

Glasgow's name is said to mean 'dear green place'. The city has a wide variety of parks and open spaces, from the **Botanic Gardens** with their Victorian glasshouses, to the **Victoria Park and Fossil Grove**, with its fossilised stumps of 330 million-year-old trees. *Both open: daily.*

The 'new' Glasgow is one of Britain's most entertaining cities.

GLENCOE
HIGHLAND (ARGYLL)

The dramatic landscape of Glencoe was created by ancient volcanic activity which formed rocks that were later scoured and gouged by massive glaciers. Yet Glencoe is noted for a dreadful crime, as well as its breathtaking scenery. In 1692, many of the Macdonald families living in the glen were brutally murdered by a company of Campbell soldiers, acting for the government in a botched attempt to punish a recalcitrant clan whose chief was late with an oath of submission. The Campbells were billeted with their Macdonald hosts at the time. There is a visitor centre at the north end. *Open: daily (NTS).*

GLENFINNAN MONUMENT
HIGHLAND (INVERNESS-SHIRE)
■ NEAR THE A830, 18 MILES (29KM) WEST OF FORT WILLIAM ■

By 1815, the Jacobites and their failed cause had begun to achieve an aura of romance and sentiment in the popular imagination. A monument was raised at Glenfinnan, recalling the escapades of Prince Charles Edward Stuart ('Bonnie Prince Charlie') who had raised some of the clans here in 1745 and led them to their doom at Culloden the following year. The story of the '45 rebellion is told at the National Trust for Scotland's **visitor centre** nearby, though many will also pause to admire the spectacular **Glenfinnan Viaduct** on the Fort William to Mallaig railway, opened in 1901. This innovative 21-span, 1,248ft (381m) long construction pioneered the use of concrete for bridges. *Open: Apr–Oct (visitor centre), NTS.*

GLENCOE

The Glencoe Massacre of 1692 has left a chilling memory behind. A party of 128 soldiers under the command of Campbell of Glenlyon arrived in Glencoe at the beginning of February that year and billeted themselves in friendly fashion on the Macdonalds, who treated them hospitably. Before dawn on 13 February, however, the soldiers had turned on their hosts and slaughtered at least 40 of them, including children and invalids. Those who ran for safety, out into the freezing night, died from exposure on the hillsides. On dark, forbidding days the famous glen seems to be brooding over its story of treachery and death.

Left: the Glenfinnan Monument marks the spot where Prince Charles Edward Stuart raised the flag of rebellion in 1745.

Below: Glencoe offers some of the most spectacular mountain scenery in Britain – though high-level excursions are only for the experienced

HADDO HOUSE
GRAMPIAN (ABERDEENSHIRE)
■ OFF THE B999, 4 MILES (6KM) NORTH OF PITMEDDEN ■

This handsome mansion was designed by William Adam in 1731. The interior today is mainly in the 'Adam Revival' style, dating from around 1880. The attractive grounds around the property – parkland, woods and mixed farmland – form 180 acres (73ha) of country park and, like the house, are cared for by the National Trust for Scotland. In the parkland are a network of winding woodland paths and a bird observation hide. One of the more peaceful properties of the Trust, Haddo receives a mere 20,000 visitors annually, which means there is little disturbance to the ambience of the family home of the Marquesses of Aberdeen. In the north-east, Haddo is also noted for its active promotion of the arts. As well as a range of facilities such as visitor centre, shop, tearoom and adventure playground, it has a theatre-cum-recital hall, which regularly features some of Scotland's top performing artistes. *Open: daily, Apr–Sep; Sat, Sun, Oct (grounds daily), NTS.*

HIGHLAND WILDLIFE PARK
HIGHLAND (INVERNESS-SHIRE)
■ OFF THE A9, 7 MILES (11KM) SOUTH OF AVIEMORE ■

Taking Scottish species, past and present, as its theme, this zoo features a drive-through **reserve**, as well as an **exhibition** telling the story of man's impact on nature in the Highlands. Wolves, European bison, wild boars, brown bears and polecats are all on display in their (former) natural habitat. *Open: daily, Apr–Oct.*

HILL HOUSE
STRATHCLYDE (DUNBARTONSHIRE)
■ UPPER COLQUHOUN STREET, HELENSBURGH ■

Cared for by the National Trust for Scotland, this house, the finest domestic example of the architectural style of Charles Rennie Mackintosh, was commissioned by the publisher W Blackie in 1902. Mackintosh, pioneer of the 'Modern Movement' in architecture which discarded historicism, designed both the house and its furniture. The result is outstandingly original in every way. *Open: daily, Apr–Dec.*

HOPETOUN HOUSE
LOTHIAN (WEST LOTHIAN)
■ OFF THE A904, 2 MILES (6KM) WEST OF SOUTH QUEENSFERRY ■

This opulent mansion, one of Scotland's most splendid, was greatly enlarged by William Adam and his son John between 1721 and 1754. Today it provides a grand setting for magnificent furniture, a fine collection of china and paintings by various Old Masters. The palatial pile is still the home of the Hope family, Earls of Hopetoun and later Marquesses of Linlithgow, whose fortunes were originally made through extensive mining interests. The grounds include formal gardens, a deer park and woodland walks, and there are also magnificent rooftop views eastward to the Forth Bridges, (both road and rail). *Open: Eas–Oct.*

Below: a pinnacle of Victorian engineering achievement, the Forth Rail Bridge opened in 1890. It is 2,765 yds (2,527m) long, except on a hot summer day when it expands by another yard (90cm). It is held together by approximately 7 million rivets.

■

■

Right: ornate plasterwork and a magnificent art collection are just two features of Hopetoun House, the palatial home of the Earls of Hopetoun and Marquesses of Linlithgow, whose fortunes were originally acquired through extensive mining interests

■

■

DON'T MISS
_____

■ The Aonach Eagach ridge (Glencoe – for experienced climbers only)

■ Steam trains crossing the viaduct (Glenfinnan)

■ The view of the Forth Bridges (Hopetoun House)

INVERARAY CASTLE
STRATHCLYDE (ARGYLL)

■ ON THE A83, NORTH OF INVERARAY ■

Right: Inveraray Castle has been the seat of the Dukes of Argyll, chiefs of the Clan Campbell, for centuries. It was the vision of the 3rd Duke which prompted the building of the castle – as well as the construction of the town of Inveraray nearby

Right: An ancient cross with ornate carving on Iona. Crosses like this were carved on the island in the 8th century AD

Inveraray Castle is the home of the Duke of Argyll and has been the seat of the Chiefs of the Clan Campbell for generations. In 1743 the 3rd Duke of Argyll commissioned the architect, Roger Morris, to build not only the castle but also the new town of Inveraray, a little distance away. The splendid interior decoration was carried out at the request of the 5th Duke, and today the castle contains a wealth of historical relics, as well as magnificent portraits. The **bridges** in the castle grounds are of architectural interest, and Inveraray has many elegant 18th- and 19th-century buildings. *Open: Sat–Thu, Apr–Jun and Sep–Oct; daily, Jul–Aug.*

INVEREWE GARDENS
HIGHLAND (ROSS AND CROMARTY)

■ ON THE A832, 6 MILES (10KM) NORTH-EAST OF GAIRLOCH ■

This extraordinary garden was created from a barren peninsula exposed to westerly gales and with the barest covering of acid peat over the bedrock. The luxuriant growth seen today owes much to the planning and hard work of the original owner, Osgood Mackenzie, who started the project over 120 years ago. Not only were tons of soil brought in, but in some cases

Below: on the same latitude as Leningrad, Inverewe Gardens' magnificent displays and wide range of frost-tender species owe much to the effect of the Gulf Stream which warms the coastline hereabouts – though salt-laden westerly gales can be a problem in winter

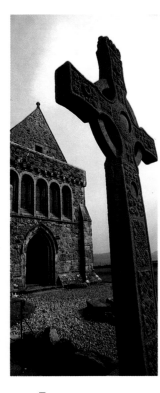

trees were only able to grow after holes had been cut for them in the bedrock. The presence of the North Atlantic Drift, part of the Gulf Stream, on this part of the coast helps to keep it frost-free to a great extent, and many tender species from temperate parts of the globe flourish here. The densely planted, exotic air in the garden causes many visitors to believe that the flowers and shrubs are actually tropical – which would certainly be a miracle on the west coast of Scotland! Instead, the exotic effect is created by plantings which feature groups of species from particular regions, for example, temperate South America, or the Himalayas. The garden is split into a number of 'rooms', each cared for by a different gardener. Visitors wandering along the winding pathways constantly encounter new vistas and ideas. *Open: daily (visitor centre Apr–Oct), NTS.*

IONA
STRATHCLYDE (ARGYLL)

Formerly the ancient burial place of Scottish kings, the cradle of Christianity and a place of pilgrimage, the tiny island of Iona is now a centre for spiritual renewal and an escape from everyday pressures. Some visitors fall in love with it instantly, and experience a palpable sense of peace. Others find the mixture of the ancient and the earnest surrounding today's Iona Community (a spiritual centre based in the restored abbey buildings), a little uncomfortable. In AD563 the high-born Irish monk, Columba, came to the island with 12 followers and founded a monastery. This settlement subsequently bore the brunt of many Norse raids (in AD806, for example, when 68 monks were killed). There is a variety of buildings to enjoy, including the ruins of a nunnery founded in about 1200. Also of interest are **St Oran's Chapel** (said to have been built by Queen Margaret in 1080) and the abbey complex, of which the **cathedral** (dating mainly from the 16th century) forms a part. Most of these structures were at one time in decay. The island came into the hands of the Dukes of Argyll in 1695 and the 8th Duke presented the ruins to the Church of Scotland in 1899. Restoration of the cathedral began in 1910, and then work started on the other buildings by the newly founded Iona Community. Today Iona absorbs not only thousands of visitors on daytrips from Mull, but also provides a place of spiritual retreat on one of Scotland's most attractive western islands.

JEDBURGH
BORDERS (ROXBURGHSHIRE)

This town's history is bound up with its strategic position on the main route from England to Scotland. It lay in the path of armies travelling north and south in the days when Scotland and England's relationship was stormy. Although in more recent times it has been a woollen-mill town, Jedburgh originally grew round its **abbey**, whose ruined shell still dominates the skyline. It was destroyed by the English Earl of Hertford in 1544, and today it is the site of an excellent visitor centre, telling the story of the role of the Border abbeys. As well as enjoying associations with famous Scottish figures such as Sir Walter Scott (who attended court here), and Bonnie Prince Charlie (who spent a night here), Jedburgh is also linked with Mary, Queen of Scots. **Queen Mary's House**, now a local museum, is popularly associated with her. The story goes that in 1566 Mary was staying at the house when she heard that her lover Bothwell was at Hermitage Castle, wounded. She made a desperate ride to see him, a round trip of about 50 miles (80km), all in one day. The town's **Castle Jail Museum** shows what the penal system was like in the 19th century. There are many other buildings of historic interest along a **Town Trail**, which visitors can follow. *Open: daily (abbey, HS): daily, Apr–mid-Nov (Queen Mary's house): daily, Apr–Oct (castle jail).*

KINTAIL AND MORVICH
HIGHLAND (ROSS AND CROMARTY)

The National Trust for Scotland cares for this 17,422-acre (7,055ha) estate, which comprises some of Scotland's wildest scenery. The Five Sisters of Kintail, a hill range with four peaks of over 3,000ft (915m), and the Falls of Glomach, among the highest in Britain with a 370ft (113m) drop, are among its attractions. This is remote countryside, and many of the excursions should only be tackled by the fit and well-shod. There is a **Countryside Centre** at Morvich Farm, off the A87. *Open: daily, May–Sep, NTS.*

■

CELTIC CHRISTIANITY

At what time in Scotland's dark prehistoric past the first Celtic peoples – Britons and Picts – entered the country is not known, but from the end of the 4th century AD St Ninian, St Kentigern and other missionaries had begun to make Christian converts in the south. In the 6th century people from Northern Ireland, the Scots, established a kingdom in Argyll on the west coast, and the formidable St Columba made Iona his missionary base. The Celtic form of Christianity was gentler in spirit than Roman Catholic Christianity, and differed from it in points of doctrine. It drew much of its artistic inspiration from Celtic paganism, and the Celtic crosses at Iona are a symbol of its ideals. Roman Catholic Christianity, imported later to Scotland from England, was eventually to overwhelm it.

■

■

Below: Inveraray Courthouse and Jail dates from 1816–20. Today it is a unique visitor attraction – a prison brought to life with guides in the role of prisoners and warders. This edifying sight in the once cramped, cold and dark old prison is, however, a model

■

■

DON'T MISS

■ The Jail (Inveraray)

■ The gardens in June (Inverewe)

■ White, sandy beaches (Iona)

THE KYLES OF BUTE
STRATHCLYDE (ARGYLL/BUTE)

The attractive little island of Bute is all but grasped by the mainland fingers of Cowal reaching down its east and west coasts. It is separated from the mainland only by two narrow, almost fjord-like channels which meet at the northern tip of the island and run into Loch Riddon. It is these twin sea lochs which are called the Kyles of Bute (Gaelic: *caolas* – a strait). The peerless views down the narrow waters with wooded slopes on each side can best be appreciated from the A8003, where there are panorama boards identifying the sights down both the East and West Kyle.

LINLITHGOW PALACE
LOTHIAN (WEST LOTHIAN)
■ ON THE SOUTH SHORE OF LINLITHGOW LOCH ■

Linlithgow Palace still retains a little of its former magnificence. It was once a fine royal residence, built round a quadrangle and incorporating a tower built by King Edward of England in the early 14th century, though much of the palace was destroyed in a fire of 1424. In fact, the palace in its final state was burned again, probably by accident, in 1746, immediately after the departure of government troops who had been billeted there during the last Jacobite rebellion. Some of the ruined apartments which visitors can see today include the late 15th-century chapel and great hall, and there is a 16th-century fountain in the quadrangle. The palace was the birthplace of Mary, Queen of Scots, in 1542. In those days, the palace and its domed headland overlooking Linlithgow Loch were more easily defended against aggressors, as the level of water in the loch was higher than it is today. *Open: daily (HS).*

LOCH LOMOND
CENTRAL/STRATHCLYDE (DUNBARTONSHIRE/STIRLINGSHIRE)

At 23 miles from north to south and 4 miles from east to west, this is the largest Scottish loch in terms of surface area and a byword for Scottish scenery, thanks to the famous song *The Banks of Loch Lomond*. Though undoubtedly an attractive area, the loch's fame must owe at least a little to the fact that it is the first Highland loch found north of the densely populated Clydeside conurbation and it has been a green escape route for generations of residents from Glasgow's conurbation. Today it offers fishing, cruising, island-visiting, water-sports and wildlife interest – though not all of these pursuits necessarily coexist happily – while the official long-distance footpath, the West Highland Way, brings yet more visitors to admire the fine oakwoods and craggy vistas along the 'bonnie banks'.

Loch Lomond also offers all kinds of geology lessons. The Highland Boundary Fault runs through it, and can easily be made out as it follows the humps of Conic Hill behind Balmaha. The fault line also runs through Inchcailloch, one of the most beautiful of Loch Lomond's islands, with an attractive canopy of oakwoods. Like its neighbours to the west, Loch Long and Loch Fyne, Loch Lomond almost became a sea-loch after the last Ice Age. It is separated by a dump of glacial material, raising the loch only about 27ft (8m) above sea level. The 'bonnie banks' of Loch Lomond were almost salty!

LOCH NESS
HIGHLAND (INVERNESS-SHIRE)

■

Above: the 27.45 sq miles (71 km²) of Loch Lomond, set in magnificent scenery, have no less than 33 islands to explore, some of which are inhabited. Shore settlements such as Luss, Balmaha and Balloch, among others, offer a choice of cruising

■

This is the largest of Scotland's lochs in terms of the volume of water contained within it. It is also the second deepest (only Loch Morar is deeper), with a central trench of around 800ft (244m) in places. But ever since a quiet week on the *Northern Chronicle* in 1930 resulted in the publication of a strange story about a mysterious disturbance in the peaty waters, Loch Ness has been famous for only one thing: the Loch Ness Monster. Hundreds of sober witnesses have witnessed the phenomenon, yet the frequency of Nessie's coming to the surface seems to be in inverse proportion to the number of cameras trained on the loch at any one time. She seems to favour still, warm conditions in summer – as do the mirages which also occur on the loch (the great volume of water has local effects on the weather). The **Official Loch Ness Monster Exhibition** is on the shores of the loch at Drumnadrochit. Other attractions in the vicinity include, on the less busy eastern shore, the **Farigaig Forest Centre**, with displays and woodland walks showing the work of the local foresters, and also the **Falls of Foyers** (above the village of Foyers). At the south end of the loch, the little town of **Fort Augustus** is a good place to observe the life of the Caledonian Canal. **Urquhart Castle**, on the west shore, is another popular spot. Blown up in the 17th century, this ruin was in its day one of the largest fortifications in Scotland and controlled the routes through the Great Glen. It also makes a good vantage point for monster-spotting. Visitors can also look for the traces of Wade's Roads in the area, built by General Wade from around 1726 onwards, to allow easy movement of his government troops while subduing the Highlands. *Open: daily (Loch Ness Monster Exhibition): daily (Urquhart Castle, HS).*

■

the mild air and benevolent climate of Galloway are ideal for frost-tender plants, such as tree ferns

■

LOGAN BOTANIC GARDENS
DUMFRIES AND GALLOWAY (WIGTOWNSHIRE)

■ OFF THE B7065, 14 MILES (23KM) SOUTH OF STRANRAER ■

The gardens of Galloway make the most of the prevailing moist and mild south-westerlies. Out on the Rinns of Gallway (the 'hammerhead' of land on the extreme western edge) the nearness of the sea helps to keep the area relatively frost-free. The Royal Botanic Garden in Edinburgh chose Logan as an outstation for some of its more tender species, and for some specialities, such as cabbage palms and exotic-looking tree ferns from the Antipodes. Magnolia, rhododendrons, azaleas, a wide range of primulas and other less-well-known species all add to the colour of this 14-acre (5.6ha) site. *Open: daily, Mar–Oct.*

MELLERSTAIN HOUSE
BORDERS (BERWICKSHIRE)
■ OFF THE A6089, 7 MILES (11KM) NORTH-WEST OF KELSO ■

Mellerstain House was transformed in the 18th century by its owner, George Baillie, whose family had been successful Edinburgh merchants. Inspired by a 'grand tour' of Europe in 1740–4, he later commissioned Robert Adam to rebuild the central block of the house as a palatial neo-classical mansion. Although the exterior resembles a series of boxes with crenellated parapets, the plasterwork and decoration inside are among the most refined and elegant in Scotland. *Open: Sun–Fri, Eas, May–Sep.*

MELROSE ABBEY
BORDERS (SELKIRKSHIRE)
■ OFF THE A6091, IN MELROSE ■

A Cistercian settlement founded in 1146, Melrose suffered the fate of other Border abbeys when it was destroyed by the English during the Wars of Independence in the early 14th century. However, some of the most lavish ornamentation to be found in Scottish stonework can be seen in parts of the nave and choir of the abbey church, which was rebuilt after 1385. Following the Earl of Hertford's destructive visit of 1545, the abbey gradually fell into disuse. *Open: daily (HS).*

NEW LANARK
STRATHCLYDE (LANARKSHIRE)
■ 1 MILE (1.6KM) SOUTH OF LANARK ■

On its approach to Lanark, the Clyde winds its way gently out of the southern uplands and then abruptly thunders through a sandstone gorge over waterfalls hemmed in by dense woodland. This was the site chosen in 1783 by the Glasgow businessman, David Dale, to build a complex of cotton mills in what became the biggest single industrial concern in Scotland. For the employees conditions were good by the standards of the day. Although hours were long, there was adequate housing and food, as well as educational facilities. Dale's philanthropic approach was further advanced by his son-in-law, Robert Owen, who had strong views on equality and social welfare. He added further educational buildings and directed his efforts towards creating a society without poverty or crime – putting into practice the fundamentals of 'Owenism'. Visitors came from all over the world to see Owen's benign capitalism at work in this obscure valley in southern Scotland.

ROBERT OWEN

Robert Owen was born at Newtown in Wales in 1771. As a child he devoured books like *Robinson Crusoe* before he was old enough to realise that they were fiction. The religious books he was given to read suggested to him that there was something fundamentally wrong with all religions. He worked as a shop assistant for a time before going into the cotton-spinning business in which he made a fortune, in Manchester and New Lanark. High-minded, utopian and benevolent, his ideas made little impact in his own time, but he is considered a forerunner of British socialism and the co-operative movement. He died at Newtown in 1858, at the age of 87.

Below: built of warm red sandstone, ruined Melrose Abbey has a peaceful atmosphere that appealed greatly to Sir Walter Scott. Among the abbey's ornate stone carvings is a pig playing bagpipes

Far left: Robert Owen gave his name to 'Owenism' and practised his belief in benign capitalism and an ideal society at New Lanark (below)

By the middle of the 20th century the mills had mostly fallen silent, but thanks to the New Lanark Conservation Trust's restoration work the community is thriving again today. A major visitor centre tells the story of this unique experiment. The woodland and the roaring river remain as attractive as ever.

OBAN
STRATHCLYDE (ARGYLL)

Gateway to the Hebrides, Oban is a busy west coast resort offering a good choice of ferry excursions and cruises. There is also a variety of things to do in or near the town. A few examples include visits to pottery-, glass- and whisky-making concerns, or to **Dunstaffnage Castle**, a former Macdougall stronghold 4 miles (6.4km) north of the town, with outstanding views of the sea and mountains.

PERTH
TAYSIDE (PERTHSHIRE)

Built on the river flats or 'inches' of the River Tay, Perth became a royal burgh as early as 1210, and as one of the chief towns of the kingdom until the mid-15th century it was an important religious centre. Perth is associated with the fiery Reformer John Knox, whose 1559 sermon at **St John's Church** is said to have started the Reformation in Scotland. Today this handsome, bustling town, built on a grid pattern, offers a good range of places to visit. Among them are the **Black Watch Museum, Branklyn Garden, Bell's Cherrybank Garden**, a working **water-mill**, **Perth Art Gallery and Museum** and **Perth Repertory Theatre**.

ST ANDREWS
FIFE

St Andrews was formerly the ecclesiastical capital of Scotland, with a (now very ruinous) **cathedral** founded in 1160. The town displays a unique heritage and has the oldest university (founded in 1412) in Scotland. It is also the spiritual home for golfers the world over – the famous **Royal and Ancient Golf Club** was established here in 1754. There are many reminders of the past scattered through the town. Its medieval street plan can still be made out, and it also boasts a rare town gate, the **West Port**. **St Andrews Castle**, perched on a cliff edge, has a mine and counter-mine – actually a tunnel and counter-tunnel dug by the castle's defenders during a 16th-century siege. Red-gowned students and mellow university colleges add to the historical atmosphere of the city. Other attractions include a good local **museum** as well as the **British Golf Museum**, a **botanic garden**, a **Sealife Centre** and, naturally, a choice of **golf courses**. *Open: daily (sealife centre, cathedral, HS and castle, HS): daily, May–Oct; Thu–Tue, Mar–Apr, Nov; Thu–Mon, Jan–Feb (Golf Museum).*

Within easy reach of the town is Leuchars' Norman **church**, with a chancel and apse dating from the 13th century. Also, a little further north, there is a superb sandy beach at **Tentsmuir**. Southwards is **Cambo Country Park**, which has a good variety of things for children to do, from cuddling farm animals to puddling about in rock pools.

SKYE
HIGHLAND (INVERNESS-SHIRE)

Skye has a romantic charm that is much enjoyed by visitors – especially if they see the island under blue skies. The largest and most northerly of the Inner Hebrides is perhaps best known for its breathtaking mountain scenery. The Cuillin Hills offer a challenge to even the most experienced rock-climber and are no place for low-level strollers. There are superb views of the Cuillins from Sligachan on the Portree road, from the road to Glen Brittle and also from Elgol across Loch Scavaig. The ancient lavaflows and landslips which characterise the northern peninsula of Trotternish also offer scenic delights: for instance, north of Portree the curious pinnacle of the Old Man of Stoer stands out from the tumbling cliff. Even more spectacularly, at the Quiraing beyond Staffin, landslips of ancient lava have created a jumble of rocky fangs, towers and tables along the line of cliffs. Here stolen cattle were formerly hidden away. Apart from its landscape spectacles, Skye is also associated with the escape of Prince Charles Edward Stuart ('Bonnie Prince Charlie') after his disastrous rebellion of 1745–6.

■

Right: Castle Moil, the slight remains of a 13th-century keep, overlooks the narrows of Kyle Akin and the five-minute ferry crossing from Kyle of Lochalsh to Skye. The castle is said to have been built by the daughter of a Norse king in order to levy a toll from shipping using the strait

■

Below: the Cuillin Hills from Elgol, looking across Loch Scavaig, form a jagged ridge of dark rock known as gabbro – hence their name, the Black Cuillins

■

Flora Macdonald, a local girl who gained romantic fame for helping the Prince to avoid capture, is buried at Kilmuir in the north.

Equally romantic are some of the tales attached to **Dunvegan Castle**, seat of the chiefs of the Clan Macleod. Among the treasured possessions in this porridge-coloured pile is the famous Fairy Flag, an ancient magic cloth that has the power to save the clan if waved in times of dire need. According to tradition, it still has potency for one more use. In the misty, magical Isle of Skye anything is possible. *Open: daily, Mar–Oct (castle). Visitors should note the variety of Skye ferry options, to and from Mallaig and the Western Isles, as well as Kyle of Lochalsh.*

STIRLING
CENTRAL (STIRLINGSHIRE)

Stirling was once the lowest bridging-point of the River Forth. Upstream and westward lay great marshes. Above, the Ochil Hills still present a steep scarpface to the northbound traveller. Southwards are the Campsie Fells, more uplands that bend the routes towards Stirling. In short, before great bridges were built and marshes drained, almost all roads between Lowland and Highland passed through Stirling, in those days a strategic centre with a castle that was the key to the kingdom. Small wonder that the Battle of Bannockburn, which freed Scotland from England's domination for almost 400 years, was fought within sight of its walls in 1314. **Stirling Castle** today is the setting for summer programmes of pageants and historical plays which recapture the vanished splendours of the royal Scottish court. An authentic atmosphere can be found in the Old Town below, where tolbooth, mercat cross and restored 18th-century domestic architecture recall the everyday life of an old Scottish burgh. Though much has been rebuilt and swept aside in the name of progress, Stirling seems more conscious of its heritage than many other sizeable Scottish towns. Its history, evident in its castle, old town, and Victorian developments, can be gauged simply by strolling downhill from Castle Esplanade to the Thistle Centre, a modern shopping mall. *Open: daily (castle, HS).*

Stirling entertains its visitors with changing events at the **Smith Art Gallery**, and with varied theatrical and cinematic offerings at the **Macrobert Centre** on the beautifully situated university campus a couple of miles north of Stirling at Bridge of Allan. There is plenty to interest history buffs at the **Bannockburn Heritage Centre**, which tells the story of events leading up to the famous battle of that name in 1314. More history can be found at the **Wallace Monument**, a Victorian memorial to the first of Scotland's freedom-fighters, William Wallace. The views from the top of the tower on **Abbey Craig** are also well worth the exertion involved in climbing the poorly maintained road and then the claustrophobic spiral staircase. *Open: daily (Smith Art Gallery): daily, Apr–Oct (Bannockburn Heritage Centre).*

SWEETHEART ABBEY
DUMFRIES AND GALLOWAY (KIRKUDBRIGHTSHIRE)
■ OFF THE A710 AT NEW ABBEY, 7 MILES (11KM) SOUTH OF DUMFRIES ■

Looming over the village of New Abbey is the roofless ruin of Sweetheart Abbey, built in warm red sandstone. It was founded, like Balliol College, Oxford, by Lady Devorgilla of Galloway in 1273 in memory of her husband, John Balliol. Somewhat grotesquely, his embalmed heart was buried with her here in 1290. Though damaged by both Anglo–Scottish warfare and a lightning strike in the 14th century, which caused a fire, Sweetheart continued covertly to offer Roman rites even after the Reformation, up until the 17th century. Eventually an early conservation movement, 'desirous of preserving the remainder . . . as an ornament to that part of the country', bought the abbey in 1779. A parish church stood on the site until 1877. Visitors to the ruin today can see impressive masonry with restrained Cistercian designs, and a boundary wall of huge granite boulders. *Open: daily (HS).*

TRAQUAIR HOUSE
BORDERS (PEEBLESSHIRE)
■ OFF THE B709, 8 MILES (13KM) SOUTH-EAST OF PEEBLES ■

Thought to be the oldest continually occupied house in Scotland, Traquair dates back to the 12th century. It is a fortified mansion of considerable charm. The exterior of the house still looks very much as it did at the end of the 17th century – tall, grey and austere, with small windows and rounded towers and turrets. Inside there are stone-flagged passages and winding stairs and a secret priest's room with an escape stairway. This very complex building has many other notable features, among them examples of 17th-century panelling, a late 16th-century painted ceiling and Jacobean embroidery. There is also a variety of relics associated with the 27 English and Scottish monarchs who are said to have visited the house, notably Mary, Queen of Scots. Bonnie Prince Charlie stopped here during the rebellion of 1745. *Open: daily, Eas–end Apr; Sun, Mon, May; daily, Jun–Sep.*

Below: Sir William Wallace gazes out from the Wallace Monument, opened in 1869. In 1298 the Scottish patriot won a famous victory at Stirling Bridge against English occupying forces, but was eventually captured and hanged, drawn and quartered in London

■

THE ARGYLL AND SUTHERLAND HIGHLANDERS

The Argyll and Sutherland Highlanders, whose museum is in Stirling Castle, are one of the army's most celebrated regiments. Battle honours include the Thin Red Line at Balaclava (1854) and the Relief of Lucknow in the Indian Mutiny (1857). The old 91st regiment of foot became the 'Argyllshire' in 1820 and the 93rd Foot became the Sutherland Highlanders in 1861. The two Scottish regiments were merged in 1881. The Argylls always had a connection with the Campbell clan, and the regiment's badge united the boar's head crest of the Argylls (the chiefs of Clan Campbell), with the mountain cat symbol of the Sutherlands. On the collar badge myrtle (the Campbell emblem) is entwined with butcher's broom, the badge of the Sutherlands.

■

Traquair House has two main drives, in parallel. An impressive quarter-mile sycamore lined avenue forms the main approach to the house, though it has been unused for more than two centuries. At its end are the Bear Gates, impressive iron gates with bear decorations on the gate-pillars. (Bears were once hunted in the local forests.) Tradition states that Bonnie Prince Charlie was the last person to go through the gates in 1745, during the last Jacobite rebellion. The sympathetic 5th Earl of Traquair swore that they would not be opened again till the Stuarts were restored. They have therefore been closed ever since.

■

■

Above: Traquair House claims to have entertained no less than 27 monarchs in its long history. In addition to exploring this fascinating house, today's visitors can enjoy craft workshops, pleasant grounds and a brewhouse selling strong Traquair ale

■

■

DON'T MISS

■ The view of the Cuillin Hills (from the road to Glen Brittle)

■ The view (Stirling Castle)

■ The summer programme of historical re-enactments and pageantry (Stirling)

THE TROSSACHS
CENTRAL (PERTHSHIRE)

The Trossachs are a byword for craggy Scottish scenery. As early as 1794 a minister in Callander, the gateway to the Trossachs, wrote that 'the Trossachs are often visited by persons of taste, who are desirous of seeing nature in her rudest and unpolished states'. In fact, the area became popular with the rise of the cult of the 'picturesque', part of the Romantic movement of the late 18th and early 19th centuries. English Romantic poets found their way here – notably Wordsworth in 1803 – but it was the publication of Sir Walter Scott's long verse-narrative, *The Lady of the Lake*, in 1810 that really set the seal on the Trossachs' popularity. For generations after, crowds flocked to see the **Silver Strand**, **Ellen's Isle** and other readily identifiable landmarks around which Scott's story takes place.

With the visitors came 'infrastructure', hotels and improved transport links such as **Dukes's Road** (the A821), the main road through the Trossachs which was opened as recently as 1932. Two other factors contribute to the Trossachs' popularity. The wooded slopes and winding loch for which the area is renowned are certainly romantic, but not austere; and because the whole area lies just beyond the Highland boundary fault (a well-defined geological line which separates the northern hills from the softer Lowlands), the Trossachs are easily reached from some of Scotland's main centres of population. They are an easy journey from Edinburgh or Glasgow, and have been so since the days of rail and steam – though most visitors come by road today. The main circuit comprises an approach from **Callander**, and then a turn westwards before **Ben Ledi** to reach **Brig o' Turk** (from the Gaelic word *tuirc*: wild boar) via **Loch Venachar**. The heart of the Trossachs lies a little way to the west, between **Loch Achray** and **Loch Katrine**. **Duke's Road** then climbs southwards to the highest point of the route, which gives good views over acres of dense conifer plantation. From here the road drops towards **Aberfoyle**, via the **Queen Elizabeth Forest Park** with its visitor centre. Much of the Trossachs lies within the Forest Park, where there are many forest walks and drives. A historical character associated with the area is Rob Roy MacGregor, a real-life Robin Hood who has become a Scottish folk hero. He was born at **Glen Gyle**, at the north-west end of Loch Katrine, more than 300 years ago. Many of his adventures, such as outwitting the Lowland authorities and robbing the rich of their cattle, took place in the Trossachs. Today, his story is told at the **Rob Roy and Trossachs Visitor Centre** in Callander. *Open: daily, Mar–Nov; Sat, Sun, Dec–Feb.*

WESTER ROSS
HIGHLAND (ROSS AND CROMARTY)

Wester Ross, the western section of the old county of Ross and Cromarty, sweeps far northwards beyond the **Kyle of Lochalsh**, the ferry gateway to Skye, to **Ullapool** where, amid the curiously shaped peaks of **Inverpolly Forest** to the north, it meets the old county of Sutherland. Wester Ross includes some of the most dramatic mountains in Scotland, notably those of the **Torridons**, the area around peerless **Glen Torridon**. This is an area where even the most casual visitor becomes aware of geological forces. The long sandstone flanks of **Ben Eighe** (pronounced to rhyme with 'say') are dredged with white Cambrian quartzite, while the loch-pitted landscape beyond Ullapool on the Wester Ross/Sutherland border is an ancient, glacier-scoured gneiss (a coarse-grained, branded bedrock), which acts as a kind of plinth. On this the sandstone mountains stand discreetly, their summits guarded by steep cliffs, among them **Ben More Coigach** or **Cul Mor**. Others have steep slopes splintering into sandy rubble, like **Stac Polly**. Geology certainly means drama in these regions. The wild scenery also promotes interesting flora and fauna. A fenced-in section of **Rassal Ashwood**, south of **Shieldaig**, shows how natural woodland and plantlife regenerate if sheep are excluded, while slightly to the north-east by **Loch Maree**, is **Beinn Eighe**, Britain's first national nature reserve. It was given this status partly because of the importance of the old Caledonian pinewood growing on its slopes. Following the nature trail on the shoulders of Beinn Eighe is a good way to understand the landscape. Start on the western shore of Loch Maree (sometimes described as Scotland's largest natural loch, since so many others have been dammed for hydro-electric schemes). The trail offers outstanding views of **Slioch**, through the remnants of the old Caledonian pine forest. This majestic mountain (3,217ft, 981m) on the eastern shores of Loch Maree, commands stupendous views from its summit, given the considerable blessing of a clear day.

Corrieshalloch Gorge near Ullapool is another popular attraction, not only for its rich woodland, but also for the dramatic 150ft- (48m-) high **Falls of Measach**. Golden eagles, pine martens, wildcats and other Highland specialities can be encountered in many parts of Wester Ross. However, apart from the main settlements of **Gairloch** and **Ullapool** and a few other villages, this is primarily an empty landscape – the section of the A832 between **Little Loch Broom** and **Braemore** is known as 'Destitution Road', recalling the days in 1851 when it was built to give work to starving locals. Poor soils and remoteness led to steady depopulation over the centuries. Even so, these austere landscapes exert a strong pull on southerners today. Many have come to run craft shops, hotels or restaurants, fascinated by the curious magic of the landscape.

INDEX

Page numbers in italics refer to captions and/or side text

A

A La Ronde 10, *10, 11*
Abbeydale Industrial Hamlet 185
Abbot Hall Art Gallery 167
Abbot Hall Museum of Lakeland
    Life and Industry 167, *167*
Abbotsbury 10–11, *10, 11*
Abbotsford House 194, *194, 195*
Aberdeen 194, *194, 195*
Aberdulais Falls 126, *126, 127*
Abney 115
Acton Scott Historical Farm 126
Albert Dock 172
Alloway 196
Alnwick 154, *155*
Alresford 48, *49*
Alton Towers 90, *90, 91*
Alum Bay 62, *62*
American Museum 13
Anfield football ground 173
Angel Corner 95, *95*
Angelsey Sea Zoo 126, *126, 127*
Angus Folk Museum 195
Anne Hathaway's cottage 120
Apsley House 66
Arlington Court 11, *11*
Armstrong Energy Centre 160, *160*
Arreton Manor 63
Arundel 48, *49*
Ashmolean Museum 76, *77*
Ashurst 75
Athelhampton House 11
Attingham Park 146
Auchindoun 201
Audley End 48, *48, 49*
Avebury 11, *11*
Aviemore 197
Axe Edge Moor 114
Ayscoughfee Hall 118
Aysgarth 190, *190*

B

Baddesley Clinton 90
Badgeworthy Water 28, *29*
Bagpipe Museum 175, *175*
Bakewell 115
Balmoral Castle 195, *195*
Bamburgh 154, *154, 155*
Bankfield Museum and Art Gallery 163
Bannockburn Heritage Centre 217
Bar Convent 189
Barnard Castle 154
Bass Museum of Brewing History 91,
    91
Bateman's 48, *49*
Bath 12–13, *12, 13*
Battle 49
Beacon Fell Country Park 162
Beamish 176
The Beatles Story 172
Beaulieu 49, *49*
Beaumaris Castle 126, *127*
Beck Isle Museum of Rural Life 179
Bedford 49
Beer 34
Beinn Eighe 219
Belton House 91, *91*
Belvoir Castle 91, *91*
Bembridge 63
Ben Nevis 204, *205*

Berkeley 14, *14*
Berkeley Castle 14, *15*
Berney Arms 94, *95*
Berrington Hall 127, *127*
Berwick-upon-Tweed 154–5
Beverley 155
Beverley Minster 155, *155*
Bewdley 127, *127*
Bickleigh 14, *15*
Biddulph Grange Garden 92
Big Ben 68, *69*
Big Pit Mining Museum 128
Bishop's Palace, Wells 42
Black Country Museum 102, *102, 103*
Blackpool 155, *155*
Blair Castle 195, *195*
Blenheim Palace 50, *50*
Blickling Hall 92, *92, 93*
Blist's Hill Open-Air Museum 138
Blue John Cavern 97, *97*
Bluebell Railway 50, *50*
Boat Museum 155, *155*
Bodelwyddan Castle 128, *129*
Bodiam Castle 50, *50*
Bodleian Library 76
Bodnant Garden 128, *129, 129*
Bodstone Barton Farmworld 29
Boldre 75
Bolling Hall 156
Bolton Castle 156
Bolton Priory 191
Bo'ness & Kinneil Railway 196
Border History Museum 165
Boscastle 14–15, *14*
Boscobel House 129, *129*
Bosherston 142
Boston 92
'Boston Stump' 92, *92*
Bosworth Battlefield 93, *93*
Boulby Head 179
Bourneville 95
Bourton-on-the-Water 15, *15*
Bovington Camp 40, *41*
Bowes Museum 154, *155*
Bowood House 15, *15*
Bradford 156, *157*
Brading 63
Brantwood 156, *156*
Breamish Valley 177
Brecknock Museum 129, *129*
Brecon 129
Brecon Beacons National Park 130, *130*
Brecon Mountain Railway 130
Brentor 25
Bressingham Live Steam Museum and
    Gardens 93, *93*
Bridestones Nature Reserve 178, *178*
Bridgnorth 131, *131*
Bridlington 184
Brighton 50, *51, 51*
Brimham Rocks 191
Bristol 16–17, *16, 17*
Bristol Industrial Museum 16–17
British Golf Museum 215
British Museum 66, *66*
Broadfield House Glass Museum 102
Broadland Conservation Centre 94
Broadlands 80, *80*
The Broads 94, *94*
Brockenhurst 75
Brontë Parsonage Museum 164–5
Brougham Castle 156–7, *156*
Broughton Castle 52
Browne's Hospital 119
Brympton d'Evercy 15, *15*
Buckfast Abbey 15
Buckfastleigh 15

Buckingham Palace 66–7, *66*
Buckland Abbey 18, *18, 19*
Bucklers Hard 75, *75*
Bunyan Meeting Library and Museum
    49
Burford 52
Burghley House *118, 119, 119*
Burns Cottage 196, *196*
Burrell Collection 207, *207*
Burton Constable Hall 157, *157*
Burton-upon-Trent 91
Bury St Edmunds 95, *95*
Butterfly World 63
Buxton 115
Byland Abbey 179

C

Cabinet War Rooms 71
Cadbury World 95, *95*
Cader Idris 148
Caerlaverock Castle and Nature
    Reserve 196, *197*
Caernarfon 131, *131*
Caerphilly Castle 131, *131*
Cairngorms 197, *197*
Caister Castle 94
Calbourne 62
Calderdale Industrial Museum 163
Caley Mill 111
Calke Abbey 96, *96*
Cambo Country Park 215
Cambridge 98–9, *98, 99*
Cambridge colleges 98, *98, 99*
Cambridge and County Folk Museum
    99
Camelot Theme Park 157, *157*
Canal Museum 97, *97*
Cannock Chase 96, *96*
Canons Ashby House 96, *96*
Canterbury 52, *52*
Canterbury Cathedral 52–3, *52, 53*
Captain Cook Memorial Museum 187
Captain Cook's Schoolroom Museum
    178
Cardiff 132
Cardiff Castle 132, *132*
Carisbrooke 62
Carlisle 157, *157*
Carlton Towers 158, *158*
Carnforth 185, *185*
Carrawburgh 163
Cars of the Stars Motor Museum 169
Castell Coch 132, *132*
Castle Combe 18, *19*
Castle Drogo 18, *19*
Castle Howard 158, *158*
Castle Rising 97
Castlerigg Stone Circle 169
Castleton 97, *97*
Catalyst Chemical Museum 158
Cawdor Castle 198, *198*
Centre for Alternative Technology 133
The Chains 28
Charles Dickens Birthplace Museum 79
Charles Rennie Mackintosh Society 207
Charleston Farmhouse 53, *53*
Chartwell 53, *53*
Chatham Historic Dockyard 53, *53*
Chatsworth House 100, *100*
Chatterley Whitfield Mining Museum
    119, 119
Chawton 53, *53*
Cheddar Gorge 18–19, *18, 19*
Cheltenham 19, *19*
Chenies Manor House 54, *55*

Chepstow 133
Cheshire Military Museum 159
Chesil Bank 10
Chessington World of Adventures 54,
    54, 55
Chester *158, 159, 159*
Chesters Fort and Museum 163
Chichester 54
Chichester Cathedral 54, *54*
Chilham 55, *55*
Chillingham Castle 160, *160*
Church Stretton 146
Chysauster Ancient Village 20
Cider Museum 137
Cirencester 20, *20, 21*
Cirencester Park 21
Clandon Park 55
Claydon House 55, *55*
Clearwell Caves Ancient Iron Mines 27,
    27
Cleeve Abbey 28
Cley Hill 33
Clifton Suspension Bridge 16
Clive House Museum 146
Clovelly 20, *20, 21*
Clywedog Gorge 133
Coalbrookdale 138
Coalport China Museum 138
Cockermouth 169
Colchester 56, *56*
Colour Museum 156, *157*
Combe Martin Motorcycle Collection
    29
Combe Martin Wildlife Park 29
Combe Sydenham Country Park 28
Commonwealth Cemetery 96
Compton Acres Gardens 20
Coningsby's Hospital 137
Conisbrough Castle 160
Coniston Water 169
Conwy 133, *133*
Cookham-on-Thames 56, *56*
Corbridge 163
Corfe Castle 21, *21*
Corinium Museum 20, *20, 21*
Cornish Seal Sanctuary 21, *21*
Corrieshalloch Gorge 219
Corsham Court 21, *21*
Cotehele House 22, *23*
Cothey Bottom Heritage Centre 63
Cotswold Farm Park 22
Cotswold Wildlife Park 56, *56*
Coughton Court 100, *101*
Countisbury Common 29
Courage Shire Horse Centre 56, *56*
Covent Garden 66, *67*
Cowes 62, *62*
Coxwold 179
Cragside House and Garden 160, *160*
Craigievar Castle 198, *198*
Crathes Castle 198, *198*
Craven Museum 191
Criccieth 134, *134*
Crich 110
Cricket St Thomas 22, *22, 23*
Croft Ambrey 134
Croft Castle 134
Cromford 100, *101*
Croxteth Hall 173
Cruachan Power Station 198, *199*
Cuillin Hills 216, *217*
Culbone 29
Culloden Battlefield 199, *199*
Culross 199
Culzean Castle and Country Park 200,
    200, 201
Cutty Sark 67, *68*

D

Dalby Forest Drive 178
Dales Countryside Museum 190
Dales Way 190
Dalmeny House 200
Dan-yr-Ogof Showcaves 134, *134*
Dartmoor 24–5, *24, 25*
Dartmouth 22, 23, *23*
Dean Forest Railway 27
Deene Park *100*, 101, *101*
Derwent Water 168, *168, 169*
Dickens' House 67
Didcot Railway Centre 56, *57*
Dinas Bran 139
Dinosaur Museum 23, *23*
Dobwalls Family Adventure Park 23, *23*
Dolaucothi Gold Mines 135
Dolgellau 148
Dorchester 23, *23*
Dorney Court 57, *57*
Dorset County Museum 23, *23*
Dorset Military Museum 23
Dove Cottage 160, *169*
Dover 56, *57, 57*
Downing Street 71
Dr Johnson's House 67
Drayton Manor Park and Zoo *100*, 101
Drumlanrig Castle 201, *201*
Duddingston 203
Dudley 102
Dudley Zoo 102, *102*
Dufftown 201
Dumfries 201, *201*
Duncombe Park 179
Dunfermline 201
Dunkery Beacon 28
Dunrobin Castle 201, *201*
Dunstaffnage Castle 215
Dunster 23, *23*
Dunvegan Castle 216
Durham 161
Durham Cathedral *160*, 161, *161*
Durham Light Infantry Museum and Arts Centre 161
Duxford Airfield 102, *102*
Dyson Perrins Museum 151, *151*

E

Earsham 112
Easby Abbey 181
East Bergholt 102–3, *103*
Easton Farm Park 103, *103*
Edale 115
Edinburgh 202–3, *202, 203*
Edinburgh Castle 202, *202, 203*
Elgar's Birthplace Museum 151
Elgin 204
Ellesmere Lakes 135
Ellesmere Port 155
Elsdon 177
Ely Cathedral 103, *103*
Erddig 135, *135*
Etal Castle 177
Eton 86
Exbury Gardens 58, *58*
Exeter 26, *26, 27*
Exeter Cathedral 26, *26, 27*
Exeter Maritime Museum 26, *26*
Exmoor 28–9, *28, 29*
Exmoor Bird Gardens 29
Eyam 115
Eyam Moor 115

F

Fairfax House 189
Falkland Palace 204, *204*
Falls of Foyers 213
Farigaig Forest Centre 213
Fawley Court 58
Felbrigg Hall 103, *103*
Fenton House 68
Ffestiniog Railway 136, *136*
Fingle Gorge 25
Fishbourne Palace 54
Fitzwilliam Museum 99
Flamingo Land 162, *162*
Flatford Mill 103
Fleet lagoon 10
Floors Castle 204, *204*
Ford 177
Forde Abbey 27, *27*
Forest of Bowland 162, *162*
Forest of Dean 27, *27*
Fort Augustus 213
Fort Victoria Country Park 62
Fort William 204, *205*
Forth Rail Bridge 209
Fountains Abbey 162, *162*
Fox Talbot Museum 31, *31*
Framlingham Castle 104
Freshwater 62
Frogmore House 86
Furzey Gardens 75
Fyvie Castle 205, *205*

G

Gaping Gill 191
Garman-Ryan Collection 104
Gaulden Manor 28
Georgian Theatre Royal 181
Gilbert White Museum 82, *82*
Glamis 195
Glasgow 206–7, *206, 207*
Glastonbury 27, *27*
Glen Roy 205, *205*
Glen Torridon 219, *219*
Glencoe 208, *208, 209*
Glendurgan Garden 27
Glenfiddich 200, 201, *201*
Glenfinnan Monument 208, *208*
Glenfinnan Viaduct 208, *209*
Gloucester 30, *30, 31*
Gloucester Folk Museum 30, *31*
Godshill 63
Gondola steam yacht 168
Goodwood 58, *58*
Goyt's Bridge 114
Grace Darling Museum 154
Granada Studios Tour 174, *174, 175*
Grasmere 160, *169*
Grassington 190
Great Ayton 178
Great Barn Museum of Wiltshire Life 11, *11*
Great Dixter 58, *59*
Great Glen 205
Great Malvern 140
Great Orme 139
Great Witley 136
Great Yarmouth 94
Green Howards Museum 181, *181*
Green Park 70
Greenwich 67–8, *67*
Grime's Graves 104, *105*
Grimspound 24–5
Grindleford 115

Gustav Holst Birthplace Museum 19
Gweek 21

H

Haddo House 209
Haddon Hall 104, 105, *105*
Hadleigh 105
Hadrian's Wall 162, 163, *163*
Halifax 163
Hall of Aviation 82
Hall's Croft 120
Ham House 68
Hammerwood Park 58, *59*
Hampstead 68
Hampstead Heath 68
Hampton Court 68, *68*
Hancock Museum 176, *176*
Hanley 119, *119*
Hardknott Roman Fort 169
Hardraw Force 190
Hardwick Hall 105, *105*
Harewood House 164, *165*
Harlech Castle 136, *136*
Harlow Carr Botanical Gardens 164
Harrogate 164, *165*
Harveys Wine Museum 17
Harvington Hall 136, *136*
Hatfield House *58, 59, 59*
Haughmond Abbey 146
Hawes 190, *191*
Hawk Conservancy 60, *61*
Hawkshead 169
Haworth 164–5, *164, 165*
Heacham 110, 111
Heart of Midlothian 203
Heavy Horse Centre 22, *22*
Helmsley Castle 179
Hereford 137, *137*
Herschel House 13, *13*
Hever Castle 60, *60, 61*
Hexham 165
Hickling Broad 94
Hidcote Manor Garden 31, *31*
Highclere Castle 60, *61*
Highgate Cemetery 68–9
Highland Wildlife Park 209
Hill House 209
Hill Top 169
HMS *Belfast* 69
HMS *Victory* 79, *79*
Holburne Museum 13
Hole of Horcum 178
Holker Hall 165, *165*
Holkham Hall 105
Holme Pierrepont Hall *105*, 112
Holmfirth 165
Holmfirth Postcard Museum 165, *165*
Hopetoun House 209, *209*
Horner Vale 28
Horning 94
Horse Guards Parade 71
Hospital of St Cross 85
Houghton Hall 106, *106*
Hound Tor 25
Houses of Parliament 68, *69*
Housesteads Roman Fort 163, *163*
Hoveton Great Broad 94
How Hill 94, *94*
Howgill Fells 191
Hull 166, *166, 167*
Hull and East Riding Museum 166, *167*
Huntly House 203
Hutton-le-Hole 179
Hyde Park 70, *70*

I

Ickworth 106, *106*
Ightham Mote 61, *61*
Imperial War Museum 69, *69*
Industrial Heritage Centre 13, *13*
Inveraray Castle 210, *210*
Inveraray Courthouse and Jail 211
Inverewe Gardens 210–11, *210, 211*
Iona 210, 211, *211*
Ironbridge 138, *139*
Isle of Wight 62–3, *62, 63*
Isle of Wight Steam Railway 63

J

Jackfield Tile Museum 138
Jedburgh 211
Jenner Museum 14
Jervaulx Abbey 166, *167*
Jodrell Bank 166, *166, 167*
John George Joicey Museum 176
John Knox House 203
John Rylands University Library 174
Jorvik Viking Centre 189
Judges' Lodging Museum 170

K

Keats' House 68
Kedleston Hall 106
Keighley and Worth Valley Railway 165
Kelvingrove Art Gallery and Museum 207, *207*
Kendal 167, *167*
Kenilworth Castle 106
Kensington Gardens 70
Kentwell Hall 109, *109*
Kenwood House 68
Keswick 169
Kettle's Yard 99
Kew Gardens 69
Kielder Water 177, *177*
Kiftsgate Court 31
Kilburn 179
Kilburn White Horse 179
Killerton 31
Killhope Wheel Lead Mining Centre 167, *167*
Kilnsey Crag 190
Kilpeck Church 138, *138*
Kinder Scout 115
King's College 98, *98, 99*
King's Lynn 107, *107*
Kintail 211
Kirknewton 177
Kirkstall Abbey 170
Knebworth House 61, *61*
Knightshayes Court 31, *31*
Knole 64, *64*
Knowsley Safari Park 173
Kodak Museum 157
Kyles of Bute 212
The Kymin 141

L

Lacock 31, *31*
Lady Lever Art Gallery 167, *167*
Lady Waterford Hall 177
Laing Art Gallery 176
Lake District 168–9, *168, 169*

Lamb House 81
Lancaster 170, *170*
Land's End 32, *33*
Langthwaite 190
Lanhydrock House 32, *32, 33*
Lavenham 107
Laxton 107
Layer Marney Tower 64
Leeds 170, *170*
Leeds Castle 64, 65, *65*
Leeds Industrial Museum 170
Leighton Hall 170, *170*
Leonardslee Gardens 64, 65
Leuchars 215
Levens Hall 170, *170*
Lichfield 107, *107*
Lightwater Valley Theme Park 170, 171
Lilla Cross 178
Lincoln 108–9, *108*
Lincoln Cathedral 108, *108,* 109
Lindisfarne Castle 171, *171*
Lindisfarne (Holy Island) 170, *171*
Linlithgow Palace 212, *212*
Little Moreton Hall 171, *171*
Liverpool 172–3, *172, 173*
Llanberis Pass 148, *149*
Llandaff Cathedral 132
Llandudno 139, *139*
Llangollen 139
Llangorse 130
Llanthony Priory 130
Llanystumdwy 134, *134*
Llechwedd Slate Caverns 139
Lloyd George Memorial Museum 134
Llyn Padarn Country Park 141
Loch an Eilein 197, *197*
Loch Katrine 218, *218, 219*
Loch Lomond 212, *212, 213*
Loch Ness, 212, *213*
Lodmore Country Park 37
Logan Botanic Gardens 212, 213
London 66–71
London Transport Museum 67
Long Melford 109, *109*
Longleat House 32–3, *32, 33*
Longshaw Park 115
Longthorpe Tower 113
Loseley House 72, *72*
Lotherton Hall 173, *173*
Lower Broadheath 151
Lowestoft 94
Ludlow 140, *140,* 146
Lullingstone Silk Farm 45
Luton Hoo 72, *72*
Lydney Park 27
Lyme Park 173, *173*
Lymington 75
Lyn and Exmoor Museum 29
Lyndhurst 75
Lynmouth 29
Lynton 29

M

Macclesfield Silk Museum 173, *173*
Madame Tussaud's 69
Malham Cove 191
Malham Tarn 191
Mallyan Spout 178
Malmesbury House 36
Malvern Hills 140
Malvern Priory 140, *140, 141*
Manchester 174, *174*
Manchester City Art Gallery 174, *175*
Manchester Jewish Museum 174
Manchester United Museum 174

Manorbier 143
Mapledurham House 72, *72*
Mappin Art Gallery 185
Marble Arch 70
Margam Country Park 141
Martinhoe 29
Marwell Zoo 72, *72*
Mary Rose 79
Mathematical Bridge 98
Melford Hall 109
Mellerstain House 214
Melrose Abbey 214, *214*
Merrivale 25
Merseyside Maritime Museum 172
Middleham Castle 190
Millom Folk Museum 169
Milton Abbas 33
Minehead 29
Minstead 75
Minster Lovell 73, *73*
Mirehouse 169
Mompesson House 36, *36*
Monmouth 141, *141*
Montacute House 33, *33*
Morpeth 175, *175*
Morvich 211
Morwhellam Quay 33, *33*
Mount Edgcumbe 34
Mount Grace Priory 179
Moyse's Hall 95
Muker *191*
Muncaster Castle 175, *175*
Muncaster Mill 169
Museum of Army Transport 155, *155*
Museum of Automata 189
Museum of Bookbinding 13
Museum of Childhood 126
Museum of Costume 13, *13*
Museum of Costume and Lace 26
Museum of Costume and Textiles *112*
Museum of Dartmoor Life 25
Museum of Domestic Life 82, *83*
Museum of the Duke of Edinburgh's
    Royal Regiment 36, *37*
Museum of English Naïve Art 13
Museum of Iron 138
Museum of Lincolnshire Life 109
Museum of North Craven Life 191
Museum of Packaging and Advertising
    30, *31*
Museum of Science and Engineering
    176
Museum of Science and Industry 174,
    174, 175
Museum of Smuggling History 63
Museum of the South Wales Borderers
    129
Museum of Transport 207
Museum of Waterpower 25
Museum of Witchcraft 15

N

National Centre of Photography 13
National Collection of Model Soldiers
    59
National Dairy Museum 83
National Gallery 69
National Gallery of Scotland 203
National Horseracing Museum 109, *109*
National Maritime Museum 68
National Motor Museum 49, *49*
National Museum of Labour History
    174, *174*
National Museum of Photography,
    Film and Television 156, *157*

National Museum of Wales 132
National Portrait Gallery 69
National Railway Museum 189
National Tramway Museum 110, *110*
National Waterways Museum 30
National Wireless Museum 63
Natural History Museum 69, *69*
Needles Old Battery 62, *62*
Nene Valley Railway 113, *113*
Ness Gardens 175
New Forest 74–5, *75*
New Forest Butterfly Farm 75
New Lanark 214–15, *214, 215*
Newark-on-Trent 110
Newburgh Priory 179
Newby Hall 175, *175*
Newcastle upon Tyne 176, *176*
Newmarket 109
Newport 63
Newstead Abbey 110
Nidderdale Museum 191
Norfolk Broads 94, *94*
Norfolk Fire Museum 93
Norfolk Lavender *110,* 111
Norris Castle 62–3
North of England Open Air Museum
    176, *176*
North Wales Quarrying Museum 141
North York Moors National Park 178–
    9, *178, 179*
North Yorkshire Moors Railway 179
Northumberland National Park 177,
    177
Norwich 110, 111, *111*
Nostell Priory 180, *180, 181*
Nottingham 112, *112, 113*
Nottingham Lace Market 112
Nunnington Hall 179

O

Oare Church 28, *28*
Oates Museum 82
Oban 215, *215*
Offa's Dyke 146
Official Loch Ness Monster Exhibition
    213
Okehampton 25
Old Bailey 69
Old Royal Observatory 68
Old Sarum 36
Orford 112
Oriental Museum 160, *161*
Osborne House 63
Otter Trust 112, *113*
Oxburgh Hall 113, *113*
Oxford 76–7, *76, 77*
Oxford colleges 76, *76, 77*

P

Packwood House 113, *113*
Painshill Park 73
Painswick Rococo Garden 34, *34*
Palace of Holyroodhouse 203
Paradise Mill Silk Museum 173
Parcevall Hall 190
Parke 25
Parke Rare Breeds Farm 25
Peak Cavern 97
Peak District 114–15, *114, 115*
Pecorama Pleasure Gardens 34, *34*
Pembroke Castle 141
Pembrokeshire Coast 142–3, *142*
Pencil Museum 169

Pennine Way 190
Penrhyn Castle 143, *143*
Penrhyn Railway Collection 143
Penshurst Place 72, 73, *73*
Perth 215, *215*
Peterborough 113
Peterborough Cathedral 113, *113*
Petticoat Lane 69
Petworth 78, *78*
Pevensey Castle 78, *78*
Peveril Castle 97
Piccadilly 70, *70*
Pickering 179
Piece Hall 163
Pilkington Glass Museum 180, *181*
Pittville Pump Room 19
Planetarium 70
Plas Newydd, Clwyd 139
Plas Newydd, Gwynedd 143
Pleasurewood Hills American Theme
    Park 116, *117*
Plymouth 34, *34*
Plymouth Hoe 34, *34*
Poldark Mine 34, *35*
Polesden Lacey 78
Pontcysyllte Aqueduct *138*
Port Lympne Zoo Park 78, *79*
Port Sunlight Heritage Centre 167
Porth-yr-Ogof 130
Portmeirion 143, *143*
Portsmouth 78, 79, *79*
Potter Heigham 94
Powderham Castle 35
Powis Castle 144, *144*
Priest's House Museum 44

Q

Quarry Bank Mill 180–1, *181*
Quarry Gardens 146
Queen Elizabeth Forest Park 218, *219*
Queen Mary's Dolls' House 86
Queen Mary's House 211
Queen's House 68
Queen's Royal Surrey Regimental
    Museum 55
Quince Honey Farm 34, 35, *35*

R

Raby Castle 181, *181*
Radcliffe Camera 76, *76*
Radipole Lake 37
Raglan Castle 144
Ranworth 94
Ravenglass and Eskdale Railway 169
Ravenscar 179
Red Lodge 17
Reeth 190
Regent's Canal 70
Regent's Park 70
Regimental Museum of the Royal
    Welsh Fusiliers 131
Regiments of Gloucestershire Museum
    30
Rhondda Heritage Park 144, *145*
Rhuddlan Castle 144, *144*
Richmond 181, *181*
Richmondshire Museum 181
Rievaulx Abbey 182, *182*
Ripon 182, *182*
Ripon Prison and Police Museum 182
Rob Roy and Trossachs Visitor Centre
    218, *218*

Robert Burns Centre 201
Robin Hood's Bay 179
Roche Abbey 182
Rochester 80, *80*
Rockingham Castle 116, *117*
Roman Baths Museum 13
Romany Folklore Museum 82, *82*
Romsey 80, *80*
Ros Castle 160
Rosedale 179
Rothiemurchus 197
Rotunda Museum 183
Rougemont Gardens 26
Round Church 99
Rousham House 80
Royal Academy of Arts 70
Royal Albert Memorial Museum 26
Royal and Ancient Golf Club 215
Royal Botanic Garden 203
Royal Crescent 12, *12*
Royal Mews 67
Royal Museum of Scotland 203
Royal Naval College 67–8
Royal Naval Museum 79
Royal Pavilion 51, *51*
Royal Pump Room Museum 164, *165*
Royal Shakespeare Theatre 120, *120*
Royalty and Empire 86, *86*
Rufford Old Hall 183
Rufus Stone 75
Ruskin Gallery 185, *185*
Rydal Mount *182*, 183, *183*
Ryde 63
Rye 81, *81*
Ryedale Folk Museum 179

S

St Albans *80*, 81
St Andrews 215, *215*
St David's 145, *145*
St Fagans 132
St George's Chapel 86
St Helens 180
St James's Park 70
St Michael's Mount *34*, 35, *35*
St Non's Well 145
St Paul's Cathedral 70, *71*
Salisbury 36, *36*, *37*
Salisbury Cathedral 36, *36*, *37*
Salisbury and South Wiltshire Museum 36, *37*
Saltram House *34*, *34*
Samuel Johnson Birthplace Museum 107
Sandown 63
Sandringham House 116, 117, *117*
Satrosphere 194
Scarborough *182*, 183, *183*
Science Museum 70
Scotney Castle 81, *81*
Scott Polar Research Institute 99
Sealife Park 37, *37*
Seaton Delaval Hall 184
Sedbergh 191
Selborne 82, *82*
Selworthy 28
Settle 191
Severn Valley Railway 145
Sewerby Hall 184, *185*
Sezincote 37, *37*
Shaftesbury 37
Shakespeare's birthplace 120
Shandy Hall 179
Shanklin Chine 63
Sheffield 184–5, *184*, *185*

Sheffield Botanic Gardens 185
Sheffield Industrial Museum 185
Sheldon Manor 37, *37*
Sheldonian Theatre 76
Sheppy's Cider Farm 38, *38*
Shibden Hall Folk Museum of West Yorkshire 163
Shoe Museum 38, *38*, *39*
Shottery 120
Shrewsbury 146, *146*
Shropshire Hills 146, *147*
Shropshire Regimental Museum 146
Shropshire Union Canal 135, 139
Shugborough Hall 117, *117*
Shuttleworth Collection 82, *82*
Sir John Soane's Museum 71
Sizergh Castle 185
Skipton Castle 191
Skye 216
Sledmere House 185, *185*
Slimbridge Wildfowl Refuge 38, *39*
Snowdon 148, *148*
Snowdon Mountain Railway 149, *149*
Snowdonia National Park 148–9, *148*, *149*
Snowshill Manor 38–9, *39*
Somerleyton Hall 117
Somerset Rural Life Museum 27
South West Coast Path 29, 32
Southampton 82, *83*
Southsea 79
Southwold 118, *119*
Spalding 118, *118*
Speaker's Corner 70
Speedwell Cavern *96*, 97, *97*
Speke Hall 172–3
Spetchley Park Gardens 147
Springfields Gardens 118
SS *Great Britain* 17, *17*
Stackpole Quay 142–3
Staindrop Church 181
Staithes 179, *179*
Stamford 118–19
Stanford Hall 119, *119*
Stanley Spencer Art Gallery 56
Steamtown Railway Centre 185, *185*
Sticklepath 25
Stirling 217, *217*
Stoke Bruerne 97
Stoke-on-Trent 119
Stokesay Castle 147, *147*
Stonehenge *38*, 39, *39*
Stonor Park 83, *83*
Stott Park Bobbin Mill 186, *186*
Stourhead 39, *39*
Stowe Landscape Gardens 83, *83*
Strangers' Hall 111
Stratfield Saye 83, *83*
Stratford-upon-Avon 120, *120*, *121*
Street 38
Strid 190–1
Studley Royal 162
Styal 180
Sudeley Castle 40, *41*
Sulgrave Manor 121
Swaledale Folk Museum 190
Swanston 203
Sweetheart Abbey 217
Sygun Copper Mine 147

T

Tan Hill Inn 190
Tank Museum 40, *40*, *41*
Tarr Steps *28*
Tate Gallery 71

Tate Gallery Liverpool 172
Tattershall Castle 121, *121*
Tatton Park 186, *186*
Techniquest 132
Temple Newsam House 170
Tenby 143, 150, *150*
Tenement House 207
Tennyson Down 62
Tewkesbury 40–1, *40*, *41*
Theatre Museum 67
Theatre Royal 95
Thorpe Park Theme Park 83, *83*
Thursford Collection 121, *121*
Tintagel Castle 41, *41*
Tintern Abbey 150
Tolland 28
Totnes 41, *41*
Tower of London 71, *71*
Town Docks Museum, Hull 166, *166*, *167*
Townend 169
Trafalgar Square 71, *71*
Traquair House 217, *217*
Treak Cliff Cavern 97
Tredegar House 150, *150*
Trelissick Garden 41, *41*
Trerice 41
Tretower Court and Castle 150
Tring 87
Trinity College 98
Tropiquaria 28
The Trossachs 218, *218*
Troutbeck 169
The Trundle 58
Tullie House Museum 157
Twycross Zoo 121, *121*

U

Ullswater 168, *169*
Urquhart Castle 213
Usher Gallery *108*, 109

V

Vale of Llangollen Railway 139
Valle Crucis 139
Valley of the Rocks 29
Ventnor 63
Vicars' Close 42
Victoria & Albert Museum 71
Victoria Park and Fossil Grove 207
Vindolanda Fort *162*, 163

W

Waddesdon Manor 84
Wade's Causeway *178*
Walker Art Gallery 172
Wallace Monument 217, *217*
Wallington 186, *186*
Wallsworth Hall 41
Walsall 104
Warkworth Castle 186, *186*
Warwick 122, *123*
Warwick Castle 122, *122*, *123*
Warwick Doll Museum 122
Warwickshire Museum 122
Washford 28
Wast Water 168
'Watercress Line' 48, *48*
Watermeet 28
Weald & Downland Open Air Museum 84, *85*

Wellington Country Park 83
Wells 42, *42*
Wells Cathedral 42, *42*, *43*
Welsh Industrial and Maritime Museum 132
Welsh National Folk Museum 132
West Highland Museum 204, *205*
West Park Museum 173
West Wycombe 84, *84*, *85*
West Wycombe Park 84
Wester Ross 219
Westminster Abbey 71
Weston Park *150*, 151
Westonbirt Aboretum 43, *43*
Wet Withins 115
Weyhill 60
Wharfedale 190
Wheal Martyn Museum 43, *43*
Whipsnade Zoo 84, *85*
Whitby *186*, 187, *187*
Whitby Abbey 187
White Scar Caves 191
Whitehall 71
Whitworth Art Gallery 174
Widnes 158
Wigan Pier *186*, 187, *187*
Wightwick Manor 123, *123*
Wilberforce House 166
Willow Tea Rooms *206*
Willy Lott's Cottage 103
Wilton House 43, *43*
Wimborne Minster 44, *45*
Wimpole Hall 123, *123*
Winchester 85, *85*
Winchester Cathedral 85, *85*
Windermere 168
Windermere Steamboat Museum 168
Windsor 86, *86*
Windsor Castle 86, *86*, *87*
Windsor Great Park 86
Windsor Safari Park 86
Wisley Gardens 87
Witley Court 136
Woburn Abbey 87, *87*
Wolferton 117
Wolseley Garden Park 123
Wood End Museum 183
Woodbridge Tide Mill 123
Woodhenge 38
Wookey Hole 44–5, *44*, *45*
Woolly Monkey Sanctuary 45, *45*
Worcester 150, *151*, *151*
Worcester Woods Country Park 150
Wordsworth House 169
Wordsworth Museum 160
Worldwide Butterflies, 45, *45*
Wroxeter Roman Town 146
Wye Valley 137

Y

Yeavering Bell 177
York 188–9, *188*, *189*
York Castle Museum 189, *189*
York Minster 188–9, *188*
Yorkshire Carriage Museum 190
Yorkshire Dales National Park 190–1, *190*, *191*
Yorkshire Dales Railway 191
Yorkshire Museum 189

Z

Zennor 45, *45*
Zoological Museum 87, *87*

ACKNOWLEDGEMENTS

■

The Automobile Association would like to thank the following photographers, libraries and associations for their assistance in the preparation of this book:

J Allan Cash Photolibrary **18** *Cheddar Gorge,* **65** *Leeds Castle,* **74** *New Forest ponies,* **82** *Shuttleworth Collection,* **86** *Windsor changing the guard,* **97** *Stoke Bruerne,* **110** *Tram, Crich,* **111** *Norwich market,* **117** *Shugborough Hall,* **118** *Float, Spalding,* **159** *Chester,* **162** *Flamingo Land*

Cadbury World **95** *Exhibit and poster*

City of Plymouth Museums & Art Gallery **18** *Drake's drum*

City of Sheffield Museum **184** *Scissors*

Clark's Shoe Museum **38** *Shoe Museum*

Dean & Chapter, Durham Cathedral **161** *St Cuthbert wall painting*

FCB.TCB Advertising **151** *Lea & Perrins Worcester sauce label*

Granada Studio Tours **174** *Coronation Street*

V K Guy Ltd **131** *Caernarfon Castle,* **168** *Derwent Water*

D Hardley **172** *Liverpool,* **173** *Beatles sculpture*

Hatfield House **59** *Elizabeth I*

Highclere Castle **61** *Interior of castle*

Holmfirth Postcard Museum **165** *Postcard*

Mary Evans Picture Library **16** *Brunel,* **30** *Gloucester,* **36** *Salisbury,* **42** *Wells,* **48** *Rudyard Kipling,* **52** *Pilgrims,* **55** *Florence Nightingale,* **93** *Richard III at Bosworth,* **101** *Lord Cardigan,* **105** *Bess of Hardwick,* **107** *Lichfield Cathedral,* **110** *Lavender,* **120** *Shakespeare,* **129** *Charles II,* **146** *A E Houseman,* **151** *Worcester Cathedral,* **156** *John Ruskin,* **187** *Vampire bat,* **199** *Bonnie Prince Charlie,* **212** *Mary, Queen of Scots*

E Nagele **148** *Llyn Mymbyr*

National Motor Museum, Beaulieu **49** *Motor Museum*

National Museum of Photography, Film & Television **157** *Poster*

National Trust **41** *Trelissick,* **180** *Nostell Priory*

National Trust for Scotland **198** *Crathes Castle,* **205** *Fyvie Castle*

Nature Photographers Ltd **75** *Butterfly (C Carver)*

Pilkington Glass Museum **181** *The Laughing Friar*

Royal Shakespeare Company **120** *Shakespeare's Henry IV*

Sheppy's **38** *Cider labels*

Spectrum Colour Library **17** *Cabot Tower, Bristol,* **25** *Dartmoor ponies,* **50** *Bluebell Line,* **54** *Chessington, Safari Skyway,* **57** *White cliffs of Dover,* **58** *Exbury Gardens,* **80** *Dickens Festival,* **81** *Rye,* **116** *Sandringham and statue,* **118** *Burghley House,* **155** *Blackpool illuminations,* **159** *Town cryer, Chester,* **161** *Durham Cathedral,* **200** *Stills, Glenfiddich,* **218** *Loch Katrine*

Tate Gallery **78** *Turner's Dewy Morning*

The Mansell Collection **14** *Jenner,* **26** *Exeter,* **31** *W Q H Fox Talbot,* **83** *Wellington,* **184** *Sheffield,* **196** *Robert Burns,* **199** *Battle of Culloden,* **214** *Robert Owen, New Lanark*

The Needles Pleasure Park **62** *Coloured Sand*

The Sporting Life **19** *Cheltenham Gold Cup*

Thorpe Park **83** *Thorpe Park*

Wales Tourist Board **132** *Castell Coch, Cardiff Castle,* **136** *Ffestiniog railway,* **142** *Marloes*

Warwick Castle **122** *Warwick Castle*

Zefa Picture Library UK Ltd **204/5** *Fort William & Ben Nevis,* **216** *Isle of Skye*

All remaining pictures are held in the Association's own library (AA Photo Library) with contributions from the following photographers:

M Adleman, M Allwood-Coppin, A Baker, P Baker, J Beazley, A W Besley, M Birkitt, E A Bowness, P & G Bowater, J Carney, D Corrance, R Czaja, R Eames, P Eden, P Enticknap, D Forss, S Gibson Phot, V Greaves, A Grierly, A J Hopkins, A Lawson, S & O Mathews, E Meacher, A Molyneux, C Molyneux, R Newton, D Noble, G Rowatt, P Sharp, V Sinhal, B Smith, A Souter, F Stephenson, R Surman, T D Timms, M Trelawny, A Trynor, R Victor, W Voysey, R Weir, H Williams, T Woodcock, J Wyand